NEWSPRINT METROPOLIS

HISTORICAL STUDIES OF URBAN AMERICA

Edited by Lilia Fernández, Timothy J. Gilfoyle, Becky M. Nicolaides, and Amanda I. Seligman James R. Grossman, Editor Emeritus

A complete list of series titles is available on the University of Chicago Press website.

NEWSPRINT METROPOLIS

CITY PAPERS AND THE MAKING OF MODERN AMERICANS

JULIA GUARNERI

The University of Chicago Press
Chicago and London

Publication of this book has been aided by a grant from the Neil Harris Endowment Fund, which honors the innovative scholarship of Neil Harris, the Preston and Sterling Morton Professor Emeritus of History at the University of Chicago. The Fund is supported by contributions from the students, colleagues, and friends of Neil Harris.

Publication of this book has been supported by Furthermore: a program of the J. M. Kaplan Fund.

Furthermore:
a program of the J. M. Kaplan Fund

The University of Chicago Press, Chicago 60637
The University of Chicago Press, Ltd., London
© 2017 by The University of Chicago
Published 2017.
Printed in the United States of America

26 25 24 23 22 21 20 19 18 17   1 2 3 4 5

ISBN-13: 978-0-226-34133-0 (cloth)
ISBN-13: 978-0-226-34147-7 (e-book)
DOI: 10.7208/chicago/[9780226341477].001.0001

Library of Congress Cataloging-in-Publication Data
Names: Guarneri, Julia, author.
Title: Newsprint metropolis : city papers and the making
of modern Americans / Julia Guarneri.
Other titles: Historical studies of urban America.
Description: Chicago ; London : The University of Chicago Press, 2017. |
Series: Historical studies of urban America | Includes bibliographical references.
Identifiers: LCCN 2016058657| ISBN 9780226341330 (cloth : alk. paper) |
ISBN 9780226341477 (e-book)
Subjects: LCSH: American newspapers—History—19th century. | American newspapers—
History—20th century. | American newspapers—Social aspects. | News audiences—United
States. | City dwellers—United States. | Cities and towns—United States—History. | Urbanization—
United States—History—19th century. | Urbanization—United States—History—20th century.
Classification: LCC PN4864 .G83 2017 | DDC 071/.309034—dc23
LC record available at https://lccn.loc.gov/2016058657

♾ This paper meets the requirements of ANSI/NISO
Z39.48-1992 (Permanence of Paper).

CONTENTS

Plates follow page 154.

INTRODUCTION

In February of 1911, identical ads appeared in the newspapers of fifty-six different American cities. "We need *your* viewpoint," the ads said, "and we ask you to answer these six questions":

1. What local newspaper do you read regularly?
2. How are your opinions influenced by its editorials?
3. Do you as a rule believe what you read in the news columns?
4. What feature or department do you value most?
5. What criticisms, if any, have you to make?
6. Which local newspapers exert a good, and which a bad, influence on your community?[1]

Collier's Weekly magazine was conducting a national survey of newspaper readers as part of a year-long investigation into the history and influence of the press. The ads offered fifty-dollar prizes for the best essay from each of the fifty-six cities. In the three months before the deadline, *Collier's* received ten thousand essays from every state and territory in the nation.

Collier's began by asking people *which* local newspaper they read regularly because nearly all American cities housed multiple daily papers. "Like true Americans," explained Egmont H. Arens in his essay for *Collier's*, "the citizens of Albuquerque must have the news. It is an essential of modern life. Everybody in town has one of the papers, and a great many of us read both the morning and evening sheets."[2] Of course, some essay writers complained that even with two (or four or seven) papers to choose from, they could not find the kind of news they wanted. But others seemed to revel in their choices. Curtis C. Brown of Kansas City reported that he occasionally read the *Journal* and the *Post*, and always read the *Star* and the *Times*.[3] O. H. Chamberlain of Chicago called the *Chicago Tribune* "his" paper, but commented knowledgeably on Chicago's *Record-Herald*, *Daily News*, *Post*, *Journal*, and *Inter-Ocean*.[4] Because early twentieth-century papers had grown fat with new sections, ads, and special features, readers could easily find something to love in each of them.

The ten thousand responses to the *Collier's* contest sounded some consistent notes. Readers tended to believe the news reports printed in their papers, but insisted that the editorials did not influence them. They scorned the sensationalism that had spread from San Francisco and New York papers into their hometowns, but they appreciated the investigative reporting these same papers performed. Essay writers clearly felt that their choice of newspaper spoke to the kind of person they were. Mr. Chamberlain believed that, by choosing the *Chicago Tribune*, he was choosing self-improvement: "It brings to a mind like mine, which has a breadth of thought on things current, the depth which it needs."[5] Edward Broderick of Pittsburgh read the *Chronicle-Telegraph* in the evening and the *Gazette-Times* in the morning "because they alone, among our seven, have a flavor of intellectuality."[6]

Readers formed intensely personal relationships with the papers they had chosen. "The editorials of the 'Times' have been a source of pleasure and interest to me," wrote May V. Godfrey, *New York Times* reader. "Every morning I have lengthy arguments with the man who writes them. Often I praise him because he is so catholic in his knowledge, so fair in his judgment.... Occasionally he displays such a lack of insight of information that I box his ears, shake him, scold him because his view-point is not the same as mine."[7] Frederick Thomas Bowers, a *New York Evening Post* reader, wrote that "to read the 'Post' regularly is like meeting every day your broadest-minded, best-informed friends, the people who are concerned with things worth while. Your faith in humanity is stimulated, your interests expand, your knowledge grows."[8] Curtis Brown explained that the *Kansas City Star* and *Times* "are the papers that come into my home, welcomed with a spirit of confiding friendship."[9]

Readers turned to their newspapers not just for companionship and familiarity but also for guidance. For Mr. Chamberlain of Chicago, John McCutcheon's cartoons in the *Chicago Tribune* provided a daily reminder of what was right and good: "Kindly, intelligent, sincere, and delightfully funny, they bring to each one at our breakfast table something needed to begin the day on."[10] Newspapers helped other readers to envision success and imagine how they might achieve it. Marjorie Van Horn, reader of the *New York Journal*, loved the pictures of glamorous "Brinkley Girls" in the Sunday magazine; these pictures became many women's beauty icons in the 1910s and 1920s. "The pictures which Miss Nell Brinkly puts in this paper is some thing elaborate," she wrote. "I have many of those beautiful pictures framed and placed around on the walls of my room which shows great skill done by her, also the advices which Miss Fairfax gives are very good indeed, they aid the lovers just what to do and how to win love."[11] Van

Horn did not even have to write in to Beatrice Fairfax's advice column to feel that the columnist was helping her toward love and happiness.

Readers isolated in their offices, homes, or neighborhoods explained that their newspapers connected them to the greater workings of the city and the world. Ms. Van Horn worked during the day and only got the chance to read a paper in the evenings. "Now if it was not for the evening journal being a nights paper I would not know nothing about what is going on in the large cities," she wrote.[12] May Godfrey's tuberculosis kept her homebound, but her daily *New York Times*, she said, connected her to the wider world. In one of *Collier's* 1911 investigative articles on the newspaper, journalist Will Irwin argued that to read the news was to plug into global circuits, to be a part of a larger system, to be alive. "We need it, we crave it," he observed. "This nerve of the modern world transmits thought and impulse from the brain of humanity to its muscles."[13]

The *Collier's* editors may have thought it common sense to structure the contest around fifty-six cities, for newspapers were fundamentally urban institutions. Papers' offices stood at cities' busiest intersections. They sent dozens or hundreds of reporters out each day to take the city's pulse. Reporters "covered" cities, and so did the papers they produced. The *Collier's* questions assumed that all newspapers influenced their cities, for better or for worse. And in both its initial ad and in follow-up reminders, *Collier's* appealed to newspaper readers' sense of civic duty. "If you do not care about the prize, please write anyway. These letters are a piece of public service," the magazine explained. "We want letters from you, the intelligent citizen who has the well-being of his city at heart."[14]

As the scale of the response to the *Collier's* contest makes clear, newspapers were flourishing in the turn-of-the-century United States. Between 1880 and 1930, both the number of individual newspapers and the number of copies they printed reached record highs. Whereas the country's existing daily newspapers had printed fewer than one copy for every two U.S. households in 1880, they printed one and a half copies for each household by 1915.[15] The issues themselves grew fatter and fatter. In 1880, urban daily papers had run about twelve pages. By 1930, those papers would run perhaps forty or sixty pages, with their Sunday editions topping one hundred. Many turn-of-the-century Americans read several papers a day, and some families had two copies of the same paper delivered each morning—one to take to work, one to keep at home. Millions of women had recently picked up the newspaper habit, and working-class Americans—seamstresses, mill hands, steel workers—had become, in an era of mass literacy, dedicated consumers of news.[16] Marjorie Van Horn's effusive letter may have won the *Collier's* contest in part because a working woman so perfectly represented the newspaper reader of modern times.

The growth of U.S. cities stoked Americans' appetites for news. Many

American cities doubled or even quadrupled in population between 1880 and 1930, swelling with migrants from farms and small towns and with immigrants from abroad. Cities built up manufacturing economies and developed into centers of both wholesale and retail commerce. Their citizens adapted to the era's new urban technologies: streetcars, electric lights, subways, and skyscrapers. As cities became richer and more diverse, so too did their media. Major cities boasted a dozen or more dailies each. Cities such as Chicago and New York, with their large suburban peripheries, printed more newspapers than they had residents.[17] In bustling metropolises, explained New York journalist John Given, "apparently the thirst for information is in the air. In the crowds that ride to the offices, stores, and factories in the morning there is scarce a man or a woman who does not carry a paper, and in the home-going crowds those who are not reading, or carrying papers as evidence that they intend to read, are so few that unless sought for they are overlooked."[18]

Newsprint Metropolis tells the linked histories of newspapers and the cities they served between 1880 and 1930. It tracks two simultaneous processes: how cities made newspapers, and how newspapers made cities. It therefore treats newspapers not just as historical records but also as historical actors, not just as repositories of information but also as instruments of change. The book reaches beyond the front pages and into the colorful world of feature news, which entertained readers while teaching them how to deal with this urban world of diversity and possibility. Newspapers circulated the local logistical information that enabled readers to conduct their lives within cities and city-centered metropolitan regions. They presented readers with place-based definitions of class and community, sophistication and success. They facilitated an imaginative relationship to city and region, conjuring the experiences, qualities, and commitments that supposedly bound readers to their metropolitan neighbors.

In the 1920s, toward the end of this story, newspapers began to come a bit unmoored from their urban context. Distribution of news articles and images through syndicate services or through chains enabled newspaper editors to piece together satisfying papers without commissioning much local news. But while newspapers never again focused as intensely on their own cities, their heyday as city organs left a lasting mark. The civic campaigns, the commerce, the fast pace, and the variety in turn-of-the-century cities all combined to create the newspaper model that endured through the twentieth century and that we might still recognize in today's media.

LOCAL MEDIA, COMMERCIAL MEDIA

In 1792, the congressmen of the very new United States saw newspapers as more national than local organs. In the Post Office Act of that year, they set extraordinarily low postal rates for newspapers, so that delivery cost would not dissuade anyone from subscribing to a paper printed hundreds of miles away. The act enabled editors to exchange newspapers through the mail for free as well, encouraging the constant sharing and reprinting of national (rather than local) news. If Americans kept track of one another's doings, congressmen reasoned, they might learn to think of this agglomeration of territories and peoples as a coherent unit. In the early years of the United States, newspapers' editorials and their letters to the editor discussed national and state politics more often than they discussed city affairs, and that focus made sense in what was still an agrarian nation. Yet the only people who determined state and national laws, and who were therefore explicitly welcome in this public sphere, were those who could vote—white men of property.[19] Federalist, Whig, and Democratic-Republican newspapers vied for these voters' loyalty and attention.

Over the course of the nineteenth century, as native-born and immigrant Americans flocked to cities, editors began to recognize those cities as lucrative markets for newspapers and as rich sources of news. Readers eagerly bought papers that both portrayed and decoded their cities for them. In the biggest cities, this process started early. In the late 1830s, New York City newspapers began reporting on urban crimes and using those articles to explain secret worlds—brothels, jail cells, politicians' backrooms—for cities' own readers and residents.[20] In the second half of the nineteenth century, newspapers increasingly hosted civic dialogues, not just national ones, over issues such as street lighting, slumlords, utility costs, or the construction of new city buildings. These urban issues affected many city dwellers, regardless of whether they could vote, so newspapers' civic conversations expanded their reading audiences. By the last decades of the nineteenth century, newspapers had rooted themselves much more deeply in cities.

Publishers never issued newspapers solely as a civic good—they intended to turn a profit. In the nineteenth century, publishers cobbled together their budgets and their profits from a combination of subscription prices, support from their chosen political party, and advertisements. The advertisements in early nineteenth-century newspapers coordinated the markets for land, labor, and shipping services. They did a business in smaller goods as well, though the trade was often wholesale, for barrels of molasses or bags of wheat. Newspapers' classified sections functioned as nodes within far-flung mercantile economies, in which the goods or labor advertised inside might start or finish in a nearby town, a western territory, or a Caribbean island.

As the United States urbanized, however, newspapers' advertising clearinghouses concentrated on city markets. Papers could bring in plenty of ad revenue simply by hosting urban commerce. Advertisers, too, could benefit from the access to denser economies. Instead of selling barrels of molasses to out-of-town merchants, shopkeepers or manufacturers could market individual tins of molasses directly to urban readers and reap most of the profits for themselves. Newspapers that had once facilitated mercantile exchange became organs of new consumer economies.

In the late nineteenth century, advertising for consumer goods and entertainment became so important to publishers' bottom lines that they reconsidered their target audiences and redesigned their articles to better fulfill advertisers' wishes. Advertisers wanted to pitch to any and all prospective buyers, not just the white male partisan readers of most nineteenth-century papers. So publishers began crafting features that explicitly invited women, immigrants, teenagers, and children into their reading audience. By focusing the new "feature news" on topics such as fashion, cooking, real estate, or travel and by making the composing room aware that advertisements needed to run alongside relevant content in the paper, publishers increased ad sales. They also hired a more diverse news corps as they tried to draw in a more diverse audience. White middle-class men may have dominated papers' editorial boards and city newsrooms, but new types of workers, such as female freelance writers and self-taught immigrant illustrators, contributed a wider variety of voices to daily papers.[21]

We—like the editors of the turn of the century—might be tempted to see the new, advertiser-subsidized business model as an unfortunate if understandable tradeoff. Ad income kept subscription prices down and subsidized the spread of what many people deemed the truly important information, the "hard" news and the editorial columns. But this view ignores the fact that many readers enjoyed the features, and even the advertisements, more than the regular news. The vast majority of front-page stories—news of international diplomacy, tornadoes, national politics, or egregious crime—did not reflect readers' everyday experience. By contrast, the women's page, Sunday magazine, classified advertisements, and wedding announcements spoke to readers about how to live their lives and gave them basic tools to get through a city day. Men jump-started their morning with jokes from the sports pages. Children stole away with the comics section on Sundays. Teenagers trusted their most intimate questions to newspaper advice columnists. Because these new categories of news often struck readers as personally relevant, it was this material to which many people grew most attached.[22] Readers' responses pushed newspapers to further expand the features. As letters and queries poured into advice columns, editors created more of them. As readers snapped up the Sunday papers with the best comic strips, editors created entire separate comics sections, and the funnies were born.

Readers' embrace of spectacularly commercial newspapers forces us to question the idea that advertising simply corrupted public dialogue. Without pressure from advertisers, twentieth-century newspapers might never have broken from the nineteenth-century newspaper mold, which was visually bland, stridently political, intended only for white male readers, and, generally, no fun. With the birth of ad-driven newspaper features, the phrase "the news" shifted its very meaning; it no longer indicated just international events or national politics, but also the latest sports scores, the current fashions, and advertisements themselves. Those in the industry might refer to this material as "leisure news," but many readers regarded it as news all the same—up-to-the-minute information about changing events and conditions in the modern world. All of this resulted in a new breed of newspaper and, by extension, a new kind of public sphere: more commercial, to be sure, but also more colorful and more inclusive.

THE WORLD THAT NEWSPAPERS MADE

Readers used their daily newspapers as maps that could help them navigate the modern city and the modern world. Many looked to their papers for guidance on how city people ought to behave. In the late nineteenth century, when most city papers served niche audiences, those standards could be fairly class specific and may have actually sharpened class boundaries within cities. By the early twentieth century, as advertisers exerted similar pressures on nearly all papers, class-specific advice began to disappear. The new model of newspaper attracted readers with particular features— a sports section, a Sunday magazine, a favorite columnist—rather than with class or party loyalties. Editors sorted city dwellers into separate interest groups to whom they could pitch specific goods, and these categories became lenses through which readers might think of themselves: sports fans, cyclists, cooks, homeowners. These sections created communities in which buying became a signal of belonging; they wove consumer goods into definitions of modern manhood, womanhood, middle-class respectability, and metropolitan style. As publishers deemphasized their papers' class and party affiliations, they paved the way for the newspaper mergers in the first years of the twentieth century. After these mergers, readers often found a great deal of variety *within* their newspapers but much less variety from one newspaper to the next.

As papers guided readers through the details of daily life, they also sketched a bigger picture, offering a sense of the place—the community—that readers belonged to. "Community" may seem an odd concept to apply to cities of five hundred thousand or a million people. The term appears an easier fit for smaller groups within cities: migrants from the South, Italian immigrants in a single neighborhood, or the workers at a particular factory. Yet news features let readers interact, through the paper, with their fellow city residents. They consciously mimicked the in-person experiences of neighborly conversation, market bartering, sidewalk wandering, and restaurant eavesdropping. Through those re-creations, newspapers allowed readers to grasp and join a newsprint metropolis when the physical city had grown too large to fully explore or comprehend.

Articles often depicted cosmopolitan cities whose vitality and distinctiveness derived from the interactions among their polyglot populations. But they also consistently placed city residents in hierarchies of importance and belonging. Similarly, many varieties of local news fostered a climate of civic responsibility and modeled a relationship with the city that involved charity and political activism yet seemed only to speak to the white, middle-class residents that editors assumed made up the bulk of their readership.

Newspapers forged bonds between people with print interactions rather than in-person encounters. They offered secondhand rather than firsthand knowledge and created one-sided and unequal relationships between news readers and news subjects. None of this sounds like "community" in any traditional sense. But this is the point. Newspapers cultivated a new model of urban community, in which residents understood and interacted with their cities not simply by living in them but by reading about them.

Feature news rarely addressed politics head-on, yet newspaper features do illuminate the broader political arc of the early twentieth century. Newspapers offer one explanation for how the fragmented cities of this era, riven with racial, ethnic, and class tensions, continued to cohere at all. Etiquette columns taught readers new habits that marked them as urbanites and also helped to maintain the peace on crowded streetcars and sidewalks. Papers' question-and-answer sections fashioned open public forums that made the city legible to immigrants and rural migrants, as well as urban natives. Newspapers' articles collectively encouraged municipal pride, a consciousness of "how the other half lives," and a sense that all urban residents shared a common fate. In this, newspapers were integral to the rise of Progressive politics.

In the early twentieth century, urban newspapers broadened their circulations into suburbs, small towns, and rural hamlets. As they expanded, newspapers reoriented readers to a larger metropolitan geography. City papers followed their readers as they moved to the city's perimeter, offering suburban delivery service and suburban news coverage. Further afield, canvassers pushed metropolitan papers on small-town and rural residents. When daily newspapers expanded into broader regions, they whet appetites for urban goods and connected formerly isolated populations to elements of mass culture. But as newspapers sent urban information into small towns, they also brought the region into the city. Newspapers' real estate sections promoted the suburban ideal and stoked suburban growth. Agriculture sections and regional society notes brought small-town life to urban readers. By facilitating flows of people, goods, and information, metropolitan papers functioned as economic infrastructure and enabled coordinated regional economies. And by circulating definitions of regional character among widely dispersed readers, newspapers helped to build metropolitan regions and turned Americans themselves into metropolitans, bound to their regional neighbors by both real and imaginary ties.

Even as newspapers expanded their local coverage outward into suburbs and regions, they were abandoning other kinds of local newswriting. Beginning around the turn of the century, the nation's largest newspapers formed syndicates, which sold news material to dozens of smaller papers. By the 1910s and 1920s, most of the articles that Americans read in their local papers had either been bought on the national news market or distributed through a chain. Newspapers never gave up on local news completely, since it was their tie to a particular place, and their daily publication schedule, that distinguished them from magazines. But the center of gravity shifted within newspapers, and especially in their features, from local and specific to national and generic.

The nationalization of news through syndication and chain distribution was more accidental than purposeful. The directors of syndicates and chains did not see their work as part of a patriotic project; they sought only to expand their markets and capitalize on economies of scale. Yet because of national chain distribution and syndicated news, Americans across the country read the same headlines, bought the same products, cooked the same recipes, and laughed at the same jokes. City newspapers played even more subtle roles in the spread of mass culture as they advertised national brands, reviewed Hollywood movies, and printed national radio broadcast schedules. Urbanites may not have realized that they were coming to live their lives in parallel with residents of other cities, and suburban and rural people may not have noticed how urban their information diet had become. When wartime propaganda marshaled residents' pride in the American way of life, however, or when radio or television pandered to audiences' commonalities, each used the shared vocabularies and shared values that newspapers had helped to spread.

Newspapers, through the late nineteenth and early twentieth century, often claimed to be for and about everyone. Some called themselves "voices of the people." Others turned their editorial pages into public forums in which seemingly any reader could broadcast opinions to the city at large. By the 1910s and 1920s they were circulating images of an America that all readers were meant to recognize as their own. But daily newspapers did not actually speak for everyone, nor did they welcome all readers. Most papers catered to specific classes, spoke to specific political persuasions, and ignored the poor and minority audiences that they did not care to reach. While many papers began to subtly accommodate immigrant readers in the 1890s and the early 1900s, they still relegated African Americans to the help-wanted ads and to derogatory depictions on the humor page through the 1910s and 1920s. Each of these editorial decisions reflected publishers' assumptions about who belonged in the public sphere and what kind of part each person ought to play there. Each also reflected newspapers' roles not as civic instruments but as commercial organs. Editors, focused on ad revenue, did not see all Americans as equally desirable readers.

Because metropolitan dailies failed to cover and cater to all populations, many readers turned to other kinds of papers made especially for them. Foreign-language papers, African American papers, religious weeklies, neighborhood weeklies, and suburban newsletters all thrived in the turn-of-the-century metropolis. The collective circulations of foreign-language papers rivaled those of English-language papers in several cities, and African American weeklies' circulations usually reached across several states. These other kinds of papers can help us better understand metropolitan dailies' omissions, weaknesses, and—significantly—their power. The influence of big-city papers was so strong that black papers and foreign-language papers, while reflecting the priorities and desires of their specific audiences, could look and sound strikingly similar to metropolitan dailies.

This book tells the history of a local medium, so it takes a local approach. The story unfolds through studies of four U.S. cities: Philadelphia, New York, Chicago, and Milwaukee. Each chapter focuses on a particular city in order to study the relationships between cities and their news. The first chapter is the only one that is uniformly national in scope; it examines critical changes in the late nineteenth-century news industry that launched newspapers into a more prominent place in urban life. Chapter 2 investigates metropolitan newspapers' roles as advice manuals that taught different modes of urban living to men and women, to the working class and the middle class, in Philadelphia. The third chapter turns to New York and examines the print community that emerged in features such as "human interest" stories, urban travelogues, reprinted church sermons, and letters to the editor. Chapter 4 takes the example of Chicago to show how newspapers fueled suburban and regional growth but also kept those outlying regions tethered to downtown. The fifth chapter reveals how newspaper syndicates and chains created and distributed national culture. A smaller city, Milwaukee, illustrates this process. The epilogue paints a portrait of the news industry of the interwar years. Buyouts and mergers produced behemoth newspapers that took the innovations of the preceding decades and refined them into a model with true mass appeal. The resulting corporate newspaper model and the consolidated national newspaper field was to endure for decades.

It is impossible to separate the history of one city's papers from those of all others. Newspapers constantly exchanged information, ideas, and employees, so while each paper ran local news and catered to local tastes, that content appeared within a template that varied little from one city to the next. Editors subscribed to each other's papers, responded to each other's opinions, and adopted each other's inventions. Under pressures to maximize profits, editors employed the same technologies: the rotary press, the half-tone, the linotype machine.

Cities' histories, too, cannot be entirely separated from one another. Across the Northeast and Midwest, cities expanded and industrialized at roughly the same time. Urban growth in the South and West looked a bit different from that in the Northeast and Midwest: Southern cities attracted fewer immigrants from Europe and Asia, and most Western cities did not develop dense urban cores. These differences rendered some eastern newspaper trends irrelevant, but Southern and Western editors still borrowed plenty from their peers. Everywhere, the challenges of city life created niches for newspapers to fill, whether that meant schooling readers in office etiquette or circulating daily prices for department-store goods. The closing section of each chapter brings in examples from many cities to show how news patterns played out across the country.

The newspapers of the turn of the century were sprawling, chaotic, and wildly contradictory documents. Because editors tried to craft papers that provided something for everyone, a single newspaper issue might contain articles on thrifty housekeeping but also advertisements for luxury purchases; the details of a grisly murder but also the heart-warming tale of a local hero; a culturally curious profile of an immigrant community but also gross ethnic stereotypes in a humor column. As is still true today, advertiser-approved "feature" news subsidized "hard" news, and the two types of material could be completely at odds with one another. What newspapers offered does not cohere, but it does matter.

Between 1880 and 1930, as Americans witnessed astonishing changes, they turned to newspapers to keep track of and understand the shifts around them. They read about the tides of immigrants settling in American cities, adapting to American ways and changing the nation in the process.

They read about a new Progressive politics that attempted to rein in the excesses of capitalism while limiting the influence of immigrant politics and cultures. They learned that the U.S. population had shifted, by 1920, from majority rural to majority urban. And they read about the United States' entrance onto a world stage, first with imperial outposts in Cuba and the Philippines, later with intervention in World War I.

But daily newspapers did not just tell Americans about these shifts—they participated in them and enabled their readers to do the same. The quotidian ritual of skimming newspapers' varied offerings, when repeated by millions of people over many decades, transformed cities, regions, and the nation.

1: A NEW NEWSPAPER MODEL

"The American newspaper is distinctly ahead of its English contemporaries," announced William Thomas Stead, one of the most celebrated newspapermen in England, in 1901. "To begin with, there is more of it, more news, more advertisements, more paper, more print," he explained. "Hence the busiest people in the world, who have less time for deliberate reading than any race, buy regularly morning and evening more printed matter than would fill a New Testament, and on Sundays would consider themselves defrauded if they did not have a bale of printed matter delivered at their doors almost equal in bulk to a family Bible."[1] The sheer quantity of news necessitated some sort of organizing system. Stead analyzed and praised one American solution, the large headline—or as he called it, the "scare-head." Scare-heads made reading more efficient, allowing people to glean information in only a few seconds and to choose the articles they wanted to read in full. But headlines also, thought Stead, made the news more appealing. "The scare-head is like the display in the show window in which the tradesman sets out his wares," he wrote. "Good journalism consists much more in the proper labelling and displaying of your goods than in the writing of leading articles. The intrinsic value of news is a quality which does not depend upon the editor, but the method of display."[2]

Stead had encountered a new newspaper business model, in full flower in turn-of-the-century American cities. Faster presses suddenly made it possible to print Bible-sized papers, and revenue from advertising kept those papers affordable. For the first time, publishers could sell their product for next to nothing yet still reap healthy profits. Under this system, urban daily newspapers cut their prices, expanded their offerings, and grew their circulations. Stead was witnessing newspapers' transformations into true mass media whose influence reached across thousands or even millions of readers' lives.

To turn out such large newspapers, publishers had to grow their companies. They constructed new buildings, hired large corps of news workers, and purchased massive machines. Newspapers—as organizations as well as objects—became emblems of the modern era, whose profitability, efficiency, and sheer size garnered popular attention and outright awe. Stead noticed that, as newspapers grew, they provided more information than anyone could actually use; they made the "busiest people in the world" even busier. Newspapers contributed to urban information overload; they circulated pages full of clashing messages and eye-catching images and filled city streets with newsboys' loud pitches and reporters' hard-hitting questions.

Stead chose an apt metaphor, the shop window, for newspapers had indeed become more commercial products than ever before. Stead described the articles themselves as products to be consumed, each one vying to be chosen and read. Newspapers became shop windows more literally, when editors ran elaborate ads, crafted features that focused readers' attention on consumer topics, and persuaded local merchants to advertise. By the turn of the century, publishers regarded even their own audiences as products to be sold. Publishers boasted about the numbers, the wealth, and the spending habits of their readers and then sold the attention of those readers to advertisers.

The huge new papers of the turn of the century came in for both praise and criticism, as Stead's defense suggests. But they were unqualified successes. Fast, lucrative, efficient, and abundant, newspapers became beacons of a new era in urban America. They also entwined public dialogue with commerce so thoroughly that readers could not disentangle the two.

"MORE NEWS, MORE ADVERTISEMENTS, MORE PAPER, MORE PRINT"

When a man or woman in 1880 paid two cents for the daily paper, he or she walked away with four pages absolutely crammed with information. Printers chose small type for the titles, smaller type for news, and minuscule type for the classified ads. Many printers dispensed with titles altogether, printing only the broadest of headings: "The Latest News" or "Local Affairs." Wherever extra space remained, printers tucked in one more tidbit—an anecdote, a statistic, or an advertisement.

These papers were products of nineteenth-century technology. Rags, the raw material for newsprint at the time, yielded sturdy and long-lasting paper but were relatively expensive and in constant short supply. Editors had to perpetually weigh whether information was worth the cost of the paper it would be printed on. The painstaking printing process also forced publishers to keep their papers to a modest size. "The circulation of a daily newspaper was imperatively limited by the number of pulls one pair of arms could give a Washington press," explained Whitelaw Reid, editor of the *New York Tribune*. A large and successful paper might circulate only four hundred copies.[3]

Nineteenth-century publishers relied on advertisements as well as subscriptions for revenue, and assumed ad printing to be part of their job. Indeed, papers in dozens of different cities took the name *Commercial Advertiser* and crowded their entire front pages with ads. Advertising, however, still carried with it a shady reputation. In a world where people made most of their purchases and sought most services from people they knew, readers treated items advertised in the paper with caution. Why would they buy something of unknown origin? Why would they take advice on what to buy from a stranger? Advertisers often did have something to conceal, whether touting the benefits of a "health tonic" or trying to sell an arid patch of farmland.[4] So most urban daily newspapers kept advertisers to certain parameters, requiring that they use extremely small typeface, insisting that they keep their ad the width of a single column, and permitting them to illustrate only with a tiny symbol indicating the type of good or service offered. This formula minimized the space that each individual ad took up—important in the era of expensive newsprint—and kept advertisements from overshadowing the news. And crucially, it was the vertical lines between columns, when placed on the printing frame, that physically held the type together. Without the column marker wedged between, the letters simply fell out.[5]

The newspapers that resulted from these conventions are almost impenetrable to the modern eye. They offer no pictures, large headlines, or boxed advertisements to break up the monotony of tiny text. To the nineteenth-century reader, though, it did not much matter what the paper looked like. If a man had an hour to spare and a paper in hand, he would likely start at the beginning and work his way through the whole issue. In the sea of text, he would discover spots of relevant, entertaining, or absorbing news. He might laugh at a prickly letter to the editor, note that a neighbor had been admitted to the hospital, and pay special attention to news from his parents' home country. Perhaps he balked in disagreement at some of the editorials—but more likely he nodded in approval as he read, for he knew which paper spoke for the city's Democrats or its Republicans, and he bought the opinion he wanted to hear.

Other readers might pick up a paper in a tavern after work. They, too, read through from start to finish, and then perhaps discussed the increase in railroad rates with an acquaintance at the bar. Still others brought the paper to work with them. Cigar rollers or seamstresses took turns reading aloud to one another or allotted the task to the best reader among them. The reader might stop at a description of a greedy landlord's trial and relay

1.1 Hoe Rotary Press at the *Milwaukee Journal*, 1912. This same technology was already in place at the biggest papers in the 1890s. Wisconsin Historical Society, WHS-119169.

her own similar troubles, linger over an intriguing personal ad, or weigh out loud the reasons for and against immigration restrictions. Families, too, might take the news this way, in a post-supper circle around a father or daughter reading aloud. Each member could tune in and out, and sometimes comment, as they smoked, sewed, or washed the dishes.[6]

This entire mode of reading the news would disappear when cheap newsprint rendered the four- or eight-page newspaper a thing of the past. Manufacturers gradually perfected a new process that used wood pulp rather than rags as raw material, and the newspaper business developed a voracious appetite for it—in 1897 the *New York World* went through a spruce forest four times the size of Central Park.[7] Over the course of the 1890s, the annual per capita consumption of newsprint rose from six to sixteen pounds, as daily papers grew fatter and fatter.[8] Abundant supplies of newsprint also gave publishers far more freedom to experiment. They could use large and artistic typefaces, print expansive illustrations, and still charge the same price that they had for the old-fashioned four-page paper.

With cheap newsprint, editors could afford to print large papers; with fast presses, they could churn out enough of those larger papers to meet demand. Richard Hoe introduced his rotary press (fig. 1.1) in the 1840s, which spun off seamless reams rather than individually stamping out sheets. Over the following decades, several more inventions sped things up. Printers learned to cast molds, called stereotype plates (fig. 1.2), from hand-set type and then fit the plates to rotary presses. The Mergenthaler Company perfected the linotype machine, which allowed workers to type out newspaper columns rather than hand set them (fig. 1.3). Autoplate machines, developed around 1895, prepared images for Hoe presses in record time.[9] Rotary newspaper presses grew larger and larger, until many papers housed mammoth double-decker machines that worked at staggering speed and volume. In 1905, the *New York World*'s presses could print 720,000 eight-page papers in a single hour.[10] Only the largest and wealthiest newspaper offices purchased these giant presses at first. Once publishers had installed them, though, they often began to think more ambitiously about their readership, for a well-equipped printing room could meet any demand that advertising and circulation staff managed to drum up. And because Hoe presses could

1.2 Stack of stereotype plates, *New York Herald*, 1920s. These half circles would then be fitted together into cylinders, to spin off sheets of paper in a rotary press. The word "stereotype," invented to describe this technology, only later took on its metaphorical meaning. William Thompson Dewart Collection of Frank A. Munsey and *New York Sun* Papers, Image 90970d, New-York Historical Society.

1.3 Linotypists at the *Milwaukee Journal*, circa 1912. When the typist hit a letter key, that letter in metal type slid down the machine's diagonal chute, where it aligned with and then fused to the other typed letters. Wisconsin Historical Society, WHS-119172.

easily print, fold, and stack separate sections, they freed publishers to cre-ate sprawling, multipart papers.

Newspaper publishers and readers alike celebrated this new printing technology as a modern wonder. The *New York Herald* built glass panels into the lower level of its building on Thirty-Fourth Street in 1893, so that passersby could see the presses in action.[11] The managing editor of the *St. Louis Post-Dispatch* reported to his boss, Joseph Pulitzer, after he opened the paper's new printing plant: "As I write, there are at least 75 people in the country room watching the presses work, while there are crowds about the front of the building admiring the presses in operation."[12] When the *Milwaukee Journal* ordered eight linotype machines, a line of visitors shuffled through the composing room for two and a half hours to see how they worked.[13] School children began to visit on field trips. When the *New York World* produced its first color supplement in 1898, it took the opportunity to show off the color press itself. An illustration showed visitors observing the press in action; the accompanying text described the machine's parts and abilities in detail (plate 1). When readers visited a press or viewed a lino-type machine, they showed their interest in not only the product but also the process of news. They wanted to understand the astounding technology that produced their daily paper and that also seemed to herald a new age of mechanical precision and speed.

Income from advertisements—alongside cheap paper and fast presses—enabled publishers to dramatically expand their papers. By the turn of the century, advertisements had lost much of the stigma that had led so many editors to give them only minimal space and attention. In cramped apartments, migrants no longer had the space or supplies to mill their own soap, grind their own flour, or even sew their own clothing. And unlike those in small towns or rural communities, city dwellers did not always have the option of sourcing goods from familiar faces. Other urbanites wished to live as they imagined their richer or more "American" neighbors did, and their aspirations could not be satisfied in their neighborhoods' shops. Many urban Americans were ready to listen to anyone who could tell them what to buy and where to buy it.

In 1880, American companies spent thirty million dollars on advertising. By 1910, that number increased twentyfold to six hundred million dollars, a full 4 percent of the national income.[14] New trade magazines like *Printers' Ink* and the *Advertising World* counseled salesmen. Advertising agencies sprouted up in major cities, first advising their clients on where to place advertisements and, later, helping them craft effective pitches.[15] "Fill the advertisement so full of hooks that the glancer is likely to get caught," advised one expert in the field.[16] Only this way would readers come across items that, until then, they perhaps had not known they needed.

Advertisers' new eye-catching images and flamboyant text could not be made to fit within the old newspaper model—though some tried (fig. 1.4).[17] Gradually, editors conceded more of what advertisers wanted, allowing them to spread out over a half or a full page. Once stereotypes and autoplates made it easier to print unconventional images or unusual typefaces, editors permitted illustrated, attention-grabbing ads.

Newspaper publishers gained some of their advertising savvy by watching their peers and competitors: monthly magazines. In the late 1880s and early 1890s, a handful of entrepreneurs launched magazines, such as *Cosmopolitan*, *Munsey's*, *McClure's*, and the *Ladies' Home Journal*, that targeted a large and growing national middle class. These magazines offered highbrow literary fare, such as one might find in *Harper's* or the *Atlantic*, but wove in more personal, practical features such as household advice and etiquette columns and more fanciful material such as travel stories and romantic fiction. The whole package sold for ten cents, or a dollar a year. These new monthlies proved a runaway success; by 1905, enough magazines sold each month to put four on the coffee table of every American household.[18]

Magazines demonstrated that advertisements, far from being unwanted

THE SUN, THURSDAY, MARCH 11, 1880.

1.4 Advertisers bent the rules by setting letters in eye-catching patterns, in this case forming small letters into large text. *New York Sun*, 11 March 1880, 4. Other strategies included printing a message one hundred times in a row, using capital letters to spell vertical messages through blocks of horizontal text, or constructing images (such as a Christmas tree) out of words.

distractions, could actually increase profits and attract readers. Instead of confining ads to a segregated space, magazine editors spread them over a whole issue. They offered advertisers prime space in the front pages, or gave them the full back cover, and charged them a correspondingly higher price. Magazines also helped merchants advertise by streamlining their ads' typeface or adding illustrations.[19] So beautiful and imaginative were magazine ads that readers regularly tore out their favorite ads before tossing away the magazine; one writer quipped that articles had become mere "space-fillers" between the ads.[20]

As newspaper publishers adopted these magazine strategies, they charged more for highly visible ad space and turned ads into part of newspapers' appeal. This slowly changed the look and purpose of newspapers. By 1900, ads often took up more than half of the pages in daily papers. "If bulk alone is considered," admitted circulation manager William Scott in 1915, "the title should be changed from 'news' paper to 'ad' paper."[21] Ads also remade newspapers' operating budgets. Advertising revenue had provided 44 percent of periodicals' total income in 1879; by 1909 it provided 60 percent.[22]

Relying so heavily on advertising money opened many new possibilities to newspaper publishers. Advertisements paid for larger papers, bigger presses, and more skilled staffs. [23] But in relying on ad money, newspapers went from selling one product to selling two. They sold a newspaper to readers; they also sold their readers' attention to advertisers. And advertisers wanted the attention of as many readers as possible.

READERS BECOME CUSTOMERS

During the nineteenth century, many newspaper editors had carved out niche audiences within urban reading populations and contentedly catered to those loyal readers. But by the turn of the century, that strategy no longer worked. Many editors felt compelled—by expenses or by competition—to drum up new readers to please advertisers. New York City's cutthroat newspaper business bred some of the era's most innovative selling strategies, but editors in San Francisco, Saint Louis, Chicago, and a host of smaller cities experimented too, aggressively marketing themselves to readers. They hired bigger corps of reporters to provide more thorough and timely news. They drew readers in with scandals and stunts and kept them reading by promising something even better in the next issue. Editors sought out sectors of the city's reading population that they had earlier ignored and created new content just for them. These new practices turned newspapers into a daily habit for all kinds of people and, for the first time, forged a truly mass audience.

Newspaper publishers began to think like advertisers, and developed schemes to get their product into the public eye. Where newspapers' personalities had once surfaced in their editorial voice and opinion, publishers now crafted their papers into recognizable brands. Much like detergent companies and department stores, newspapers used slogans and packaging to distinguish themselves from the competition. When William Randolph Hearst bought the *New York Journal* in 1895, he dubbed it "A Modern Newspaper at a Modern Price." The *New York Times* followed with "All the News That's Fit to Print" in 1896, and the *Chicago Tribune* claimed first to be "The People's Paper," then "The World's Greatest Newspaper" on its front page. Publishers adopted unique typefaces and mastheads, to give their papers distinctive looks.[24]

Nearly every major daily hired a circulation manager and set aside a budget for publicity.[25] Publishers then plastered city surfaces with ads. They distributed color posters for news vendors to hang up and placed ads on streetcars.[26] New York's *World* constructed a sixty-foot-wide electric sign on the roof of a five-story building at Fifth Avenue and Twenty-Fifth Street to announce its circulation of over five million a week.[27] Publishers had no qualms about infringing on competitors' territories; they used each other's

1.5 A *New York Journal* poster on scaffolding on Twenty-Third Street, 1896. The poster uses the Yellow Kid to advertise the paper's color comic supplement. The men in the foreground are rag pickers; they suggest that the market for rags survived even after newspapers started using wood-pulp paper instead. Photograph by Alice Austen, courtesy of the Alice Austen House.

pages to advertise.[28] And whenever newspapers ran special features, they drummed up interest through previews, advertisements, and posters. The *New York Journal*, for example, pasted images from its upcoming Sunday comic strips on construction scaffoldings (fig. 1.5).

All of this newspaper advertising helped to build a new kind of city landscape, in which every surface communicated a message and every image called out for attention. City newsstands were riots of print; giant headlines shouted from stacks of newspapers and six-foot-long posters announced the day's features.²⁹ Newspapers' flashing electric signs, which one on-looker described as "striking and almost startling to behold," overwhelmed the buildings behind them and cast a glow on cities' plazas and passersby.³⁰ City landscapes—plastered with signs, saturated with leaflets, strewn with newspapers and magazines—gave the eye no calm place to rest.³¹

Newspapers' in-person sales tactics, too, created a more stimulating and chaotic city. Circulation managers dispatched salesmen on house-to-house canvassing campaigns, offering subscriptions for twelve cents a week.³² They equipped the salesmen with scripts that listed dozens of sell-ing points to rattle off, so that customers might agree to take a subscription out of sheer argumentative exhaustion.³³ Much like posters and flashing signs, the hundreds of newsboys on city corners added to the quantity of stimuli in metropolitan life. In 1885 a New Orleans writer described a typi-cal city newsboy, who "shocks nervous people by screaming like a steam whistle."³⁴ Boys yelled out headlines from the paper as impromptu adver-tisements, filling the streets with shrill announcements of fire, warfare, and murder. These sales methods succeeded in enlarging newspaper audi-ences; they also helped to create a new kind of market that could be harsh not only on competitors but also on consumers. "The reader does not seek the paper," explained Don Seitz, business manager of the *New York World*; "the paper lets no possible reader escape."³⁵

Publicity campaigns could attract steady audiences only if newspapers then provided satisfying reading. So publishers did everything they could to print more and better news than their competitors. Publishers—especially those of sensational papers—hired the best reporters away from rivals, and they stationed these reporters all over the city.³⁶ In 1907 a New York City journalist listed eleven places that the papers "watched constantly," another fourteen that they watched "carefully but not continually," and dozens that reporters checked in on at least once a day.³⁷ Special reporters kept a finger on the pulse of each different urban scene, from cities' charity bureaus to chambers of commerce, from harbors to labor unions. "A city is now 'covered' by a machine as fine and complicated as a rotary press," ex-plained reporter Will Irwin in 1911.³⁸

Editors also outfitted their papers to "scoop" competitors as often as possible. Charles Dana, editor of the *New York Sun*, found that news of a fire added ten thousand readers, the results of a sports race added twenty-five thousand, and the outcome of a presidential election added eighty-two thousand readers.³⁹ Any paper that scooped such events would thus profit handsomely. Editors provided a handful of reporters with the freedom and the funds to do whatever it took to get the freshest, juiciest bits of news.⁴⁰ Some editors also paid any person who brought them an eyewitness ac-count, and paid up to five times more if that witness promised not to share the news with any other paper. This instilled a habit in some city people of rushing to a newspaper office as soon as they had witnessed an accident or a crime.[41] Printers, meanwhile, developed a mechanism called a "fudge" to insert breaking news into a paper even while the press was rolling. "If New York City Hall were to fall down," predicted journalist John Given, "both the *Evening Journal* and the *Evening World* would, in all probability, have 'fudge extras' on the street within four minutes."[42] Editors of afternoon papers had so little time to write up the day's news that they would occasionally prepare two different articles—both "Yale Wins" and "Harvard Wins"—and insert the accurate one into the press as soon as they received reports.[43]

If extensive publicity and broad news coverage did not hook readers, contests and other short-term lures could do the trick. Many in the business considered the so-called forcing of circulation a cheap tactic, but that did not stop them from doing it. The *Baltimore Sun* asked readers to vote for the bravest local fireman; the *Philadelphia Evening Item* asked readers to nominate their favorite trolley conductor.[44] Readers would buy one copy of the paper to get the ballot and then would keep buying copies to follow the results. Editors slipped in special inserts, from trading cards to art reprints to sheet music, prompting newsstand rushes on those issues.[45] Newspapers could also "force" circulation by running addictive ongoing features. The *New York Sun* sent a reporter on a frantic trip around the world, and readers bought issue after issue wondering whether she would finish her journey in less than eighty days.[46] Reporters also turned news stories into sensational dramas that spilled over from one day's issue to the next; some readers bought newspapers just to follow these dramas. "Take for example the strange disappearance of Miss Dorthy Arnold," wrote Marjorie Van Horn, a reader of the *New York Evening Journal*. "This is a case that I have followed up ever since I first saw its appearance in the journal and I expect to follow it to its end. I am very anxious to know where Miss Arnold is and whether she has become the bride of Mr. George Griscom."[47] The longer the *Evening Journal* could string this story out, the longer Marjorie Van Horn would keep buying her daily copy.

The most effective method of all for expanding reading audiences was to identify and target populations who did not yet buy the paper. By marketing to these groups and creating content that would appeal to them specifically, publishers could boost sales by thousands or tens of thousands. Publishers pursued these readers so relentlessly that by the early twentieth century they had spread the newspaper habit to nearly all corners of urban society.

In 1880, few newspapers made any real effort to attract women readers. Many women did read the general news and used the paper's contents in their daily lives. They learned of local marriages, births, and deaths, scanned the help-wanted columns for positions as chambermaids or laundresses, and read the notices of ships' arrivals in hopes of a husband's return.[48] Yet many genteel families thought that the violence, crime, and politics contained in newspapers made them unsuitable for women readers. William Dean Howells detected traces of this attitude in himself and others as late as 1902: "I saw a pretty and prettily dressed girl in the Elevated train, reading a daily newspaper quite as if she were a man. It gave me a little shock."[49]

The rise of the 1890s "new woman"—strong enough to handle disturbing news stories and politically engaged enough to follow current events—may have opened publishers' eyes to the possibility of female newsreaders. But ultimately, pressure from advertisers and competition from magazines prompted newspaper editors to more energetically pursue female readers. Advertising professionals, writing in journalism trade magazines, pointed out that women spent the household's money and were therefore more likely to become customers for advertised goods. "An advertisement has not one twentieth the weight with a man that it has with a woman of equal intelligence and the same social status," explained advertising expert Nathaniel Fowler to his industry colleagues in 1892. "Woman buys, or directs the buying of, or is the fundamental factor in directing the order of purchase, of everything from shoes to shingles."[50] One reader's suggestion to the *New York World* seemed to confirm this: "Why not put all the advertisements of the dry-goods houses on one sheet?" she asked. "Then when the ladies of the family wish to read the (to them) most interesting part of the paper they will not have to wait until the males of said family devour the baseball news."[51] Monthly magazines demonstrated that a female focus could be profitable. The *Ladies' Home Journal*, for instance, built up a large national audience, and then demanded more from advertisers. By 1903 the magazine was taking in an unprecedented one million dollars per year in advertising revenue.[52]

When newspaper editors focused on women readers, they made corresponding changes all over the paper. "Every story with a woman in it is 'played up,'" explained the circulation manager of New York's *Commercial Advertiser* in 1905, "and it has become largely a question of 'the woman in the case'; or, as the detective stories put it, 'look for the woman.'"[53] Some of those woman-centric stories thrilled readers with tales of divorces, jewelry heists, inheritance swindles, and jealous murders. Because they intrigued men as well as women and boosted overall readership, scandals like these moved into the regular front-page rotation. Less sensational newspapers commissioned investigative reports on food processing plants and patent medicine companies, knowing that the subjects of family health and diet lay near to many women's hearts. Behind the front pages, editors expanded coverage of city art exhibitions, theater productions, and music recitals. They ran highly detailed descriptions of weddings, tea services, and charity balls. They asked their New York and Washington correspondents to comment on society and arts happenings as well as on politics.

Starting in the 1880s and 1890s, editors also created the first women's sections. Most metropolitan dailies, from the *Cincinnati Tribune* to the *Boston Globe*, ran women's columns by 1895; by around 1905 those columns had become multipage illustrated spreads. The special sections were meant to invite women's attention and also to signal that the newsroom kept them especially in mind. "The women always find just what they want to read in The Wisconsin," announced the front page of the 1893 *Evening Wisconsin*, a Milwaukee paper. "It is the paper for the ladies."[54] In the 1890s, newspapers in several cities ran extraordinary poster campaigns to attract women readers to these sections and to the newspaper habit more generally. In full-color art nouveau prints, papers showed glamorous young women buying, carrying, and reading newspapers (plate 2).

Meanwhile, in their search for more readers, daily newspaper publishers also trained their sights on the working class. Newspaper reading had been a working-class habit at least since the 1830s, but only the biggest cities tended to print newspapers aimed at working-class tastes and budgets.[55] By the late nineteenth century, this was changing. E. W. Scripps, for example, was gradually expanding his chain of short, cheap papers meant for working-class readers in cities such as Cleveland, Cincinnati, Saint Louis, and Kansas City. Scripps and his contemporaries all knew that, for a paper to succeed among the working class, it had to be published in the afternoon. Factory workers did not have the time to linger over a newspaper at breakfast, since they started their shifts at seven or eight and either walked to work or commuted on crowded streetcars. Instead, most bought a paper on the way home. Some editors of morning papers began producing separate afternoon editions to capitalize on this market, while many other publishers began issuing independent afternoon sheets. Afternoon papers accounted for 79 percent of the increase in the number of American daily newspapers between 1880 and 1910.[56]

Around the turn of the century, any bid for working-class readers was also a bid for immigrant readers. The United States admitted over five million immigrants in the decade between 1881 and 1890; it accepted 8.7 million between 1901 and 1910.[57] The 1910 census indicated that 15 percent of all Americans had been born in another country.[58] The tides of immigrants changed the makeup of newspapers' potential audiences. Southern and eastern Europeans were replacing waves of Irish and British immigrants, so a greater portion of new arrivals spoke no English. Many read newspapers printed in their native languages, such as New York's *Jewish Daily Forward*, Chicago's *Skandinaven*, and Milwaukee's *Germania*. But even in their own countries, most of these new citizens had not read a daily newspaper. About 12 percent of them could not read at all.[59]

A few innovative editors tailored their papers to appeal to immigrants of varying reading abilities as well as to the native-born working class. Joseph Pulitzer, editor first of the *St. Louis Post-Dispatch* and then of the *New York World*, perhaps drew on his own experience as an emigrant from Hungary and as a new reader of English when he revamped both papers. He printed headlines in very large type. Underneath the lead phrase, he added a few subheadings in simple language that allowed readers to grasp the basic outline of the story before they reached the article's main text. The Scripps chain carried the emphasis on simplicity down to the vocabulary of the news. An editor at a Scripps paper said that he used basic language "not only to save space but also to make the meaning plainer to the man on the street, the man with the pail who quit school at twelve or thirteen. I would use 'pm' instead of 'afternoon' . . . ; 'aid' instead of 'assistance'; . . . 'wounds' instead of 'lacerations'; 'chances' instead of 'opportunities.'"[60] These words made newspaper articles less intimidating to the "man with the pail"; they could be equally helpful for those just learning English.

Editors interested in attracting immigrant readers took the logical next step and put illustrations all over their papers. Pulitzer often devoted a quarter of the front page to a single image and made sure to place it in the top half of the page, so that newsstand customers could see it even when the paper was folded. He scattered smaller images throughout the paper, some of which depicted the action of a news article from beginning to end. This format not only helped readers to grasp the crux of a story, it also served as English practice, letting readers check their understanding of the article against the pictures.[61] Pulitzer's paper succeeded in attracting immigrant readers, but it also grew so spectacular with caricatures, city scenes, celebrity portraits, puzzles, games, and advertisements that even native English speakers might find themselves spending more time on the pictures than on the words.[62] Scripps's illustrations were not so extravagant; he insisted that his pictures always convey information rather than simply dazzle the reader. Still, in the medium-sized cities where he operated papers, he far out-illustrated his competitors.[63]

A few illustrators experimented further with drawings of sequenced action, and in the process developed a new genre: the comic strip. Starting in 1884, artists at both the *New York World* and the *New York Daily News* tried dividing their images into several related sections, depicting a cluster of moments in time.[64] Pulitzer separated these images from articles and launched the first comics section in 1889. One of Pulitzer's early comics,

1.6 A San Francisco newsstand displays the comics sections as well as the front pages, 1925. Major metropolitan dailies began printing separate (often color) Sunday comics sections like this as early as 1902. San Francisco History Center, San Francisco Public Library.

Hogan's Alley, followed the goofy-looking "Yellow Kid" and his adventures in New York City tenement alleys. When the feature became a runaway hit, William Randolph Hearst, publisher of the rival *New York Journal*, hired the Yellow Kid's creator away from the *World*. Eventually both papers printed a Yellow Kid, drawn by different artists.[65] So many readers bought the papers for *Hogan's Alley* that people dubbed the Hearst-Pulitzer style "yellow journalism." A Pulitzer employee claimed that the comics section alone boosted the *New York World*'s circulation from 250,000 to 500,000.[66]

The comics proved a runaway success among all kinds of readers; they also provoked anger and disgust. A 1906 *Atlantic* article described them as "humor prepared and printed for the extremely dull," filled with "the clamor of hooting mobs, the laughter of imbeciles, and the crash of explosives."[67] Many comic strips took immigrants as their subjects: the Irish Yellow Kid; the German Katzenjammer Kids; Jewish Abie the Agent. Comics tread the line between affectionate ribbing and cruel caricature, but they continually put immigrant humor at the center of the newspaper. And whether readers found them hilarious or offensive, comics seemed a harbinger of a new entertainment age. They drew on the old-fashioned format of vaudeville routines but depicted life in fragmented narrative bits that echoed a fast and fractured urban experience. Their loose language, incorporating ethnic dialect and action words ("wham!"), reflected the hybrid, slangy vocabularies of urban neighborhoods. Comic art played in sophisticated ways with readers' sense of time and perspective, but still often pandered to the basest levels of humor, with fistfights and bawdy jokes. No wonder so many city readers could not seem to look away.

With comics, newspapers captured one last untapped audience: children. The bright colors and slapstick humor appealed to young readers, and many of the comics' protagonists—Little Nemo, Buster Brown—were children themselves. Editors noticed that children who loved a certain comic could successfully badger their parents to buy a particular paper.[68] Many parents disapproved of their children poring over comic strips, though. Mothers' groups and education leaders criticized newspapers for running comics at all, and the International Kindergarten Union staged a strike in 1907 to protest violent content in the comics.[69] Newspapers aiming for a middle- or upper-class audience began to run tame children's pages, full of puzzles, poems, and bedtime stories, as more palatable alternatives to the comics. "It is a source of pleasure for us to place this high-class material in their hands," commented one parent on the *Philadelphia Public Ledger*'s children's page, "instead of the usual low-class, vulgar 'slapstick stuff.'"[70] Sanitized children's material could build circulation just as the comics did. Managers hoped, too, that children might grow up to be loyal readers, so they started clubs for young readers, printed games and activities that could be cut out and constructed from newspaper pages, and included coupons for dolls or paint boxes.[71]

Mass-circulation newspapers had discovered a lucrative new business model. Their extensive news coverage and special features attracted thousands or even millions of readers. The revenue from advertisements allowed publishers to sell their papers at below the cost of production; in the eighty-page Sunday *Journal*, the newsprint alone cost William Randolph Hearst more than the three cents he charged for the newspaper.[72] The low price further expanded readership. The ad contracts that were to make this whole system possible, however, did not come rushing in. In merchants' eyes, working-class readers did not shop enough to warrant the expense of advertising to them. Advertising men soon realized this and warned each other in the trade press about "mushroom circulation," "cheap circulation," and even "worthless circulation."[73] "Of readers alone a newspaper may get too many for its own good," explained journalist John Given in 1907, "for a large circulation unaccompanied by advertising receipts in proportion is a costly luxury."[74] With their attention spread so thin over scores of pages, readers did not necessarily notice every ad, either. Merchandisers suspected that their pitch might get lost in a sea of riotous illustrations and text. So while newspaper publishers had bent over backward to increase circulation, ultimately they could not keep enough advertisers on the strength of their circulation alone.

By the early twentieth century, publishers had reconfigured their papers to help sell advertisers' products. They added sections and issued new afternoon and Sunday editions, all in service to this selling mission. An ad in the 1909 *Philadelphia North American* paraded the paper's commercial role within plain sight of all readers:

Selling Power! What is it? It is the ability of a newspaper to sell your goods—
To create in the minds of its readers the desire and the willingness to buy—
To reach the buying public—
To go right into the homes of the people.[75]

It became a widely known fact inside the industry, and a fairly common comment outside of it, that, as E. W. Scripps put it, newspapers were "fashioned for advertisers."[76]

Perhaps the most important concession to advertisers was the creation of separate feature sections. Editors initially commissioned women's columns hoping to boost circulation and to get women to look at the advertisements sprinkled throughout the paper. By around 1900, though, most editors had turned their women's sections into shopping forums. They used the sections' columns to talk about beauty, fashion, or cooking and then surrounded that material with ads specifically targeting female buyers. Sports pages, while not originally intended to sell things, gradually became equivalent sections for men, where articles on boxing ran alongside advertisements for shaving lotion and chewing tobacco. Editors created other sections, such as those for automobiles, bicycles, real estate, travel, and gardening, due to advertiser demand alone.[77] For manufacturers who tended to advertise seasonally, newspapers printed special editions; a typical 1915 paper might put out numbers for spring fashion, summer resorts, back to school, and autumn real estate.[78] These sections furthered advertisers' goals not only by creating designated space for advertisements but also by turning people's attention toward certain subjects and away from others. Newspapers encouraged readers to think about beauty routines, business investments, and vacations; they rarely urged readers to consider spiritual questions or think about improving their working conditions. Simply by editing and organizing daily information into consumer-oriented categories, newspapers pushed consumer habits on news-reading Americans and turned readers into customers.

Many advertisers migrated toward papers with extensive feature sections; many also preferred to buy space in afternoon papers. Afternoon papers attracted working-class readers of both genders—not particularly desirable in advertisers' eyes—but they also tapped a middle-class female audience. Many men who bought morning papers at newsstands threw them away at work. By contrast, men buying afternoon papers often carried them home, where wives and daughters might also read them. Advertisers reasoned that women running households were more likely to have time to read at night than in the morning. "The morning paper," explained a writer in *Advertising World*, "will never be the home paper so long as women are confronted with household duties. When it is fresh, they are too busy to read it and when they are at leisure, it is old."[79] Thus, many merchants preferred to advertise in afternoon papers, which became quite profitable. Many papers actually lost money on their morning sheets, which were heavier on news and lighter on advertising, but made it up in the afternoon, when they recycled much of their morning news and loaded up pages with ads.[80] The *Milwaukee Sentinel* was able to sell its afternoon paper for one cent less than its morning edition; the extra advertisements in the afternoon subsidized the price.

Editors expanded their Sunday papers to turn them into especially effective vehicles for advertisements. Advertisers initially lobbied for space in Sunday papers in the 1870s and 1880s, when Americans began to treat the day differently. No longer content to spend their Sundays in church and in prayer, Americans started to spend their one work-free day visiting amusement parks, taking in exhibitions, ice skating, and riding bicycles. Trolley and steamship companies shuttled day trippers to the countryside or the beach, no longer halting their routes in observation of the Sabbath. Ministers found they needed to give more entertaining sermons in order to compete with cities' enticing menus of Sunday activities.[81] Because more Americans were using Sundays for leisure, they had more time to read a paper on that day. Independent Sunday weeklies saw their sales double; sensing demand, daily papers began printing Sunday supplements too.[82]

Advertisers bought so much space in Sunday newspapers that editors had to commission more Sunday news and feature content just to keep up. Editors fashioned separate book review supplements, extended the sports pages, and printed fiction in Sunday installments. They created glossy magazine inserts. In an 1898 advertisement for New York's *Sunday World*, the Sunday paper appeared as a kind of swirling carnival (plate 3). "Laymen may assume that the Sunday newspaper has more space for advertising because it carries so much more news and feature reading," explained one circulation expert. "As a matter of fact, the extra news and special features really are carried because the paper has so much more advertising patronage and the displays must be sandwiched with reading matter."[83]

Sunday editions swelled to fifty pages, then eighty pages, then over a hundred. One reader of the *New York World* commented in 1889 that Sunday alone did not afford enough time to take in the Sunday paper. "A grand idea is to have no edition of THE WORLD on Monday morning. Give the people a chance to read your Sunday WORLD through."[84] Overwhelming as these papers may have been, readers could not resist their wealth of attractions. Papers' Sunday circulations outpaced their weekday numbers by tens of thousands.[85]

Publishers accommodated advertisers' needs within their papers but also went one step further by actively recruiting new advertisers. These publishers not only produced an overtly commercial form of media but also took transactions out of neighborhoods and onto the page, drawing individuals and businesses into citywide, print-coordinated economies. Publishers were perhaps most keen on attracting classified ads; unlike other advertisements, classifieds facilitated a dialogue among readers themselves, and a large classified section could guarantee newspapers a steady audience. The *Chicago Tribune* sent men out in teams to canvass neighborhoods for new classified ad takers.[86] Other papers placed decoy ads in their pages to make their classified section appear popular.[87] Several newspapers schooled readers in exactly how and why to take out a classified ad, encouraging them to search for a job, piano lessons, or a used automobile in the newspaper. "Mr. Commuter," said an ad in the 1907 *Philadelphia Record*, "if Fall charms in the suburbs have been insufficient to hold your maid, try this: Telephone your Help Wanted advertisement to 'The Philadelphia Record.'"[88] Classifieds seemingly put the whole city's opportunities at the fingertips of any reader, while perhaps reinforcing city dwellers' tendencies to view many relationships as mere transactions. "5,000 OFFERS to hire, work, buy, sell, rent, exchange," announced the 1905 *New York World*. "See Sunday World's Want Directory To-Day!"[89]

Publishers hired advertising managers at higher salaries than any other employees and gave ad salesmen expense accounts to wine and dine potential advertisers.[90] These managers and salesmen used aggressive strategies with local merchants, such as insisting that any merchant who did not advertise would soon be eclipsed by competitors who did.[91] Nathaniel Fowler, advertising specialist, estimated that 75 percent of all periodical advertising came in from these active sales.[92] Newspapers waged campaigns for advertising in their own pages, too. The *Chicago Defender* listed dozens of reasons why people should buy newspaper space, including:

Advertising Shows Energy
Advertising Shows Pluck
Advertising is "Biz"
Advertising or Bust[93]

The *Philadelphia North American* ran short articles that taught readers how to write better ads. "The nearer advertising writing can come to just plain conversation," it advised, "with that dash of conscious art which a tactful person would inject into casual conversation, the nearer it will get to the mind of the reader."[94] The American Newspaper Publishers' Association, an industry consortium and lobbying group, issued short daily "talks" on advertising for members to publish.[95] These talks often singled out particular organizations—banks, insurance companies, magazines, churches—and explained why they ought to consider advertising.[96]

Newspapers sometimes won ad contracts with local merchants by providing the services of ad agencies, scaled to a local clientele. Newspaper offices kept distinctive typefaces on hand for advertisers, so each could choose a signature look. Papers designed advertising strategies for merchants and wrote ad copy for them. "If you are not an 'ad writer' yourself," advised R. Roy Shuman in a manual for newspapermen, "employ a bright young man or woman who shows taste and talent in that line, and make advertising easy for those of your patrons who wish to be relieved of the drudgery of preparing the copy."[97]

Newspaper publishers pushed advertising to improve their own bottom lines, yet their actions had broader consequences. By pressing local retailers to enter the mass market, publishers stoked a new kind of economy in which small businesses either grew their operations or lost out to larger competitors. "We must reach out and out and out for wider fields. The advertisement is the natural and most effective way of reaching out," explained Frank Munsey, owner of several major newspapers. "It means that the big houses will get bigger, and that the small ones will disappear."[98] Department stores fully embraced this strategy; by running detailed daily announcements of new items and sales in their local papers, they turned themselves into emporiums with citywide customer bases. William F. King, the president of the New York City Merchants' Association, even credited newspaper advertising for the very creation of the department store.[99] Businesses that did not advertise might suffer simply because they remained out of sight and out of mind of city people, who had learned to look to newspapers for information about the goods and services they needed.

Around 1900, several newspaper editors took up a new and counterintuitive strategy to help boost their advertisers' sales; they began rejecting certain advertisements. When *Collier's Weekly* collected readers' essays about their newspapers in 1911, the most common complaint was "bad advertising" for patent medicines and miracle cures.[100] Some editors began to screen out ads for products that genteel readers might consider vulgar—from dandruff shampoo to alcohol—and rejected those that made obviously false claims. The Scripps-McRae newspaper chain, for example, appointed an ad censor in 1903 who inspected every potential ad and product.[101] This tactic boosted newspapers' circulations among families. "I read the other Kansas City papers—the 'Journal' and the 'Post'—occasionally," explained a Kansas City resident, "but the 'Star' and 'Times,' clean in sentiment and appearance, void of all whisky, beer, fraudulent, fake, and patent-medicine advertising, are the papers that come into my home."[102] Newspaper editors screened ads as much in deference to the highest-paying advertisers as to readers. Waldo P. Warren, advertising manager for Marshall Field's department store, clipped out a piece of medical hokum from the *Chicago Daily News* in 1902 and sent it to the paper's editor with an angry note. He dangled the promise of higher profits if Lawson censored ads: "Think of the value of having the News spoken of and thought of as 'The cleanest paper in Chicago.' . . . I feel safe in saying that if such a standard of dignity was reached by the News it would call forth a great deal more of our higher class advertising."[103] Papers that screened their ads often did find that they gained more money than they lost, and advertisers were indeed willing to pay more. A merchant who made it into a screened "pure food" section declared: "It is as if you delivered our message from a high place to a waiting and eager multitude."[104]

By the first decade of the twentieth century, the search for bigger audiences and the quest to sell more ads had created an entirely different kind of newspaper. The Sunday paper, especially, had become a day's entertainment in itself. The new abundance and diversity of turn-of-the-century metropolitan newspapers turned them into apt organs for the era's cities. The colorful pages reflected the polyglot metropolitan populations that newspapers served. As W. T. Stead described, "Just as the people have wide and varied tastes, and the interests of the whole community have to be catered for, everything goes in."[105] The clashing messages within the paper echoed the noise and spectacle of city streets. And as feature writers wove product recommendations through their articles and focused readers' attention on advertiser-approved topics, they implied that commerce and consumption ought to be central concerns in readers' lives.

Yet these new metropolitan newspapers offered city people a more solitary reading experience than they had once known. At a price of one or two cents, more Americans could afford to purchase a daily paper of their own. So rather than listening to a brother or a coworker read steadily through the paper's jumble of information, they now flipped through the pages themselves. And because news came in separate sections, readers could parcel out those sections and exchange pieces of the paper to read silently. Newspapers' visual appeal, their length, their skimmable headlines, and their separate sections all discouraged people from reading papers from start to finish. As Stead noticed, "No reader is expected to do more than assimilate just such portion of the mammoth sheet as meets his taste."[106] Hundreds of thousands of people might read the same edition of a city newspaper, but when they perused the various sections, they all experienced that paper a little differently.

NEWSPAPERS REMAKE THEIR CITIES

As newspapers attracted ever-larger audiences, they grew into formidable institutions, with large buildings, intricate production and circulation systems, and huge numbers of employees. Newspapers' operations catalyzed cities' transitions into centers of industry and of mass culture. They increased the scale and the volume of urban production and sped up the pace of urban life; they changed the makeup of workplaces and the feel of city streets.

Publishers eager to boost their newspapers' reputations built large and distinctive headquarters that staked a claim to their papers' broader importance. In the 1880s and 1890s, several publishers grew dissatisfied with their plain urban storefronts, which seemed too humdrum for the brash and confident newspapers they housed. Metropolitan papers were also outgrowing those storefronts as they acquired large presses and hired more workers. Publishers commissioned fifteen- or twenty-story skyscrapers, competing to construct the tallest building in the city. They adorned the towers with signature details—baroque domes, copper turrets, or elaborate clocks—that made them easy to spot from far away.[107] The *New York Tribune* carved its name into the marble at the top of its clock tower. The *New York World* invited the public up to its top story for a panoramic view of the city and sent them away with brochures detailing the *World*'s newsgathering prowess.[108]

Publishers were attempting to create the monuments of their age: testaments to American ambition, wealth, and appetite for information. Senator Chauncey Depew, speaking at the laying of the cornerstone of the *New York World* building in 1889, picked up on this: "The Pyramids and obelisks of the past, the national monuments of every age, are symbols of force and conquest. These splendid structures built by the modern newspaper, are the results of a combination of brains and business, of mental vigor and culture, of ability in the conduct of affairs, of statesmanship and common

1.7 Headlines being written up at the *New York Tribune* (*right*) and *New York Tele-graph* (*left*) during the Spanish-American War. Image from Henry W. Baehr, *The New York Tribune since the Civil War* (New York: Dodd, Mead & Company, 1936), opposite page 226.

sense, which makes possible American literature and perpetuates American liberty. Yonder rises the stories and towers which will tell to all succeeding generations the story and the glory of Greeley and Raymond, of Bennett and Bryant and Dana."[109] In their efforts to turn their new buildings into urban icons, some newspaper owners lobbied to officially rename their districts. Detroit had a Times Square, named for the *Detroit Times*; Baltimore had Sun Square. In New York, the intersection of Thirty-Fourth and Broadway became Herald Square, and Longacre Square was rechristened Times Square with the arrival of the *New York Times* in 1904.

Publishers staged events that put their buildings at the center of the action. Newspapers' staff wrote the latest headlines on chalkboards in the windows or on large marquees over their doors, which encouraged people to stop by the building.[110] When especially exciting events were unfolding—such as a major baseball game or an election—crowds gathered to read every update (fig. 1.7). During a highly anticipated 1897 boxing match in Nevada, the *New York World* placed puppets in a ring in front of its building. The puppeteers received telegraphic reports of each punch and re-enacted the match for a crowd of twenty-five thousand people.[111] Postings on sports and politics attracted mostly working-class men, who dominated much of the nineteenth-century streetscape. But by the turn of the century, newspaper buildings welcomed other types of visitors. Women entered newspaper lobbies to place classified advertisements, middle-class and wealthy visitors traveled to the tops of newspaper buildings for the views, and various urban professionals rented out offices there. Publishers thus turned their offices into hubs of activity for a cross section of city dwellers.

Meanwhile, newspapers' expanding production and distribution networks demonstrated the capabilities of the industrial metropolis. The largest papers kept more than a thousand regular workers on the payrolls and employed perhaps two thousand as part-time and freelance workers.[112] Publishers invited the public into their just-in-time manufacturing operations, showing off the modern and wondrous processes that generated their dailies. Many papers proudly explained their production methods within their own pages; the *Milwaukee Sentinel* lovingly described every stage in preparing newspaper images and included detailed illustrations of its workers and equipment.[113] Magazine articles also sated readers' curiosity about the inner workings of the news. "The superintendent of delivery has to know exactly when he must have the first papers in order to catch the first mail," explained Lincoln Steffens in a *Scribner's Magazine* article. "The foreman of the press-room must say how little time he needs to run off the first thousand copies; the foreman of the stereotyping-room times his process to a second; and so on back to the news department, which has to be ready for the night editor's 'make-up' in season to 'go to press' at the moment determined by the closest reckoning of each chief of staff."[114] (See figs. 1.8–1.10.) These articles alerted readers to the increasing speed and scale of production and turned the reading of the newspaper from a mundane daily ritual into a small way to participate in an impressively modern drama of industrial urban life.[115]

Meanwhile, the people who reported and sold the news carried a fast-paced modern style out into city streets. Poor and working-class children, hired to sell their papers on street corners, became the consummate urban hustlers. Young workers gauged exactly how many papers they thought they could sell, for news offices would not buy back any leftover copies. Some papers trained newsboys in sidewalk or door-to-door salesmanship techniques; other newsboys figured out on their own how to stake out the busiest intersections, how to find the likeliest buyers for their paper, or which headlines would grab the attention of passersby.[116] Thanks in part to the newsboy heroes in Horatio Alger's popular novels (that appeared starting in the 1860s), newsboys became icons of street smarts, shrewd business sense, and up-by-the-bootstraps success. However, while from one angle newsboys look like nascent businessmen, from another they seem more

1.8 "The Press Room," illustration by W. R. Leigh, in J. Lincoln Steffens, "The Business of a Newspaper," *Scribner's Magazine* (October 1897), 450.

like the pawns of large corporations. Newspapers' sales structure, in which newsboys ate the cost of any unsold papers, shifted that financial burden onto the young workers who could least afford it.[117] And sales managers employed newsboys in part because they knew customers were more likely to buy a paper from a small child who needed the half-cent profit from each copy than to buy from an adult being paid a real salary.[118] The children hawking and delivering newspapers, then, served as poignant symbols of the promise and peril of cities' competitive economies.

Newspapers' reporters modeled a bold new way of inhabiting the urban world, and their presence changed the character of city streets. During the day, reporters tracked down newsworthy citizens and often asked them the questions that they least wanted to answer. They scanned birth notices for evidence of illegitimate children, marriage notices for indications of elope-

1.9 "Receiving Papers from the Elevators," illustration by W. R. Leigh, in J. Lincoln Steffens, "The Business of a Newspaper," *Scribner's Magazine* (October 1897), 451.

1.10 "The Mail Room," illustration by W. R. Leigh, in J. Lincoln Steffens, "The Business of a Newspaper," *Scribner's Magazine* (October 1897), 452.

1.11 These images from a 1911 magazine article show a reporter not only visiting the expected news-generating places, such as the legislature (*a*), a fire (*b*), and a hospital (*c*), but also more energetically and creatively pursuing stories. Here the reporter interviews a construction worker (*d*), gets secrets from a servant in the middle of the night (*e*), and jumps on the back of a car (*f*), perhaps to gather information about the man inside it. Will Irwin, "The American Newspaper: A Study of Journalism and Its Relation to the Public," pt. 7, "The Reporter and the News," *Collier's Weekly*, 22 April 1911, 21–22.

ments, and obituaries for hints of suicides; they then worked to uncover the details of events that people usually wanted to keep secret.[119] They appeared at the scenes of crimes and accidents, prying for details. They did not wait for widows to grieve or for victims to recuperate but insisted on interviewing people while emotions were still raw. Readers usually welcomed the news that these reporters were able to extract. News subjects, however, did not feel so kindly toward reporters (fig. 1.11).

The reporting lifestyle seemed to offer young men all of the romance and danger of the modern metropolis. Authors and academics recommended reporting work as a quick way for any young man to learn the truths of a city and of the wider world. Aspiring writers moved to big cities hoping to prove themselves and perhaps make their names at a metropolitan paper.[120] Like other types of workers in turn-of-the-century cities, reporters occupied their own spaces, lived by their own schedules, and spoke their own particular language. They worked late hours and ate midnight suppers in news districts while debating politics and literature. Adding to reporters' mystique was the notion that they touched the heart of the city, witnessing all facets of urban life. "Its excitements, its outlook upon the world, its opportunities for knowing men, and the sense of power that comes from being a part of such an engine of civilization," explained reporter Edwin Shuman in 1903, "these things create a spell which the born journalist is loath to break."[121]

But journalism could be an unforgiving career path, and the profession demonstrated the hazards of a fast-paced, high-stakes urban economy. Seven out of eight migrants from small papers, warned a former employee of the *New York Sun*, would fail to find a position at a big-city paper.[122] Even those who did get work were probably destined for a "short and brutish" career, as reporter John Reed put it.[123] Theodore Dreiser, one of the many men who failed to ascend the ranks of New York City reporters, explained that "men such as myself were mere machines or privates in an ill-paid army to be thrown into any breach."[124] Like industrial-age cities themselves, newspaper offices seemed to prize youth, energy, and resilience. "Reporting involves so much 'leg work,' requires so much spurring from the buoying sense of adventure, that, as a rule, only very young men do it successfully," wrote journalist Will Irwin in 1911. "A reporter's useful life is about contemporary with that of an athlete."[125] Newspapers' corps of eager young reporters and their ranks of older, discarded workers together epitomized the labor cycle of modern urban life.

While the newsroom chewed up and spit out male reporters, it also gradually expanded to include female reporters. Many daily papers noted the success of early women columnists such as Jennie June Croly, Grace Greenwood, and Fannie Fern and took on a handful of women writers in the 1880s and 1890s.[126] Yet editors often kept women "reserved," as one reporter described, "for such dainty uses as the reporting of women's club meetings and the writing of fashion and complexion advices."[127] The majority of women news writers made their livings by writing about traditional female roles, but they pushed boundaries in their own ways. Each time a woman's name appeared at the top of a column, in the highly public and traditionally male forum of the newspaper, it announced women's professional arrival.

By the turn of the century, more women were taking up reporting jobs and "male" subjects.[128] Women ran city desks, wrote political editorials, and challenged the status quo in muckraking articles. They went undercover as servants, recent immigrants, factory workers, or shop girls in order to expose substandard working or living conditions. Women reporters deliberately covered events, such as hangings, that genteel women were not supposed to witness. They went places, such as downtown streets at night, that genteel women were not supposed to go. Because of this, such authors came to epitomize the seemingly fearless "new women" of the age.[129] In New York, Kate Carew (whose real name was Mary Williams) led an especially public career as an interviewer and caricaturist. The *World* and other papers sent Carew to speak with celebrities, from Jack London to Pablo Picasso to the Wright brothers (fig. 1.12). When Carew and other women reporters ventured onto the streets alone, asked questions, and presented themselves as proficient newsgatherers, they helped to create a world in which women increasingly operated as professionals and public figures.

Newswomen also accustomed people to a female presence in an overwhelmingly male work space, a trend that would continue as more and more women took jobs in city offices and shops. Women news workers sometimes provoked resentment among male editors and reporters, who suddenly felt more self-conscious about their newsroom culture of curse words, dirty jokes, and alcohol.[130] Reporter Flora McDonald wrote that she felt forever "a fish out of water" in the male-dominated newsroom.[131] Many of the first women journalists avoided newsrooms by working from home, bringing pieces to their editors once a week or sending them in by mail.[132] Yet other women simply adjusted. Isabel Worrell Ball, a congressional reporter for the *Topeka Capital*, put it this way: "If a man wants to smoke in her presence when she is at work, or keep his hat on, or take his coat off, or put his feet on the desk, or do any of the things which she would order him out of her parlour for doing, she must remember that it all goes with the place she is in."[133] The *Journalist*, a trade publication, was more pointed: "The girl who has it in her to survive for newspaper work will cry the first time a man swears at her, grit her teeth the second time, and swear back the third time."[134] Female journalists forced men to recognize that women could tolerate, and even thrive in, male-dominated offices.

Editors in need of feature news and illustrations hired large corps of freelance writers; these writers diversified the types of voices heard within the paper but were rarely treated as equals to their full-time counterparts. The specialized nature of feature writing lent itself to a freelance structure. No paper needed a staff reporter who concentrated solely on boxing, cooking, or philanthropy, but a freelancer could build a career by picking one of those topics and writing about it for a number of newspapers. Freelancers worked from locations all over the country, but they concentrated in New York, selling work to magazines and Sunday papers nationwide.[135] Freelance jobs offered more flexibility than salaried jobs; women could write even while raising children at home.[136] Freelancing, however, offered none of the job security, oversight, or training that salaried journalism provided.

1.12 Kate Carew's caricatures always depicted both her subject and herself. Unlike most cartoons of women at the time, she appeared neither as a young fashion plate nor as a dowdy housewife but as an inquisitive, slightly shy, bespectacled interviewer. Carew worked for the *New York World* in the 1890s and 1900s, for the *New York Journal* in the early 1900s, and for the *New York Tribune* in the 1910s. *New York Tribune*, 19 May 1912, sec. 2, 1.

The freelancers who pitched articles and the editors who bought them treated news as a commercial product. Unlike a salaried worker, a freelancer was likely to draw a direct line from an idea to the profit it might produce when written up. "It does not matter where you live," stated a 1910 brochure for a correspondence course in journalism. "Wherever there are people there is news, and my instructions teach you how to turn it into money."[137] Writers learned to describe their work to editors as appealing merchandise. "All the news of every kind from Oklahoma and Indian Territories, by mail or wire, always *fresh, brief* and *reliable*," advertised one freelancer in a trade magazine. "Indian news and sketches a specialty. You state what you want, I'll do the rest."[138] The structure of freelancing pushed writers to treat their own names as brands to be continually promoted and to treat their pieces as goods to be purchased and consumed.

As newspapers adopted a twenty-four-hour schedule, they subtly altered the rhythms of urbanites' lives. Newspapers took it as their responsibility to report all important events and so kept their office doors open, their telegraph lines ready, and their reporters working through the night. The *New York Herald* even kept its classified offices open until 10 P.M.[139] Newspapers required intense labor at night in order to get their papers out by morning, so their employees worked staggered shifts. Most writers reported for work in the early afternoon and finished after midnight. As those writers headed to supper clubs in the neighborhood (which stayed open late just to serve the news industry), the compositors set the news into print. Printers, working from perhaps midnight until six in the morning, turned out the finished product, and the papers' distribution force then shuttled papers around the city at dawn.[140] As newspapers took to printing several editions per day—anywhere between two and ten—they had to engineer even more round-the-clock operations, using a second set of reporters, compositors, printers, and distributors.[141] Cities that housed major newspapers became cities that truly never slept.

The all-hours nature of the news industry likely affected city dwellers' sense of time. No event occurred too late or too early to be picked up by the news; thus was no city hour entirely private. Nor was any hour truly quiet and still, for there was always a fresh edition of the paper to be read and digested. Some readers found these constant editions comforting and came to rely on them. "As long as I have been a reader of the evening journal it has been a great comfort to me," explained reader Marjorie Van Horn. "Nights when coming home from work I would feel very down hearted and when I would get this paper and read it I could go to rest with great ease."[142] Others might find the arrival of new editions relentless—far too much to keep up with. Whether readers welcomed or resented them, the stacks of fresh papers on newsstands reminded everyone that all through the day and night, dramas had been unfolding, presses had been churning, and the city had been making news.

THE OBJECTIVITY QUESTION

Until the late nineteenth century, most papers had operated under the auspices of a single owner or a primary owner plus several investors. The owner usually served as the paper's editor; he also purchased all of the equipment, paid the employees, pocketed any profits, and suffered all of the losses. A handful of these owners operated independently. More of them enlisted support from a political party, in the form of equipment, free rent, volunteer labor, or cash. In return, editors stuck to party lines in their editorials and talked up the causes that local party bosses championed.[143] However, by the 1880s and 1890s, to stay competitive in an expanding industry, many newspaper publishers needed more funds than local party leaders or a few wealthy investors could provide. Thus, publishers would invite several hundred investors to own a small part of the paper and share in its gains or losses, incorporating the papers as joint-stock enterprises.[144]

Editors, when entrusted with shareholders' money, often acted conservatively. "Some editors are fortunate enough to be able to make their papers pay on lines conforming with their own ideas in most matters, but there is none who has not had to suppress many of his private views," explained Edwin Shuman in 1903. "He is only one of many whose money is invested in the paper, hence he has no right to wreck it for the sake of any idea, however dear to him."[145] If profits began to slip, the newspaper's board could ask an editor to step down. Jointly held papers could remain political organs, but more often they expressed moderate views in an attempt to attract readers from all parties. The corporate model clearly discouraged experimentation. The greatest newspaper innovations of the late nineteenth century came from papers still operating under sole proprietors. Neither Joseph Pulitzer nor William Randolph Hearst, for example, issued stock for their newspapers.[146]

Corporate structures pushed newspaper editors to approach their work like businessmen, to treat an editorship more like a salaried position than like a crusade or a calling. "What I want is the reader who likes to talk," said a newspaper manager in an 1897 interview, "and then I want to set him talking; to make him turn to the next man and ask him if he has read something in my paper. That advertises the paper and sells it, which is the thing I am after. I have no mission, you know."[147] Many editors chose their line of work because they loved the news and hoped to shape public opinion; they would never go so far as to say they had "no mission." But by the early twentieth century, most editors had to balance their own views with the business needs of their large, corporate papers. Managing editors, and lower-level editors as well, might feel more accountable to their shareholders, their supervisors, and their customers than to their own convictions.

Corporate newspapers' emphasis on moderation and steady profits gave rise to a new reporting ideal: objectivity. Highly structured corporate papers found it safest to produce neutral news. Eventually, reporters embraced this objective role, putting it at the center of their professional identity. "Tell the truth and dare to stand back of it," urged a 1906 manual for reporters. "Be impartial, unprejudiced."[148] Journalists issued pamphlets with titles like "The Ethics of Journalism" to standardize codes of conduct, and some reporters were so wedded to the objectivity ideal that they refused to register as members of any party, since it would give readers an indication of their personal political sympathies.[149]

While corporate structure encouraged nonpartisan news coverage, advertising revenue helped make objectivity financially viable: money from ads could substitute for the income once received from political parties. Melville Stone, editor of the *Chicago Daily News*, articulated this platform for his independent newspaper. "In its every phase as a news-purveying organ, or as a director of public opinion, it must be wholly divorced from any private or unworthy purpose," he argued. "It must have only two sources of revenue—from the sale of papers and the sale of advertising."[150]

"Objectivity," however, was a misleading term for the new newspaper ideal. In truth, newspapers traded one set of obligations for another, swapping partisan ties for a more generalized and pervasive commercial influence. "'Big business' is a complex web, binding this near department store to that remote trust company, this near insurance corporation to that far bank," described Will Irwin. "Since the metropolitan newspaper also is a large commercial venture, involving millions in capital, hundreds of thousands in annual profit or loss, it follows the rule."[151] When editors embedded themselves in this "complex web" of big business by borrowing money from businessmen in order to buy a new press or expand a department, they sometimes wrote more sympathetically about their creditor. The joint-stock model also opened newspapers up to business influence more than ever before. Business barons sometimes bought shares in newspapers in order to tilt reporting in their favor.[152] Finally, when publishers invested the profits from their newspapers in other companies and sat on boards of other corporations, their involvement could sway their papers' coverage. Upton Sinclair accused Joseph Pulitzer, for example, of dropping his populist crusades once his fortune was invested in telegraph and railroad companies.[153]

The rise of a new journalism institution, the press club, aided the transition away from personally and politically motivated journalism and toward business-friendly reporting. Press clubs sprouted up near newspaper offices and furnished reading rooms, billiards, bars, and dining rooms to all who paid the annual dues. The clubs provided some security in a notoriously unstable profession; they used the pool of dues to aid elderly, infirm, or unemployed members and to pay for funerals.[154] Press clubs also allowed reporters from different papers to read one another's work, discuss their jobs, and debate news standards, thus fostering ideals that spanned the industry.[155] At the same time, the clubs put journalists in regular contact with their cities' businessmen. At Philadelphia's Clover Club, businessmen bought dinners or drinks for cash-strapped journalists. At New York's Blue Pencil Club, merchants befriended editors, then invited them to join private yacht trips or offered them exclusive investment opportunities.[156] The Milwaukee Press Club enjoyed summer feasts hosted by Pabst Brewery.[157] In ways large and small, the ties formed at press clubs put journalists in businessmen's debt.

By the early twentieth century, it had become common for editors and reporters to move in and out of corporate jobs. As a result, business sympathies were likely to surface in news writing. Real estate editors took positions with realty offices, newspaper ad managers became advertising directors for department stores, and bicycle merchants took jobs editing papers' cycling pages.[158] The managing editor of the *New York Morning Journal* resigned in 1906 and took a job as a press agent with Standard Oil for a staggering salary of $20,000 a year.[159] Any writer hoping for such a position was unlikely to report very negatively on a potential future employer. Freelancers, too, often cobbled careers together from both newspaper and publicity work. Feature illustrators, for example, took jobs illustrating advertisements. Some feature writers ran businesses on the side, such as a beauty department editor who simultaneously ran a cosmetics company.[160] "Greater Grub Street is utilitarian," concluded one freelancer. "That which propels it is not Art, but Advertising—not Clio or Calliope, but Circulation."[161]

Finally, new methods of journalism training oriented writers toward commercial writing and commercial careers. In the apprentice system of the time, writers worked their way up through positions at a single paper, hewing to its viewpoint and style. But at journalism schools—which cropped up from the 1880s through the early 1900s—students were trained to write neutrally, so that they could work anywhere. Journalism schools simultaneously trained their students in commercial and reportorial work. Hundreds of students took courses in ad copy writing, learning to think and write like advertisers.[162] Early twentieth-century journalism manuals and correspondence courses, too, trained aspiring writers in both the art of the report and the art of the pitch.[163]

48   CHAPTER ONE

Personal ties, professional overlap, and dependent relationships all contributed to business's corruption of the news. "We depend upon the advertisers to pay your salaries in the editorial room, and we can't afford to make enemies of them," explained one publisher to his employees. "In other words, no matter what anyone says, a man can't afford to quarrel with his bread and butter."[164] Advertisers' influence often resulted in omissions and silences in the news. Several papers maintained "keep-out" books or lists, naming all the prominent people reporters ought not to mention.[165] "Is there a newspaper in America which will print news unfavorable to department-stores?" asked Upton Sinclair in his book *The Brass Check*. "If the girls-slaves of the local department-store go on strike, will the newspaper maintain their right to picket? Will it even print the truth about what they do and say?"[166] Papers devoted little or no space to civic campaigns against bad working conditions, inadequate trolley service, or utility monopolies. Perhaps the one exception was the *Day Book*, E. W. Scripps's short-lived Chicago daily that printed no advertising at all.[167] When the merchandising manager at Marshall Field's department store found *Chicago Daily News* coverage of his store unsatisfactory, he wrote right to the editor. "I am well aware that is your policy to keep your advertising and editorial departments separated and heartily approve of the policy," he wrote, "but I have just had occasion to sign a bill for advertising for the month of November to the Chicago Daily News Company amounting to $18,155.26. Would it not seem that we deserve a little better treatment?"[168] Advertisers clearly expected special care in the news.

The appearance of the press agent in the late nineteenth century further blurred the boundaries between journalism and business boosting. Agents drummed up good press for corporate clients; some agents were actually paid per line of positive notice that they generated.[169] Sometimes agents simply worked their way into reporters' good graces. Railroad press agents routinely mailed free passes to journalists on New Year's Day, good for the entire year.[170] Agents also wrote articles about their clients and offered the text free to editors, who were often desperate for material. Press agents' influence surfaced in articles praising the inventions of a certain car company, in women's page pieces describing a certain elegant department store, in consistently positive reviews for the shows at an advertiser's theater. "Such a thing as an independent and educative review of a moving-picture is not conceivable in my local newspaper," observed Upton Sinclair in 1919. "Nine out of ten of these plays are unspeakable trash, but from the notices you would think that a new era of art was dawning upon Pasadena. All this is 'dope,' sent out by the moving-picture exploiters."[171] Press agent material also prompted papers to speak enthusiastically about business prospects, as John Given explained: "A paper may print a long article in its news columns, saying that oil has been discovered on property owned by Blink, Blank & Co., 'the well-known brokers.' The public, reading this, thinks how lucky Blink, Blank & Co. are, and John Smith, Henry Brown, and others hasten to the offices of their brokers to invest their money in these same oil lands, which is just what Blink, Blank & Co. had planned."[172] News offices benefited so much from this system that the press agent became an accepted part of the trade. "The press agent is a valuable and necessary factor," declared an *Editor & Publisher* editorial in 1907. "While he was sneered and scorned at only a few years ago he is now welcomed by editors, that is if he really knows his business and quite a number do."[173]

While some news publishers capitulated to advertisers in their coverage, almost all publishers worked with and accommodated advertisers by muddling ads and news. Many newspapers ran paid advertising columns, which were odd hybrids of news and sales pitches. The *Milwaukee Sentinel*, for example, printed a front-page column every day called "What Milwaukee Merchants Are Offering," with "news" such as:

The Ellis Floral Company has a large stock of flowers for carnation day to be observed in memory of President McKinley. Its office is in the Wells building.

E.F. Pahl & Co. suggests that there is no better time than this for having baby carriages repaired and repainted ready to take out when the pleasant days arrive.[174]

Some papers interspersed actual news items with these paid advertising "puffs" to bait readers, forcing them to skim through the ads for nuggets of real news. Upton Sinclair described the disorienting experience of reading such puffs: "You read a headline about an aviator just returned from France, and what you learn about him is that Jones & Co. have put out twenty thousand pictures of him in twenty thousand boxes of 'Frizzlies.'"[175]

Publishers allowed advertisers to mimic news formats. "Make the readers look to your announcements as they look to news," advised M. M. Gilliam, advertising director for Wanamaker's department store in Philadelphia.[176] Gilliam structured his ads like newspaper pages, with headlines, subtitles, columns, and illustrations (see fig. 1.13). He took out a full page every day and printed a small weather forecast in the corner of the daily ad, turning these Wanamaker's pages into regular newspaper features that readers could expect and even depend on.[177] Gilliam wrote breezy, appealing dispatches on inventory, fashions, and sales:

Some of the selling counters were crowded all of yesterday in spite of the rain. You don't crowd around in such weather just to look at tons and

1.13 An ad for Wanamaker's department store echoes the format of a news page, and deems the store's specials and sales "news." *Philadelphia Public Ledger*, 1 May 1900, 11.

car-loads of stockings. There must be another magnet than bulk to draw and hold you at such a time.

There was. There will be while this Hosiery exposition lasts. The magnet of perfect, seasonable goods at the price of imperfect, unseasonable things.

That was what made such a jam of water-proofed women at so many of the counters yesterday. It's what'll keep a jam at the counters while the sale lasts—with waterproofs if need be, without if may be.[178]

The text deployed the hook, explanation, and resolution more artfully than most news articles of the time, and communicated to the reader that she was missing out were she not at the hosiery sale. Wanamaker's model became the standard for department store ads all over the nation.

Unlike the more subtle business influences on news coverage that seeped in through press clubs, press agents, and writers and editors sympathetic to the business world, these advertising strategies were relatively transparent. Puffs could be detected after careful reading, and few readers actually mistook a department store ad for reporter-written news. When newspapers allowed or helped advertisers to blur the lines between news and ads, though, they strengthened the impression that newspapers existed in part to fulfill a commercial role. "An advertisement is simply business news," explained Edwin Shuman, clearly at ease with this arrangement. "Its object is not to divert, or to amuse, or to startle, but to inform."[179]

The party affiliations of nineteenth-century newspapers had existed in the open, but early twentieth-century papers made no overt announcement of their corporate affiliations. It took disillusioned insiders to expose these ties. Hamilton Holt, editor of the *New York Independent*, gave a public talk in 1909 in which he recounted all of the ways he had refused to accommodate advertisers and all of the ad contracts he had lost as a consequence.[180] Will Irwin wrote a series of highly critical articles about the news industry for *Collier's Weekly* in 1911, describing advertisers' abuses of power. *Collier's* also published a damning article, "Confessions of a Managing Editor," by an author who chose to write anonymously.[181] Upton Sinclair self-published his book *The Brass Check* in 1919, in which he detailed all the ways that newspapers silenced the left while boosting big business.

Whistleblowers like Holt, Irwin, and Sinclair alarmed readers and embarrassed newspapers. Angered citizens and politicians attempted to regulate advertisers' influence on the news with laws such as the Interstate Commerce Commission's 1907 ban on issuing railroad passes in exchange for advertising.[182] Newspapers began to self-police as well. The American Newspaper Publishers' Association began a drive to purge papers of free publicity in 1909.[183] At the association's urging, a young congressman introduced the Newspaper Publicity Act of 1912, under which any newspaper that wanted a subsidized mailing rate had to remove paid advertising from news and editorial columns and to label all advertisements that resembled news articles.[184] These laws created baseline standards for reporting that would stand independent from corporations' publicity campaigns. Yet they could not keep a more general pro-business attitude from shaping the news. Papers nearly all tended to boost the major businesses and manufacturers of their region, because their own prosperity was so intimately tied to these businesses' success. A 1909 *Philadelphia North American* article advised readers to mistrust "what New Orleans says of sugar, or Pittsburg of steel, or San Francisco of fruits, or Chicago of packing-house products. And it is common knowledge that what almost every big New York paper says is an echo of Wall Street."[185]

As publishers and whistleblowers argued over what level of business influence was permissible in the "hard" news, almost no one seemed to object to the overwhelmingly commercial nature of "soft" feature news. Readers may have accepted motoring sections or theater reviews as commercial by nature and perhaps never expected to find objective information there. Readers and publishers alike may also have set their expectations differently because they realized that advertising paid for feature sections. "The American newspaper at one cent is unquestionably the greatest value sold anywhere in any age," wrote William Scott in 1915. "For this nominal admittance fee, the buyer enters a forum where he may hear the news of the world, where through special features he will be entertained with fiction, pictures, and miscellany, and where he may meet every merchant or producer with whom he may need to deal. It is worth one cent to have any one of these three services, but he gets them all for one cent, and the advertiser foots the bill."[186] While the outright buying of opinion and the disguising of paid publicity struck most readers as dishonest (and it became the exception rather than the rule by the 1910s), the more general tendency for newspapers to promote businessmen's causes—and the perfect harmony between feature sections and advertisers' needs—became a widely accepted fact.

But advertisements and consumer-focused sections did not just subsidize the "real" news. They also added a sheen and allure to newspapers that readers enjoyed. A devoted reader of the *Chicago Record-Herald* wrote to *Collier's*, without irony: "I do not know of any criticism to make of this paper except that it does not contain enough department-store advertisements."[187] Editor E. W. Scripps tried to stand above this fray; he refused to rely too heavily on advertising revenue in a bid to preserve his papers' editorial independence. He insisted that all advertisements appear small and inconspicuous, and he did not steer his feature writers toward advertiser-friendly topics such as fashion or automobiles.[188] Many of Scripps's papers found steady audiences in smaller cities, but in Chicago, San Francisco, and Los Angeles, Scripps's compact papers never earned as much affection as those of his competitor, William Randolph Hearst.[189] Hearst packed his papers full of advertising material, lavish illustrations, and consumer advice, which made them longer, more commercial—and much more fun. So even though readers seemed not to want their hard news too tainted by businessmen's influence, many thoroughly enjoyed the consumer topics, colorful images, and breezy tone that business and advertising influence brought to the feature news and, ultimately, to the whole package.

*   *   *

In the three decades following 1880, city newspapers transformed themselves. Papers' audiences swelled in step with city populations, with the biggest newspapers reaching well over one million people per day.[190] Papers drew in whole new populations of urban readers, including working men and women, recent immigrants, housewives, and children. Publishers greatly expanded their range of topics, motivated by the need to sell copies and to attract ads. The influx of advertising revenue enabled more colorful, expansive papers, while giving rise to a world in which civic dialogue went hand in hand with business boosting.

Metropolitan dailies' news gathering, manufacturing, and distribution practices changed city landscapes and city culture. Newspaper offices saturated streets with pushy newsboys and papered newsstands with loud headlines, helping to turn cities into places where people and print constantly jostled for residents' attention. Reporters' aggressive, even invasive working styles made privacy and solitude still scarcer in city life, while newspapers' women employees and women visitors started to habituate city people to work and leisure spaces where men and women mixed. Newspapers' campaigns for advertising drew manufacturers, merchants, and customers away from small-scale, in-person networks and into a larger-scale, growth-oriented world. Over the course of these decades, newspapers became engines that propelled cities into a modern age. But they also became guidebooks to the very modern cities that they had, themselves, helped to create.

2: MAKING METROPOLITANS

"There are lots of things that you don't know that it would be well for you to know," stated an advertisement in the 1899 *Philadelphia Inquirer*.[1] The ad was selling the *Inquirer*'s almanac, a thick compendium of information that had been printed in the paper but that readers might want to keep for reference. Newspapers had always been in the business of telling readers things that they did not know—they published "news," after all. But something changed toward the end of the nineteenth century. Newspapers took the leap from telling people about facts and situations to advising them on everyday routines. For much of the nineteenth century, partisan papers had told readers how to vote but stayed silent on other facets of readers' lives. By the turn of the century, papers were running advice columns, fiction, advertisements, and cartoons that illustrated an entire metropolitan way of life.

While editors surely had ideas about how readers should behave, it was readers, more importantly, who sought direction on the rituals of city life. Many readers had recently arrived from farms or small towns and needed to learn how to feed, clothe, and house themselves and their families in urban neighborhoods. If readers aspired to middle-class lives, they needed to learn the places to go and the things to do that would mark them as "respectable." Even those Americans born and raised in cities sought out instruction at this moment. For the first time, Americans were living in high-rise apartment buildings, dining in cafeterias, riding elevators, boarding electric streetcars, and taking jobs on industrial shop floors or in white-collar offices. All of these brand-new urban spaces carried their own unspoken rules of conduct, and the rules had to be learned.

City residents drew on all types of experiences and resources to determine how to behave. They observed how the people around them navigated the sidewalks, ordered at restaurants, or dressed for the office. They took informal lessons from their more streetwise or socially adept friends. They listened as bosses, school teachers, and nosy neighbors all passed along opinions about proper conduct. Many members of the disoriented middle class bought books of advice for extra guidance. Women bought house-keeping manuals that advised on cooking, cleaning, and home decoration. Young men bought character manuals from door-to-door booksellers and read up on how to succeed in a newly competitive work world.[2] The aspiring elite read etiquette manuals with titles like *Sensible Etiquette of the Best Society* and learned how to dress and dine as elegantly as European royalty.[3] Presses churned out five or six new advice manuals every year between 1870 and 1917, marking these as peak years for the advice industry.[4] They fed, but did not sate, Americans' appetite for advice.

The urban poor and working class, including many immigrants, tended to turn to different sources for guidance than did the middle class. New arrivals relied on friends from their hometowns (whether in the U.S. or the Ukraine) to walk them through the basics of life in the city. Immigrants subscribed to newspapers in their native languages, which guided them to the services they needed. If poor, working-class, or immigrant city residents wanted more instruction, they could turn to one of the many middle class-run organizations that tried to instruct the less fortunate. They might enroll in settlement-house or YMCA courses in English, housekeeping, or child rearing. They might look over pamphlets that the Urban League handed out in train stations, teaching African American migrants about proper public conduct. They might open their doors to social workers doing home visits in their neighborhoods.

Yet metropolitan newspapers offered uniquely accessible and useful urban guidance. One writer in 1878 noted that people bought advice manuals "with an uneasy sense of shame, read them *sub rosa*, and keep them out of sight."[5] Yet newspapers delivered advice as part of a larger package, so no reader had to admit to actually needing it or seeking it out. Unlike the Salvation Army or the YMCA, newspapers offered seemingly neutral advice, free of religious agendas. And rather than forcing lessons down readers' throats, newspapers offered to answer readers' own questions. Columnists spoke in friendly, sympathetic tones, unlike those scolding social workers. Newspapers' advice was also locally specific and, hence, potentially more useful than advice from magazines and manuals. Papers told readers exactly where to shop, which agency could help them find a job, and where they ought to vacation. Readers could take in advertisers' pitches without feeling pressured to respond right away, in contrast to door-to-door salesmen or department store staff. Last, in an era of constantly shifting norms, newspapers revised and updated their advice every single day.[6]

Of course, newspaper advice did carry out some agendas. Editors and journalists used advice articles to spread their own standards for urban behavior. And much of newspapers' counsel came through advertisements, whose images and slogans suggested how city people ought to dress, eat, shop, and play while using the advertised product. Over time, editors and advertisers worked ever more closely together, and newspapers narrowed the range of reader questions and opinions that they printed. Still, newspapers' amalgam of slick selling, preachy instruction, and responsive counseling proved satisfying enough to attract and hold onto their tens of thousands of readers.

From the 1880s into the early 1910s, newspapers tended to cater to specific classes and to communicate class-specific standards of behavior. Each paper guided its readers toward particular spaces in the city, cultivated their distinct interests, and encouraged them to purchase certain things. In the 1910s and 1920s, however, a series of mergers erased many of the distinctions between newspaper types. The resulting mass-media papers forged a common metropolitan culture for a diverse readership. They loosened class boundaries by speaking more openly about upward mobility. Perhaps assuming that their readers had, by the 1920s, mastered the basics—that they had assimilated—newspapers stopped giving so many authoritative instructions on urban living and, instead, began to delve more deeply into the dilemmas and disappointments of Americans' personal lives.

This chapter turns to the city of Philadelphia to examine newspaper advice in the American metropolis. In the late nineteenth century, Philadelphia was a sprawling industrial city with a still-visible colonial past. Much of the city had been built on a very small, preindustrial scale. Narrow streets, laid in a grid, were bisected by even narrower alleys, and its trinity houses (three small rooms, stacked on top of each other) could seem miniature in comparison to houses in other cities. Machine shops, textile mills, tanneries, breweries, and sugar refineries dotted the landscape. An unusually high proportion of Philadelphia women worked in industrial jobs, turning out carpets, lace, hosiery, suits, and hats.[7] The port along the Delaware River, the second largest one on the East Coast, employed tens of thousands of workers.[8] The center of the city was slowly moving westward, away from the port; in the late nineteenth century, downtown lay halfway between the Delaware and Broad Street. At the intersection of Broad and Market, the city's biggest streets, sat city hall, still under construction. Enormous, expensive, and topped with an almost comically large statue of William Penn when it was completed in 1900, the building seemed a symbol of "corrupt and contented" Philadelphia, a phrase coined by Lincoln Steffens.[9] This was a city, according to Steffens, in which politicians profited from streetcar monopolies and siphoned money from city hall's construction budget, yet where many residents were comfortable and prosperous enough not to care.

Turn-of-the-century commentators often called Philadelphia a truly American city not only because of its starring role in the nation's founding but also because of its relatively small incoming stream of immigrants. In all years between 1870 and 1920, about 25 percent of Philadelphia residents had been born abroad; this contrasted to 30 percent in Boston, 40 percent in New York, and even higher percentages in newer cities such as Cleveland, Chicago, and San Francisco.[10] Philadelphia still grew impressively in these years, approaching two million residents by 1930. White migrants came from rural Pennsylvania and surrounding states, while black migrants came from the upper South and from other cities on the Eastern seaboard.[11]

Philadelphia's class structure, its ethnic makeup, and its physical layout combined to create a population ready—even eager—to read advice in newspapers. The city's layout often put people of different classes within view of each other; each glimpse of a different mode of living could whet Philadelphians' appetites for advice on etiquette and upward mobility. Through much of the eighteenth and nineteenth centuries, builders had constructed large row homes on Philadelphia's wider streets and smaller homes on the streets behind. Many working-class Philadelphians, then, looked out their windows at middle-class homes, and vice versa. "Company towns" within the city (such as Manayunk and Tacony) housed workers in lowlands and managers on hills above, but the two groups lived very much within sight of each other.[12] Even suburban-type neighborhoods such as Germantown and Mount Airy housed people of varying incomes in their mixes of apartment buildings, small row homes, larger twin houses, and sprawling single-family homes. When Philadelphians went downtown to shop, they could not help but see people of other classes. Arch Street catered to a working-class clientele, Market Street to the middle class, and Chestnut Street to the upper class, but these three streets lay parallel to each other, just a few blocks apart. When middle-class shoppers passed by upper-class Chestnut Street, they may then have wondered what it would take to climb up a rung on the class ladder.

At the same time, Philadelphia could be an extraordinarily insular place—and that insularity created a distinctive market for newspaper advice. Many Philadelphians shopped, worked, and socialized within a radius of four or five blocks. Families from Kensington, in northeast Philadelphia, spoke of downtown as a forbidding place, and years could pass with no family member traveling there.[13] Women who took in piecework, sewing tags onto coats, hemming pants, or crocheting curtain pulls, worked at home and thus missed the chance to travel outside their neighborhood or to meet other workers.[14] About one-quarter of Philadelphians, from the 1880s through the 1930s, married someone who lived no more than five blocks away.[15] The abundance of neighborhood weeklies attests to the self-sufficiency of these districts within the city. In 1890, Kensington, Manayunk, Oakdale, and West Philadelphia each published a weekly; Nicetown published two, and Frankford and Germantown each published four.[16] In these insular neighborhoods, a metropolitan newspaper might be the only way to learn about life in the rest of the city.

Early settlers, and then developers, had built row homes in order to fit many people onto small, narrow lots. This created a seemingly endless supply of single-family houses. The dominance of the single-family unit, combined with multiple-income families and with immigrants' desires to own land after generations of tenancy, gave Philadelphia one of the highest rates of homeownership in the nation.[17] Buying a house usually gave a family more space and put them in a more prosperous neighborhood than the one where they had rented. It was not hard to interest such a family in advice on how to become middle class. As Russian Jews moved from eastern South Street to the more gracious Society Hill, and African Americans moved from Lombard Street to the much greener northern reaches of West Philadelphia, they found that their new surroundings demanded new skills: furnishing a foyer, dressing children for their new schools, hosting the neighbors for tea.

In 1880, all nineteen Philadelphia dailies printed local, national, and global news. Only the editorial columns, however, resembled "advice," regularly instructing readers in how to think or act.[18] Otherwise, newspapers rarely spoke to readers about their own lives—about their work, family, health, food, friendships, or free time. This would change over the next several decades, when papers made their first halting efforts to speak to women.

ADVISING WOMEN

In the mid-nineteenth century, newspapers had made their first bids for women's attention by printing small columns of fashion notes. These notes often read as straightforwardly as the rest of the paper, but they contained some real daily-life advice (for example, "In combination one rule must be observed—if there is a difference in color, then the drapery and bodice must be alike").[19] Readers might follow or disregard such notes—but they made their decisions against the backdrop of newspaper opinion. George W. Childs, editor of the *Philadelphia Public Ledger*, took newspaper advice one step further when he asked a woman on staff to write a few extra paragraphs for women readers. The *Ledger* was a morning paper popular among well-to-do Philadelphia families, so Childs could expect that women in *Ledger* households would have the paper delivered to their doorsteps and that their days were leisurely enough to allow for some newspaper reading. The first women's column, "In and Out of the Household," aired early in 1880.[20]

The *Ledger*'s column assembled a user-friendly guide to urban domestic life, written in an intimate tone, like a conversation in a kitchen or a parlor. Writers described how to remove the stains on wallpaper, how to make a hamburg steak, and how to filter the muddy water coming from the spigot after a heavy rain. Almost immediately, women wrote into the "Household" with questions. How could they clean out a clogged chimney? Store eggs so they would not spoil? Many women sought the type of household wisdom that a grandmother would pass on to a granddaughter or that one might learn from helping a seasoned housewife with the laundry. Yet many Philadelphia women did not have grandmothers, or even mothers, nearby. They followed jobs or husbands to the city and no longer lived in intergenerational households. Prosperous women may have felt especially stranded; while their husbands headed to work each day, they stayed home with the children, and their somewhat spacious homes with separate back lots meant that they were not forced into contact with their neighbors.

Many readers needed local information that even a grandmother could not have provided. They asked the paper to explain how ash collection worked in the city, or whether it was safe to open the door for peddlers, or where they could find someone to recard a wool comforter. Writers tracked down answers or responded with the addresses and hours of relevant businesses. The "Household" column also received a steady stream of letters on civic issues—indicating pent-up demand for a space where women could air grievances and suggest solutions to city problems. The letters called attention to dangerous intersections, inadequate street cleaning, irresponsible waste dumping, and unlit streetlamps. Writers asked for better treatment of bicycle riders and complained that their children's teachers sent them on errands during the school day. When possible, the paper referred complaints to the mayor's office or the school board.

Readers quickly made clear that they wanted advice not only on how to get by but also on how to fit in. "Dear Household," wrote one reader, "Should cake and bread be bitten, cut with a knife or broken with the fingers? Should a teaspoon be left in the cup while drinking or put in the saucer, and should a napkin be spread over the knees or simply placed unaltered upon the knee?"[21] Women asked about the complicated rituals of urban middle-class life: calling cards, engagement rings, theater outings, wedding gifts, and anniversary presents. Because this was the only space in the paper that fielded social questions, a few men wrote in, too. Readers' hunger for answers to etiquette questions led the *Ledger*, and most other metropolitan papers, to create specific etiquette columns by the early twentieth century.[22]

The *Ledger*'s column did not merely dispense advice; it also created a space for readers to advise each other. Individuals asked where they might send unneeded clothes or old magazines, and workers at women's charities wrote to accept the donations. Directors of city organizations wrote to publicize their services and invite readers to meetings. Debates unfolded over issues like equal pay or the consistent price gauging of the gas company. When a young woman wrote in to complain that even as a college graduate, she could find no work to support herself, the paper received a host of letters offering suggestions, jobs, and even free places to stay.[23] Letters inspired articles, and articles prompted letters in return. The column became a female public forum and clearinghouse, remarkable in its range.

Collectively, the *Ledger*'s women's material—questions, answers, articles, and ads—drew a map of middle-class spaces where women would feel welcome. For much of the nineteenth century, genteel culture had required women to tend their homes, travel in enclosed carriages, send servants out for errands, and only brave the streets with a husband or male relative for protection.[24] By the 1880s and 1890s, though, some city women found it unappealing or even impossible to remain so cloistered. Many Philadelphia women did their own errands, often at the public market houses that dotted the city or under the canvas awnings stretched over market streets. Many women left their houses every day for their jobs as seamstresses at H. Daroff & Sons or saleswomen at Wanamaker's. Married middle-class and upper-class women ventured out for public lectures at the Academy of the Fine Arts, meetings of the National Consumers' League, and shopping excursions along Market Street.[25] Yet city streets remained uncertain territory for many middle-class women. If a Market Street shopper wandered onto nearby Vine Street, she could find herself in the city's red light district. And Philadelphia spaces could be hard to read. Some boarding houses offered safe, comfortable homes for single women; others functioned as houses of prostitution. Some lunchrooms had separate floors for ladies; others were male spaces, raucous and alcohol soaked. Women's middle-class status was fragile, and they could not risk being seen in the wrong place at the wrong time. When the *Ledger* mentioned a specific streetcar line, concert hall, or boarding house, it informed readers that women—respectable women—went there. The *Ledger*'s women's material accommodated (rather than protested) the system that linked women's reputations to the spaces in which they were seen. But it helped women to navigate the streets and, therefore, to venture out of doors with confidence.

When the column's writers laid out views that a reader needed to share in order to feel included, they implicitly set standards. "The need of 'variety' is one of the greatest worries of the housekeeper," noted one writer. "Even the best of meats and the ever-returning breakfast dish gets to be unpalatable by very sameness."[26] The writer thought that she was offering solutions to a problem, but for some readers used to serving the same meal every Tuesday, she had perhaps created a problem. When an article walked the reader through the four steps of nightly face washing, it alerted readers that a round of soap and water was inadequate.[27] The daily menus in the "Household" helped some readers draw up market lists and plan family meals, but they also created a definition of a standard lunch or dinner that did not fit with every woman's family traditions or budget. Not everyone could afford beefsteak rolls for dinner and meringues for dessert, nor would everyone prefer that dinner to their family's traditional cornbread, spaetzle, or goulash.

While some of the column's pieces set very high standards, other pieces slyly questioned those standards. Writers recognized how difficult, and even absurd, it could be to try to behave as a respectable woman should. An 1880 column criticized the expectation that women remain perfectly graceful at all times—even as they corralled children, traveled in long skirts, or carried packages through the rain.[28] Tiny shoes, one writer said, "are causes of genuine torture to the saleswoman behind the counter as well as to the finely dressed customer before it."[29] Another writer referred with barbed humor to her corset. "It feels like getting into chain armor," she lamented. "But, as we have to be straight and slim to be correct, we have, of course, to take steps to become so, at whatever cost of personal discomfort."[30] Readers likely placed greater trust in the *Ledger*'s column when it sympathized with the daily trials of their lives.

After a few years of running "Household" columns, the *Ledger* debuted a new section, "Women's Interests." This was not pitched as an advice column, yet by showcasing women's behavior, it may have expanded the range of activities, careers, and goals women readers considered for themselves. The column profiled the first woman to win a state scholarship at the Massachusetts Institute of Technology, and the first woman to argue before the Wisconsin Supreme Court. In a typical column in 1892, the *Ledger* told readers about a Californian woman who was studying to be a rabbi and a woman composer who had made her debut at the Paris Opera.[31] The "Women's Interests" column joined other forces in the late nineteenth and early twentieth centuries that were breaking down the Victorian paradigm of separate spheres, in which women stayed in the home and men labored in the wider world. Women graduating from Bryn Mawr College, just outside of Philadelphia, or getting degrees at the Woman's Medical College sought meaningful ways to apply their skills. These highly educated women founded the city's Civic Club, where committees investigated issues such as public schools, free kindergartens, and sanitation. They lived in the University Settlement House and Philadelphia College Settlement, trying to help the residents of Philadelphia's desperately poor Third Ward.[32] The "Women's Interests" column trumpeted these women's achievements, while also acknowledging the more utilitarian nature of most women's work. Even here, the column saw strength in numbers; it proudly calculated that fifteen thousand women typists worked between Canal Street and the Battery in New York City.[33] These newspaper notes could help working, professional, and activist women feel that they were in good company.

The *Ledger*'s women's material sent mixed messages about how to be an urban woman. It seemed to encourage civic involvement and urged readers to take pride in women's roles as paid workers. It occasionally criticized the double standards women lived by. Yet it continued to advise readers on baking techniques and flower arrangements. While contradictory, the mix of material surely helped it to draw in a range of readers. And when taken all together, the *Ledger*'s women's material gave readers a spectrum of acceptable ways to behave—while still indicating certain arenas in which they did or did not belong.

When other papers in Philadelphia and around the country noticed the interest that readers took in the *Ledger*'s women's column, and when they noticed advertisers' pressing new interest in reaching women, they started up their own women's pages. The *Inquirer* began printing a "Women's Gossip" column in 1891 and answered "Women's Queries" by 1895. The *Philadelphia Record* called its column "The Interesting Sex" and was celebrating women's accomplishments in "The Doings of Women" by 1903.[34] From women's columns, advice spread even further into newspaper pages. In the 1890s and the first decade of the 1900s, papers' new automobile sections sprouted advice columns, sports pages offered exercise tips, and advertisements modeled suave urban fashions. In each instance, newspapers built on the women's pages' model that mixed collective comfort with prescriptive counsel. Yet as different sections of newspapers began advising readers, they (like the women's pages) set standards that were difficult to maintain, and drew lines of distinction between those who lived by papers' rules and those who did not.

DEFINING THE WORKING, MIDDLE, AND UPPER CLASSES

In a city with nineteen daily newspapers, readers might choose their paper for its political affiliation, its religious leanings, or its particular features. But Philadelphia readers also chose their newspapers based on class. Working-class papers, mass-readership papers, and elite papers included very different—and different quantities of—material about how to behave.

Working-Class Newspapers

Of Philadelphia's working-class papers, the *Evening Item* and the morning *Record* proved the most popular and enduring.[35] The *Item* squeezed all of its news and classified columns into a mere eight pages. Its penchant for gossip, scandalmongering, and huge headlines mark it as a predecessor to the twentieth-century tabloid. The *Record* printed a longer and slightly more restrained daily; it claimed the most readers in Philadelphia through the early twentieth century. The paper boasted an impressive staff of daily reporters and subscribed to the Associated Press for national and international news. Advertisers did not clamor for space in either of these papers, since working-class readers were likely to buy their food, household supplies, and even their clothes at pushcarts or dockside stalls. Both papers derived most of their income, instead, from newsstand sales and hundreds of daily classified ads. This business model made room for a distinctive, relatively independent working-class culture to take shape in newspaper articles.

Working-class papers tended not to provide much advice on how to best go about daily life in the city. The *Item* and the *Record* did not need to please advertisers by running advice features, and their readers did not necessarily want to read those kinds of articles anyway. Readers may have been too concerned with finding work, raising families, and making do to worry much about mastering etiquette rituals. They may have felt they were already learning what they needed to know from their friends and neighbors. Working-class Philadelphians may have resented the preachy instructions they got from social workers, dispensed by the Octavia Hill Association or the Southwark Settlement. Or they might have been tired of hearing bosses lecture them on proper behavior. Employees of North Philadelphia's Stetson Hat Company, for example, were asked to eat their lunch in the company cafeteria (rather than in neighborhood saloons), to start a savings account in the company bank, to buy a home in the neighborhood, and (if they were immigrants) to attend Americanization classes.[36]

Working-class newspapers did outline parameters of behavior—not in features but, instead, in their news and their directories of goods and services. This material seemingly condoned behavior that middle-class and upper-class Philadelphians publicly shunned, from gambling to late-night dancing to drinking in mixed company. Each paper printed extensive horse-racing reports so that readers could place their bets wisely. Both papers invited readers to skating rinks, orchestra concerts, steamer excursions, restaurants, and theater productions. The *Item* printed a full page called "The Dancing World" on the back of its Sunday paper, where waltzes, cakewalks, and contests promised to keep people dancing until midnight or later. By 1910, an *Item* column called "Some Pleasant Resorts" listed saloons and hotel bars and welcomed women by noting which ones provided separate ladies' entrances.

Classified ads in the *Record* and the *Item*, meanwhile, displayed a surprising frankness about human needs and desires. Ads hawked dye for gray hair, phrenology readings, bust-building regimens, electrolysis, psychic consultations, massage parlors, and short-term hotel rooms for trysts. Philadelphians left secretive messages for each other in the classifieds: "Jack—one Wednesday afternoon (you know which one); drop me a line or see me. Will be at A. Thursday. Annie."[37] Matrimonial clubs promised to put lonely hearts in correspondence with each other. Maternity services offered places where pregnant, single women could give birth, recover, and leave a child for adoption if they wished. Ads that offered "Female Regulating Pills" or that called to "Ladies in Trouble" both promised, in a veiled way, to abort a pregnancy. Readers would not likely take the classifieds as models of ideal behavior, but in them they saw a cross section of their neighbors' businesses and behaviors.

The *Item* and the *Record* cultivated a subtle pride in being working class by making fun of the city's rich and famous. The *Item*'s society column referred to the city's stylish classes as "swelldom" and their excitement over invitations as "silly flutter."[38] Unlike more decorous papers, the *Item* noted when a member of Philadelphia's upper crust was running out of money, and the *Record*'s theater column informed readers that one actress's rich husband had financed her entire production.[39] Both papers criticized rich Philadelphians' conspicuous consumption. An *Item* society column that followed a pair of wealthy girls on their weekly round of pedicures, manicures, shampoos, and Turkish baths had sharp words for them. "The way these smart girls deliver themselves up nowadays to specialists just to keep themselves clean and well groomed is extraordinary," it commented. "The cost of it is prohibitive to poorer people, so that it is the hallmark of high fashion, so to speak, to have different people take care of different parts of your person."[40] Thank goodness, these papers implied, their own working-class readers were not slaves to such rituals of distinction. Again, working-class papers' business model made this attitude possible; if the gossipy society notes or disrespectful dispatches about the city's elites alienated advertisers, these papers would still have steady sources of revenue.

By reporting closely on local events, these papers reflected (and reinforced) working-class culture's local focus. Both of these papers chronicled city politics, city crimes, and locals going to court. They printed copious notes on ordinary Philadelphia residents, devoting columns to marriages, divorces, and obituaries. The *Record* printed lists of Philadelphians admitted to hospitals the day before; the *Item* listed every public bathhouse visitor on the week the baths opened. All of this detailed listing and reporting helped readers keep track of what was going on with the people they knew. Both papers printed news on the wider world as well, but because it bore less immediate relevance to readers' lives, reporters took pains to make it hugely entertaining. A typical *Item* front page from 1902 sported these headlines:

PATERSON UNDER GUARD OF STATE MILITIA!

LORD BERESFORD ROASTS THE BRITISH NAVY FOR ITS INEFFICIENCY!

SOFT COAL MINERS WILL STAND BY THE ANTHRACITE WORKERS!

HORRIBLE DOUBLE TRAGEDY![41]

The capital letters, exclamation points, and enormous typeface made far-off events seem urgent and exciting. The paper strung such stories out over days or weeks and printed the latest developments almost like chapters in serial fiction. Both the *Item* and the *Record* treated faraway events as useful sources of melodrama rather than as developments with possible consequences for readers' lives.

The *Philadelphia Tribune*, the city's African American paper, also shied away from outright advice and instead functioned as a directory of activities and products. That directory, assembled through ads for barbershops, law offices, and seaside resorts, mapped out safe spaces for black Philadelphians. The *Tribune* may have avoided giving much explicit daily-life advice for different reasons than the *Item* or the *Record*. The *Tribune*, publishing only on Saturdays, did not try to thoroughly cover happenings in national or international news but, instead, focused on events within Philadelphia's African American community and on racial politics and progress nationwide. Editors knew that much of their reading public likely took both the *Tribune* and one of the city's mainstream dailies, so they did not try to assemble a full-service paper.[42] Additionally, the public pages of a newspaper may not have seemed like the best place for African American Philadelphians to talk to each other (either within classes or across classes) about how to behave. In an environment in which the actions of a single black resident could be taken as representative of the whole black population, any discussion of subpar behavior risked shaming the community.[43] The advice that readers did receive (and in this, the *Tribune* resembled nearly all of America's black weeklies) contained conflicting messages. Editorials urged readers to take pride in their race and their community, but illustrated ads for skin creams and hair tonics indicated to female readers that they ought to think about lightening their skin and straightening their hair.

Both the *Item* and the *Record* did print a sprinkling of direct advice to readers. The *Item* ran short columns with guidelines on how to pack a trunk, how to mix a cocktail, and how to throw an afternoon tea. It sometimes discussed basic etiquette, warning readers not to be rude to shop girls or to avoid divulging personal secrets to new friends. The *Record* printed a column called "Household Knowledge" with short notes on fashion, a handful of recipes, and practical tips on how to whiten linens or treat coughs. But mostly, Philadelphia's working-class papers gave readers lessons in urban behavior by giving them indexes of where to go and what to do. The relative absence of advice indicates that these papers did not cater to a segment of the working class that was particularly intent on gentility or upward mobility. Those who were interested in such things could turn elsewhere—to mass-readership papers.

Mass-Readership Newspapers and Middle-Class Behavior

Beginning in the 1890s, Philadelphia's *Evening Bulletin* and the morning *Inquirer* adopted a "something for everyone" model that combined thorough news coverage with entertaining features. Using this formula, the *Bulletin* and the *Inquirer* grew their circulations and approached that of the reigning *Record* in 1905. The *Record* then started to imitate the mass-readership model. All three papers drew readers from the city's growing middle class but also from those who hoped to work their way into it. The *Inquirer*, the *Bulletin*, and the twentieth-century *Record*, more sober and more censored, would have been called more "respectable" than their working-class competitors. Their pages brimmed over with advice outlining middle-class rituals, values, and consumer choices, teaching immigrants' children, newcomers, and social climbers how a reputable and comfortable metropolitan resident ought to behave.

The early twentieth-century *Inquirer*, *Bulletin*, and *Record* all carved out space for wide-ranging question-and-answer sections. These functioned as informal, utterly practical newspaper advice columns. The columns grew out of a nineteenth-century tradition in which newspapers served as encyclopedias for their readers. Because papers kept large collections of reference books and maintained archives of news articles, they could usually answer readers' queries about historical facts or scientific discoveries. They printed answers on their editorial pages and even assembled the most-requested information into almanacs that they distributed free to subscribers each year. Over time, readers began to send in a wider variety of queries, turning to newspapers to decipher city bureaucracies, legal obligations, and social rules. If a couple married in another state, was their marriage now valid in Pennsylvania? If a man died without a will, who should inherit? What did it take to attain and prove citizenship? Papers responded by creating titled columns of questions and answers, such as the *Bulletin*'s columns "Social Problems," "Legal Queries," "Points in Etiquette," and "Ethical Problems." These columns, no longer confined to the women's section but placed on the editorial page, guided newly arrived Philadelphians through the frustrations and bafflements of city living, and directed them to city services. Philadelphia's turn-of-the-century reformers had created some institutions, such as the Gaskill Street Baths, the Central Soup Society, and visiting nurse services, to help city people in need. Yet it often took a newspaper to match citizens to the appropriate agency:

"Constant Reader."—(1) If you have a lease you cannot be removed.
(2) The office of the Society to Protect Children from Cruelty is at No. 1406 Chestnut street.[44]

While question-and-answer columns passed on essential information, headlines and advertisements provided a subtler type of guidance. Editors at the *Inquirer*, the *Bulletin*, and the twentieth-century *Record* ran tamer headlines than those in the *Item* or the early *Record* and screened out the most dubious advertisements, communicating middle-class tastes in the process. Meanwhile, articles and ads instructed readers in broader middle-class values of self-improvement and appreciation for great works and achievements. The *Inquirer* reported on sculpture exhibits in New York, and its book department sold volumes of art reproductions that promised "The Paris Salon Brought into Your Home."[45] The *Record* printed stories on the latest scientific patents and feats of engineering. The *Inquirer*'s feature called "The Home Study Circle" cycled through topics in government, literature, art, and European history.[46] The *Inquirer* published and sold its own edition of the complete works of Shakespeare and a great books series for young readers. The ads for these series highlighted middle-class values of studying the literary canon and of respecting experts' authority.

Newspaper ads sold education both as a means to help families improve their children's job prospects, and as a route into middle-class culture, which placed a high value on cultivating the mind. Some ads promised refinement, such as those for lessons in piano playing, singing, painting, or a foreign language. Others, like the Master Builders' Mechanical Trade School or the Quaker City Civil Service School, offered career training.[47] Ads for private primary and high schools harnessed parents' aspirations and persuaded them to enroll their children in selective and expensive academies. Newspapers created information bureaus where readers could write in for school recommendations—though only from among those schools that paid to advertise.[48]

Mass-readership papers offered lessons in basic etiquette, which could help readers blend into (and move up within) the urban middle class. "There are somethings [sic] that a well-bred young lady never does," lectured the 1892 *Inquirer*:

She never turns around to look after anyone when walking on the street.
She does not permit a man to join her on the street unless they are intimate acquaintances.
She never forgets her ball room engagements, or refuses to dance with one man and immediately dances with another.
She never snubs other young ladies, even if they happen to be less popular or well-favored than herself.[49]

Instead of being put off by the lecturing or superior tone of such newspaper advice, readers seemed to eat it up. They flooded newspaper offices with further etiquette questions. What was a proper reply to "glad to have met you"? What did one serve at a formal versus an informal dinner party? Newspapers instructed readers in everything from how to pronounce certain words to how to address one's superintendent. And papers responded carefully even to questions that would have seemed embarrassingly basic (or embarrassingly intimate) to most middle-class Philadelphians. When readers wanted to know how to groom their eyebrows or how often to bathe, newspaper writers told them. The *Bulletin*'s "Ethical Problems" and "Social Problems" columns aired hundreds of tales of romances and friendships gone wrong due to jealousies, betrayals, or too much alcohol and gave gentle advice on how to patch things up.[50] Advice writers seemed intent on bringing errant readers into line with middle-class standards of conduct.

In addition to sketching out middle-class values and etiquette, newspapers provided readers with the logistical know-how for upward mobility. By the turn of the century, boys no longer simply inherited their fathers' trades. Instead, young men (and some women) found themselves choosing from among industrial jobs or professional careers that their parents barely understood. This turned newspapers into many readers' best sources of career advice. "Sir: Which would you suggest, a trade, a profession or a business education for a boy of sixteen?" asked one letter in the *Bulletin*. "If a trade what trade would be preferable?"[51] Readers requested advice on starting up in their chosen field, for urban professional careers seemed to require ever more specialized training and certification. Which school should a country girl attend if she wanted to become a nurse? What subjects would an aspiring civil service chemist need to know for the entrance exam?[52] Newspapers helped readers jump through all the hoops required for entry to the professional middle class.

Advertisers bought space in newspaper pages in order to embed their products into middle class life, often while capitalizing on readers' ambitions and their insecurities. "If you ask a well dressed man where he gets his clothes you'll always find he deals with a good Tailor," stated an ad for E. O. Thompson, clothier.[53] An Estey Player Piano ad explained that "the hostess who entertains her guests with selections on this instrument has achieved not only success as a capable hostess, but has placed herself . . . deep in the hearts of her listeners."[54] From browsing the illustrated advertisements in any one of these papers, readers would gather that a middle-class household ought to have certain things: a piano, a coordinated set of heavy wooden furniture for the dining room and the living room, oriental carpets, ornate table linens, and leather-bound editions of classic literature.

One particularly successful, coordinated campaign won readers over to the ritual of the summer shore vacation. Because so many hotels bought ad space, newspapers started to run descriptions of resorts along the Jersey, Maryland, and Delaware shores in springtime. When summer arrived, papers' society writers decamped to these resorts. Soon Philadelphia papers, and the department stores that advertised in them, were offering home delivery to shore towns.[55] By the early 1900s, most papers had created resort information bureaus that suggested destinations and hotels tailored to the reader's particular taste and budget. News features and ads did not merely aim to sell vacations to anyone who would buy. Instead they spoke about vacations as a way to become middle class and to perform middle-class status. The first rule in a *Bulletin* list of "Don'ts for Travellers" was "Don't travel unless you can afford it."[56] The *Bulletin*'s list went on to detail middle-class standards for travel:

Don't permit your children, if you have any with you, to annoy people by ill-bred behavior . . .
Don't return civility with its opposite.
Don't forget that you owe a duty to every human being, the duty of looking pleasant and being gracious.[57]

These instructions stressed that travel was something readers must work their way up to, by saving up money and practicing good manners.[58]

Starting in the 1890s, a new, fantastical strain appeared in newspapers' advice material, most often in the women's pages. Newspapers' artists started to picture perfectly outfitted homes, where songbirds perched on women's kitchen windowsills and delicate wisps of steam trailed from pies just out of the oven. Fashion illustrations depicted women who were ever longer and leaner. The women that appeared in this material seemed to have no trouble cooking, cleaning, or caring for children while remaining impeccably dressed and entirely at ease (see, e.g., fig. 2.1). Such newspaper material was of a piece with a broader consumer culture emerging in Philadelphia and other cities at this time. Window displays at Gimbels or Strawbridge & Clothier, glossy advertisements in the *Saturday Evening Post* or *Century Magazine*, billboards next to train platforms, and posters on Pennsylvania Rapid Transit streetcars all conjured an alternate universe—a world where women were beautiful, men charming, homes cozy, and biscuits impossibly fluffy. These images of contentment, glamour, and ease conjured up deep longings for many people. They then attached those longings to material goods.[59]

Like home economics courses and manuals of the same era, many newspaper articles devalued women's inherited knowledge and intuitive sense by insisting that there was a "right" way of doing every household and personal task. Pieces such as "Right and Wrong Way of Watering Plants" and "Do You Know How to Sweep?" informed readers that various mundane chores actually had precise rules.[60] Seemingly innocuous choices could have disastrous consequences, according to advice writers; a bit of sun could ruin a fair complexion, and a quick dip in saltwater threatened to destroy hair's color and texture. Fashion was especially perilous. Articles instructed women with large hips, a plump figure, or unshapely feet to avoid certain styles at all costs. And minor shortcomings would draw attention. The *Bulletin* quoted a man of high society in an article outlining the steps of a proper manicure: "I can forgive a plain face in a woman, but I can not forgive ugly hands."[61] Articles set standards so high that they could undermine women's confidence in their own abilities to make things, choose goods, take care of others, and present themselves—which, of course, made them even better consumers.

Newspaper material that stressed the importance and difficulty of consumer decisions apparently reached an interested audience; readers continually asked for guidance in the world of goods. When the *Inquirer* instituted an advice columnist on the women's page, readers wrote in to ask exactly how to trim a dress or which colors they ought to pair together. Readers asked beauty columnists how to brighten tired eyes, how to plump thin hands, and how to make hair glossy.[62] In 1911, the *Inquirer* began a column called "Harmony in Homecraft." "Are you in doubt about the color of your new wall paper?" asked the columnist. "Do you know the very latest

2.1 This 1915 article on useful tools for the kitchen shows an elegant housewife using each one with perfect grace and poise. The cook simultaneously models fashionable outfits, few of which would have been practical in a real kitchen. *Philadelphia Record*, 28 May 1915, 6.

in table decorations? Are you in a quandary over your summer slip covers? Bring your problems, big or little, to Anne Carrington. She is here to help you."[63] The popularity of Carrington's column—as well as Wanamaker's fashion shows and YWCA cooking classes—showed that the messages in the paper had sunk in.[64] Philadelphia women tried to, and even wanted to, live up to the standards being set for them.

The consumer focus did not permeate every feature of mass-readership papers. Other portions criticized and spoofed consumer culture and let readers know that they did not necessarily have to follow the strict guidelines put forward in advice columns and advertisements. Some cartoons laughed at those who lived for fashion.[65] Others poked fun at the housekeeping advice of the day's newspapers and magazines:

MRS. NEWWED — "I've been working in the kitchen all morning."
MR. NEWWED — "Doing what?"
MRS. NEWWED — "Preparing one of those 'Fifteen-minute luncheons' that the Nicckel-out Magazine tells about."[66]

Other features—in contrast to always optimistic advertisements—spoke cynically about readers' chances at happiness. Dorothy Dix, whose columns appeared in the *Bulletin* and in many other U.S. newspapers, could deflate any fantasy that a reader harbored. "This one thing is certain—there are no bargains in life," she stated in a 1916 piece. "Success, fame, riches, friendship, family ties—we must pay for them in blood and sweat if we get them."[67] This advice ran directly counter to the messages of consumer culture, which insisted that readers could find perfect happiness by simply choosing the right goods.

Mass-readership papers, then, offered readers a grab bag of material. They constructed fantasy worlds but also dispensed hard-nosed truths; they gamely answered readers' practical questions while teaching them the impractical routines of middle-class respectability. The jumble of voices and messages in mass-readership papers did not really merge into a single coherent message, but they did not need to. As businesses, mass-readership papers worked—they sold products and kept people reading. In assembling such mixes of material, they established standards for behavior and consumption among the urban middle class, even as they expressed mixed feelings about those very standards.

Elite Newspapers

Philadelphia's elite newspapers served an audience that lived by fairly elaborate codes of behavior. Yet they offered surprisingly little instruction in exactly how to act upper class. Elite papers did not print practical tips on metropolitan life or discuss basic social rules, because their desired readers already knew everything about basic urban conduct. These newspapers, then, acted as class gatekeepers. They made themselves legible and interesting only to those who already knew the rituals of the city's upper tier.

By 1890, mass-readership papers had won over many of the middle-class people who once read the *Public Ledger*, but the *Ledger* held onto the city's wealthiest subscribers through the 1910s.[68] Meanwhile, the *North American* grew into a major paper after Thomas Wanamaker (son of John Wanamaker, the department store owner), bought it in 1899. He made a name for the paper with populist politics and muckraking, but Wanamaker eventually adopted a pattern similar to the elite *Ledger*'s, concentrating on thorough news coverage and consumer-focused features.[69]

Elite papers were more beholden to advertisers than working-class or mass-readership papers. They charged advertisers high rates for the privilege of reaching a small but select group of readers with substantial spending money. To make their ad space worth the price, however, elite papers needed to be sure that their readers bought the advertised goods. So these papers, whenever possible, used their content to push readers toward purchases. Editors of elite papers also tried not to offend their advertisers in features or even in their regular daily news, for a canceled ad contract severely hurt their bottom line. They often obliged their advertisers' requests for good publicity and handily omitted news that might hurt advertisers' business.

The reporting in the *Public Ledger* and the *North American* reflected the national and international interests of Philadelphia's elite. Neither paper had to kindle interest in those subjects through eye-catching headlines or scandalous stories, because so many upper-class readers' livelihoods and fortunes were bound up with national and global affairs. Philadelphia bankers, lawyers, and manufacturers scanned the news for developments that would affect their investments, clients, and customers. The wives of these men read the society reporting in the *Ledger* and the *North American*, trying to keep abreast of their real (or wished-for) national and international social circles. The *Ledger*'s society page announced events not just in Philadelphia but in Baltimore, New York, and Washington, DC. "Peggy Shippen," the *Ledger*'s society columnist, constantly noted the European royalty, business tycoons, or famous authors who were passing through Philadelphia, and she assumed her readers were versed in foreign ways. She relayed one conversation with a visiting luminary: "He says every one says of American efficiency: 'Mais, ces Americains, c'est epatant.'"[70] She wrote to an imagined audience of elite Philadelphians who would not need a translation.

Where mass-readership papers stressed a middlebrow regimen of education and self-improvement, elite newspapers emphasized association with exclusive national institutions. The *North American* printed the names, hometowns, and fellowships won by each local graduate at commencement time and issued detailed columns of University of Pennsylvania news.[71] The *Public Ledger*'s "College Notes" column did not build a narrative around each dispatch but, instead, assumed that the reader would take an interest.[72]

For all the elements of upper-class culture that a reader might learn about in newspaper pages, there were many more components that never appeared, for elite papers kept some class secrets. Papers such as the *Ledger* and the *North American* did not teach readers the meaningful details that would mark them as insiders or outsiders—the particular accents, necklines, postures, or jokes. Their etiquette columns never outlined rules of courtship, refined table manners, or proper introductions. Advertisements never invited the public to join the Manufacturer's Club—a six-story townhouse on Pine Street where factory owners socialized—nor did they publicize the club's suburban golf course.[73] Meanwhile, the advertisements for luxury goods and high-end services did not instruct readers the way that *Inquirer* and *Bulletin* ads often did. Some excluded through price alone: the *Ledger* printed an advertising "Guide for Americans Abroad" with hotels in exotic destinations from Vienna to Cairo that a middle-class Philadelphian could never afford.[74] Others excluded by withholding information. Unlike the copiously illustrated ads for the goods in mid-priced department stores, boutiques' ads for jewelry, furs, or fine stationery did not picture the goods.[75] Omitting the prices signaled that they would be high. Omitting illustrations meant that the shopper would have to enter the store and ask a salesperson to display the item—a routine that only Philadelphia's "carriage trade" would feel comfortable with. Some shops' advertisements mimicked formal event invitations or calling cards by printing only their name, trade, and location in elegant typeface.

The *Ledger*'s women's material, once relatively open and wide-ranging, had narrowed its focus by the turn of the century. Articles on women making professional strides and conducting civic campaigns did not help to sell anything, so editors gradually pushed them off of the women's page.[76] Instead, women's page writers spoke as if women's emotional lives revolved around consumer goods. Articles rarely touched on the ups and downs of friendship but harped on other topics such as table settings, finger sandwiches, and parlor games that would delight friends at teatime. They did not dwell on issues of marital strife or disappointment but, instead, contemplated the items that went into a perfect bride's trousseau. The world of upper-class women, as interpreted by the *Ledger*, was much like the one advertisers pictured—glittery, cheerful, and shallow.

In the early twentieth century, the *North American* and the *Ledger* discontinued open query columns and instead adopted a new mode: the themed advice column. This gave editors more control and allowed them to point readers toward advertisers' products. Fictional personalities such as "Anne Rittenhouse" or real women like Kathleen Norris presided over columns on topics such as beauty, etiquette, child rearing, or relationships. These women wrote in distinctive voices—warm and maternal or sharp and no-nonsense—and often addressed the reader as a friend and confidante.[77] These themed columns originated in elite papers and then spread to nearly all the city's dailies by the 1920s, shutting down more open discussions not only in the highly consumer-oriented *Ledger* and *North American* but also across the entire newspaper field.

Editors and advertisers imagined somewhat distinct audiences for working-class, mass-readership, and elite newspapers, but in practice, these audiences overlapped a bit. Working-class papers offered the most comprehensive classified ads, so a diverse group of Philadelphians probably consulted them. Other well-educated readers bought these papers to indulge an appetite for sensation or slapstick.[78] Elite papers, meanwhile, often cost no more than any other paper in the city. Upwardly mobile Philadelphians may have purchased these papers as both status symbols and as windows into the more prosperous world they hoped to join. And many people sampled a range of newspapers every day, browsing for the highlights of each one.[79] Factoring in some overlaps in readership, though, late nineteenth-century news seems remarkably class specific—though that specificity was to dissolve in the 1910s and 1920s.

TEACHING TECHNOLOGY

Philadelphia's turn-of-the-century newspapers provided varying instructions in everyday urban behavior. When it came to new technologies, however, nearly all newspapers instructed their readers in the same way. Upper-class and working-class readers alike were encountering toasters and electric irons for the first time, so there was no stigma attached to not knowing how to use them. Newspapermen framed these technology "lessons" as a public good. "Advertising must teach new ways of sweeping the carpet, new ways of furnishing the home, new ways of promoting cleanliness and health, new ways of enjoying life," explained ad man Truman DeWeese. "In the newspaper we have daily lessons in the art of doing things better than our forefathers did them."[80] Partly because merchants advertised their technologies as equally essential to working-class, middle-class, and upper-class city people, newspapers began to print less class-coded advice. At the same time, when newspapers sold readers on household appliances and prepared foods, they gave rise to an urban way of life that relied on the labor and expertise of specialists. These trends—toward mass consumption and away from doing things oneself—were already visible in the first years of the twentieth century and accelerated through the 1910s and 1920s.

As newspapers introduced new technologies for the kitchen, they helped construct what we would now recognize as the twentieth-century American diet, full of processed and refrigerated foods. For most of the nineteenth century, home cooks and servants had made nearly everything from scratch, from cakes to ketchup. When local merchants offered prepared food, they had often made it themselves, aging cheese, baking bread, or brining pickles in the back rooms of their shops. In the late nineteenth century, though, entrepreneurs began to apply techniques of mass production to food. They built huge bakeries to churn out biscuits and shortbreads. They devised methods to safely and reliably can perishable goods like vegetables and fish. Using refrigerated warehouses and railroad cars, slaughterhouses and dairies processed and shipped much larger quantities of meat and milk. Mass production reduced the prices of most staple foods, putting ingredients like white flour and refined sugar within reach of most household budgets.[81] Still, because city people had relied on small-scale urban merchants and on their own (or their servants') recipes, they did not automatically embrace mass-produced food.

Ads appearing in working-class, mass-readership, and elite newspapers alike spelled out the attractions of these processed foods for skeptical readers. They described the delights of *not* cooking. "Soup is the best start of the evening meal," explained an ad for Anderson's ten-cent soups, "but not if someone has to stand over a hot stove to make it and get too tired to eat at all."[82] Prepared foods meant "Less Work for Mother," as one slogan put it, and allowed women to sit down to dinner relaxed and refreshed.[83] Ads claimed that, with prepared foods, Philadelphians could relive memories of countryside meals and grandparents' tables. "Do you remember how good fresh green corn tastes?" asked one ad. "Baker's Sugar Corn will help you"—even though the corn came from a can.[84] "You don't know pancakes," another ad insisted, "unless you know Heckers' Old Homestead Pancake Flour."[85] If women decided to buy these new foods, they still might not know quite what to do with them. Newspaper ads and articles again stepped in to explain. Ads for canned olives or shredded coconut included recipes or assured readers that they would find recipes on the package. Cooking columns incorporated recipes that used prepared foods such as condensed milk.

Newspapers also slowly weaned women of their habit of buying only what the family would consume in the next few days. "It's such a relief not to have to go to market every day," exclaimed a woman in a refrigerator advertisement.[86] Columns urged shoppers to keep an "emergency shelf" for unexpected guests and told them exactly what canned provisions belonged there.[87] Finally, ads tried to accustom cooks to the odd idea that packaged foods kept for ages and could be eaten in any and all seasons. "Always fresh in moisture and dust proof packages," described an ad for crackers. "Therefore Oysterettes are in season every day in every month of every year."[88] Slowly, material like this accustomed women to shopping for food in tin cans and in plastic bags.

Newspaper advertisements lobbied readers to adopt other technologies of this era, like gas heat and electric light, that would radically change their home lives. Ads explained in detail the benefits of an electric-wired or gas-heated home to readers who had never experienced one. "No need to suffer eye-strain," explained the United Gas Improvement Company, "when you can have a light of wholesome quality almost like daylight."[89] Ads featured testimonials from fictional customers who raved about their new labor-saving systems: "I've stoked my last furnace! What a joyful thought that is."[90] Illustrations showed men and women looking relaxed and satisfied as they stocked the icebox, laundered their clothes, or shaved with hot water straight from the tap. Ads worked in tandem with a Philadelphia Electric campaign to wire Philadelphia's modest row homes; by the end of the 1920s, nearly all Philadelphia families had electricity.[91]

Newspaper advertisements of the 1910s and 1920s managed to sell one new technology that made little sense in urban circumstances: the automobile. Between Philadelphia's narrow row houses and its narrow streets, there was hardly room to drive or park cars. Outlying neighborhoods, meanwhile, had been constructed around rail stations, so even those residents might not automatically see the need for an automobile. Initially, when Philadelphians first drove in the city, cars created more problems than they solved. Drivers expecting to speed down Market Street wound up stuck behind horse carts or streetcars. Traffic fatalities became commonplace in a city without stop signs, traffic lights, or even an expectation that drivers keep to the right side of the road. Yet auto section articles, written to accompany the copious ad space that car companies bought, made cars seem glamorous. They profiled racecar drivers and described a new car as a way to win a woman's heart or to earn more respect in the business world.[92] Papers then eased Philadelphians into the world of car ownership by answering their questions about auto mechanics and driving rules.[93] Philadelphians went to Bush Hill auto dealerships and bought Hupmobiles, Fiats, and Cadillacs. They then lobbied for wider roads. Benjamin Franklin Parkway, a massive diagonal boulevard built in 1918, combined with East River Drive (now Kelly Drive) to funnel white-collar workers from northwestern neighborhoods to their downtown jobs.⁹⁴ Car companies' ad campaigns, and newspapers' cooperation, helped to create a more car-centric city infrastructure and, starting in the 1920s, a more sprawling city.

Newspapers' material dealing with new products subtly guided readers away from doing things themselves, ultimately decreasing the material skill that city life required of residents. Automobile and radio sections at first encouraged readers to experiment with new technologies. In columns such as the *Inquirer*'s "The Automobile Speaks," auto experts told readers about potential causes of a noisy starter, how to protect the brass surfaces of a car with lacquer, and the ins and outs of the cooling system.⁹⁵ Within a short span of time, though, many papers phased out columns on auto logistics; advertisements directed readers toward professional mechanics instead. Newspapers' radio sections went through a parallel shift. Early radio sections tackled readers' questions in highly technical advice columns: "On which side of the storage battery is the rheostat placed for filamental control?" asked one typical reader.⁹⁶ These forums for amateur mechanics gradually ceded space to daily broadcast schedules and ads for upcoming music programs and radio dramas. Readers should leave the baking to industrial kitchens, papers advised, and leave the furnace problem to a utility repairman. By the 1910s, newspapers' contents seemed to insist that truly competent city people were not those who could cook a fricassee, change a tire, build a table, sew a dress, or stop a faucet leak. The most competent city people, newspapers indicated, were those who knew how to choose products and services—those who knew how to shop.

Advertisements and articles, across all types of Philadelphia newspapers, spoke of shopping as both essential skill and enjoyable pursuit. Advertisers quoted smart shoppers who improved their families' lives by choosing the right goods, from fresh butter to vacuum cleaners. The *Public Ledger*'s cooking column explained the need to be discerning when buying packaged cheese: "You must be sure to get the best brands, for some are made from skim milk and are proportionally less nutritious."⁹⁷ A skilled shopper safeguarded her family's health; she could also have fabulous fun in the shops. The quote under an image of well-dressed women sipping tea in a Wanamaker's ad read: "It will take half the afternoon to do the new dress goods justice. And, oh! Let's see the Guerlain perfume exhibit. I'm told that Frenchman makes some extracts that sell at upwards of twenty dollars a bottle. Wonder if it's so?"⁹⁸ Spending half a day looking at dresses, or squinting at cheese labels, may have struck some readers as dull or a waste of time. Newspapers, however, insisted that these activities were both necessary and pleasurable.

The kind of shopping that newspapers encouraged could be unfamiliar, even daunting. It required readers to venture downtown to a showroom or

2.2   The shopping scenes here are meant to entice customers to the new store, but they also show what kinds of customers the owners would like to attract and preview how goods will be displayed and sold. Castelberg's ad, *Philadelphia North American*, 5 November 1905, 8.

department store or to enter the gleaming interior of a franchise grocery store. People used to haggling at a street stall, visiting a dressmaker in a cramped apartment, or buying sacks of potatoes at a general store might easily be intimidated by the spaces, the staff, and the other customers at a downtown emporium. For this reason, retailers used their newspaper advertisements to soothe and draw in new shoppers. Many ads pictured the exact interiors of stores (fig. 2.2) and reassured readers as to exactly what kind of counters, displays, and staff waited inside. Ads sometimes mimicked displays in stores by showing goods on mannequins, with prices attached. An illustration of a salesman rolling out a carpet for a woman shopper or answering a couple's questions about a refrigerator indicated what readers could expect. These ads let readers preview new rituals from the comfort of their own homes.[99]

At the same time, ads gave readers tools that would help them to feel like expert shoppers. Some department store ads included directories to all of the stores' different sections.[100] Others noted exactly where readers would find the advertised item, pointing them, for example, to the north arcade of the main floor. Ads' written descriptions allowed shoppers to speak knowledgeably about the products they wanted. "There are flattering wide brims; there are tiny brims—there are hats with dashing off-face effects," described a Lit Brothers department store ad in 1925. "Velvet, Satin, Velour, Felt. Richest of shades, including black prince, Epinard, pencil blue, sapphire blue, Mexico, phlox, wild aster—and navy and black."[101] A reader might not know what shade "Epinard" was, but she could still go to the counter and ask to see a velour hat in Epinard and feel that she fit into the sophisticated surroundings.

Last, giving readers all the price information beforehand in an ad laid down basic rules for both shopper and salesman. Philadelphians in this era sometimes clipped newspaper ads and took them on their shopping trips.[102] The printed prices let these readers enter the store confident that they would not be swindled by salespeople who took them for gullible newcomers. The prices made salespeople's lives easier, too, for they warned away those shoppers who could not afford the goods and alerted readers that haggling would not be welcome. In the 1920s, the *Inquirer* even started providing prices from the vegetable dealers in the Reading Terminal Market. This gave shoppers a baseline for judging a good deal in the terminal or anywhere else in the city and gave merchants outside of the market a sense of what they could reasonably charge.

Newspapers encouraged readers from the working, middle, and upper classes all to adopt new technologies and to substitute shopping for skill. This shift paralleled the city's transition from a production-based to a consumption-based economy. Already, by the early twentieth century, Philadelphia factories were outgrowing their urban plants and relocating outside the city. Many of the new jobs of the 1910s and 1920s were in the service sector—filling Sears catalog orders, for example, or working as a switchboard operator for Bell Telephone.[103] Papers' more uniform recommendations began to create a mass market out of urban consumers. Other changes in newspapers' advice through the 1910s and 1920s both reflected and expedited this shift toward mass culture. Newspapers dropped much of their class-specific advice and outlined new parameters of behavior for metropolitan men and women who were growing ever less certain of how they ought to behave.

TOWARD A MASS AUDIENCE

In Philadelphia, as in the nation as a whole, the number of different newspapers declined steeply in the 1910s and 1920s, even as total newspaper circulation rose. The startup costs for new papers had grown prohibitive; few rookie publishers could afford to purchase new equipment, buy Associated Press or United Press news, and secure the syndicated feature contracts that would attract readers. And without a large subscription base, new papers had trouble selling the advertising space that helped to bankroll the whole operation. When publishers realized that they were safe from upstart competition, they engineered mergers and formed newspaper chains to take advantage of greater economies of scale.[104] Adolph Ochs, owner of the *New York Times*, bought the *Philadelphia Public Ledger* and the *Philadelphia Times* in 1902 and merged them. Cyrus Curtis then took over the *Ledger* in 1913 and proceeded to buy and close three of its competitors: the *Telegraph* in 1918, the *Press* in 1920, and the *North American* in 1925. After scooping up what he wanted—national press contracts and a handful of features—Curtis let the laid-off reporters, columnists, and printers scatter to the city's remaining dailies.[105] Curtis started up an evening edition of the *Ledger* in 1913, supplanting smaller evening papers like the *Call* and the *Item*.

Any Philadelphian walking down Chestnut Street in the 1920s would sense the changes of the past decade. The offices of the *Call*, *Telegraph*, *Press*, *Item*, and *Times*, all between Sixth and Eighth Streets, had shuttered. Philadelphia's remaining papers had moved into monumental new headquarters. The *Ledger*'s building (fig. 2.3), completed in 1924, took up the entire city block at Sixth and Chestnut, and the eighteen-story Elverson building on North Broad Street, completed for the *Inquirer* in 1925 (fig. 2.4), became one of the signatures of the Philadelphia skyline.

The era of the class-specific paper was over. Only the tabloid *Philadelphia Daily News*, founded in 1925, noticeably catered to one class (the working class) more than another.[106] The rest of the city's newspapers tried to move beyond their niches by running content that appealed across class, gender, and political lines. The *Bulletin*'s masthead in the 1920s read: "In Philadelphia, nearly everyone reads the *Bulletin*"—a claim that no nineteenth-century paper would ever have tried to make.[107] Yet because they all sought to dominate the field in the same way, Philadelphia's major newspapers started to resemble each other more and more. The *Record* and the *Bulletin*, which had been strong on local stories, started printing more national and international news. The *Ledger*, especially in its evening paper, abandoned its staid reputation and commissioned more sensational pieces. Newspaper editors also strove to offer products and information for people of widely varying tastes and incomes. The *Inquirer* gave readers of its cooking column two options, printing a weekly menu and market list for both a $10 budget and a $25 budget.[108] Auto sections in these papers advertised Rolls-Royces, Jewett's "Thrifty Six" model, and used cars all at once.

2.3 The *Philadelphia Public Ledger* building, circa 1924. Library of Congress.

Wanamaker's took out pages in the same newspapers for both their regular store and their bargain basement.

The *Philadelphia Tribune*, the city's black weekly, never became a mass paper, for of course it never aimed to serve all Philadelphians. And yet it followed many of the trends of the era and mirrored the mass-market dailies in several ways. In the late 1910s and 1920s, the *Tribune* began running more features: recipes, cartoons, beauty advice, and humor columns. Many mass-market companies placed the same ads in the *Tribune* that they placed in other papers. In the 1920s, a number of black Philadelphians began taking the *Pittsburgh Courier*, which also showed signs of catering to a mass audience—one that spanned cities and classes.[109] It published a full page of Philadelphia news and ran up to twenty-four pages a week instead of the *Philadelphia Tribune*'s sixteen. The *Courier* seemingly catered to working-, middle-, and upper-class blacks all through the mid-Atlantic and Midwest. It printed extensive society notes, columns for college students, and ads for cruise vacations; but its ads for blues records and its advice column letters indicated a working-class readership as well. Even within the niche market of African American papers, many editors seemed to adopt the one-size-fits-all approach.

2.4 The *Philadelphia Inquirer* building, completed in 1925, photographed in 1954. Parker & Mullikin Collection, Philadelphia Free Library.

The rise of mass-audience newspapers formed part of a broader shift toward mass entertainment in American cities. Where Philadelphia's upper and lower classes once went to opera houses or music halls, respectively, both groups began listening to the same radio programming on WIP, which started broadcasting in Philadelphia in 1922. Where some Philadelphians once shopped in elegant department store food emporiums and others went to bustling street markets, shoppers of many different classes and ethnicities started to frequent chain stores. American Stores and A&P, combined, owned over fifteen hundred stores in the Philadelphia area by the mid-1920s. Horn & Hardart Baking Company operated forty-six lunch-rooms and automats in Philadelphia by 1932.[110] Newspapers popularized these many forms of mass culture as they printed radio broadcast schedules, advertised chain stores' low prices, and suggested middlebrow titles for book clubs in their literary supplements. Their advertisements started using a "bandwagon" pitch, telling readers that they ought to try what everybody else was trying. "So many, many people here in New England demand Fruit-Nut cereal," said one ad in the 1922 *Bulletin*, "and won't be satisfied till they get it."[111] The idea that one product could satisfy *everyone* would have seemed a little silly in an era of more rigidly defined classes, but in an era of mass marketing it would come to seem like common sense.

Mass media and mass marketing worked alongside key events of the 1910s and 1920s to level out a few of the differences among classes. The World War I years humbled Philadelphia's elite families, introducing them to scarcity and sacrifice. Because of the rising demand for women workers in war production work (at Philadelphia factories like General Electric and Midvale Steel) and in offices where male employees had been drafted, fewer women were willing to take jobs in domestic service. Having lost their servants, many middle-class and upper-class women attempted to do all of their own housekeeping and child rearing. Government propaganda urged American households to consume less meat and wheat, in order to send more food to famine-ravaged Europe. "Phila. Society Women to Restrict Meals," reported a 1917 *North American* article. "Pledge Themselves to Three Courses and One Meatless Day a Week. Stand by President."[112] Price increases for food and fuel forced even the well-to-do to budget carefully. In 1917, the *Ledger*'s relatively well-off readers sent thirty letters a week asking for advice on how to feed a family cheaply. "Dorothy's Shopping Service" in the *Ledger* started to point out sales and discounts rather than just the latest and chicest items. Newspapers ran expansive spreads on American-made fashions, helping to divert elite consumers' appetites away from European clothes made scarce by the war.

While the war taught American upper-class families to make do with less, the 1920s economic boom then led working-class and middle-class families to expect more. Incomes, especially urban incomes, rose substantially between 1917 and 1929.[113] Philadelphia women continued to leave jobs as servants for positions in Sears's new distribution center in North Philadelphia, the Curtis Publishing Company's offices downtown, and the Artcraft Silk Hosiery factory in Tacony. Some of Philadelphia's formerly working-class women stopped working, since their families could now live comfortably on a husband's single salary.[114] Families living in cramped quarters in center city or North Philadelphia moved into larger homes in newly built neighborhoods like Feltonville and Overbrook. Some used the newly completed Delaware River Bridge to drive to suburban homes in southern New Jersey. Having achieved more comfort and security, working-class Philadelphians were ready to read about (and selectively adopt) the social and material ways of the middle and upper classes.

Mass-audience newspapers opened up elite rituals and elite goods for public perusal and consumption, and in the process, they redefined "elite." What was once an inherited status became a trait that could be learned and a good that could be purchased. Publishers likely tried to attract middle-class and working-class audiences with their instructions for upward mobility. They may have also believed that they were elevating readers' tastes and ambitions. Yet it was advertisers who had the strongest incentive to teach readers the habits of the middle and upper classes. The more they could kindle desires for luxurious products, the more profits they would reap. A 1923 Gimbels ad articulated this concept: "Philadelphia starts another year as the most prosperous of cities—a time when all can sensibly gratify their tastes and longings."[115] If newspaper readers believed that they really could afford to gratify their tastes and longings, Gimbels would make out very well.

Newspapers in the 1910s and 1920s offered readers precise guidelines for building their savings into real wealth. While ads in mass-readership papers had begun hawking financial services like insurance and bonds around 1900, only in later decades did newspaper ads give readers detailed instructions on how to get rich. A 1930 ad for Integrity Trust Company offered services "for persons in every stage of financial progress":

SAVINGS for the beginner, and for the prompt reinvestment of dividend income.
CHECKING for those who have made substantial progress.
SAFE DEPOSIT for protection of valuables.
INVESTMENT for the building and administration of permanent capital.
TRUST which provides for professional management and conservation of life accumulations.[116]

A reader with nothing but some cash under the mattress, and who knew no one with a bank account, here received a map toward security and prosperity. For those bewildered by financial terms and products, newspapers provided explanations. The *Record* printed a daily feature, "Money Problems of Women," that answered questions such as: "What are Mortgage Certificates?" and "How does one go about the investment of trust funds?"[117] The financial education available in newspapers was flawed and incomplete, to be sure. Financial ads sometimes swindled readers or gave the false impression that anyone could build a fortune with a few smart investments. Still, newspapers democratized finance in that they opened the promise of wealth to readers with cash and some curiosity, rather than to only those with the right connections.

In keeping with this new openness about money and status, journalists in the 1910s and 1920s provided frank, almost sociological explanations of the American class system. For decades, papers had printed society columns that pictured the season's debutantes, yet they never explained what a debutante was. In 1916, however, an exasperated reader wrote to the *Evening Ledger*'s advice columnist to ask what those society columns meant by phrases like "made her coming out," and the columnist gamely described the system. Debutante balls were just one of the ways that elite Philadelphians had devised to separate themselves from the masses, she explained. "There must always be a change of fashion, in every phase of manners," she wrote, "or else the distinction between the 'most refined' and the others will be lost, which would, of course, mean the disintegration of society."[118] Such a sarcastic answer would never have appeared in the *Ledger* a decade or two before; it made fun of the rituals and hierarchies that the earlier *Ledger* held dear. The *Evening Ledger*'s etiquette columnist Deborah Rush also wrote explicitly (though without irony) about class distinction. She told readers that certain common expressions betrayed "a vulgarity of the ordinary, and only ordinary persons use these phrases."[119] Good etiquette, she made clear, was meant to distinguish people from the masses, to prove individuals better than the crowd. For the first time, newspaper material was publicly discussing exactly how class worked.

Newspaper etiquette writers then taught readers to perform social rituals with grace. The *Evening Bulletin* started a small feature, "How's Your Grammar?" that versed readers in topics like "'Ain't I' and 'Aren't I?'"[120] In her *Evening Ledger* column, "Good Form," Deborah Rush printed correspondence templates for readers to copy for common occasions:

My dear _____,

Perhaps you will not be surprised to hear my news. My engagement to Mr. _____ will be announced in the papers on _____, but as you are an old and loved friend I wanted you to hear the news directly from me. I am anxious to have you meet my fiance, for I am sure then you will appreciate how happy I am.

Your loving friend _____.[121]

Rush, evidently raised in an upper-class or upper-middle-class household, sometimes assumed that readers shared her background, as when she referenced thank-you notes in a 1916 column without explaining what they were. Readers unfamiliar with them sent a deluge of follow-up questions. Was a thank-you letter required after a simple luncheon? A dinner party? A week-long visit? What should it say? As they answered questions like these, etiquette columns of the 1910s and 1920s began teaching upper-class routines to all interested newspaper readers, regardless of the class they came from.

Alongside articles that taught readers refined behavior ran newspaper advertisements that blatantly sold status. Instead of targeting the upper class, the way that minimal *Ledger* ads had done at the turn of the century, ads in the 1910s and 1920s encouraged anyone to dream of affording elite goods someday. Ads offered horseback riding lessons and French language magazines, tempting readers to buy their way into the culture of the rich.[122] A Rolls-Royce ad offered readers the opportunity to join an elite circle through a discerning choice of car. "A list of Rolls-Royce owners reads like Who's Who or The Social Register," claimed the 1924 ad. "Kings and princes, bankers and social leaders, manufacturers, publishers, statesmen—all those who insist on the best that civilization affords in their homes, and in every material detail of their lives, choose the Rolls-Royce as a matter of course."[123] Advertisements in the 1920s began to print the tagline "Sold only at the finest shops." Though this line attempted to conjure an air of exclusivity, it actually initiated a far *less* exclusive shopping system than that of the previous era, in which the finest goods were not advertised at all.

"Affordable luxury" products allowed readers to dip in and out of certain classes as they tried different products, rather than living with the set of goods that family and tradition required. Department store advertisements labeled their girls' clothing "Junior Debs," as if all shoppers were soon-to-be debutantes.[124] Ads pictured women attended by French maids in ruffled outfits, couples chauffeured in sleek cars, and parties of well-dressed people greeted by footmen at the entrances to estates. (See, e.g., fig. 2.5.) Bourjois cosmetics declared their cake of face powder the essence of "True Patrician Smartness." The ad listed the company's address as No. 28 Rue de la Paix, Paris, France, even though that was useless to any Philadelphian, who would likely ask for the powder at the Gimbels counter.[125] Twentieth-century advertisements did nothing to even out Americans' incomes and, thus, equalize Americans' abilities to afford these products. But they did open up channels for anyone to want, and potentially buy, luxury consumer goods. By smoking Egyptian Deities cigarettes or sipping Clicquot Club ginger ale, readers could buy a little bit of glamour—and a small taste of upper-class life.

2.5 An ad for Lux soap implied that its customers employed a maid to do their washing. Advertisements usually pictured young, white maids, even though African American women made up a large proportion of domestic workers. This was yet another way of signaling luxury; young, white women were more expensive employees. *Philadelphia Inquirer*, 8 June 1919, 9.

SHAPING MODERN MEN AND WOMEN

Between 1915 and 1930, newspaper advice lost much of the certainty it had conveyed in the preceding fifteen years. Earlier on, the anonymous voice of the paper itself—in the form of answers to questions on the editorial pages—had seemed to guide readers through established rules of conduct.

By the 1910s and 1920s, that voice of authority stayed surprisingly quiet. Instead, newspapers began presenting a smorgasbord of material that laid out acceptable parameters of behavior without insisting on a single "right" way. When newspapers presented readers with options, they reflected somewhat loosened moral codes and also a heightened emphasis on choice that came from the world of advertising. Advertisers who stressed variety and choice discovered that they could sell more goods; each new (often unnecessary) variation allowed customers to purchase a different experience, look, or lifestyle. Newspapers' discussions of modern manhood and womanhood usually kept to this kind of reasoning, portraying gender roles as a series of individual and exciting decisions rather than as constricting societal norms or shared struggles.

The features and ads of the post–World War I era always communicated that men and women had very distinct roles to play in urban life. Papers kept running employment ads in separate "male" and "female" sections. Men columnists served as newspaper doctors, pastors, and financial advisers, while women columnists counseled on relationships, etiquette, and home decoration. Even so, this material aired a relatively wide range of ways that men and women could behave.

Many advertisers, feature writers, and illustrators of the 1910s and 1920s continued to advance an alluring vision of womanhood that revolved around consumer goods. The *Evening Ledger* called its shopping department "Adventures with a Purse," and the writer fantasized aloud about unlimited charge accounts at the city's jewelry counters.[126] The *North American*'s fashion feature pictured young women who arranged their whole social lives around favorite outfits.[127] In humor sections, meanwhile, husbands or fathers balked at women's frivolous purchases and their inexhaustible interest in fashion, reinforcing the idea that all women did, and should, love to shop. Yet in the same newspapers, a parallel set of features encouraged women to find meaning and independence through wage work. During the war, salaried work shed a bit of the stigma it had carried among middle-class women. The *Ledger* women's page, which had once focused exclusively on domestic work like cross-stitch, now reasoned that "every woman—in office, shop, home, store—should begin at once to study the machinery associated with her work and to ground herself in mechanical principles, for there will surely arise a need and opportunity for her to use this knowledge."[128] A "Woman's Exchange" column in the 1920s *Evening Ledger* directed career-minded correspondents to the appropriate schools and employment bureaus. And ads recruited women aggressively. The Philadelphia School of Filing's advertisement described how a Miss Morgan took a night course, found a position, and "now feels that she is doing something worth while."[129]

Newspapers offered women readers previews of the working world, bringing them on tours of workplaces and introducing them to a range of careers. Early on, the *North American* ran a series of articles, "Women's Ways of Making Money," that described the day-to-day demands of professions such as stenography or teaching.[130] In the 1920s, *Evening Ledger* columnist Vivian Shirley tried out a different job every day and reported on her experiences.[131] Comics *Tillie the Toiler* (plate 4) and *Somebody's Stenog* chronicled the office adventures of 1920s secretaries.[132] The comic strips could reinforce gender stereotypes; in the final frames, women stood shocked by men's stupidity, or men sat aghast at women's vain habits. Still, the comics let readers visually tour an urban office setup and familiarized readers with the idea of women and men sharing a workplace.

By advising modern working women, newspaper features helped to normalize women's work. Articles discussed budgeting for the working girl and offered menus geared toward single women cooking in apartments rather than mothers cooking in family homes. "The Modern Well-Dressed Woman of Business," in the *Inquirer*, told readers where to find bargains on work clothes, which colors were office appropriate, and how to turn a work outfit into an evening one with a change of a blouse.[133] The *Evening Bulletin*'s regular women's page feature "Getting On at the Office" printed fictional dialogues among workers in offices or at shop counters. Though the stories never finished with a moral, the dialogues brought readers inside office dilemmas such as unwanted pressure from coworkers or a boss's request for confidentiality.[134]

In the 1920s, many papers picked back up on the kind of confidence-boosting, women-focused reporting that the *Ledger* had done back on its early women's page. The *Inquirer* printed "World of Women" columns listing women's global achievements:

Ohio has a woman game warden who does not hesitate to use a gun when
  it is necessary.
The last session of the Japanese Diet removed the embargo on women
  attending political meetings.[135]

After women's suffrage passed into law, the *Ledger* started a feature titled "The Woman Citizen," and the *Record*'s column "Money Problems of Women" took up questions that independent women faced, such as whether and how to travel alone.[136] The *North American* asked readers to nominate "Women of Mark" for the paper to profile in its Sunday magazine.[137] Papers in the 1910s and 1920s rarely tried to reconcile apparent conflicts between all the different activities—shopping, homemaking, wage work, and politics—that appeared in their pages. But the range of roles discussed in newspapers expanded, and women had the option to read and take the advice that suited them best.

Newspapers offered a host of possibilities for modern male behavior as well, illustrated in male-targeted sports sections, business sections, and editorial pages. Newspaper features and ads pointedly defined the modern man as self-made and independent, a definition that not only harmonized with a widespread American up-by-the-bootstraps ethos, but that meshed well with the beliefs of advertisers and publishers. The *Record*'s editorial-page series, "The Story of My First Job," profiled prominent men around the city—attorneys, prosperous real estate brokers, corporate presidents—and described their climb up the career ladder.[138] The *Record* also constantly reported on scientific innovations and the men who were turning them into profitable enterprises. One 1924 ad for a filing cabinet depicted a businessman as a superhero, soaring through the city sky.[139]

Newspaper publishers and their advertisers likely hoped to steer readers away from a more political understanding of labor. Strikes had paralyzed the nation in the 1890s, and government and business leaders feared immigrant-imported radicalism during World War I. Advertisers and newspaper publishers both employed large workforces in their factories and printing presses. They would rather win those workers over to the idea of an individualistic capitalist contest that rewarded hard work than plant the idea that collective action could improve salaries and conditions.[140] So features avoided talking about systemic issues that might hamper men's career progress (the slim chances of moving from the factory floor to management, for example) and implied that every worker had total control over his career choice and business success. "You and Your Habits Are Masters of Your Fate," advised the *Evening Ledger*.[141]

Failure, too, appeared the fault of individuals—not systems—and was curable through helpful products that renewed individual drive. "Success starts in right thinking," counseled the *Evening Ledger*. "Failure comes when you think you cannot succeed."[142] While ads and features taught men to blame themselves for any failures, they also reassured them that products could fix problems. Advertisements for gasoline, beer, cigarettes, and even chocolate milk implied that the reader might not be man enough to handle the challenges of the days ahead but promised that the product could boost him back into the ranks of successful men. "It's not only brains, but the pep and energy to carry things through that wins success today," explained one ad. Next to the image of a dashing man with a glass in hand appeared the slogan: "Ovaltine—It Makes a New Man of You."[143]

Newspapers portrayed men's leisure time as purposeful, productive, and decidedly middle class. Ads framed men's shopping as a limited task rather than an expansive pleasure and encouraged men to become connoisseurs of only a few types of goods: tobacco, automobiles, and perhaps well-tailored clothes. Papers rarely spoke of—and never promoted—the effete tastes of the urban artist or the flamboyant fashions of the dandy. Men's ads tended to emphasize workmanship and value over aesthetics. "Successful men are the largest buyers of LOUIS MARK SHOES," claimed a 1920 ad, "because, from experience, they have learned that every dollar they spend here buys 30% more value."[144] Men only purchased the items women would not buy for them, according to newspaper material, and did so on efficient errands rather than leisurely days of browsing.[145] Men's material tried to channel readers toward sedate, respectable leisure activities that profited newspaper advertisers: motoring in the country, following sports, or enjoying a good cigar at home. These visions of male leisure left out the favorite pastimes of rowdy urban working-class culture such as gambling, amateur boxing, or rounds of drinks at saloons (made illegal from 1920 onward), and omitted the long ambling walks favored by the urban drifter. Instead, they rendered a world of dutiful laborers who, in their spare time, pursued pleasures that would not interfere with the next day's work.[146]

Like the images of physical and domestic perfection in the women's pages, the images of men in the sports pages and in the ads set exacting standards. Turn-of-the-century sports pages had run only the occasional team photo of a football league, but in the 1920s such pages displayed photographs of boxers ready to punch, sprinters in motion, and football players in a tackle. The men in advertisements had square jaws, broad shoulders, aquiline noses; they were trim but muscled and impeccably groomed. On the sports pages, writers commented on men's prowess. "Tilden's great stamina was a big factor in his victory over his opponent, whose physique, while powerful, cannot compare," explained the *Daily News* under a photo of the boxer.[147] Images of brawny men sold everything from tires to fishing vacations. Newspapers of the 1920s also hinted that readers could actually achieve impressive physiques with enough hard work. Editors hired sports coaches to write articles on how to train for football, long-distance running, swimming, or basketball.[148] The articles primed men to follow the regimens and buy the products—from sports equipment to health tonics—that would get them closer to the modern chiseled, agile ideal.

Comic strips offered some relief from the overwhelming expectations elsewhere in the newspaper, since they rejected and parodied the masculine ideals of the 1920s. Men in the comics were either stick-skinny or doughy and round, with pug noses and no shoulders to speak of. They slouched through the city with scraped knees, scuffed shoes, and hair that stuck straight up, untamable.[149] Many 1920s comics characters—Darius Dubb (fig. 2.6), Jerry on the Job, Smitty, Barney Google—entertained read-

2.6 Comics characters such as Darius Dubb entertained readers with their ineptitude. *Philadelphia Inquirer*, 2 November 1915, 13.

ers with their sheer ineptitude. They misinterpreted the boss's orders, they botched their plans to get rich quick, and they offended every woman they tried to talk to. Lacking any street smarts or business sense, comic strip characters were exploited right and left by salesmen and by employers. They got cheated out of paychecks, fired for accidents that they did not cause, and talked into bad investments. The sagas of working-class characters critiqued the myth that all men could work their way up in an open and fair economic system. They labored as cogs in a bureaucratic machine or drifted from one odd job to another.[150]

The strips following upper-class characters were equally skeptical toward the ideal of bootstrapping success. Jiggs—from the strip *Bringing up Father*—and Barney Google had both lucked into their money and did not quite know what to do with it. They were incurably working class, their millions notwithstanding. Readers could interpret the strips as send-ups of the concept of meritocracy or of the upward mobility promised elsewhere in the paper. The comics got away with such criticism and pessimism because they were only jokes. But they did provide a respite from and an alternative to the relentless capitalist optimism that appeared in the rest of the men's material.

Newspaper features of the late 1910s and the 1920s paid more attention to marriage and family than they had previously and spoke in much more intimate detail. The social upheavals of the era partly explain this new focus. Marriages and families were going through a rocky phase, between women's new rights and roles and the birth of a more rebellious youth culture. The relative prosperity and security of the era may also have fueled the public discussion of private life. In the strong economy of the 1920s, many Philadelphians (and other Americans) had been able to achieve a number of milestones: an education for themselves and their children, a stable job, a home of their own. Yet with all of this in the bag, life may not have felt perfect or even easy. Why not? Americans may have asked themselves. What could they do about it? And was this situation normal?

In the 1910s and 1920s, nearly every Philadelphia paper ran features that turned ordinary people's marriages into entertainment. Husbands and wives suddenly cropped up everywhere—bickering in comic strips, learning to live together in fictional vignettes, and insulting each other in humor columns. The *Philadelphia Record* printed readers' answers to the questions "What Does Your Husband Do?" and "What Does Your Wife Do?" "My husband takes both hands off the steering wheel and yawns and stretches and frightens me to death," reported Mrs. C. H. P. "My wife wears my pajamas if all hers happen to be in the laundry," shared G. W. B.[151] The *Public Ledger* and the *Daily News* both ran a feature, "The Marriage Game," with a "his" and "hers" take on marital problems. Once each party had made their case, a referee declared a winner.[152]

In newspapers of the past, marriage had appeared as the happy ending in serialized fiction and in the society pages' wedding announcements. While this material continued to run in the 1920s, new features spoke much more savagely about the institution. In newspapers' humor columns, husbands drank, lied, and insulted their wives; wives chatted endlessly, spent money on trifles, and pestered their husbands. Short dialogues painted depressing pictures of love and marriage:

WIFE— Do you know, I have a very little mouth. In the glass it doesn't look
    large enough to hold my tongue.
HUSBAND— It isn't.[153]

HE— How'd you like a pet dog?
SHE— Now, George, haven't I told you that I don't intend to marry?[154]

Nagging wives featured in dozens of the era's most popular comic strips, including *Bringing up Father*, *The Gumps*, *Mutt and Jeff*, and *Doings of the Duffs*.[155] Another cartoon chronicling a marriage ran under the title *The Padded Cell*.[156]

The 1920s was a time of both raised romantic expectations and dashed hopes. The median marriage age fell in the 1920s, to around twenty-two.[157] Young people with good jobs could afford to marry early; they may also have been made more eager for romance by celebrity magazines, crooning love songs, and especially movies, which were selling 95 million tickets a week to a population of just over 120 million Americans by the end of the 1920s.[158] Movies could foster outsized romantic expectations. As one nineteen-year-old woman explained in a 1929 survey: "I got an idea . . . that people who were in love married and lived happily ever after, in a little rose-covered bungalow. The movies gave me a lot of foolish ideas which my imagination accepted as facts."[159] Movie plots usually portrayed all of the fluttering emotions of courtship and then conveniently ended before the daily realities of marriage set in. Yet most moviegoers were already married and perhaps faced a lifetime spent with a spouse who paled in comparison to the movie stars.

Newspaper material, then, provided something of a corrective to pop culture fantasy. Movies and romantic fiction rarely suggested that relationships might need fixing, for example, but 1920s newspaper material began to talk about ways readers might improve their marriages. Beatrice Fairfax, an advice columnist, recommended marriage vacations, with spouses taking occasional weeks apart.[160] Columnist Elsie Robinson suggested that women cultivate individual interests and activities rather than sharing every passing thought and expecting a husband to do the same.[161] Although a few features discussed the possibility of ending a marriage—the *Record*'s psychology column talked to readers about "Divorce: Why and When?"— more often, newspapers told readers how to reconcile their idealized concepts of marriage with their real-life situations.[162] Dorothy Dix consistently urged readers to content themselves with humdrum marriages. "The majority of us are no more capable of the grand passion than we are of singing in grand opera," she declared, "nor do we find many people whose attractions justify any overwhelming devotion."[163] In a piece called "The 'Next Best' Husband," a *Philadelphia Record* writer explained how to find contentment in a practical, rather than romantic, marriage.[164]

Newspaper features began acknowledging discord between not just husbands and wives but between parents and children as well—sometimes attempting to instruct parents, and sometimes simply reassuring readers that all this fighting was normal. Newspapers had advised readers on the care of babies for decades, but only in the late 1910s and 1920s did they start to talk about children's less-than-perfect behavior and how to handle it. The *Philadelphia Record* ran a daily feature that alternated titles: "That Problem Girl of Yours" and "That Problem Boy of Yours." The author told readers how to curb girls' sarcastic remarks and how to teach boys good streetcar manners.[165] Syndicated columnist Angelo Patri told parents how to get children to clean up after themselves and how to calm tantrums.[166] Papers were less forthcoming with explicit advice about (and for) teenagers, but readers asked for it anyway. Mothers wrote in to advice columnists, wondering how tightly to monitor their daughters' spending habits and social lives, and daughters used columnists to second-guess their parents' rules. "A boy friend of mine gave me a bar pin for a present," explained one letter, "and my mother says I ought not to keep it; that a girl should not take jewelry from a boy. What is your opinion on this?"[167] Comic strips turned the generation gap into entertainment: *Harold Teen*, *Switchboard Sally*, and *The Bungle Family* all featured teenagers who wore clothes that their parents disapproved of, stayed out past their curfews, and groaned about having to go on family vacations. Comic strips depicting parents and teens did not take sides but simply aired squabbles that many families would recognize.

When newspapers opened up forums on the new practice of dating, they widened the scope of discussable, and acceptable, behavior. The *North American*'s fashion feature suggested that its young heroine could hardly keep track of all the men flirting with her: "Mitzi sits with Tom, Dick or who-is-it under the blooming tree and listens sympathetically."[168] One woman reader responded to another in an advice column:

Read your piece, and must say I agree with you as far as necking goes. I think it is just common slang and really think the girls and fellows ought to have more pride in their language, also think the fellows ought to have more respect for a girl than to expect to mush the first time they meet. I am a collegian girl. Have been around a lot, but I do not let every Tom, Dick and Harry hug and kiss me, I am not called slow either. I have a lot of good times and I like dancing.[169]

Even though this reader insisted that she did not go as far as other girls, she danced with, dated, and kissed many a man without getting engaged to any of them. A letter like this would have been scandalous for a newspaper to print fifteen years earlier; that the *Evening Ledger* even published it indicated to readers how much the rules for relationships had changed.

By the 1920s, features spoke in looser, more open ways than the prescriptive articles of earlier decades. But the material in mainstream daily newspapers in no way reflected the full spectrum of people's experiences. The *Pittsburgh Courier*, the most widely read African American weekly in 1920s Philadelphia, took a noticeably different approach. *Courier* features sometimes harped on the same themes as mainstream dailies. The paper ran a comic strip, *Aggravatin' Papa*, that followed the beautiful, vain teenager Bess and her bumbling father. It printed ads for a publication called the *Book of Good Manners* that promised to teach readers how to escort a lady, accept an invitation, and cultivate charm.[170] But the *Courier*'s advice column, "Friendly Advice to Girls" by Mary Strong, was far more open about life's disappointments and difficulties than any column ever printed in a metropolitan daily paper. It advised readers toward stable relationships and conservative conduct, but it acknowledged and included those who struggled to meet such standards.

Truly painful problems surfaced in the column in part because many African Americans faced terrible choices that their white contemporaries never had to make. "I am in love with a young man who is very dark and really want to marry him," wrote one young woman. "I want children, but I hate to bring a dark child into this world to be buffeted about, as he will doubtless be."[171] A reader wrote to ask whether she could risk a trip to the South to visit her relatives; she lived in the North as white and worried that if her husband discovered her black family, he would leave her.[172] Alongside race-specific problems, though, the column brought up universal dilemmas that mainstream dailies simply never discussed. "I have been deceived by one of my classmates who tells me he cannot marry me now, as he must finish his education," explained one letter writer. "Please tell me where to go that I may get through with my confinement far from the world's eye."[173] Another wrote in cryptic language, seemingly about her marriage to a gay man:

Dear Mrs. Strong:

I have not been married very long, but long enough to know that I have made a bitter mistake. What I have learned is not a matter that I can make public, yet I feel that you can sense the situation. Surely it would be foolish to continue on playing the part of a wife before the world when the reverse is true. I am wondering if I should get a divorce, or if I should just bury myself for life?[174]

Through the contrast with a column like this we see how many issues—premarital sex, accidental pregnancy, suicide, homosexuality, abortion, drug addiction—mainstream papers kept out of their pages.[175] The exclusions themselves became a form of advice, telling readers what they ought to never do—or at least never talk about.

Philadelphia's newspaper material advanced competing ideas in these years. Advice personalities and women's sections reinforced notions of separate spheres for men and women, even as some features encouraged women to enter the male-dominated work world. Articles and ads told men how to make their way in a capitalist market, even as comics vented frustrations with a rigged system. Daily papers' features presented a range of ideas about how to be a modern urban man or woman, and the fact that they offered a range may have seemed exciting or even liberating to many readers. Yet newspapers' instructions on how to behave could just as easily alienate and exclude, since so many situations and dilemmas never appeared in newspaper features at all.

*   *   *

"The modern American newspaper is our national educator of the plain people, young and old."[176] So concluded James Edward Rogers in his 1909 study, *The American Newspaper*. Rogers believed immigrant and working-class "plain people" had to be taught middle-class values and work habits to successfully assimilate into the native-born middle class but that those "plain people" could be hard to reach. "We can enlighten the children by means of compulsory school acts but we cannot force knowledge upon adult men and women," Rogers assessed. "The one institution however that is coping with this problem and getting practical results," he explained, "is the press."[177] Rogers praised newspaper departments that taught readers improved everyday habits in cooking, sewing, cleaning, and exercise.

Rogers rightly noticed that newspapers had taken up the task of guiding readers through the rituals of daily life. But his analysis mistook the true nature and function of newspaper advice. Newspapers were not top-down enterprises run by benevolent and paternalistic reformers but utterly commercial media that evolved to appeal to readers while serving the needs of advertisers. Their varying forms of counsel did establish standards, goals, and limits for urban behavior, but they hewed more to readers' interests and businessmen's wishes than to any reformer's agenda.

When the *Public Ledger* initiated its women's section, it demonstrated the potential of advice material to capture an audience's attention and to steer readers toward purchases. Papers all over the country debuted their own women's pages in the 1890s, which often evolved through the same basic phases. The *Boston Globe* section "The Woman's Hour," for example, quickly developed into a forum in which readers exchanged ideas, opinions, and recipes. However, like the *Philadelphia Public Ledger*, the *Globe* eventually shut down those wide-ranging conversations, trading them for columns on advertising-friendly topics like "Feeding the Baby" and "Hints on Care of Flowers."[178]

Editors across the United States built on the success of women's pages by incorporating advice material into many portions of their newspapers. In the 1890s and in the last decade of the 1900s, it was mass-readership papers that were most likely to serve as advisers. The *New York World*, for instance, gave readers explicit lessons in city etiquette and customs in a series of fictional letters from "city cousin Edith" to "country cousin Bessie."[179] The *Atlanta Constitution* advised ambitious young men on the pros and cons of various trades.[180] Denver's *Rocky Mountain News* ran a "Summer School at Home," offering middle-class self-improvement through articles on science, economics, and literature.[181] Meanwhile, working-class papers tended to reinforce the local focus of readers' lives in their news columns. Like the *Philadelphia Item*, many of these working-class papers relied on revenue from classified ads rather than major advertisers, and so could afford to make fun of high society and consumer culture when they wished. An 1889 *New York Sun* article, "A Five O'clock Tea in Town," at first appeared to instruct readers on the art of hosting a perfectly correct tea. But the article quickly turned into a parody: the tea in fact tasted terrible, the guests were bores, and the hostess and the servants wound up hoarding the alcoholic punch for themselves.[182]

Upper-class papers across the nation knew that their readers prized comprehensive, "big picture" news that reflected the national and international scope of their investments and careers. When a reader of the highbrow *New York Evening Post* praised his paper's reason and judgment, he also described the attitude he himself aspired to: "The 'Evening Post' looks at life with the eyes of a man who wants to understand the large happenings in his own city and country, and in the world at large. With a mere glance it dismisses the unessential and the ephemeral, or omits to notice them at all."[183] A Pittsburgh reader insisted on papers that matched "my good taste and my sense of proportion."[184] No matter how high-minded, though, upper-class papers were beholden to advertisers. The *San Francisco Bulletin* stated as much in 1896: "For reaching the purchasing class it is unexcelled and is therefore THE advertising medium par excellence of the evening papers of the Pacific Coast."[185]

The niche papers of the late nineteenth century, which often outlined class-specific behaviors and attitudes, were swiftly subsumed by a mass-market model in the early twentieth century. In cities all over the country, major papers did everything they could to shut down or take over their smaller competitors. They temporarily slashed their prices in circulation battles, relying on their advertising contracts and financial reserves to keep afloat; this drove smaller dailies out of business.[186] Other large papers simply purchased smaller ones outright. The *Chicago Herald* acquired the *Chicago Times* in 1895, the *Chicago Record* in 1901. George T. Oliver bought the *Pittsburgh Gazette* and merged it with the *Pittsburgh Times* in 1900. In 1909, the total number of daily newspapers in America came in at around twenty-six hundred; from then on, the number fell each year.[187]

The ensuing mass newspapers often fused working-class, middle-class, and upper-class strains of urban culture by speaking to readers as if they all desired the same things and spent their time in the same ways. Newspaper material of the 1910s and 1920s also began breaking down a few class boundaries. In New York, the "Evening Journal Investors' Service" opened up conversations about stocks to all readers, whether or not they came from families with investments. "I am a reader of your paper and want to buy stock," wrote a reader in Jersey City. "What is your opinion of a purchase of Technicolor?"[188] Newspaper ads started to offer "exclusive" goods to any reader with enough cash, rather than to a strictly upper-class clientele. An ad in the *New York Times*, for example, offered "Hats for Aristocrats" to even the paper's most humble readers.[189]

In the 1920s, newspaper features did a bit less advising and instructing on the "right" way to behave and, instead, aired a spectrum of possibilities. The more critical and honest depictions of relationships may well have felt empowering, especially for women; the *Chicago Tribune* illustrated its weekly feature "Husbands under Scrutiny" with an image of a woman inspecting a little man under a magnifying glass.[190] Yet papers' new willingness to discuss changes in men's and women's lives did not mean they happily answered any question or tackled any subject. The *Detroit News*'s column "Experience" shut down questions about teenage kissing and about partners who lived together without marrying.[191] When a reader asked the *Baltimore Sun*'s advice column "Is there any place where I can get a complete flirtation code?" the column did not supply one.[192] The editing and sanitizing of newspaper advice, in itself, set parameters for urban behavior and defined papers' desired audiences. Advice columnists showed themselves willing to advise only a segment of the population that they considered *already* reasonably well behaved.

Even though newspapers limited the scope of their advising, readers still wrote to advice columnists in droves. In 1926, the *Chicago Tribune* received 4,113 letters for its "affairs of the heart" column, 24,047 letters for its health column, and 14,570 letters for its beauty column.[193] Some readers may have recognized how narrow—and commercial—newspaper advice had become by that time. Other readers may have stopped noticing. Because papers stated every day that romance, health, and beauty (as well as cars, athletics, vacations, fashion, and home decor) mattered deeply, readers may have absorbed the lesson that these facets of life deserved particular attention.

Newspapers gave readers portraits of city people and explained the behavior and purchases it took to be one of them. At the same time, papers offered visions of the places that readers, as city dwellers, belonged to. Metropolitan newspapers informed readers not just how to be city people but also how to belong to a metropolitan community.

3: BUILDING PRINT COMMUNITY

In 1909, sociologist Charles Horton Cooley was investigating social life in America and, in the process, found himself defending the importance of the American newspaper. "The bulk of its matter," he explained, "is best described by the phrase organized gossip. The sort of intercourse that people formerly carried on at cross-road stores or over the back fence has now attained the dignity of print and an imposing system.... We are gratifying an old appetite in a new way."[1] Newspapers' circulation of seemingly mundane gossip, Cooley argued, served a vital purpose—it bound communities together. "The decried habit of reading the newspapers contributes much to a general we-feeling... pervading the world with a conscious community of sentiment."[2] In an era when many Americans worried that big cities would dissolve community entirely, and in which city dwellers hotly debated who belonged in the urban public, newspapers had a vital role to play in creating, as Cooley put it, a "we-feeling" or a "conscious community."

The ties that bound turn-of-the-century metropolises together necessarily differed from those that bound neighborhoods and towns. In small towns, years of interactions and shared experiences might make residents feel empathetic toward, and responsible for, one another. Daily chats and small favors could bond urban neighbors as well, but such intimate exchanges could not unite entire cities. Metropolitan residents who lived in different neighborhoods, practiced different professions, and moved in distinct social circles might never encounter each other or even walk the same city streets. If urbanites were to feel themselves a part of a metropolitan community, they would have to assemble their understanding of that community out of something other than in-person experience and interaction. Newspapers formed the raw material for that project.[3] By distributing shared vocabularies, images, and stories, newspapers could help convince readers that they and their neighbors shared a single urban reality.

Columns of letters to the editor hosted much disagreement and debate. Yet those editorial-page debates often took as their starting point a set of shared interests and investments among participants. Most obviously, readers and contributors might share an allegiance to a particular political party, but more subtly, they might also assume a common future, a sense of mutual responsibility, and an ethic of interdependence. Surprising and varied portions of newspapers—not editorial pages but events listings, muckraking articles, travelogues, and charity drives—built up that sense of common interest and shared fate for hundreds of thousands of city readers.[4]

The "conscious community" depicted in turn-of-the-century newspaper pages can seem, at first glance, remarkably inclusive. The poor, the rich, immigrants, and even criminals all appeared in newspaper articles as legitimate and permanent members of the urban public. Articles often treated these subjects as readers' neighbors, about whom they ought to be curious, and whom they might strive to help. Civic campaigns spotlighted issues that concerned (and therefore bound together) all city dwellers, while newspapers' charity drives created the impression of a cohesive urban community that cared for the city's neediest. When these articles assumed that readers would take an automatic interest in the state of their cities' politics, infrastructures, and most vulnerable populations, they fostered a culture of civic stewardship.

A few populations did fall outside the scope of papers' curiosity and concern, however. The newspapers of many eastern cities remained nearly silent on African American community life, behaving as though that population simply did not exist. Other regions' papers intermittently excluded Asians and Hispanics as well, either through silence or through vitriolic campaigns. More often, newspapers assigned ethnic and racial minorities specific places in a fairly rigid social hierarchy. It seemed that only the reader, assumed to be white and middle class, could move freely through cities' varied spaces and populations. Thus newspapers' renderings of urban communities were inclusive but not egalitarian; they depicted cities made up of actors and subjects, central citizens and peripheral characters.

Judging from the front pages, turn-of-the-century cities were harsh places. Articles showcased the greed, violence, loneliness, and poverty that governed many city dwellers' lives. Because newspapers reported so much bad news, it is in some ways surprising that they also managed to depict cities as places that readers might want to claim as their own, in which they might even take some pride. But editors and reporters took great pains to emphasize other, less sensational kinds of urban stories, in which city people treated each other with generosity and warmth. The new genre of the human-interest article encouraged readers to empathize with a wide variety of urban lives and to appreciate moments of grace as well as of tragedy.

Newspapers' sunnier depictions of cities could provide escapes from real life. Readers might take refuge in a print version of the metropolis that was far more knowable, navigable, and welcoming than the real thing. They could feel reassured by portraits of cohesive communities, unrealistic as they were. But newspapers' sometimes-utopian civic visions did not exist in simple parallel to urban reality. Newspapers had real power to alter how people thought about cities and their places within them. When articles explained the rewards of urban observation and pointed out especially interesting neighborhoods, they could launch readers out into city streets. When they supplied data and some critical distance, newspapers equipped city dwellers to change their cities in systematic and organized ways. Remarkably, news articles taught each reader to think of millions of metropolitan neighbors as members of his or her community. This is evident even in the least knowable, least coherent city in the nation, New York City.

The island of Manhattan alone qualified as the nation's largest city for most of the nineteenth century. When the city then formally incorporated the Bronx, Queens, Brooklyn, and Staten Island in 1898, it grew from roughly one and a half million people to three and half million, and from twenty-three square miles to 303 square miles.[5] The consolidated city was one of the largest in the world.

New York City's growth further separated the city into wealthy and poor neighborhoods, into ethnic enclaves and specialized commercial quarters. Well-off New Yorkers moved farther and farther uptown, into ever more exclusive and homogenous districts.[6] New immigrants who joined their relatives and countrymen in Manhattan neighborhoods swelled the population of each one, so that by 1890 reporter and photographer Jacob Riis could map out swaths of the Lower East Side that were overwhelmingly Italian, Polish, Jewish, or Chinese.[7] The city's African American center relocated from portions of lower Manhattan to the much larger Harlem, which by the 1920s stretched more than thirty-five blocks from south to north and from Amsterdam Avenue to the East River.[8] In New York's dense yet stratified boroughs, residents living in one type of neighborhood might rarely interact with residents of others.

In fits and starts, New York City's patchwork of boroughs and islands fused into a more integrated metropolitan region. The monumental Brooklyn, Williamsburg, Manhattan, and Queensboro Bridges brought New Yorkers across the East River. Subway lines connected Manhattan to the Bronx in 1904, to Brooklyn in 1908, and to Queens in the 1920s.[9] A flurry of construction in the 1910s and 1920s then opened up bridges, tunnels, and roads to automobile traffic. Better transit facilitated urban mixing, in one sense, allowing people to easily visit different areas of the city. At the same time, the room for expansion resulted in even more specialized neighborhoods. Working-class Polish families moved to Sunset Park, middle-class Italians to Bay Ridge, middle-class Orthodox Jews to Borough Park, and working-class Jews to Brownsville. Jamaica filled with African American families seeking more space than Harlem could offer, while planned communities in Jackson Heights and Sunnyside filled up with native-born New Yorkers starting families and commuting to work in Manhattan.[10]

The enormous reach of the city and the diversity of its people suggest that residents might have a difficult time fashioning a coherent identity for the metropolis and that they would feel little kinship with their millions of fellow New Yorkers. Even as dense urban development spread, the city remained so vast that it still held almost every possible type of settlement. A New York address could indicate an estate on Staten Island, a dairy farm in Queens, a seaside summer home on Far Rockaway, or a towering skyscraper in midtown. And yet New York managed to cultivate a distinctive personality of its own and to inspire fierce loyalty among its residents.

Because newspapers saturated New York, they played an especially important role in familiarizing readers with the broader city and in making the metropolis feel like a village.[11] The *New York World* and the *New York Journal*, at the peak of their popularity in the late 1890s, each printed enough copies to reach one in every three New Yorkers, or three of every four Manhattan residents. The *World* and the *Journal*—and later, in the 1920s, the *New York Daily News*—circulated so widely that they provided common languages for residents. Other papers carved out more specialized, niche audiences. The *New York Tribune* attracted wealthy suburban Republicans, the *Globe* appealed to middle-class women and mothers, and the *Morning Journal* earned the nickname "the washerwoman's gazette."[12] Working-class conservatives read the *Sun*, most businessmen read the *Times*, and the intellectual elite took the *New York Evening Post*.[13] The city offered nine dailies in foreign languages (four German, two French, and one each in Czech, Yiddish, and Italian).[14] Neighborhood, ethnic, trade, religious, and political groups' weekly papers added to the panoply. And the borough of Brooklyn printed three daily papers of its own. All of these papers created and strengthened smaller communities within the city.

Even the biggest papers did not reach the entire urban population, so no single vision of New York's identity and community made its way into the lives and minds of all of the city's residents. But every New York paper, from the *Amsterdam News* to the *Jewish Daily Forward* to the *Herald Tribune*, offered a vision of New York as a whole, a print version of the city that residents browsed, criticized, and partially adopted as their own. Each cast its readers in relationship to the wider city. The city and the citizens that appeared in newsprint helped New Yorkers to envision a metropolitan community and to make meaningful places for themselves within it.

A CONCERNED PUBLIC

The mass metropolitan dailies of late nineteenth-century New York sketched an urban community for readers in part through their civic reporting known, in its most aggressive form, as "muckraking." Editors embraced muckraking partly out of self-interest, for these articles boosted newspaper sales by uncovering previously hidden, and often scandalous, urban problems. Yet muckraking—and its counterpart, the newspaper charity drive—changed city culture and altered urban lives in very real ways. Together, these two types of material established the idea that the urban public, regardless of class or political party, shared both concerns and responsibilities.

In mid-nineteenth-century journalism, class and party loyalty had trumped any broader civic identity, and the newspapers took it as their job to choose a side, not to solve a problem. When New York's newspapers covered the 1836 murder of Helen Jewett, for example, the *Sun* rallied its working-class readers in solidarity with the poor prostitute Jewett, while the slightly more genteel *Herald* asked its readers to stand with Richard Robinson, the wealthy patron suspected of her murder.[15] Neither paper looked at the case through a wider civic lens. Neither one examined the police system that allowed prostitution to thrive along Thomas Street, and neither one discussed any systemic change that might prevent women like Jewett from winding up in such a dangerous occupation.

In the late 1880s and the 1890s, New York editors endeavored to expand their audiences beyond a single party or class—which meant that they had to enlist readers' loyalties in new ways. Some papers tried to make New Yorkers feel that whenever they bought an issue, they were joining a community of readers who chose "the best" paper in the city. "An exclusive story is supposed . . . to instill in the reader interest and pride in 'his paper's' triumph," explained Lincoln Steffens. "It is to the new journalism what common opinion was to the old, a good shared by the reader with his paper."[16] Both Joseph Pulitzer and William Randolph Hearst used their newspapers' size and popularity to make readers feel like a part of something important, trumpeting their circulations on their papers' mastheads and on signs on their buildings.[17]

Late nineteenth-century New York papers also began to use populist—not partisan—language that drew many different kinds of readers together rather than setting them against each other. In 1883, Joseph Pulitzer de-

scribed his paper's mission in politically independent language: "An institution that should always fight for progress and reform, never tolerate in-
justice or corruption, always fight demagogues of all parties, never belong
to any party, always oppose privileged classes and public plunderers, never
lack sympathy with the poor, always remain devoted to the public welfare,
never be satisfied with merely printing news, always be drastically independent, never be afraid to attack wrong, whether by predatory plutocracy or
predatory poverty."[18] This manifesto aligned the *New York World* with the
interests of the great majority of New Yorkers and defined the enemy as just
a handful of demagogues, plunderers, and privileged urbanites. Pulitzer's
paper created a *we* that was far more expansive and inclusive than that in
partisan papers and asked the reading audience to unite in pursuit not of
party goals but of public welfare.[19]

The *New York World*, and also its rivals the *New York Journal* and the *New
York Sun*, adopted populist stances with an eye to expanding their circulations. But when these papers stated their intentions to watch out for all city
people's interests, readers began turning to them to solve urban problems.
"If you have any fault to find with anybody or anything of a public nature,"
stated the 1889 *New York World*, "put it in as concise form as possible and
address it to 'The Grumbler.'"[20] Respondents complained about all kinds
of urban irritations, from noisy gangs of boys who kept the neighbors awake
all night to streetcar conductors' bad breath. An 1889 survey taken by the
New York World indicated readers' confidence in newspapers' abilities to
effect change through investigations and editorial campaigns. When the
World asked readers what it could do to improve itself, dozens of readers
wrote in not to suggest changes to the paper's format or its beats but instead to suggest specific causes the paper ought to take up. They wanted it
to reform the city's garbage business, to investigate factories for evidence
of contamination, to campaign for better treatment of animals. The most
imaginative readers pictured the *World* as a national or even international
force, asking the paper to build a bridge across the Atlantic Ocean or to
change the country's name to the United States of Columbia.[21]

Partisan papers had purposely avoided reporting on municipal problems, for they did not want to call attention to their own parties' flaws. Partisan papers had also failed to investigate local concerns because they were
too busy talking about their party's state- or national-level platforms and
campaigns.[22] And while New York City's entrenched political system had
caused large-scale urban problems to go underreported, the city's sheer
size and complexity had also obscured them. Information often failed
to travel through the city's many layers. Working-class immigrants used
filthy equipment in meatpacking plants or worked under exploitative conditions in garment factories, but their knowledge rarely traveled beyond

their circles of friends and coworkers. Politicians themselves knew about the graft and corruption that ruled New York's intricate system of wards, aldermen, and commissioners, but that corruption remained hidden from most voters. Such a complex and stratified city sheltered plenty of secrets for reporters to uncover, especially if they were willing to break free of partisan politics.

New York's newspapers came into their own as civic stewards when they began exposing exploitation and fraud—when they began muckraking. The muckraking model required that reporters not simply wait for news to surface but that they go looking for hidden problems. Some of these reporters dug up dirt on city, state, and national political systems. Others exposed city businesses' immoral practices, from watering down milk to fixing prices for railroad tickets.[23] Elizabeth Cochrane, who wrote under the name "Nellie Bly" for the *World*, routinely went undercover to expose terrible conditions in insane asylums, prisons, hospitals, factories, and nursing homes.[24] Jacob Riis, who covered the police headquarters for the *New York Tribune* and then the *New York Sun*, wrote about the misery he witnessed in the tenements, sweatshops, and flophouses of the city's poorest neighborhoods.

Muckraking articles offered voyeuristic pleasures, and they could be doubly shocking when they exposed political corruption or dire poverty that existed right under readers' noses. Riis's photographs, later published in his book *How the Other Half Lives*, were clearly intended to both stun and fascinate middle- and upper-class readers with their images of squalid barrooms and alleyways.[25] Yet muckraking reporters also assumed and expected that readers would feel a sense of connection to their city as a whole—not just to their own class, party, neighborhood, ethnicity, or trade—and that the connection translated into a duty to solve city problems. Their articles consistently spoke of interconnected and interdependent cities. An 1897 *World* editorial described the spreading dangers of the slums: "It is in such places that small-pox, measles, scarlet fever, diphtheria, consumption and all the most deadly diseases breed, to spread until the cleanest and wealthiest quarters are involved. . . . The old proverb which says that it is our concern when the next wall is burning fits this situation exactly. If we do not drag up the slums, the slums will drag down New York."[26] In this urban vision, a problem in one part of the city became everyone's problem.[27]

Though New York City newspapers toned down their fiery language and energetic exposés in the 1890s and early 1900s, their model of civic-minded, activist, nonpartisan news coverage slowly became standard in mainstream metropolitan papers nationwide. Newspapers also passed the torch to magazines, which further developed muckraking into both a literary genre and a national sensation.[28] When newspapers positioned themselves as crusaders for the public good, they joined many Progressive organizations that were circumventing traditional party politics and establishing new structures for addressing urban problems. Settlement houses, city clubs, housing commissions, and business bureaus all tried to improve conditions in cities through independent monitoring and action. Reformers established new appointed government positions—such as city managers, school superintendents, and health commissioners—so that officials would spend more time fixing endemic problems and less time worrying about their chances for reelection. As newspapers inspired some of these efforts and publicized others, they catapulted cities into an age of energetic reform and established a norm of nonpartisan problem solving.

Metropolitan newspapers assumed even more involved roles within their communities when they founded charities of their own. Churches' donations and services were failing to meet the needs of the growing and diversifying turn-of-the-century cities. Churches in homogenous new urban or suburban neighborhoods had little contact with needy populations in urban slums, and Protestants often neglected the city's Catholic and Jewish populations.[29] Neighborhood congregations could seem too small to effectively counter cities' large-scale problems such as tuberculosis, malnutrition, and child labor. Meanwhile, many older municipal aid organizations, such as asylums, poor houses, orphanages, and free hospitals, had atrophied into mere warehouses for the poor. Newspapers, by contrast, were often well positioned to channel aid to those who needed it. Editors might know more about the city's poor than most churches or volunteer organizations, since their reporters covered the city's slums each day. And on their pages, they could mount large-scale campaigns that raised funds from hundreds of thousands of readers at once.

Newspaper charities became vehicles through which readers could engage with and improve their communities. In 1882, the *New York Tribune* sponsored the first long-running newspaper charity, the Fresh Air Fund, which sent tenement children on two-week vacations in the countryside. The *Tribune* kept the fund's director on salary; he wrote articles that appeared in the paper nearly every day through the spring and summer, soliciting donations.[30] The *New York World*, *Journal*, and *Herald* followed in the *Tribune*'s footsteps. During the depressions of 1893 and 1897, those papers set up funds providing free ice, clothing, coal, and food. By 1900, the *New York Times* was running appeals for both the Sick Children's Mission and the Little Mothers' Aid Association.[31] The *New York Times* and the *Brooklyn Eagle* later instituted "Neediest Cases" drives that ran during the holiday season.[32]

Though all of these charities cast readers as community members who cared for each other, their approaches differed. The charities of the *World*, the *Journal*, and the *American* offered temporary relief for acute crises, distributing coal to poor families during a frigid spell in winter or taking up a collection for the family of a slain police officer.[33] In this they resembled the mutual aid societies of working-class communities. The middle-class and upper-class readers of the *New York Times* and the *New York Tribune* meanwhile, steeped in a culture of Progressive reform, were likely to value highly systematic aid efforts, and they had the money to sustain those efforts over years or even decades. Readers of these papers might also be relatively unfamiliar with (and potentially quite interested in reading about) the poor.

Charity articles offered readers a risk-free way to learn about and sympathize with New York City's poorest residents. On the street, middle-class and prosperous New Yorkers often kept their guard up against the poor, expecting them to beg, peddle, or even steal. When reading the newspaper, those same New Yorkers could let down their guard, for print protected them from the unpredictability of an in-person encounter. Writers often focused on child subjects because they seemed less threatening to readers than poor adults and because few readers would be likely to blame children for their own poverty. Articles encouraged readers to see subjects as deserving, lovable individuals rather than as mere types. "No one can help liking 11-year-old Jimmy Sharp, and no one can help smiling into the joyous little face, with its brown eyes, wide mouth, and straight, narrow nose," explained one 1918 "Neediest Cases" profile.[34] The *New York Tribune* cannily printed letters from the beneficiaries of its Fresh Air Fund, putting readers into intimate (print) relationships with those receiving aid. "Dear Mama: I think that you would not have a good time as I have in a 100 years—a boy and me is getting lots of apples under the trees but we don't take the apples off the trees, and how are you getting along—I am getting along very nice and did you hear anything of grandma's foot—I hope it is well."[35] This child's enthusiasm and stream-of-consciousness writing may have reminded some readers of their own children.

In charity articles, editors deftly rendered the fragmented city as a caring community. Readers could participate in and join that fantasy of New York by donating to newspapers' causes. Nearly all charity drives printed lists of donations every day or week. A list of Fresh Air Fund donors in the 1890 *Tribune* read:

The Parsonage ... 7.00
Mrs. W. H. Vanderbilt ... 1,000.00
H. N. G. ... 5.00
Sunday-school class of young girls of the Congregational Church, Durham,
    Conn. ... 2.25[36]

By gathering such different names together on a page, around a shared cause, these lists conjured a community in which every member mattered. At the same time, newspaper charities showcased New Yorkers' generosity and caring by reprinting the letters that came in with donations. "Please give this money to the Neediest Cases," wrote Elihu Robinson of Newark, in a letter received and then reprinted by the *New York Times*. "My sister and I saved it for Christmas gifts for our family, but we decided that these cases need it more."[37] When their drives finished, editors detailed the heartening changes made possible by readers' donations. "The widowed mother whose seven children were weak and ill from malnutrition now has enough food for them," explained a follow-up article. "The children look like a different family, so healthy and rosy are they, and even the feeble grandmother of this home seems to have renewed her youth."[38] Every time newspapers attributed their charities' successes to readers' collective actions, they made contributors feel part of a benevolent and effective group.

Newspaper editors did not start charities out of generosity alone; they founded them to improve their public image. Metropolitan papers had grown into powerful corporations by the turn of the century, and critics accused publishers of profit-mongering tactics no different from those of oil or steel barons. Critics also charged newspapers' sensational stories with debasing public morals. One relatively simple way that an editor could improve his paper's reputation was to found a charity. "We invite the attention of chronic pessimists," said the *New York Tribune* in 1890, "who are constantly complaining that the press is an organized agency for assailing private reputation, debauching public morals and popularizing frivolous gossip and personalities, and that it possesses no redeeming features, to the following tabulated results of thirteen years' successful operation of the Fresh-Air Fund."[39] Papers cast themselves as heroes when they printed melodramatic stories and images in which newspaper workers swooped in to rescue desperate families (fig. 3.1).[40] Charity efforts that focused on children also helped to counter newspapers' reputations for exploiting child workers. Distribution managers hired very young boys, sometimes orphans, to sell their papers on street corners. The boys worked for low wages, and many slept on the sidewalks. If New Yorkers were not already aware of newsboys' troubles from encountering these boys themselves, they learned about their situation from Children's Aid Society founder Charles Loring Brace, who took up their cause in the 1850s, or from novelist Horatio Alger, who turned newsboys into plucky heroes in serialized stories and bestselling books.[41] When the *Times* publicized the Sick Children's Mission or the *Tribune* promoted its Fresh Air Fund, each paper cast itself as a benefactor—rather than an enemy—of children.

It seems that New York City newspapers successfully positioned them-

NEW YORK JOURNAL, FRIDAY, JANUARY 29, 1897.

JOURNAL RELIEF WAGONS BRINGING HELP THROUGH THE STORM TO THE POOR OF A GREAT CITY.

The arrival of the Journal relief wagon in Monroe Street.

Bringing food to the Starving Sheridans, 105 Orchard Street.

HUNGRY AND COLD
FED AND WARMED.

The Journal Provides More Food and Fuel for the Most Miserable of the City's Poor.

Five Wagons Busy All Day Carrying to the Starving and the Sick Edibles to Which They

3.1 The background of this image shows the *Journal*'s delivery wagon fighting through the wind and snow with its cargo of food and fuel. Captions under the round images say "The arrival of the Journal relief wagons in Monroe Street" and "Bringing food to the starving Sheridans, 105 Orchard Street." *New York Journal*, 20 January 1897, 8.

selves as generous and caring institutions, for needy New Yorkers began to turn to newspaper editors for help. Files of letters to Joseph Pulitzer include hundreds of requests for jobs, money, and publicity. Some correspondents praised the *World*'s charitable reporting before asking for assistance. "You have been the means of helping so many by stateing [*sic*] their case in the columns of your valuable paper. I am in hopes you will help me a little," wrote Mrs. Louisa Baker. "Will you please state my case to the public and receive all contributions?"[42]

Muckrakers focused readers' attention on urban problems that politicians and partisan papers had neglected for years and encouraged readers to think critically about how to solve them. Newspaper charity articles, in contrast, acted as more temporary salves. They did not examine the causes of poverty, hunger, or child labor but simply aimed to ease the suffering of victims. Still, both types of news created similar expectations that filtered into New York's political and social world. Jacob Riis's articles and photographs inspired citizens and politicians to pass child labor laws, to construct city playgrounds, and to expand the Croton aqueduct that supplied the city with uncontaminated drinking water.[43] Elizabeth Cochrane's exposé prompted an investigation and overhaul of the city's insane asylums. The *New York Times*'s crusade against abusive business practices at the New York Life Insurance Company persuaded legislators to reform the industry.[44] Charity articles successfully mobilized New Yorkers; readers of the *New York Tribune*, for example, donated anywhere from $18,000 to $52,000 to the Fresh Air Fund in every year between 1882 and 1912 and sent between four and fifteen thousand tenement children annually on countryside vacations.[45] Newspapers' vision of urban community was in many ways just that—a vision, one that never even reached many residents. Yet by stressing the idea that city dwellers ought to care about the health and welfare of all others, New York newspapers did fashion their reading audiences into more involved and reform-minded publics.

INSIDE THE CITY'S MANY SPHERES

At the turn of the century, New Yorkers' everyday lives took place within a diminishing slice of a vast city. If residents wanted to envision and grasp the entire city, they had to use their imaginations. Daily newspapers exposed readers to many facets of the city that they never saw in person, and thus helped them to imagine the city as a whole. Papers chronicled the city's cultural expansion, describing many new professions, entertainments, and specialties. They also reported on its physical expansion, familiarizing readers with the streets of its new neighborhoods, the tops of its skyscrapers, and the depths of its sewer system. Over the years, reporters developed sophisticated techniques to not only tell readers what had happened at a particular place and time but also to make readers feel as though they had been at the scene. These articles did not call explicitly on New Yorkers' sense of community, nor did they rally for change the way that muckraking and charity articles did. Yet their information could deepen readers' attachment to, and investment in, the city as a whole. Right when the city seemed to outpace readers' understanding, metropolitan newspapers took it on as their job to report on all of New York's facets, constructing "conscious community" not from small-town gossip but from big-city news.

Even basic newspaper reporting offered a more complete view of one city day than readers could ever get through direct experience. As early as 1835, the *New York Herald* had promised to take readers everywhere at once:

"We shall give a correct picture of the world—in Wall Street—in the Exchange—in the Post Office—at the Theaters—in the Opera."[46] The *New York Sun* printed urban dispatches under the title "Life in the Metropolis. Dashes Here and There by the Sun's Ubiquitous Reporters."[47] These "ubiquitous" reporters became readers' eyes and ears all over the city. Announcements of everyday events, too, carried readers far and wide. The 1887 *New York Tribune*'s column of "What Is Going on To-Day" listed:

Board of Aldermen, noon.
Irish National League, No. 61 Union Square, 8 p.m.
Knights of Labor conspiracy case, Yorkville Police Court.
Brooklyn Microscopical Society reception, Adelphi Academy, 8 p.m.
Knickerbocker Bowling Club reception, Tennis Building, 3 p.m.[48]

While listing gatherings that readers might want to attend, the column also gave them an overview of the day's happenings—a bird's eye picture of the day that only reading, not experience, could provide.

In the mid- and late nineteenth century, writers covering the day's biggest civic functions and most important meetings used special reporting techniques to mimic in-person experience, giving readers more of a stake in each event. Reporters painted the settings of a Unitarian book club meeting or a Board of Trade banquet, so that readers could visualize where the action had played out. They listed several dozen names of the most prominent people presiding or attending. They then printed the meetings' speeches, toasts, and conversations verbatim, so the reader heard nearly as much talk as an actual attendee: "'Suppose we adopt this badge. The world won't stop if we change it next year.' 'That's it!' 'That's the talk!' came from the different members."[49] In another article genre, which emerged in the 1870s and which flourished well into the twentieth century, a curious reporter sought out and interviewed some New Yorker familiar with a specialized slice of the city. Reporters described their entrance into the scene, so that readers, too, could feel that they had stumbled across an interesting urban happening. "A WORLD reporter tramped across the sands of Long Beach, L. I., the other day and made a call on Capt. Van Wicklin, who is in command of Station 33, with a watchful eye to the wind for the slighted signs of an approaching storm," began an 1889 article.[50] Reporters recorded their questions as dialogue, which allowed each reader to adopt the questions as his own:

"Are there many bald people in New-York?"
"A great many more than is dreamed of," said the wig-maker, with a
    significant smile."[51]

As reporters interviewed the city's specialists and mined their expertise, they turned readers into momentary connoisseurs of rarefied city realms. The worlds of wig makers, circus performers, rescue workers, and casting directors all briefly opened up to them.

By the turn of the century, many papers started to move beyond "you were there" coverage of civic meetings and "curious reporter" interview articles and experimented with illustrations. At first, editors printed a few pictures alongside articles, helping readers to imagine the scene. The 1889 article on the Long Beach rescue workers, for example, showed the inside of the station house and depicted the men launching a boat.[52] When the halftone process made it possible to reproduce photographs, the *World* used photomontage to create detailed, atmospheric pictures of Coney Island evenings and days in Central Park (plate 5). In glossy rotogravure sections, editors reproduced paintings currently on display in the city's museums and galleries, allowing readers to briefly "visit" each exhibit. These illustrations tackled the same task as papers' descriptive articles, carrying readers to new places as vividly and realistically as possible.

Editors turned their papers into even more exciting portals to urban experience as they crafted separate sections for theater, sports, and business. Each of these sections promoted readers' interest and investment in especially rich veins of urban life. Larger theater sections, emerging around the turn of the century, gave reporters space to write much more in-depth commentary. (See fig. 3.2.) Papers turned their reviews into entertaining dramas in themselves, as they outlined plays' premises and principal characters, then revealed the characters' secrets: "They are horror-stricken at discovering, in the first act, that she has fallen victim to the charm of a married army officer named Aynesley Murray," explained a 1906 review in the *American and Journal*, "and is about to bear him a child."[53] The *New York American* even printed entire scenes from plays currently running on Broadway.[54] One New York newspaper reader, housebound by illness, explained why she appreciated this thorough coverage. "As it is not possible to visit art shows, theater, opera concert, or lecture," she said, "I am able to keep informed by the criticisms of pictures, the plots of the new plays, the actors who are to appear and the famous singers. Armed with the information gleaned from the newspapers, I am prepared to discuss any of these matters intelligently."[55] Theater sections also provided an up-close perspective that turned readers into Broadway insiders. Reporters took readers backstage and let them listen in on industry conversations in columns such as "Theatrical Gossip" or "Heard in the Greenroom."[56] Articles described the tricks of the theatrical trade, specifying the methods that actors used to work themselves up into an onstage fury or explaining how actors fashioned elegant-looking costumes out of paper, paint, and fabric

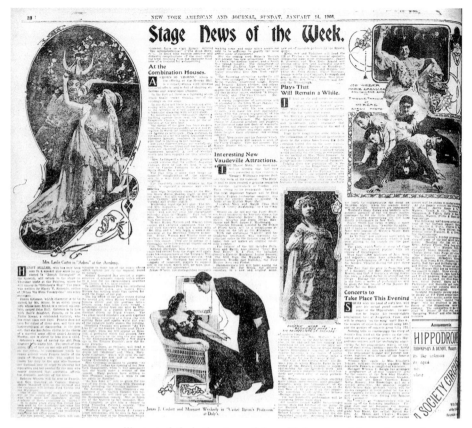

3.2 Newspapers illustrated their theater articles with images of the actors and actresses appearing onstage and with pictures of dramatic scenes. *New York American and Journal*, 14 January 1906, 38.

scraps.[57] A *New York Times* article on the coming opera season pictured not just the opera stars but the elegant occupants of the box seats and the more boisterous crowds in the cheap seats as well.[58] When the 1913 *World* caricatured and named New York's theatergoing "first nighters," all of whom never missed an opening performance, readers could feel as if they knew the Broadway regulars.[59]

Sports sections deployed similar techniques to describe the city's many races and matches, transforming readers into spectators and fans. Where sports articles early in the nineteenth century had reported only the bare facts, late nineteenth-century reporters went into much greater detail.[60] A reporter covering an 1889 handball match first described the physique of each player: "Lawlor is about the medium height, weighing about 160 pounds. His well-knit form showed off well in his tight-fitting blue uniform, and was in striking contrast to his small opponent."[61] The writer then relayed the match minute by minute: "Lawlor had rolled up 15 aces on his first hand, when he lost the ball on a short stroke," he explained. "On Courtney's second hand he did considerable to cut down the big lead of his heavier opponent. He piled up eight aces, when Lawlor got the ball away from him by sending it far back over his head."[62] Soon, New York newspapers were routinely printing a paragraph for every inning of a Yankees or Dodgers game, every round of a highly anticipated boxing match.[63] Slang-filled, energetic descriptions of sports pages in the 1910s and 1920s conveyed, maybe even exaggerated, all the excitement of the live event. A 1917 article in the *Sun* described a hockey match: "A few seconds later from a hot scrimmage in front of the Green earthworks, Jewitt caged the rubber and in 10:15 Peabody smashed a shot that caromed off Garon's shins into the Winged Fist cage. On the next face off Smith whizzed down the ice, darted from behind the net and smashed a sizzler past Smart."[64] By the 1910s, papers were also printing spectacular action shots that conveyed some of the energy and thrill of the game (fig. 3.3).

Sports articles not only brought the reader to the scene but also inducted that reader into a community of sports fans. To begin with, game reports created a sense of shared interests by using language that aligned writer, reader, and spectator behind the home team. "Up to the time we went in to bat in the ninth it looked like a shutout," reported the 1908 *New York Times* on a Giants-Reds baseball game. "Our Master Doyle had made a presentation in a brief but well-chosen error in the second inning and the two runs scored in that frame looked like all the official recorders would be called upon to set down. But such was not the case. We made two runs in the ninth."[65] Words like "we" and "our," the "enemy" and the "champs" placed the reader in a loyal group of New York sports fans. Newspaper articles brought readers into New York's fierce and loyal cheering squad by sharing inside knowledge and vocabulary. They drew up tables of batting, pitching, and fielding records. The 1920 *Daily News* showed readers exactly how Brooklyn's pitcher hurled the ball, how the centerfielder gripped the bat, and how the shortstop caught line drives.[66] After looking at the sports pages, readers would know New York's baseball coaches as "Robbie" or "Uncle Wilbert." They would know the Yankees' Babe Ruth as the Sultan of Swat, Tarzan of the diamond, or the Bambino.[67]

When an 1889 world championship series pitted New York against Brooklyn, newspapers played up the rivalry but did not choose sides. The *World* ran two separate accounts of each game, in parallel columns, told from the Brooklyn and New York points of view:

Princeton Varsity Eleven Engaged in Spirited Scrimmage with Scrub Team in Preparation for Battle with Stevens

3.3 Newspapers of the 1910s printed action shots conveying the energy of the game. *New York American*, 2 October 1910, sec. L-2, 5.

The brave Brooklyn boys appeared on the grounds a little before 2:30 and were warmly welcomed. They warmed up with a brilliant fifteen minutes' practice, and then sat down to watch the New Yorkers try to imitate them. They muffed and everything.

When the bell rang, the Brooklyns shambled out to their positions like nine prize oxen at a country fair. Did they look like winners? Well, scarcely. There was not a man among them who did not handle himself like an overgrown fumbled school-boy.[68]

Even though this series played out before Brooklyn joined metropolitan New York, the paper treated the Brooklyn team, and Brooklyn fans, as equal members of the greater New York community. Newspapers' sports coverage made clear that fans' more local and personal loyalties could be compatible with a broader New York identity.

Even business sections, dry as they might seem, could strengthen readers' bonds to the city by letting them vicariously participate in one of the city's specialized realms. Reports on major New York contracts and sales allowed small-time businessmen to follow the kinds of big-business deals that they would never participate in themselves. In its regular column "What Brokers Think of the Market Outlook," the *New York American* interviewed various firms for market assessments and predictions. Readers could weigh Marshall, Spade & Co.'s opinions against those of J. S. Bache & Co., as if they had personally consulted both.[69] Columns such as "Chat from Wall Street" or "Gossip of Wall Street" offered insider opinions and alerted readers to the hot topics among brokers and bankers. "There has been a great deal of loose talk about the war materials the Allies have been buying or negotiating for in the United States," relayed the *New York Tribune*'s business column, sounding as gossipy as a theater or society article. "The trouble has been mainly that people in the financial district have had only the vaguest ideas about what a shrapnel shell, for instance, was."[70]

As New York City expanded upward and outward, newspapers carried readers into all of the city's new spaces. Newspaper features took readers up to the tops of the city's new skyscrapers and showed them the dazzling views. The *World* enlisted the men cleaning the outside of Saint Patrick's cathedral to take pictures from the tallest spires; the *Times* and the *Herald Tribune* published city views taken from blimps and planes (fig. 3.4).[71] The *Herald Tribune*'s caption under a bird's-eye shot helped readers locate landmarks that they might not easily recognize from the air—Grand Central Terminal, Penn Station, the steamship *Leviathan* at harbor.[72] Circulating a common set of images among hundreds of thousands of New Yorkers who often inhabited very different urban realms, newspapers built up shared mental pictures, visual trademarks, and an agreed-on physical reality for the city.[73] These views were of special value in New York, where the tight grid, mostly flat terrain, and relative absence of squares and plazas made it hard to get any visual distance. The images helped readers map out the paths they themselves traveled and to see how their territory fit into the rest of the city. Newspaper readers could now imagine their lives in relationship to the entire metropolis.

Real estate sections, too, gave readers a stake in the city's expansion and helped them to assemble a more comprehensive vision of the physical city. The pace and variety of construction could make downtown seem like an anarchic, never-ending construction zone. But real estate news revealed an underlying plan. Articles explained why sites were being cleared and printed sketches of the buildings that would rise there. Pictures of Flushing's blocks of apartment buildings, Bronxville's single-family homes, and Manhasset Bay's impressive estates helped readers to visualize suburban neighborhoods and understand exactly how the city was growing.

3.4 A 1910 *New York American* magazine piece tried to reproduce the feeling of standing high above the city. The caption under the photograph read: "A remarkable photograph from the thirtieth story of a skyscraper. To get its best effect, lay the page on the floor and look down on it." *New York American*, 2 October 1910, magazine section, 2.

Other newspaper material let readers get intimately acquainted with the physical city by peeling back surfaces and revealing levels, layers, and systems. Reporters shadowed sewer inspectors, tunnel diggers, and watershed engineers.[74] A 1904 *World* special subway supplement imagined city life unfolding on several levels at once; it pictured a bustling landscape above ground and an equally bustling one below.[75] A feature on New York's "Seven Levels of Transit" (fig. 3.5) showed readers the intricate infrastructures that made the city run. In each case, reporters drew attention to systems that most New Yorkers used or benefited from but never saw. "This floor is inlay Italian marble," explained the architect of the new Madison Square Garden to a reporter in 1925. "When we have our hockey or skating, we simply run the water in on it, turn on our freezing plant which is directly under the floor and we have ice before you can say Jack Robinson. Thirty-five miles of freezing pipe under your feet and you never dreamed it."[76] All of this attention to New York's hidden structures made the city more intelligible to its own residents and stoked a collective sense of wonder at the modern marvel that was New York City.

Almost every local article that appeared in New York newspapers between 1880 and 1930 included an address. Addresses mapped the news onto the city, so that each story seemed less like a random fragment and more like a piece of a larger whole. An article on a car crash, for example, might list the addresses of the drivers, the victims, and any witnesses quoted. Addresses allowed readers to place a typical story of a robbery or an elopement in relationship to themselves. And addresses not only mapped events in physical space but also mapped people in social space. An address on West 103rd Street in Manhattan, on Arthur Avenue in the Bronx, or on Pacific Street in Brooklyn each hinted at the kind of dwelling, the income

3.5 In this cross section of New York's levels of transit, elevated and surface rail lines cross the city while freight and subway tunnels run underground. The blimps and their landing stations form the illustrator's imagined seventh level. *New York World*, 14 March 1909, cover of special "Transformation of New York" section, American Newspaper Repository, Rubenstein Library, Duke University.

level, and even the ethnicity of the resident. Most literally, addresses told readers that each person belonged somewhere. They reminded readers that despite the clamor of the streets and subways, the city sorted itself out at the end of the day and everyone returned to their home address, their designated spot in the metropolis.

As newspapers pictured and explained the city in ever-greater detail, they gave readers the raw material to turn New York, enormous and mystifying, into their hometown. Regular readers of the paper knew where the city spread, what the different areas looked like, how high into the air and how deep into the ground it stretched, and how everything connected. Newspapers offered disparate groups of readers comprehensive, collective experiences of the city. They spread a shared passion for the home teams, a shared sense of pride in the city's theater or opera scene, and a shared awe at New York's impressive infrastructures and towering skyscrapers. Of course, not every New Yorker was able to (or chose to) view New York City in this way. New Yorkers reading foreign-language papers, or reading no papers at all, did not sample the same pictures and descriptions of the metropolis. But mainstream daily papers did give millions of New Yorkers the tools to define their city and to feel attached to it.

HARDENED HEARTS AND "HUMAN INTEREST"

Urban papers mounted a sensory and emotional assault on their readers. The front pages, especially, often depicted cities as places of violence, rupture, discord, and loneliness. Committed to reporting all major events, newspapers were constantly announcing deaths, robberies, and accidents. Theodore Dreiser, when working as a reporter for the *New York World*, found newspapers' renderings of extreme wealth and poverty to be, in his words, "so harsh and indifferent at times as to leave me a little numb."[77] Numbness, however, was not simply an unfortunate by-product of reporting or reading the news: it was part of the point. When newsreaders learned to block out, filter, and mediate disturbing information, they were learning a crucial urban survival skill. At the same time, editors carefully counterbalanced all of this disturbing material, inventing the human-interest genre in the process. Newspapers thus fed readers two very different narratives of the city—one sunny, one dark—each useful in its own way.

Reporters needed to jump from happy to tragic situations without letting their emotions interfere. "A general worker thinks nothing of reporting a murder, a wedding, and a missionary meeting in the afternoon and spending half the night in the street in front of the house where a widely known man is lying close to death," wrote journalist John Given. "He takes everything as a matter of course, and, thoroughly competent, never loses his head."[78] Reporters who let stories affect them deeply did not last long on the job. Dreiser, for example, was a skilled writer with an eye for detail, but he found the work so emotionally draining that he gave it up.[79]

Journalists also needed to be ruthless about cutting unnecessary information, episodes, and people from the news. "THE SUN Condensers are men who can see at a glance what is interesting in an article, and what is useful, and what is needful, and what is of no account," explained an exhibit catalog, "and they 'kill' without mitigation or remorse."[80] The importance of events for individual lives did not matter as much as their interest for readers. "If a man falls off the roof of a six-story building and is killed or badly injured, the occurrence is certainly news, although it is not very important, for accidents of this general character are of daily occurrence in the large cities," explained Given. "But were a man to fall from the top of a six-story building and escape unhurt, the occurrence would be regarded by all editors as news of far more than ordinary worth."[81] Bradford Merrill, of the *World*, showed a typical editor's skill at weighing the "news value" of events without any sign of sentiment, moral judgment, or political involvement. In his notes to his boss, Joseph Pulitzer, he discussed which scandals were first-page versus third-page material, which strikes merited two columns versus one, and whether a recent poisoning deserved a headline.[82] Journalists blocked out the tragic, momentous, or disturbing implications of their stories—which, if considered deeply, might overwhelm them—in order to concentrate on the task at hand.

The product that reporters and editors assembled required skimming and filtering by readers as well. As papers expanded to twenty, then fifty, then a hundred pages, it became impossible to read every word or every section. Yet each portion of the paper seemed to shout for readers' attention. Sensational words—"GRUESOME," "ABANDONED," "DEATH-KNELL," "SEDUCED"—called out from headlines, in capital letters. "ONE MINUTE, PLEASE!" requested a column full of local news, pleading for a moment of readers' time.[83] Reading straight through the jumble of hundreds of articles was not only disorienting but time consuming as well. "What is the use of reading the marriages and deaths in cities where you are unacquainted, advertisements where you do not mean to purchase, timetables when you do not mean to travel . . . police news of strange places, tit-bits of scandal about strange people?" asked reader Julia McNair Wright in 1882. "This reading *everything* in the paper is dangerous, as filling the mind with disconnected trifles, and rendering almost impossible a *continuous* train of thought and study."[84] Even when newspapers added headlines and sections that helped readers locate the articles most relevant to them, newspaper pages still demanded that readers constantly jump back and forth between incongruous ideas—an experience that McNair Wright found trying and even damaging.

News language and layout could shock readers; so too could the scale of the events that papers reported. The 1883 *Tribune*'s column of local news notes told readers:

The police last week made 1,496 arrests.
There were 7,157 arrivals at Castel Garden last week.
The free baths were used last week by 191,746 men and boys and 78,831
    women and girls.[85]

As such data became more available, and as the city grew ever larger, these numbers swelled to stupefying sums. In 1912, the city consumed four and a half billion pounds of food, reported the *World*. In 1916, 763,574,085 people rode the subway, noted the *Times*.[86] Next to New York's enormous sums and numbers, individual lives could seem pitifully small and insignificant. Even the classified listings could alienate and overwhelm. Each classified ad had been placed by an individual—looking for a job, trying to sell something, offering a service. But in the newspaper, each ad appeared minuscule, relatively unimportant, and almost invisible in the mass. In New York, events that would make it onto the front page in a smaller city were often shunted to the back. When the new whale at the Aquarium received twenty thousand visitors on his first day there, the *World* noted it in just a small article.[87] When the mayor and ten thousand spectators attended the opening ceremony for a new road across Jamaica Bay, "the largest vehicular trestle in the world," the *Times* reported it only briefly on page 25.[88] How important a part could an individual play in the life of New York City, a reader might wonder, if the actions of ten thousand people barely made news?

While the substance and scale of New York City news was surely unnerving, it provided useful training for the sensory overload of urban life. Just as readers had to learn to block out information if they wanted to ever finish the paper, pedestrians had to learn *not* to closely study each passerby, *not* to stop and read every sign plastered on a fence, *not* to gawk at every store window display, if they were ever to make it down a city street.[89] Newspapers' odd juxtapositions, too, rehearsed readers for urban experience. In order to step from dirty streets into luxurious shops, from grimy and squealing subway cars into silent marble libraries, contrast had to come to seem a normal, or at least a manageable, part of life. If readers could learn to glance over newspaper stories about children killed by polio alongside advertisements for mink coats, that skill would serve them well. A passage from John Dos Passos's novel *Manhattan Transfer* suggests that some readers even came to find the alarming headlines of the paper relaxing: "He sat in a deep leather chair by a window smoking a thirtyfive [*sic*] cent cigar with the *Wall Street Journal* on his knee and a copy of the *Cosmopolitan* leaning against his right thigh and, with his eyes on the night flawed with lights like a crystal, he abandoned himself to reverie: Economic De-pression . . . Ten million dollars . . . After the war slump. Some smash I'll tell the world. BLACKHEAD & DENSCH FAIL FOR $10,000,000. . . ."[90]

Daily news forced readers to incorporate disappointment and tragedy into their understanding of life in the metropolis. The city could appear utterly indifferent to the violence on its streets and to the suffering of its residents. "When the murder was committed the sidewalks were full of people passing up and down, shouting New Year's greetings and blowing tin horns," noted an 1889 *Sun* article. "No one was found who could tell of any excitement or disturbance in the region."[91] The circumstances of deaths could make the city seem a particularly lonely and cruel place. "In trying to save enough money to bring his family from Russia and from the scenes of the recent massacres at Kishineff," explained the 1903 *Tribune*, "Nathan Longbart, forty-five years old, of No. 5 Elizabeth-st., deliberately starved himself to death and died early yesterday."[92] Many New Yorkers seemed to die alone, without friends or family or even a known identity. And the *New York World* received so many reports of missing persons that it began printing a list of them every Sunday, with notes on hair color, age, and the place they were last seen.

Newspapers' dark humor helped readers to protect their emotional re-serves, teaching them to live with, and even laugh off, the cruelty, ano-nymity, and danger of New York life. In an 1898 *World* cartoon, "The Ameri-can Sky-Scraper Is a Modern Tower of Babel," every possible thing seemed to go wrong. Workers dumped cement on each other, broke out in fights, fell off the scaffolding, knocked each other with steel beams, and acciden-tally electrocuted themselves.[93] Richard Outcault, creator of the Yellow Kid, turned grim urban reality into entertainment. In his cartoon images of tenement life, people got run over by carriages, hit by automobiles, and beaten with clubs. One of Outcault's drawings, "The Day after 'The Glori-ous Fourth' down in Hogan's Alley," showed scrappy children swathed in bandages, on crutches, missing arms and legs, all due to Fourth of July fire-works. "Pleeze keep quiet," read a sign on a fire escape, "fur mickey is dern near dead."[94] These cartoons did not exaggerate. New York construction sites killed and maimed huge numbers of workers and passersby in these years, and traffic accidents took an enormous toll as well. If readers fully considered and absorbed each tragedy in the news, the newspaper would leave them stricken, paralyzed. Instead they had to learn to see the word "suicide" and not read the article or to go ahead and read it but withhold their full sympathy. Out on the streets, New Yorkers had to walk by dilapi-dated tenements without thinking too much about the people who lived in-side; to brush past street vendors and newsboys; to pretend not to see beg-gars sitting on the curb.

While newspapers' daily deliveries of bad news may have desensitized readers to the city's tragedies, contrasts, and overwhelming size, they could actually prime readers for systematic urban action. Their articles highlighted urban problems to be solved. Readers might then use their honed screening and prioritizing skills to discern patterns and to think in a detached way about solutions. The more abstract material, which turned New York into batches of numbers and images, helped readers to understand and assess the city as a whole. A *World* magazine feature called "The Busiest Hour on Earth" (fig. 3.6) provided a social scientific overview of a single hour in New York City; its statistics ("5 buildings catch fire," "123,000 ride the subway,") could be analyzed and perhaps used to improve life in the city. Most Progressive-era reformers employed this kind of surveying, categorizing, and prioritizing logic. City planners who designed municipal projects such as bridges and parks displaced thousands of city residents but improved the lives of hundreds of thousands more. Legislators who implemented zoning laws and labor laws inconvenienced some landlords, builders, and employers but benefited many more tenants and workers over time. Doctors and social workers concerned with public health stepped back from individual cases and assessed broader threats such as tainted water supplies, germ-ridden garbage, and chronic malnutrition.[95] Newspapers both paralleled and furthered turn-of-the-century trends away from moralistic and toward statistical ways of thinking, away from episodic reforms and toward more comprehensive efforts.

Among all of the bad news and overwhelming statistics, New York newspaper editors sprinkled human-interest articles—small-scale stories that would not traditionally be considered newsworthy. New York editor James Gordon Bennett pioneered the form in the 1830s, when he sent his reporters to local courts in search of entertaining domestic dramas and neighborhood feuds. In the 1870s and 1880s, the *Sun*'s editor Charles Dana refined the art of the trivial but amusing news article and regularly worked human interest onto the front page. An 1881 *Sun* front-page article called "Cupid's Work with an Egg," for example, told the story of a Tennessee poultry farmer who managed to meet and marry a Brooklyn woman by writing his address on an eggshell.[96] By the early twentieth century, human interest had become a distinct reporting genre with conventions and rules of its own. "A human interest story," explained one journalism manual, "is primarily an attempt to portray human feeling—to talk about men as men and not as names or things. It is an attempt to look upon life with sympathetic human eyes and to put living people into the reports of the day's news."[97] Claiming newspaper space for these stories—sometimes front-page space—sent the implicit message that the dramas of everyday life deserved attention,

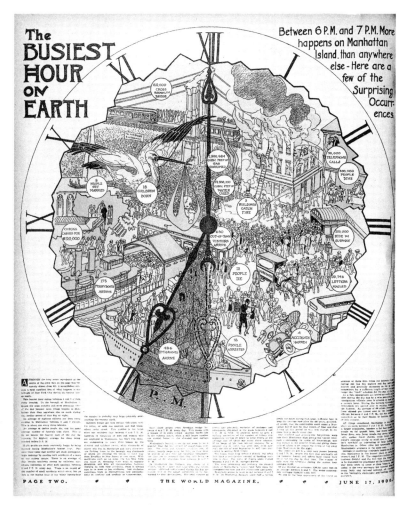

3.6 Some of the statistics in "The Busiest Hour on Earth" seem merely to entertain, such as "500,000 people dine" or "8 people get married." But others—on
fires, accidents, and arrests—seem to call for action. The clock face creates a sense
of urgency, as the viewer imagines all of these incidents unfolding as the hour
passes. *New York World*, 17 June 1906, magazine section, 2, American Newspaper
Repository, Rubenstein Library, Duke University.

even in a city as big as New York. Editors likely ran these articles to add to their papers' appeal as entertainment. Readers could handle only so many articles on local accidents and international diplomacy; surely they would appreciate some lighter fare. Yet human-interest stories offered something more than leavening for the rest of the news. They gave readers chances to rekindle a sense of empathy and to revive their faith in their neighbors.

Human-interest stories provided a respite from the high stakes and dire endings of most news articles by describing little urban moments that carried no real consequence for the subjects or the reader and where nothing at all went wrong. "A white cat peeped out of a footman's boot in the show window at 1201 Broadway on Saturday afternoon, and, after taking a leisurely survey of the store, turned her head around sedately toward the street," relayed the 1885 *Sun*. "A dozen people had already gathered to see what she was going to do."[98] Another reporter chronicled a man's spontaneous twenty-block race with a streetcar; the only point was to let readers share a moment of delightful and entertaining urban surprise.[99] In contrast to so many other news reports, human-interest stories usually turned out fine. "Hetta Holst is 5 years old and lives at 130 Hudson street, Hoboken," began an 1897 story. "She played in the street yesterday afternoon and had an unusually good time, for she found a lot of other girls and boys and wandered away with them."[100] The story described her mother's panic and all the measures she took to find her daughter—but ended with Hetta wandering right back home at the end of the day.

Such articles often pointed out the everyday generous acts of New Yorkers, providing a counterpoint to the indifference and cruelty that New Yorkers read about, witnessed, and perhaps participated in themselves. The *New York Herald Tribune* sent raggedly dressed reporters to churches in elite neighborhoods to test how well they practiced Christian charity; the articles then praised the congregations' welcoming and judicious responses.[101] Reporters noted local butchers who gave Christmas turkeys to poor families in the neighborhood; they described citizens who found and returned valuable jewelry.[102] They profiled model citizens, such as the socialite who nursed cancer victims or the volunteer emergency worker. "For twenty years he has assisted in rescues and risked his life time and again," explained the *World*. "Yes, Adolph Hofstatter has worked for the joy of working—doing some good to his fellow beings—and asking no other reward."[103]

Human-interest stories created a counternarrative to the one most visible on the front pages, a story of a city where sensitivity and kindness had not, in fact, been stamped out. A *New York Times* feature reassured readers that as violence played out in the headlines, a quieter and more generous story unfolded each day in newspaper offices:

Maybe you gentlemen will notice at times hard-luck stories in the papers—such as a woman left with a family by a man who has bolted or has been, perhaps, killed at his job by an iron girder dropping on his head. . . . Well, go into any newspaper office and ask if this isn't true—next day along comes a bunch of envelopes containing dollar bills with merely a note, unsigned, or at the most initialed which reads something like this: "Please send to the poor woman and family you mention in this morning's issue," or "-re enclosed clipping." . . . It would surprise you the amount of anonymous generosity there is in that town.[104]

Editors may have taken up human-interest reporting to revive the humanity of jaded reporters, too. "No ordinary reporter can work a police court or hospital run day after day for any length of time without losing his sensibilities and becoming hardened to the sterner facts in human life," explained journalist Grant Milnor Hyde. "Gradually his stories lose all sympathy and kindliness and he writes of suffering men as of so many wooden ten-pins."[105] According to Hyde, the task of seeking out funny and touching moments of city life rescued reporters from total cynicism and detachment. Human-interest articles did not seek to actively improve the city, as charity articles did, but they put city dwellers—both readers and reporters—on the watch for moments of grace.

Tragic news and human-interest stories, when combined, conveyed a curious mix of detachment and empathy. Yet that balance characterized the urban reforms of the Progressive era, and indeed, these strains of newspaper material schooled readers in the motivations and methods of Progressive politics and urban action. Disastrous and overwhelming news trained readers to think about urban problems. Human-interest stories reminded readers why those problems were worth solving.

MIDDLE-CLASS COSMOPOLITANS

Just as news writers traveled out to all corners of the physical city and into various specialized realms, they also crossed social divides. Reporters described the lives of the very poor and the very rich and narrated tours of New York's many ethnic enclaves. These feature articles modeled an urban cosmopolitanism, by which reporters—and, by extension, readers—felt at ease in many different social worlds.[106] To some degree, readers could carry that cosmopolitan attitude into their daily lives, perhaps growing more curious about their neighbors and more adventurous in their travels. Yet ultimately, readers still lived in a fragmented, stratified city. What newspapers offered was a vicarious experience, most often narrated from a white, native-born, middle-class perspective. And while articles seemed to tell readers that they could temporarily venture across social divides, they also emphasized a more permanent social hierarchy. Newspapers' attitudes toward class, race, and ethnicity, then, were never transgressive. Yet they could be *progressive*. Newspapers did celebrate the city's class and ethnic diversity to an unprecedented degree, and they supplied a surprisingly inclusive vision of the urban public.

Newspapers' features on New York's theater, business, and sports worlds conveyed a delight in metropolitan living, with its density of specialized spheres, its abundance of expertise. Features on immigrant institutions conveyed a delight in *cosmopolitan* living, in which residents took pleasure in the global offerings of their city. Many articles framed travels to immigrant quarters as actual journeys across the globe. "The place will prove itself a veritable treasure-house to him who cares to study foreign life in some of the aspects in which it is offered to us in New York," wrote a *New York Sun* reporter who had visited a local café full of Parisians. "They lean on their elbows over the French illustrated papers as they sip the green mixture and puff lazily at cigarettes which they manufacture themselves."[107] Years later, a *Sun* reporter making the rounds through local ethnic restaurants described the meals as "quite like making little journeys into foreign lands, with none of the expense or inconvenience of travel." Standing before an Indian eatery, she wrote, "We hesitated at the bottom of the stairs and then clambered up into Ceylon."[108]

On the one hand, reporters like this took real interest in the cultures that immigrants had brought to New York City and their detailed reporting allowed readers to take an interest, too. A 1904 article on an East Side Viennese cabaret described and illustrated the dining room, the waiters, the audience, and the actors.[109] Writers taught readers immigrant vocabulary; one reporter quoted a Williamsburg woman calling another a "mafena"—"'unfortunate one' in Yiddish," he explained.[110] Another reporter sprinkled Italian words and melodrama though his article the way that residents of that neighborhood might do themselves: "Oh, sad the day, oh, evil hour, when the stars in their courses exerted their most malefic influence and impelled Herrmann Rushmeyer into strife with Francisco and Domenico Messina, barbieri, illustrissimi, whose tonsorial parlor adorns No. 1648 Lexington avenue."[111] By taking care to familiarize readers with ethnic and immigrant cultures, reporters implied that these cultures were worth learning about.

On the other hand, reporters often treated other cultures as consumable goods, there for more privileged visitors to sample and enjoy. Reporters talked about immigrant spaces as discoveries, to be savored and kept somewhat secret. "Thus far only a handful of Americans have discovered it," said the reporter in an article on the Viennese cabaret, "and they are inclined to guard it jealously from invasion by the rabble, lest it lose its Old World flavor and acquire a Manhattanese tang."[112] And travelogue articles tended to write from the stance of an outsider who experienced immigrant cultures as entirely new and foreign phenomena. The *Sun* reporter sampling ethnic cuisines, for example, described "strange, insidious dishes."[113] The majority of readers were bound to be outsiders to any particular New York group or New York place. For this reason even reporters at the *New York World*, which sold well among immigrant readers, wrote about immigrant groups as if looking in the from the outside. Yet this perspective passed subtle judgments on both reader and subject. It positioned the imagined reader as culturally neutral and the subjects as culturally exotic.[114] It seemed that the foreign-born were always written *about*, not *for*. These articles also ignored or erased the violence and hardships that brought immigrants to New York City. Reporters were interested in foreigners not as refugees, or as economic migrants, or as subjects of a budding U.S. empire but simply as colorful characters.

New York newspapers paid far less attention to the city's African American neighborhoods than its immigrant ones. One of the only features on New York City African American life ever to appear in a mainstream newspaper was Timothy Thomas Fortune's column "The Afro American," which ran in the *New York Sun* from 1895 through 1898.[115] Fortune, himself the editor of the black weekly the *New York Age*, reported on the achievements of African Americans across the nation: lawyers, veterans, athletes, and politicians. He wove in notes on the travels and the deaths of prominent black Americans. He commented on the social and political status of African Americans, providing statistics on Southern lynchings, for example, or on black colleges. We can imagine why the *Sun*'s editors may have decided to run the column. Many black New Yorkers read mainstream daily papers, instead of or in addition to black weeklies.[116] A column devoted to African American interests and communities could potentially persuade them to buy the *Sun* rather than the *World* or the *Herald*. The column might also draw white readers who wanted to know more about happenings among African Americans. Yet the column was short-lived. We do not know whether it was the *Sun* or T. Thomas Fortune who ended its run. Perhaps the column failed to mesh with the very attitudes—curious, dilettantish— that appeared in other features about the city's minority groups. There were no colorful characters in this column, no accented English, no voyeuristic peeks into hidden spaces. For most white, middle-class New Yorkers, African American culture did not hold so much exotic appeal, at least until the era of jazz. And the column's mildly political, community-building approach meant that it did not function as pure entertainment.

As flawed as they were, news articles on New York's minority ethnic (and, to a lesser extent, racial) communities did feed a broader cultural shift toward tolerance and cultural pluralism in the early twentieth century. By keeping immigrant life in the public eye, news articles may have encouraged readers to consider to what degree immigrants would and could assimilate. Their celebrations of New York's sheer variety of ethnicities, religions, and languages helped to initiate broader debates about widening the circle of cultural inclusion and tolerance in the city and the nation. It was this intellectual climate in which writers such as Horace Kallen and Randolph Bourne proposed radically new definitions of what it meant to be an American—definitions that made room for immigrants to keep their ethnic traditions.[117]

By the late 1910s and 1920s, news reports still assumed that readers did not know about all the traditions of New York's ethnic groups, but they were less likely to depict those traditions as strange or surprising. Many immigrant communities had been established for long enough by the 1920s that perhaps they did not seem so exotic or surprising to reporters or readers; meanwhile, immigration quotas enacted in 1924 limited the influx of new arrivals. So the more neutral news tone may have reflected reporters' growing identification with (and lack of anxiety about) their immigrant subjects. An index of local events on the back page of the 1920 *Daily News* straightforwardly announced the beginning of the Jewish holiday Sukkot and a Brooklyn exhibition of Gaelic dances.[118] Similarly, when papers reprinted excerpts from the weekend's Episcopalian, Catholic, Methodist, and Jewish services, the excerpts passed no judgments and assumed no particular viewpoint.[119] Articles increasingly stressed understanding, rather than simply enjoying, other cultures. A 1920 *New York Times* reporter explained that fewer Chinatown residents wore a queue these days because the fall of the Manchu dynasty meant that the hairstyle was no longer mandatory for men in China.[120] A 1925 article on Brooklyn's Lithuanian population described the group's language, religion, political parties, and typical occupations. It explained the Lithuanian habit of wearing amber beads as a reminder of home. It even discussed the difficulties of the immigration experience, which would have been a rare topic in an earlier era. "Yes, I have been a citizen 10 years," stated one of the article's subjects, "but I always feel I am a foreigner, in the subways, on the streets, even at home."[121]

Articles on New York City's wealthiest residents, even more so than those on immigrants, were mainstays of the feature news. For the relatively few readers who belonged to the city's elite, these articles functioned as regular news and simply relayed what their acquaintances had done lately. For working-class or middle-class readers, articles on the rich welcomed them (in print) into circles where they would never be welcome in person.[122] New York newspapers followed the doings of the Rockefellers and the Vanderbilts so closely—running multipage features on their weddings, their hobbies, and their business affairs—that any New Yorker could gossip about those families the way they gossiped about their neighbors. The papers ran profiles of business tycoons that made readers feel as though they had chatted with and observed New York's richest men themselves. "If he is sitting in an arm chair he likes to rest his elbows on the arms," relayed a *New York World* profile of Jay Gould. "Sometimes he leans forward and sometimes back, and he generally throws one leg over the other."[123] In newspapers' society pages, readers could see who had sailed for Europe and which families were hosting the season's most extravagant balls. By the turn of the century, society pages printed glamorous full-length photographs of the week's debutantes and brides; in the 1910s they ran pages full of portraits of the wealthiest New Yorkers' children.

Many articles about the world of the rich let readers vicariously enjoy its pleasures. Detailed descriptions invited readers to ogle the parties, clothing, and houses of the wealthy. When newspaper photographers were allowed into the drawing rooms of the elite, they brought back images of interiors dripping with gilt ornament, hung with tapestries, and upholstered in silk.[124] The society pages' wedding announcements described the dresses, table decorations, and bouquets at fashionable young couples' celebrations. Articles reprinted indulgent menus from gatherings at Delmonico's or Sherry's.[125] By the 1920s, even real estate advertisements gave readers glimpses into the domestic spaces of the well-to-do, showing the floor plans, lobbies, and views that residents of luxury apartment buildings would enjoy. News coverage served as something of a print corrective to the city's very real social barriers. As one downtrodden character in *Manhattan Transfer* says about the paper's rotogravures of New York's glitterati: "It passes the time to look at them, I like to keep up with what's going on in New York a little bit. . . . A cat may look at a king you know, a cat may look at a king."[126]

Occasionally, news articles on the wealthy conveyed disbelief or distaste for their overindulgent ways—reinforcing papers' implicit middle-class perspective. The land it took to build the new Pell mansion on Seventy-Fourth Street, noted one writer, could fit six ordinary mansions, or ten tenement buildings: "That is to say, 928 people could live, as some New York people do live, in the space which he, his wife and the combined collections of porcelains and china will occupy."[127] A *New York World* two-page spread picturing every last Astor real estate holding in New York offered a visual representation of that family's disproportionate wealth and power.[128] A 1906 article on a society woman printed a table of her estimated yearly expenses, including her automobiles, furs, jewels, balls, stables, losses at bridge, and restaurant meals—and milked the details for shock value. "It was a startling revelation to the public," the article stated, "that a woman with no other charges upon her than her personal expenses could not live on an income greater than the salary paid to the President of the United States."[129] While articles on the city's elite might convey criticism, they rarely expressed outright anger or condemnation. It was against newspapers' interests to demonize the rich, for many of these papers' stockholders, advertisers, and editors were themselves members of the city's upper crust. Moreover, middle-class journalists and their audiences were mostly uninterested in radical critiques of a capitalist system that benefited them as well.

Meanwhile, newspapers did not shunt all of their reporting on New York City's poor into charity articles; they ran a variety of features that made slums intelligible for readers afraid or unwilling to visit in person. Writers made "beats" out of the city's pockets of deepest poverty—the Lower East Side, the Tenderloin, and Hell's Kitchen—and depicted them as foreign and forbidding places.[130] "Low openings in the street houses, no larger than a stable door, give entrance to the alley," explained a *World* reporter visiting the Lower East Side's "Murderer's Alley." "The entrances are not more than ten feet wide, paved with bits of stone covered with layers of filth."[131] The newspaper printed a map to show readers exactly where the alley lay and included sketches of the alley's fire escapes, its garbage, and its ragtag inhabitants.

Feature articles offered readers lessons in the culture of the tenements by detailing poor New Yorkers' expressions, accents, and pastimes, while again insulating readers from the risks and discomforts of personal interactions across classes. Reporters relayed conversations with street children or interviewed hobos for their life stories (fig. 3.7). The Sunday comic *Hogan's Alley* took readers into a fictional tenement neighborhood where the Yellow Kid and his band of friends staged sports matches, rallies, and fights (plate 6). On weekdays, the Kid appeared in a small column, *A Leaflet from the Yellow Kid's Diary*, in which he seemed to take the reader into his confidence as he described the daily happenings of his life. The comic strip offered an imagined friendship between the reader and the Kid—a friendship that would have been difficult to cultivate in person in the stratified, mistrustful, and splintered city.

Feature articles introduced readers to one last faction of their community—the criminal underworld. Articles on crime may have helped the city feel less like a mysterious menace, simply by bringing its darkest corners to light. Features clarified gambling terminology, explained how New York's mafia chose assassins, and schooled readers in the distinction between a "simp," a "broad," and a "moll" (different kinds of female accomplice).[132] Images took readers into spaces that criminals inhabited, from the basements where crimes were plotted to police detectives' investigation rooms

3.7 A *New York Times* reporter talked to the unemployed men who spent their days on park benches and told readers about the life paths that had brought the men there. Portraits carefully rendered the "park benchers" as individuals and let city dwellers do one of the things they had likely trained themselves never to do—stare at strangers, especially strangers who might want something from them. *New York Times*, 13 November 1904, magazine section, 7.

to the exercise grounds at Blackwell's Island.[133] Both the *New York Journal* and the tabloid *New York Daily News* regularly printed photographs of tenement crime scenes and sketched in the culprits or victims as they would have appeared.[134] Excerpts of dialogue let readers learn the vocabularies and accents of the city's toughs and addicts while keeping a safe distance. In 1915, gangsters described their purchase of counterfeit heroin: "We done it. We was crazy an' we done it. It was little brown pills. That's all they was— just little brown pills you crumble one up between your fingers and let it melt on the tip of your tongue. You gets effects immediate. It was just like the guinea said—it was better than the old stuff."[135] While editors supplied their readers with illicit-seeming information on the underworld, they simultaneously communicated a law-abiding moral code. Reporters often adopted the perspectives of law enforcers, from police cracking down on railroad crimes to detectives ferreting out hotel grafters, and sent the message that offenders would eventually be found out and punished.[136]

New York newspaper material depicted many kinds of residents as valid members of the urban public and even hinted that cosmopolitan knowledge might belong to more than just the middle and upper classes—but made it quite clear that New Yorkers could not move fluidly or permanently into other social strata. Features quoted all kinds of New Yorkers commenting on their very different neighbors. A *New York American and Journal* piece quoted a saloonkeeper's observations of the Astor family, which had visited his saloon on a "slumming" tour.[137] Richard Outcault depicted the children of *Hogan's Alley* staging mock high-society events such as operas, golf tournaments, literary societies, and dog shows. Yet such features ultimately underscored the city's social divides by showing that passing knowledge and brief contact could never erase social distinctions. The *American and Journal* printed the saloonkeeper's reaction to the Astors in dialect, emphasizing his lowly place in the city's social hierarchy. The *New York Times* quoted a museum guard who professed to see no value in the art and culture that middle- and upper-class New Yorkers held dear.[138] When the Yellow Kid went to a classical music recital, he left halfway through:

> I says come on Kitty, dis show ain't no good no how, der pyanner ain't in it. Well, I wasn't goin' ter see Kitty left on de music business, so we jist took er cable car and went downtown an' took in er show on der Bowery, where we heard singin' wot was singin'.[139]

Reporters only made entertaining features out of cross-class encounters that remained short and sweet. An 1897 *World* illustration showing Chinese immigrants visiting the Natural History Museum treated their presence as a curiosity since readers might expect to find Chinese people only in Chinatown. Because the Chinese guests were there as temporary tourists, the illustrator made light of it.[140] When New Yorkers crossed social divides in more permanent ways—for example, when they formed romantic relationships across racial, class, and ethnic lines—newspapers treated them not as admirable cosmopolitans but as scandalous and dangerous examples.[141]

The eventual disappearance of the Yellow Kid may point to New Yorkers' discomfort with those who blurred social boundaries. Artist Richard Outcault sent the Kid on an illustrated world tour in 1897. He met Europe's kings and queens, toured the Louvre, and visited Saint Mark's cathedral in Venice. The Kid certainly never blended in with his refined surroundings, but as he mixed with and thumbed his nose at the global elite, he may have made William Randolph Hearst, the *New York Journal*'s editor, a bit uncomfortable. The Yellow Kid disappeared from newspaper pages in 1898.[142] Outcault continued to devise adventures for a mischievous kid character, but his name was now Buster Brown, and he was a middle-class boy who got into scrapes and was then punished by his mother. The escapades always finished with Buster reciting a semi-apologetic, often misguided lesson. While Buster was just as much of a troublemaker as the Yellow Kid, he stayed comfortably within his middle-class world. He debuted in the *Journal* in 1902 and ran as a syndicated strip through the 1920s.

When newspaper articles assumed the perspective of the middle class looking out on the rest of the city, they suggested that the city drew its character from all of these other groups rather than from the middle class itself. It was the poor and working class whose accents gave the city its distinctive sound. It was the immigrant neighborhoods that gave the city its endless variety. It was the rich, in their carriages and furs, who made it glamorous. Articles encouraged readers to sample what all of these groups had to offer—but also to limit their interactions to brief journeys or vicarious newspaper visits. When feature news encouraged readers to pay close attention to the people around them, it did two things at once. It fostered curiosity across class and cultural lines, transitioning New York toward a slightly more open model of community and citizenship. Yet it also positioned middle-class observers as the most legitimate urban citizens. According to newspapers, it was the middle class that was best equipped to enjoy, to understand, and even potentially to change everyone else.

AN URBAN BRAND

In the 1910s and 1920s, New York papers began to self-consciously craft an identity for the city, most often in their "metropolitan" sections. While newspapers sometimes used "metropolitan" as a label for the region around and including the city, in these sections the word served as a marker of urban character. The *New York World* debuted its metropolitan section just after the turn of the century.[143] By the 1920s, nearly all of the city's mainstream dailies ran equivalent sections. Metropolitan sections and other feature stories fashioned a city identity in part by depicting an urbane and freewheeling culture taking shape in the city. Reporters, columnists, illustrators, and cartoonists of this era mixed with broader circles of actors, musicians, and producers. These New Yorkers perfected a new kind of glib sophistication; they then wrote about it in newspapers as well as in two new magazines, *Vanity Fair* and the *New Yorker*.[144] Writers displayed more detached and cynical attitudes than they had in previous decades. Their articles signaled a transition away from the sincere and moralizing Progressive culture of urban reform and toward the more private, hedonistic, and skeptical urban life of the 1920s.[145]

New York City newspapers also created an identity for the city by attempting to find the common threads that made life there distinctive.[146] In this, newspapers worked alongside other organizations that packaged and branded the city for others. Tourist agencies and business bureaus distilled and defined New York's distinctive qualities in order to attract visitors and investors.[147] Artists and filmmakers both developed a visual shorthand for New York that viewers across the nation and the world would understand.[148] Metropolitan sections communicated their urban "brand" most elegantly in their illustrated headings, which showed iconic New York scenes of bustling streets and sweeping skyline views (figs. 3.8-3.10).

Newspapers seized on the idea that the uniqueness of New York City life lay in its contrasts. A 1930 advertisement for the *New York American*'s Sunday edition riffed: "Exciting city.... City tumbling all over itself ... yet commanding the world of affairs.... City of abject poverty ... yet piled high with unprecedented wealth.... City of warm hearts, lost in its coldness ... motherly city, holding a world of sufferers to her breast.... Compelling city, intriguing in every phase of the melee which is its paradoxical life."[149] Rather than presenting the contradictory nature of metropolitan life as troubling or unsettling, the ad rendered the contradictions as true manifestations of a New York spirit. In making peace with urban contrasts in much of their feature material and especially in their metropolitan sections, newspapers signaled (and furthered) a transition away from a turn-of-the-century civic culture of zealous reform. Newspaper reporters showed less outrage at urban injustices than they had at the turn of the century; many of their articles instead paired worldliness with political complacency.

Editors carefully constructed certain 1910s and 1920s features to make the city seem like a small town—and ran others that just as deliberately depicted it as a massive metropolis. Its small-town qualities, according to these features, made New York City a friendly, connected, and intelligible place, while its size made it truly great. The *New York Times* ran a column of urban vignettes called "Our Town and Its Folk." The *Tribune* called its version of a metropolitan section "In Our Town." The *Amsterdam News* printed city observations under the title "Listen, Folks Listen."[150] By insisting that New York was a "town," full of "folks," these columns depicted the urban public as friendly and humble. The *Journal*'s 1930 column of local news read more like a conversation between neighbors and chums than ever before:

Louis Adler, who'll build that 105 story shack in the money district, looks like
　　B. A. Rolfe.
Lowell Brentano, the book man, is looking for a job.
The William Kolmers have a boy, Mozeltoff![151]

3.8 The left side of the "City Life Section" heading shows a more genteel part of town, with a hotel marquee, a line of automobile taxis, and a leafy park. The right side shows a tenement district, complete with fire escapes, an elevated train, and more humble horse carts. The image is matter-of-fact, though, avoiding the "sunshine and shadow" extremes common in the reporting and images of earlier decades. *New York American*, 2 October 1910, 1M.

3.9 A busy shopping street, as seen at night in the rain. Most of those pictured are well-off shoppers, but there are a few other urban types sprinkled in—a policeman on the corner, and a newsboy. *New York World*, 30 March 1913, metropolitan section, first page, American Newspaper Repository, Rubenstein Library, Duke University.

3.10 The Manhattan skyline, as seen from Staten Island or perhaps the Statue of Liberty. *New York Tribune*, 24 August 1919, sec. 7, page 12.

Even as the city's population topped five million, society columns still told readers when prominent New Yorkers had returned from a vacation, as if the reader would drop by and welcome them home. Papers increasingly adopted the small-town practice of reporting the everyday achievements of residents. In the 1920s, New York papers sent reporters to high school sports games for the first time. In spring, they printed graduation rosters of local colleges—even though it took multiple pages to print several thousand students' names. The lists lent the city the feel of a smaller town, where every reader could spot their nephew or their neighbor's daughter in the local paper.

Many Progressive reformers had lived uncomfortably with the scale of modern metropolises and worked to make them function more like small towns and less like massive cities.[152] Moving into the 1920s, however, newspaper editors and writers seemed to see no conflict between New York's small-town and big-city qualities and seized on New York City's size as something to celebrate. Papers transformed anything New Yorkers did into impressive statistics, from the number of eggs they ate to the number of drivers registered in the city—each time implying that the sheer size of the city made the place remarkable, extraordinary.[153] A 1928 booklet put out by the *New York Sun*, *Facts about New York*, listed the number of telephone calls placed in the city in the last year, the value of products created by the city's textile industry, and the acreage of New York's different parks.[154] Articles reminded readers that their city's structures were some of the biggest and most impressive in the world. A 1925 article on the new Madison Square Garden deemed the building New York's equivalent of the Grand Canyon.[155]

Like the travelogue articles sprinkled through newspapers in the late nineteenth century, material in metropolitan sections turned urban vignettes into a genre of entertainment. (See, e.g., fig. 3.11.) Columns with titles like "Mirror of City Life" or "Bits of Life in the Metropolis" offered quiet glimpses of single moments, such as two women carrying a chair down a nighttime alley or a grasshopper crossing the street in Times Square.[156] When readers wrote letters of appreciation for these columns, they recognized small-scale urban observation as a legitimate journalistic art. "These sketches seem to show a keen sense of observation and a vivid manner of noting the impressions," wrote one reader of the *Tribune*'s "In Our Town" section. "I thought I knew every nook and angle of this village," wrote another, "but it seems your staff are ferreting out new and interesting bits every week."[157] Metropolitan features could turn the city into an aesthetic experience, which required training to fully appreciate.

New York was a place, according to newspaper material, that could make or break anyone who lived there. As papers (along with fiction, film, and other forms of media) integrated this make-or-break quality into the city's identity, they actually bred a slow acceptance of—rather than outrage at—New York's extremes of rags and riches. Cities' potential to launch or destroy the lives of young hopefuls had been a cause of concern, even panic, in the mid- and late nineteenth century. Novels told cautionary tales of young men undone by drink and gambling, or aspiring actresses pulled into prosti-

3.11 Cartoonist Tony Sarg let readers survey all of the human dramas unfolding on a single subway platform: lost hats, lost children, collisions, crushed packages, and many, many newspapers. This image did not provide a statistical sampling of things that could be changed, as had the 1909 *New York World* illustration "The Busiest Hour on Earth." Instead, its detailed snapshot of a single city moment meant only to entertain. Tony Sarg, "The daily 5 o'clock race and riot at Brooklyn Bridge, the very vortex of New York's melting pot." *New York Tribune*, 19 October 1919, graphic section, 2.

tution.[158] Newspaper reporters seemed to confirm what many turn-of-the-century Americans had been taught to fear: that cities had the power to draw ordinary people into bad situations. Articles described young girls taken on as thieves' apprentices, men who were sucked into organized crime rings, and children who became heroin addicts after first encountering the drug on playgrounds.[159] Some obituaries profiled New Yorkers' downward spirals: "Joseph Langan, formerly a prominent politician and well-to-do business man in Brooklyn, counting as his friends the late Hugh McLaughlin and the late Judge John Courtney, shot himself in the head while confined in a cell in the De Kalb avenue police station yesterday."[160] Yet the papers also told stories of New Yorkers' breakout successes and their paths to fame. One article profiled a waiter who had been "discovered" working in a hotel and then sent to train for an opera career; another told of a man who moved from the New Mexico desert to become a football star at Columbia University.[161] Papers recounted immigrant success stories, from that of Emanuel Solari, Swiss immigrant and founder of a posh New York restaurant, to John Jacob Astor, German immigrant and real estate mogul.[162] Some obituaries repeated the narrative of upward mobility; many told readers how the recently departed had founded prosperous companies or won powerful political positions. The high stakes that seemed to hover over individual decisions and pursuits could lend a particular drama—a New York drama—to the most everyday of actions and the most humdrum of lives. Years of reading about New Yorkers' successes and failures could teach readers to view these extremes as simple facts of city life.

Metropolitan reporters of the 1910s and 1920s had become so practiced in the art of urban observation that they began to comment not just on colorful "others" but even on the group that they themselves belonged to—the New York middle class. Perhaps by the 1920s, a decade of relative urban prosperity, many New Yorkers felt secure enough in their middle-class status to laugh at it a bit. The *Times* ran an anthropological profile of New York's tribe of "white collars":

> The white collared people get little publicity. They get married occasionally and, if they live in Brooklyn, the local papers mention it. Often they are among those present at euchres and the affairs of political clubs. They report for work at 9, most of them, and quit at 5, with an hour for lunch. They spend an average of 30 cents for lunch, and often must walk four blocks for it. Sometimes the white collars lose their situations, and then they wait in outside offices and meet new baldheads, who ask more questions than a district attorney.[163]

According to such articles, a New Yorker's extensive social knowledge made him not only familiar with a wide range of New York types but self-aware and sarcastic enough to identify and make fun of his own type as well. The 1921 *World*, similarly, mocked urban professionals and their total lack of neighborliness. "New York's chiefest charm is that you don't know your neighbors. That's why I moved to New York from out among the Buckwheats," explained one writer. "I glory in my splendid isolation. . . . It's the New York idea."[164] By poking fun at the white, middle-class New Yorkers who were most likely to be reading these daily papers, metropolitan sections cultivated a reading population that could discern and lampoon nearly anything—but that was less interested in earnest engagement and efforts toward change.

Newspaper material crafted an increasingly understated and assured sense of New York City's superiority. Papers' images of soaring skyscrapers implicitly positioned the city as a modern metropolis. So did celebrations of the city's subways and its electric grid. Articles and advertisements occasionally described New Yorkers as ahead of their peers in the world of fashion and culture. "New York tailors, as usual, have slipped a season ahead of the rest of the country," said an ad for a city tailor. "Weber and Heilbroner have slipped ahead with them."[165] In 1930, the *New York American* characterized its audience as "thousands of modern-minded New Yorkers," city residents with "a zest for New York and its glamorous life."[166] New York newspapers never clamored, though, for the title of capital of the modern world. To harp too much on New York's unparalleled wealth or sleek modernity would perhaps indicate an insecurity that New Yorkers did not feel. As early as the turn of the century, New York papers kept their boasting toned down: "New-York goes about its business and knows that it is New-York, and that is enough," explained the *Tribune*. "Let the little ones crow or yelp or snarl among themselves. What is all that to a city which knows itself great?"[167] New York, the biggest city in what was becoming the most powerful nation in the world, did seem to take its rising status in stride. Yet as this self-satisfied strain appeared more frequently in newspapers, it may have encouraged readers to spend more time enjoying their marvelous city and less time thinking about how to reform or improve it.

*   *   *

New York City's journalists lived in the biggest, most diverse city in America; they seemed to try especially hard to conjure civic identity and pride in their articles and to encourage urban stewardship. Yet newspapers in dozens of other cities also told readers how to care for, cope with, and enjoy their growing cities, using tactics and trends we have seen in New York. Because most other cities were not quite as secure in their status as New York, their visions of the urban public could be less capacious.

Civic debates that surfaced in newspapers outside New York both rested on and helped to build readers' sense of "their" city. A number of papers created official columns for this civic commentary, including "Special Queries" in the 1910s *Philadelphia Bulletin*, "Thoughts of Our Readers" in the 1910s *Milwaukee Journal*, and "Friend of the People" in the 1920s *Chicago Tribune*. Muckraking articles more explicitly set the expectation that city people would care about and take responsibility for their neighbors. In 1880s' Chicago, Nell Nelson of the *Times* exposed dangerous conditions for women workers.[168] In Kansas City, the *Star* exposed an attempt to monopolize the streetcar system and successfully campaigned for public parks and free baths.[169] There remained many editors, though, who believed muckraking articles would only embarrass their cities. A reader praised the *Charleston News and Courier*'s bold opinions on national politics but wondered why it could not be similarly bold in its local reporting: "It is never looking for sensations, never sticking its nose into the nether places to find out what is wrong. For this reason Charleston is poorly informed as to itself." The city's papers, this reader believed, "do not educate their own people in political progressiveness."[170]

Like *New York Tribune* articles for the Fresh Air Fund, charity articles around the country raised money, sold copies, and depicted a print community that readers could join. A 1921 *Philadelphia North American* article that publicized its aid efforts for disabled children described the fundraising "porch parties" held all over town and printed photographs of the children who would be helped by the funds.[171] The *Cleveland News* enlisted readers and teachers to nominate needy children for its Christmas drive and ran stories on exceptionally generous donors.[172] Newspapers in smaller cities often chose to raise money for good causes without calling attention to local problems. When the *Tacoma Ledger* and the *Tacoma News* raised money for a high school stadium or a YMCA building, they improved the city without admitting that there was anything wrong with it to begin with.[173] In all cities, charity drives let readers feel good about their newspapers and themselves. Yet as the reading public watched itself come together to improve the city, the poor remained outside of the conversation, welcome to express only gratitude.

New York City's newspapers guided their readers toward an entitled and empowered cosmopolitanism, allowing them to sample the ideas, cultures, and people that had migrated to their rich and powerful city. Newspapers in other cities did not always work in quite the same way, since those cities claimed a smaller share of the nation's rising wealth and power. Perhaps especially in the South and West, newspapers were a bit more likely to write certain populations out of the feature news or even to demonize them.[174] Yet most papers did adopt some form of "travelogue" writing and used it to introduce readers to populations and neighborhoods that they might not be familiar with. These articles, even if on a small scale, stoked curiosity about ethnic difference and framed diversity as a signature urban trait. They also enshrined the white, middle-class, native-born reader as the paragon spectator and citizen and relegated all other populations to peripheral roles.

News reporters in many cities crossed widening class divides in ways that readers could not; their reports made cities temporarily traversable and intelligible to readers. When Theodore Dreiser investigated the destitute Saint Louis household where a man had murdered his family, he gave readers a voyeuristic peek into the family's bedroom, closets, and kitchen cupboards.[175] Society reporters everywhere carried readers into upper-class worlds of lavish ballrooms and expensive fashion. "Mrs. Earling will wear a gown of white lace and Miss Isabel Earling will be gowned in cerise velvet," explained the *Milwaukee Journal* in an article on a Christmas dance. "In the ball room there will be Christmas trees behind which the orchestra will be stationed."[176] Yet papers in midsize cities tended not to milk poor neighborhoods for all their horror, or to express much envy or indignation in articles about the rich. Working within the smaller social circles and smaller economies of cities like Pittsburgh, Milwaukee, and Buffalo, editors had to be careful not to lose readers, advertisers, or friends with sensational reporting and populist rabble-rousing. Editors in midsize cities may also have been reluctant to call attention to the ugly inequalities around them. New York City editors did not have to worry that their exposés would keep people from visiting, moving to, or investing in New York. Editors elsewhere, less confident in their cities' national and global status, likely worried about just that.

In nearly every city, shouting headlines, gruesome details, and overwhelming quantities of bad news could numb both readers and reporters. "I have schooled myself to scan the titles and omit the perusal of scandals and crime as much as possible," explained a reader in Saint Louis. "I find that ignorance of these subjects adds to my peace of mind."[177] Readers searching for reassurance and stability might have paid special attention to the addresses in the news. Even in cities not so logically gridded and numbered as New York (and where it thus took more knowledge to be able to place an address on a map), the practice of printing addresses helped to locate the news in space, organizing what might otherwise have felt like chaos. Editors across the country also commissioned human-interest stories to balance out the cruelty and coldness of the daily news. The editors of the 1910 *Philadelphia Evening Bulletin*, so accustomed to chronicling robberies, happily ran the headline "Found $1,000 Pin. Liveryman Picked Up Piece of Jewelry Where He Lost It."[178] A reader thanked the *Baltimore Sun* for its human-interest material: "After glancing through the daily press, recounting the toll of the tragic and dramatic happenings, this page is a relief to the mind, and appears to the wandering reader as a recuperating re-treat from the turbulence of humanity."[179] Papers' bad news, in aggregate, offered a sort of training in disinterested analysis and Progressive problem solving, while good news salvaged a sense of cohesion and community.

While few papers outside of New York printed metropolitan sections in those decades, most ran features that defined and publicized their cities' distinctive traits. Many cities constructed local identity out of local his-tory—usually that of city founders and prominent families. The *Philadel-phia Public Ledger* created fictionalized columnists—"Anne Rittenhouse," who penned fashion columns, "Girard's Topics of the Town," and "Peggy Shippen's Diary"—out of touchstone figures from the city's past.[180] Unlike New York reporters, who rarely compared their city to others, writers else-where used contrasts and rivalries to distinguish their hometowns. "Let us be glad that we are Baltimoreans," wrote H. L. Mencken on the *Evening Sun*'s editorial page. "Just suppose an unkind fate made us Pittsburgh-ers."[181] Mencken's paper fostered civic identity and civic pride through self-congratulatory contests; it gave a yearly prize for the best garden in the city and a yearly medal for the most beautiful new building.[182]

This variety of metropolitan branding left a mixed legacy for urban community. It strengthened readers' bonds to their cities by pinpointing and celebrating cities' unique qualities. But articles that slickly packaged up their cities moved urban culture away from Progressivism's earnest en-gagement and quest to improve urban community and toward a culture of urban observation, enjoyment, and self-satisfaction. Newspapers' exten-sive local coverage and their increasingly savvy presentation of their home-towns gave rise to a new phenomenon, in which anyone could experience the city, or feel that they belonged to the city, just by reading a newspaper.

4: CONNECTING CITY, SUBURB, AND REGION

In 1909, writer James Edward Rogers pointed out an unusual pattern in American news. "Traveling across the continent from New York one passes through different 'zones,'" Rogers explained. In each zone, a traveler would encounter a different city's newspapers. "On the train out of New York he is offered the New York papers—the *Times*, the *Sun*, the *Herald*, and the like. On the next day he is flooded with the newspapers of Chicago, then of Salt Lake, then of Ogden, and later of San Francisco. Returning via San Francisco on the Santa Fe, he passes through the 'zones' of the Los Angeles, the Denver, and the New Orleans newspapers."[1] These cross-country trains passed through farm country, desert outposts, mountain towns, and dense forests. Yet no matter how far he might venture from a major American city, the passenger would still get his news from a city paper.

A dozen years later, sociologists Robert Park and Charles Newcomb described the same phenomenon. Park and Newcomb mapped the reach of cities' major morning dailies and found that information from each city traveled hundreds of miles (fig. 4.1). Their map showed dailies' territories spreading outward, often edging over state borders until they bumped up against the next big-city paper's domain. Los Angeles papers, for instance, reached to the eastern border of Arizona. Minneapolis papers traveled to eastern Montana. New Orleans papers circulated in the Florida panhandle, and Chicago papers covered portions of ten different states. A handful of America's cities dominated the national news market.

In the late nineteenth and early twentieth centuries, city newspaper publishers energetically pursued readers who lived outside of city limits. The middle-class and wealthy families who moved from cities out to planned suburbs seemed like natural audiences for city papers, since they often worked in the city or visited it frequently. Residents of towns beyond the metropolitan region were more difficult to reach, yet as newspapers' advertisers expressed a desire to speak to these people, publishers did their best to draw them in. Express trains, steamships, and even airplanes sped city

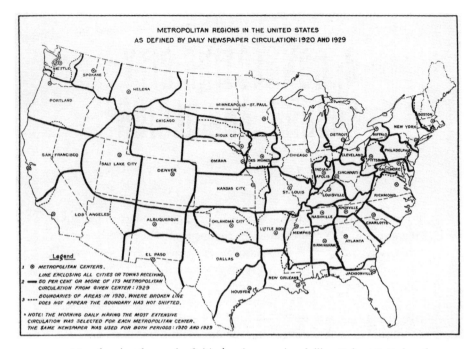

4.1 Map showing the reach of cities' major morning dailies. Robert E. Park and Charles Newcomb, "Newspaper Circulation and Metropolitan Regions," in *The Metropolitan Community*, ed. Roderick D. McKenzie (New York: McGraw-Hill Book Company, Inc., 1933), 107.

papers to readers living many miles away. Sunday papers, especially, traveled far and wide, with many metropolitan papers selling more copies outside of city boundaries than inside them.[2] Newspapers never completely saturated their broader regions, though—and this was on purpose. Papers' distribution networks simply passed over working-class suburban residents or poor farm families with little money to spend on the products that appeared in newspaper pages.

Newspapers did not just adapt to a suburbanizing trend but in fact actively created suburbs. Real estate sections grew middle- and upper-class suburbs through their advertisements for subdivisions and their mail-order house plans; they promoted the suburban way of life in features on home decor and gardening. By the 1910s and 1920s, newspapers had so integrated suburban news, images, and values that they had become truly metropolitan—not just city—media. In turn, they helped readers acclimate to the suburbs. The railroad timetables, department store ads, and help-wanted notices in papers made it possible for people to live lives that straddled city and suburb. Metropolitan papers further eased the transition to suburban life by depositing vicarious experiences of cities on suburban-ites' doorsteps.

Beyond the suburbs, city papers coordinated regional economies and drew far-flung readers into the city's cultural and economic orbit. Papers' commodity price listings and freight schedules gave farmers the logistical tools to sell their produce to city markets. Newspaper ads and features altered small-town and rural people's tastes and standards, turning them into consumers of urban products. Papers coordinated flows of not only products but people, too; they helped young men and women in small towns to imagine, and then establish, urban lives.

As their territories spread, urban papers kept readers looking to the city itself. Newspapers depicted the city as the indisputable heart of metropolitan and regional life, and the daily flow of information from downtown outward reinforced cities' centrality. Simultaneously, though, newspapers forged broader metropolitan and regional identities for their readers. Articles introduced city people, suburbanites, and country people to each other. They often outlined priorities and interests that all of these readers could share, building up regional identities. By stitching together city, suburb, and region, newspapers built an American economy, culture, and identity more tied to cities than ever before.

This chapter travels to Chicago, a city whose urban center, suburban periphery, and outlying regions all grew spectacularly through the late nineteenth and early twentieth centuries. The city's founders had envisioned it as a hub for the Midwest and even the whole western United States. They chose a site on the shore of Lake Michigan for its easy access to trade routes and to both wild and rural hinterlands. Developers hoped that products from the surrounding region—lumber from the forests to the north, livestock from the prairie, milk from nearby farms, grain from the entire Midwest—would help feed, build, and enrich the city. Chicago railroads could carry midwestern goods farther west, while boats could speed them east along the Erie Canal or south down the Mississippi. Chicago's relationship with its hinterland resembled that of many other U.S. cities. Upstate New York farmers sent their produce down the Hudson to be sold in New York City markets or shipped out through its ports. Ohio farmers sent their hogs to Cincinnati to be slaughtered, processed, and sent by rail to customers nationwide. Chicago's regional territory, though, stretched across a vast space, and its entrepreneurs dreamed on a grander scale than nearly anyplace else.[3]

Chicagoans strove for urban sophistication, and in many ways they achieved it. By the turn of the century, the city boasted the most modern architecture in the United States, an extensive transportation system, luxurious shopping districts, and landscaped parks. It had hosted the 1893 World's Columbian Exposition, the largest and most lauded fair the United States had ever seen. The city was incubating a new school of realist urban fiction and a new genre of human-interest reporting that reveled in the incongruities of urban life.[4] Yet because Chicago was so much younger than its eastern counterparts and because its economy relied so heavily on agricultural products and raw materials, Chicago's urban center bore many traces of its rural surroundings. At the downtown board of trade, brokers exchanged purchasing rights for hogs and corn. In central Loop department stores, visiting farmers gawked at the expensive goods. Some Chicagoans found their city's countrified ways embarrassing.[5] Many other Chicagoans knew, though, that their city's prosperity depended in large part on the farms and wilderness that surrounded it and embraced elements of midwestern rural culture as their own.

Almost as soon as settlers arrived in Chicago, real estate speculators began developing a suburban fringe, and the suburbs grew ever more popular as the city expanded. Chicago's population more than quintupled between 1870 and 1900, and hundreds of thousands of migrants and immigrants taking factory and service jobs crowded into the city.[6] Downtown, towering skyscrapers blocked out sunlight and high land values turned front yards and porches into unaffordable luxuries. The noise, dust, and massive scale of the city's industrial districts drove many families to seek out space and quiet in a suburban subdivision or an unincorporated, outlying district. Because Chicago's suburbs grew continuously in the late nineteenth and early twentieth centuries, the city offers examples of nearly every kind of suburb developed in those years.[7] The size and diversity of the suburban periphery also means that a large proportion of Chicagoans cycled through the suburbs at some point in their lives and experienced life not only in Chicago but also in "Chicagoland."

BUILDING THE SUBURBS, SELLING THE DREAM

Most Chicagoans' journeys to the suburbs started with a newspaper. Older methods of finding a place to live—from scouting the "for sale" or "for rent" signs in windows, to touring apartments with a local realtor, to moving into the same building as a relative—simply did not work for the suburban search. Instead, Chicagoans turned to newspapers' centralized listings, which provided space for suburban developers to speak to potential customers but also played more active roles in the process of suburbanization. Chicago dailies ran feature stories on new developments. They urged readers to browse the real estate listings, and they eventually created separate real estate sections. They commissioned countless articles on home life and countless more on the metropolitan real estate market, all of which spread suburban ideals and suburban norms.

Newspaper editors accommodated realtors in part to attract ad revenue. Editors also worked hand in hand with suburban developers because they stood to benefit from suburban growth. Every new neighborhood that sprouted up meant a broader base of potential reading customers. Finally, editors boosted suburbs and their real estate because many of them believed that suburbs offered a genuinely higher quality of life. The editors and publishers of many metropolitan newspapers lived in suburban estates themselves.[8] They were glad to partner with developers who made suburban greenery, quiet, and fresh air available to much of the city's middle class.

"Suburb," however, was a slippery concept in turn-of-the-century Chicago. The city annexed huge swaths of territory all through the period, eventually encompassing suburban, industrial, and rural areas.[9] Many middle- and upper-class districts that started as suburbs laid out by private developers, such as Hyde Park, Lake View, and Rogers Park, eventually became urban districts. These areas often retained much of their suburban character after annexation: they boasted landscaped parks and winding streets, the houses had large yards and front porches, and residents commuted to downtown for work.[10] These areas can be seen as suburban, even though Chicago came to count them as part of its municipal territory.

The suburbs also included less planned neighborhoods, where working-class residents built their own houses bit by bit, over years or even decades. These neighborhoods did not conform to the archetypal suburban image of uniform houses, neat lawns, and commuter train stations. Residents often used outhouses rather than bathrooms, raised chickens or goats, and saw the smokestacks of Chicago's outlying factories out their windows. Yet these areas—places like Melrose Park, Robbins, and Garfield Heights— were as close as many working-class families would come to the suburban dream.[11] Chicago newspapers played minimal roles in building these scrappier suburbs. Because profit margins were smaller in the business of selling cheap lots, realtors were less likely to mount major newspaper ad campaigns for such suburbs, and papers themselves probably did not clamor for that business. Circulation managers may have seen working-class suburbs as lost causes—their unpaved roads made newspaper delivery difficult, and residents were unlikely to purchase many of the goods advertised in newspaper pages. Newspapers therefore had little to do with the growth of working-class suburbs.

Newspapers had everything to do, in contrast, with the growth of home ownership as a goal and a reality for middle- and upper-class Chicagoans. Buying a home had been just one option, and not a particularly popular one, for nineteenth-century city dwellers. But in the late nineteenth century, newspaper material began making a compelling case for home ownership in the suburbs. Developers placed illustrated ads showing neat suburban tracts just waiting for customers to construct gracious homes. Classified real estate listings caught readers' attention with patterned text, bold type, and images. "Shall I buy a home?" asked an 1889 ad for a development. "Does this question haunt your waking hours? Is it disturbing your nightly rest? IT CERTAINLY SHOULD."[12] Newspapers kindled readers' interest in buying in part by pointing out the downsides of renting. "BURN YOUR RENT RECEIPTS for the last ten years; they never will buy you anything," shouted a 1913 ad in the *Record-Herald*. "Make your rent receipts represent payments on YOUR OWN HOME."[13] Advertisements also depicted rental apartments as inherently unstable places to live and commiserated with readers about the frequent moves required of renters. An 1897 *Chicago Tribune* cartoon depicted moving as akin to a game of musical chairs, in which Chicagoans went through hassles and minor traumas only to realize that their new flat was no better than their old one.[14] A full-page ad in the Sunday *Record-Herald* promised to solve renters' problems—housing instability and moving expense—in one fell swoop. "Your memory is full of the discomforts of moving day," it said. "Move just once more and then settle down to years of enjoyment in your own home."[15] Many readers, tired of neglectful landlords, noisy neighbors, and rent increases, took the bait.

Newspaper material further lobbied for suburbs by calling readers' attention to all of the amenities and conveniences that they lacked in the city. Advertisements for suburban developments depicted domestic conveniences such as wide lots, front yards, tree-lined streets, sewers, and gas heat.[16] The suburbs were shown as nature-filled alternatives to the industrial city—even though they required as much construction and maintenance as urban neighborhoods. A testimonial in an 1888 ad portrayed the Edgewater development as an idyllic haven: "There is no dust, dirt, noise, or anything unpleasant at Edgewater so far discovered. Our little children play outdoors without watching and without danger. We would think the place spoiled if the railroad ran between us and the lake, as it does on the South Side. No doctor has gone to any family in Edgewater for a single visit called by sickness. The lake bathing in summer is enjoyed by all. . . . It is cooler in summer and warmer in winter close to the lake."[17] Readers desperate to escape cramped and polluted industrial neighborhoods were primed for suburban developers' inflated promises. Live the way man was meant to live, urged the *Chicago Record-Herald*: "You Get Most out of Life in a Suburban Home" (fig. 4.2).[18]

Newspapers continued to sell the suburban idea by combating readers' fears of isolated suburban life. Every spring and summer weekend, papers ran announcements for free excursions, in which Chicagoans could hop on special trains or streetcars, tour the available properties at subdivisions, view model homes, and enjoy picnic lunches. These excursions used the promise of a pleasant Sunday afternoon to introduce city people to the plea-

You Get Most Out of Life in a Suburban Home

A suburban home is never more attractive than it is now—at no other time of the year does it seem so much like a necessity. If you have ever thought of buying suburban property now is the time to come to a decision, while your mind is naturally turned toward green lawns, garden plats and the big outdoors. Your memory is full of the discomforts of moving day. Why not respond to Spring's suggestion? Move just once more and then settle down to years of enjoyment in your own home.

Look in today's big Sunday Record-Herald. In its classified section you will find column after column of suburban property listed. There is sure to be something there that you will like. The responsible real estate dealers represented there will make it easy for you to purchase.

Real Estate Men

Now is the time to put before the people your suburban offerings. You have nature as an ally. The substantial merits of your choicest holdings—their conveniences and comforts—are backed by the irresistible call of Spring.

The Record-Herald goes into thousands upon thousands of families. Let it carry your message. It can carry it effectively into homes that can be reached through no other medium.

If you need assistance in the preparation of copy, The Record-Herald's Service Bureau will gladly help.

The Record-Herald

Telephone Franklin 44

4.2 The *Chicago Record-Herald*—not its advertisers—constructed this suburban fantasy, as it announced an upcoming real estate special issue. Beside the image of a commuter greeted by his family and dog, the text explains that, in springtime, "your mind is naturally turned toward green lawns, garden plats and the big outdoors." Sunday *Record-Herald*, 4 May 1913, sec. 2, 8.

sures of suburban life and to familiarize them with the commute. Advertisers took pains to describe the mechanics of commuting and to stress how easy and convenient travel would be. They explained that the train to the Loop took only eighteen minutes, that trains ran fifty times a day, and that the fare was a mere seven cents. Many ads printed maps that depicted their area, sometimes through sleight of hand, as close and connected to the city (fig. 4.3). In an 1888 ad for Auburn Park, rings radiated from downtown, and the text assured readers that they would have to travel through only two of these rings or "zones" to get to the Loop.[19] These ads attempted to bridge physical distances and smooth over logistical difficulties to convince readers that they could have the best of both worlds, that they could live in peace and quiet within an easy distance of cities' bustle.

In case Chicago newspapers had not convinced readers of the pleasures of suburban life, they also aggressively pushed suburban houses as wise financial investments. Speculators had hedged fortunes on Chicago's land through much of the nineteenth century, and it was largely speculators who built central Chicago. But newspapers invited average citizens to get in on the game. "This property will have a natural increase in value within the next year of from 25 to 50%," forecast an 1889 ad. "Can you afford to let so excellent a chance of making money pass you by?"[20] Ad copy sometimes played down several factors families might want to consider when choosing their homes—convenience, aesthetics, proximity to family or friends— and played up the potential for fast profit. "There's just one thing about this real estate business, young man," advised a classified ad. "That if you don't buy a lot pretty quick you'll get left."[21] By constantly talking about homes as good investments, newspapers gradually transformed suburban home buying from a means to acquire a permanent place to live into a means to get rich quick.

Newspaper material taught readers the value of one final suburban offering: neighborhood exclusivity. Advertisements promised "good homes and good neighbors" or "the best associations"—veiled references to suburbs' carefully selected, homogenous populations.[22] Ads pointed out nearby churches, letting readers know that there was a convenient congregation for them to join and indicating that the people settling there were good church-going folks. Newspapers described suburban schools in status-conscious terms. "The schools are excellent," noted one 1890 *Chicago Record* article on Hinsdale, "embracing all of the advantages of the public school system without that objectionable feature to be noticed in cities—a mixed attendance from every social grade."[23] The caliber of suburbs' residents could even raise property values, insisted newspaper ads. "A choice class of people are settling here," assured an 1889 classified ad, "and the property is increasing rapidly."[24]

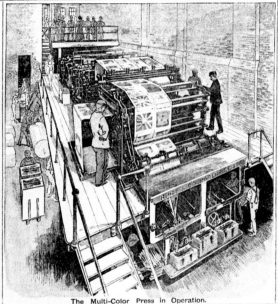

Plate 1 Here the *New York World* uses its color press to show off its color press. The text explains: "It is thirty feet long, eight feet wide and fifteen feet high, weighing about seventy tons and made up of some forty thousand separate parts, all of which move with the most perfect precision and harmony." Many newspapers opened their press and composition rooms to the public; here visitors stand on a viewing platform in the back of the room. *New York World*, 27 March 1898, back page of magazine section, American Newspaper Repository, Rubenstein Library, Duke University.

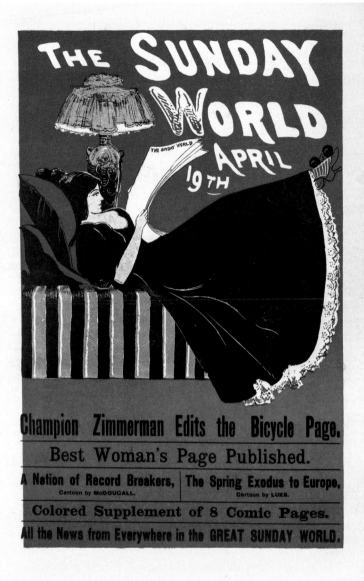

Plate 2 This 1896 poster is one of many that depicted the newspaper as a pleasant diversion and chic accessory for city women. The woman pictured here is not the kind that Americans might previously have associated with newspaper buying, such as a working-class woman looking for service jobs in the classifieds, a housewife consulting recipes, or a militant suffragette reading up on state politics. Instead, she is young, fashionable, and well-to-do. *New York Sunday World* poster, 19 April 1896, Art Posters Collection, New-York Historical Society.

Plate 3 *New York World* advertisement for the following Sunday's paper. The ad pictures a printing press transformed into a cannon, which fires off special features that explode in colorful bursts. The person operating the press is the type of reader that editors and advertisers most hoped to draw to their Sunday pages—a young woman. *New York World*, 27 March 1898, back page of magazine section, American Newspaper Repository, Rubenstein Library, Duke University.

Plate 4 *Tillie the Toiler*, which ran in the *Philadelphia North American*, chronicled the office adventures of a secretary in the 1920s. Reprinted with permission from King Features Syndicate.

Photo-Scenes of Real Life in New York City.

SUNDAY The World MAGAZINE

No. 5 in a Series on Remarkable Photo-graphs Reproduced in Four Colors.

THE MALL, CENTRAL PARK---A Sunday Afternoon Concert.

Plate 5 Photomontage of the Central Park Mall, by L. L. Roush. This was part of a series of photomontages of locations around the city that appeared in the exuber-ant, experimental first years of the *New York World*'s color supplement. *New York World*, 4 August 1901, color supplement, front page, American Newspaper Reposi-tory, Rubenstein Library, Duke University.

THE AMATEUR DIME MUSEUM IN HOGAN'S ALLEY.

Plate 6 The fun of "The Yellow Kid" lay in seeing the Kid and his friends imitate but also lampoon adult activities and in deciphering the comically misspelled and accented English, usually scrawled on signs or right onto the characters' clothes. Richard Outcault, "The Amateur Dime Museum in Hogan's Alley," *New York World*, 4 October 1896, San Francisco Academy of Comic Art Collection, Ohio State University Billy Ireland Cartoon Library and Museum.

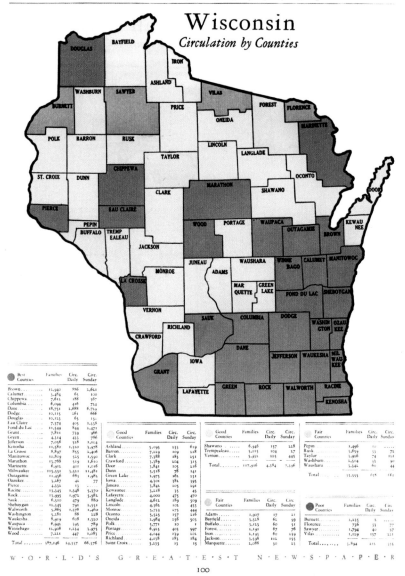

Wisconsin
Circulation by Counties

Best Counties	Families	Circ. Daily	Circ. Sunday
Brown	11,940	886	2,611
Calumet	3,484	65	100
Chippewa	7,611	188	367
Columbia	6,094	416	714
Dane	18,751	2,688	6,724
Dodge	10,115	261	666
Douglas	10,113	65	15.
Eau Claire	7,574	405	1,438
Fond du Lac	11,549	844	2,471
Grant	7,811	759	966
Green	4,114	433	786
Jefferson	7,056	528	1,104
Kenosha	11,580	1,520	3,978
La Crosse	8,897	855	2,406
Manitowoc	10,809	525	1,590
Marathon	13,788	519	1,610
Marinette	6,912	401	1,016
Milwaukee	115,551	3,522	11,481
Outagamie	11,436	683	1,982
Ozaukee	3,267	42	77
Pierce	4,312	13	..
Racine	13,545	1,548	5,370
Rock	13,995	1,972	5,982
Sauk	6,510	479	889
Sheboygan	12,345	791	2,551
Walworth	5,865	1,578	1,460
Washington	5,281	88	228
Waukesha	8,919	608	1,320
Waupaca	6,942	395	789
Winnebago	11,908	1,234	3,975
Wood	7,211	447	1,083
Total	387,146	24,337	66,376

Good Counties	Families	Circ. Daily	Circ. Sunday
Ashland	5,093	233	619
Barron	7,229	109	228
Clark	7,188	183	252
Crawford	3,389	104	315
Door	3,841	105	226
Dunn	5,518	78	141
Green Lake	2,975	162	232
Iowa	4,301	381	395
Juneau	3,841	205	291
Kewaunee	3,218	35	45
Lafayette	4,000	475	470
Langlade	4,612	289	509
Lincoln	4,361	102	433
Monroe	5,733	275	444
Oconto	5,525	157	216
Oneida	2,984	256	502
Polk	5,771	10	1
Portage	6,955	403	997
Price	4,044	139	202
Richland	4,038	183	184
Saint Croix	5,235	13	15

Good Counties	Families	Circ. Daily	Circ. Sunday
Shawano	6,346	157	228
Trempealeau	5,025	104	27
Vernon	5,351	225	445
Total	117,916	4,184	7,196

Fair Counties	Families	Circ. Daily	Circ. Sunday
Pepin	1,496	10	....
Rusk	2,659	33	72
Taylor	2,916	74	112
Washburn	2,504	33	90
Waushara	3,342	60	44
Total	12,555	615	661

Fair Counties	Families	Circ. Daily	Circ. Sunday
Adams	1,907	17	21
Bayfield	3,528	62	99
Buffalo	3,123	60	51
Forest	1,191	67	76
Iron	1,191	60	219
Jackson	1,598	112	155
Marquette	2,088	30	23

Poor Counties	Families	Circ. Daily	Circ. Sunday
Burnett	2,233	2	....
Florence	736	33	77
Sawyer	1,794	40	57
Vilas	1,129	137	111
Total	5,894	212	555

Plate 7 Map of Wisconsin counties, color-coded for wealth. The tables detail the subscription rates in each county. A few pages earlier, the *Book of Facts* explained that "ninety-six percent of the circulation of The Sunday *Tribune* is in the best counties. Three percent is in the good counties; 0.2% in the fair; and only 0.1% in the poor." Chicago Tribune, *Book of Facts, 1927: Data on Markets, Merchandising, Advertising, with Special Reference to the Chicago Territory and Chicago Newspaper Advertising* (Chicago: Chicago Tribune, 1927), quote from 95, images from 96, 99, 100, 97.

Plate 8 The *American Weekly* ran several series by illustrator Nell Brinkley. They all featured thin, large-eyed "Brinkley girls" with masses of curls, who showed off beautiful clothes while seeking adventure and romance. In the top right-hand corner is the title of the Hearst chain's Sunday magazine, "American Weekly," with a space below for the local paper to stamp its name. *Milwaukee Sentinel*, 15 November 1925. Reprinted with permission from Fantagraphics Books.

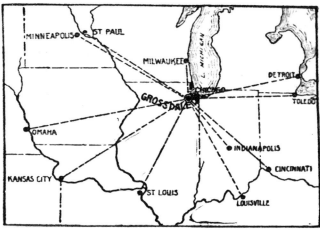
4.3 An advertisement for Grossdale pictures it at the center of the entire Midwest, and lists the distances to all of the region's major cities. The picture disguises the fact that residents could not actually travel in a straight line to any of these places, and if traveling by train, they would still have to pass through downtown Chicago. *Chicago Herald*, 16 July 1893, 23.

By the 1890s, many German families had lived in Chicago for a generation and had established themselves in a business or profession; many could pass muster in "exclusive" communities. So developers commonly placed ads in the city's German-language newspapers; readers of the 1891 *Illinois Staats-Zeitung*, for example, encountered ads for Rogers Park, Ravenswood, Irving Park, Northfield, Summerdale, and Avondale.[25] Fewer developers marketed to recently arrived, less-assimilated immigrants from southern and eastern Europe, who had less money to spend and may have been the very groups that wealthier Chicagoans were trying to leave behind.[26]

Newspaper text pointed out the benefits of homogenous, exclusive suburban communities for two reasons. On the one hand, developers and reporters believed that many urban residents would genuinely prefer to live among people much like themselves. In Chicago, as in New York, newspapers encouraged middle-class readers to visit immigrant neighborhoods as tourists, but few articles talked to readers about learning to live with immigrant neighbors. On the other hand, developers pushed a single-class model because they found it easier to lay out physically uniform neighborhoods. Most suburban developers divided their land into grids of equal-sized lots and connected each lot to the same utilities. Realtors charged all buyers the same markup for shared amenities such as schools, nearby train stations, and community parks. If developers constructed houses on suburban properties, rather than selling empty lots, they often built many variations on the same design to keep costs down.[27] Newspaper text then helped to convince Chicagoans that developers' decisions—made out of social preference and economic necessity—had actually produced the ideal living situation. Of course, advertisements sold an image and not reality. Middle- and upper-class suburbs actually housed members of multiple social classes, if only because families hired live-in domestics. Even so, suburbs dominated by one class of residents became the most common pattern in Chicago and in the United States, with help from newspapers.

Correspondingly, white realtors, developers, and homeowners drew increasingly firm boundaries around the neighborhoods where black Chicagoans could rent or buy.[28] African American readers likely knew that most suburban developments in mainstream dailies' pages—just like most of the shops and services taking out ads—would not welcome their business. Chicago's black weekly papers, though, marked out safe neighborhoods.

The *Chicago Defender*, the city's biggest African American weekly newspaper, pitched the exclusive middle- and upper-class suburban dream to its readers even though that dream might be hard to achieve. "All Are Happy and Prosperous—Most of Them Being Business Men—Place Is Like a Summer Resort," declared a 1913 feature on a South Side development, Lilydale. "Everyone Goes to Church."[29] The *Defender* emphasized suburbs' powers to uplift their residents. A 1925 serial story followed a city woman as she visited a young married couple in the fictional suburb of Ploverdale. The visitor marveled over the couple's tiled kitchen, their laundry chute, and the hot water that ran right from the tap. The story became a treatise on the transformative power of fine real estate:

> Clustered around a drive encircling an oval parkway were many beautiful homes of stucco and brick, enhanced by spacious lawns. In the center was a fountain which made a pretty picture against the smooth green oval surrounding it.
>
> Aunt Lottie Purkins was incredulous. "You ain't foolin' me, chile, so you mought as wall turn 'round an' drive down there by them railroad tracks. I know my kinda folks don't live here."
>
> "Well, auntie," laughed Isabel, whom she had come up to visit, "you forget that we are living in the 20th century. Some of our folks still live in the kind of shacks we passed there at the railroad, but there are others that are doing much better."[30]

The paper pointed out that Ploverdale selected its residents from among the well-to-do; "building restrictions prevented the erection of any but high-grade homes."[31]

An exclusive and prosperous suburban ideal appeared in *Defender* articles and fiction in spite of the few opportunities open to African American prospective buyers.[32] Those who insisted on suburban homes found just a handful of developments advertised in the *Defender*, mostly in industrial districts in South Chicago or Gary, Indiana.[33] More buyers purchased urban property—multifamily homes and apartment buildings in Chicago's black belt. These buildings offered buyers the stability of ownership and even the possibility of steady income; *Defender* ads played this up. "The road to independence is through ownership," declared an ad for a South Side real estate company. "It gives you credit and standing in the community. REAL ESTATE IS THE BASIS OF ALL WEALTH."[34] These buildings did not, however, provide any version of the leafy, leisurely suburban dream.

Newspapers played only a minor role in orchestrating both black and white working-class Chicagoans' moves to the suburbs. When developers did choose to advertise to working-class buyers, though, they made slightly different pitches. "1 block to river," stated a 1921 ad for a South Side development. "Good fishing: improved, ready for building. I.C.R.R. and electric car service; rich soil and enough to produce fruit and vegetables to cut down cost of living."[35] These developers sold homes not with images of manicured lawns but with a do-it-yourself ethos instead.

When they crafted separate real estate sections, Chicago's newspapers further accommodated suburban realtors. The size and frequency of these sections varied with the state of the market, but by the 1920s every Chicago daily ran a regular one.[36] Real estate sections played vital roles in developing Chicago's downtown, its urban neighborhoods, and its suburbs. Their listings helped many Chicagoans find rental apartments and buy businesses. Though they stimulated investment all over the city, and did not simply drain capital and residents from the center to the edges of the city, they put an enormous emphasis on the importance of homeownership. They provided the rationales as well as the logistical means for suburban growth.

Real estate sections fueled the market by conveying a relentless optimism about Chicago's potential for growth. A 1916 ad described Chicago's apparent destiny: "Yesterday, a prairie. Today—three million dollars' worth of homes, bungalows, cottages, apartments . . . Incidentally, lots have increased in value 20% to 150%."[37] The sections' articles spoke of huge demand for Chicago properties and of an inevitable rise in values. "Chicago Building Pace Called Dizzy," reported the *Daily News* in 1925. "City Growing Too Fast to Overbuild."[38] One development illustrated its ad not with images of homes but with bags of money and dollar signs.[39] Next to these euphoric statements ran more detailed listings that helped readers decide exactly where to invest. Lists of the previous day's transactions, with descriptions of the properties sold and the prices paid, could be useful to major investors deciding where to buy. But they also encouraged the average reader to think like an investor. Readers could try to predict which areas of the city were about to see the biggest growth or which styles and sizes of building would soon be in highest demand. Real estate sections' advertisements then acquainted readers with the people who could help finance their purchases: mortgage brokers who clamored for readers' attention and promised "easy terms."[40] "Lack of ready money need not stop you when you see your chance," explained one.[41] Eventually, ads appeared that invited readers to invest in bundles of other people's mortgages, predicting that the collective value of Chicago properties would increase and investors would receive hefty returns.

Even once Chicagoans had bought homes, real estate sections' material encouraged them to keep thinking about those homes as investments first and dwelling places second. The *Chicago Tribune*'s *Book of Homes*, a catalog of house plans, warned prospective builders that following personal whims might hurt the resale value of their property. "In case the owner wishes to dispose of this house in a few years," explained the catalog, "he will find that he has strayed too far from the average taste and the resale value of his house has greatly lessened."[42] The *Tribune*'s features on remodeling similarly stressed resale value over the owners' actual needs. Before diving into the details of stuccoing an old facade, the writer asked readers to "take, for instance, a house which the owner could not possibly sell for $7,000 because of its decaying, dilapidated appearance. Spend $1,500 or $2,000 on it and it becomes salable for $10,000 or more."[43] Such features taught readers to think of their homes as temporary dwellings and investments rather than permanent places to live where their own comfort and taste was all that mattered. This attitude would take deep root among homeowners in the twentieth century.

Real estate sections wrought complex transformations on the city. When they printed information about property investments, they helped to demystify and democratize the process. The mortgage brokers who found clients in the newspaper often increased the real wealth of families, for mortgages allowed many Chicagoans to purchase and then pay off properties whose values rose over time. At the same time, real estate sections' constant boosting and their promises of easy money helped create a high-turnover and dangerously volatile industry. By encouraging rampant speculation and by assuming endless growth, newspaper material inflated the real estate bubble that would burst, spectacularly, in the autumn of 1929.

When newspaper editors actively recruited advertisers who could sell products to homeowners, they boosted not only the business of home buying but of home owning as well. In nineteenth-century cities, only landlords and the home-owning upper class had needed to purchase things like roof tiles, boilers, or coal chutes. In twentieth-century neighborhoods around the city's periphery, nearly all families became potential customers for such things. And for all of the extra square feet that families gained in the suburbs, they needed more furniture, more fixtures, and more window drapes. "Those communities in which home ownership is deep-seated encourage the sales effort of the advertiser," explained the *Chicago Tribune* in its annual *Book of Facts*, which it sent to current and prospective advertisers each year. "Take a glimpse, for instance, of a few separate rooms in these *Tribune* homes."[44] The *Book of Facts* then pointed out sample products that readers might need for their kitchen, living room, bedroom, bathroom, basement, and laundry. Real estate sections of the 1910s and 1920s earned the advertising dollars of garage builders, porch screeners, roofers, interior decorators, landscapers, painters, plumbers, and utility companies, all hoping to sell products and services to homeowners.

Real estate editors supported the selling mission of their sections, and also catered to their readers' interests, by offering lessons in how to decorate, landscape, and maintain a home. In the 1910s and 1920s, editors commissioned home-decor features written by real or fictional experts, such as the *Herald*'s "Madame Maison." The *Tribune*'s "The Home Harmonious" stressed that every object in a room and every room in an entire home should coordinate. Its aesthetic encouraged readers to replace their current noncoordinating possessions with the era's marketed "ensembles" of appliances or linens.[45] Newspaper articles and advertisements both insisted, over and over, on the importance of beautiful interiors. "The labor of furnishing should be one of love, and an individual expression of self," declared one column of domestic hints.[46] A downtown department store advertised a "home beautiful service" that would create "plans in home furnishing and decoration as the requirements of individual problems demand."[47] All of these home features and advertisements fed a real interest in interior decoration. Readers used the Home Beautiful Service, bought many of the advertised products, and wrote letters to "home" editors asking for advice.[48] But by positioning home decor as a "problem," and by speaking about design as self-expression, real estate sections advanced their advertisers' agendas and primed readers to buy.

Features in real estate sections focused readers' attention on the pleasures and demands of the suburban, rather than the urban, home. They referred to spaces such as sun porches and foyers as if every reader would have one—even though most urban apartments would not. A few home decor columns, such as those appearing in the *Chicago Daily News*, made a point of discussing small spaces and ways to save money while decorating. Even so, these columns took suburban properties as the aesthetic ideal and showed readers how to make their urban apartments at least *seem* suburban. "In to-day's drawing I have shown a country outlook," explained Dorothy Ethel Walsh, the *Daily News*'s home columnist, "but even in a city apartment there is generally something worth seeing out of the windows. Maybe a branch of a tree crosses the window. Make a great deal of it if it does. . . . If only brick walls greet your gaze then plant a window box and have a vision of green."[49] Columnists assumed that readers either lived in a single-family, detached home with ample outdoor space and a yard or that they wanted to.

Gardening columns, too, established suburban norms in city papers. In 1923, the Sunday *Tribune* instituted a daily column called "Farm and Garden," which gave readers tips on keeping hydrangeas alive in winter and decorating with hyacinths. In 1926 the paper compiled the column's tips on flower and vegetable gardening and sold it as a booklet, *Suburban Gardening* by Frank Ridgway.[50] Other papers started similar features during World War I, when many civic groups urged families to start gardens, and kept publishing them through the 1920s.[51] Advertisements further set the expectation that Chicago newspaper readers had, or ought to have, gardens. Carson Pirie Scott & Company pictured spades, pruning shears, turf edgers, lawn rollers, garden hoses, and birdhouses alongside other housewares like dishes and furniture.[52] An ad in the Sunday *Record-Herald* pic-

Clark Jewel Gas Range, large oven and broiler...........59.00
Fireless Cooker, aluminum lined, with kettles, etc., 14.75 to 29.75
Refrigerators, white enamel interior...............23.75 to 44.75

4.4 Ad for Revell & Co., *Chicago Tribune*, 27 June 1920, pt. 1, 6.

tured a landscaper and a homeowner surveying a huge suburban property: "Wittbold Gardeners . . . will see with trained eyes the *unseen* possibilities of your lawn and garden."[53] These ads planted desires and aspirations in urban readers' minds for a green, suburban—and expensive—life.

Suburban imagery and expectations surfaced in many other portions of newspapers—especially advertisements. Ads for vacuums, pianos, curtains, and living room sets showed spacious homes with breezy porches, meandering driveways, and windows framed by creeping vines. Urban housewives in compact kitchens or at washbasins gave way to suburban housewives in airy kitchens with garden views (fig. 4.4). Automobile advertisements pictured glamorous motorists pulling up to suburban homes.[54] These images cropped up in the *Chicago Daily News*, even though most of its readers lived in dense urban neighborhoods, and in the *Defender*, even though most *Defender* readers did not have access to any piece of suburbia. The images lent a surprisingly suburban look to urban newspaper pages and deepened the assumption that most readers aspired to suburban-style living.

Real estate features presumed that every man planned to build his own home, and they helped him along that path. The *Chicago Daily News* titled a portion of its real estate section "The Home Builder's Clinic" and printed a regular column called "Help for the Man Who Wants to Build."[55] The columns answered home-owning readers' questions about topics such as weather stripping, attractive shrubbery, and foundation materials.[56] Both the *Tribune* and the *Daily News* printed plans for single-family homes each

4.5 Almost all of the mail-order homes offered through Chicago newspapers appeared surrounded by trees and gardens, with no neighbors in sight. *Chicago Daily News*, 12 September 1925, 15.

week, which readers could order by mail (fig. 4.5).[57] The *Tribune* even sponsored an architects' contest for five- and six-room house plans. The entries appeared in the paper's real estate section and also in a book that proved popular among Chicagoans; in 1926 alone, the *Tribune* offices sold 3,399 copies.[58] *Tribune* editors described the book of plans as a vehicle for readers to achieve their home-owning dreams: "If the homes amid its pages reach out and make their appeal," mused the booklet's editor, "bringing men and women a step beyond their dream home and a step closer to their real one, then surely its mission will have been accomplished."[59]

Newspapers' house plans, like much real estate material, did help many readers realize dreams of more spacious, healthy, serene surroundings. But like many news features, real estate sections entwined news and commerce. These sections pushed readers toward a single-family, suburban model of life, in part because that model benefited advertisers. The sections worked steadily and effectively. Chicago's suburbs could not have established such a grip on the public's imagination, nor could they have enlisted nearly so many buyers, without the constant aid of the city's metropolitan papers.

There was one much more subtle way that newspapers stimulated suburban growth: they delivered a vicarious experience of the city to readers' doorsteps each morning. The ready availability of Chicago newspapers, and the urban experience within, meant that subscribers did not have to entirely disconnect from the life of the city when they moved outside of its borders. The daily bundle of urban information eased the transition from city to suburb.

Many of the features that allowed suburban readers to imagine city life were not written explicitly for those suburbanites. Journalists tried to capture facets of urban experience that would interest people living in Chicago as well as to those living outside of it. While these features helped urbanites flesh out and interpret their own city experience, they let suburbanites imagine a Chicago life without going there at all. When the 1896 *Tribune* published columns called "Events of a City Day" or "What Some of the Chicago Preachers Said," the paper brought suburban readers into the daily life of the city proper.[60] More evocative pieces heightened the experience. George Ade wrote short "Stories of the Streets and of the Town" for the *Chicago Daily News* between 1893 and 1900, in which he sampled urban experiences. He told readers about discussions unfolding over boardinghouse dining tables or in front of paintings at the Art Institute. He described some of the city's oddest vehicles (a waffle wagon, a cobbler shop), or the city's tiniest storefronts.[61] The Sunday *Herald*'s "Humor and City Life" section printed a half page of "Tales They Tell in the Loop," and a series of illustrations, called "Our Neighbors across the Way," that reproduced the mini-dramas urbanites glimpsed through their neighbors' windows.[62] The 1920s *Tribune* ran a series of short stories on its front page, each centering on the coincidences and possibilities of life in the big city.[63]

The vicarious urban experience available in newspapers, as we have seen, rendered a print community that readers could imagine themselves a part of. It meant something a little bit different, though, to commuters and to stay-at-home suburbanites. Commuters often had very little opportunity to explore and enjoy the city, as their direct experience of Chicago might be limited to the view from the train, the walk from station to office, and a meal at a downtown lunch counter. Newspaper material could help these commuters feel connected to the cultural and social life of the city. It could make up, in part, for the urban experience they were missing when they shuttled home after work. For suburban residents who stayed home—especially women—newspapers could ease some of their isolation. The chatty society columns and the intimate women's page material provided a bit of companionship for women raising children in single-family suburban homes. Tales of urban life let these readers taste the energy and dynamism of city streets, and perhaps imagine alternate existences as city people. In these small ways, newspaper material made suburban life a bit more palatable to Chicagoans; it allowed them to move out of the city without leaving it entirely behind.

WRITING FOR SUBURBAN SUBSCRIBERS

In the beginning, all that Chicago newspapers did to cater to suburban readers was to follow them to the city's fringes. Only in the early twentieth century did Chicago papers alter their circulation strategies and adapt their reporting to appeal specifically to suburban readers. These efforts produced newspapers that felt simultaneously urban and suburban. As publishers circulated these papers across a wide swath of territory, they knit disparate communities into a metropolitan network.

In the 1880s and 1890s, Chicago publishers did not have to try too hard to get suburbanites to subscribe to their papers. After all it was newspapers, along with rail lines and streetcars, that actually made early suburban life possible. Only with access to city information could anyone live so physically separate from the city but still earn and spend money there, still work and visit downtown. Businessmen read morning sheets during their commute; papers caught them up on national events, commodity prices, and city happenings before they started their day at the office. Suburban women would use daily department store ads to plan their shopping trips downtown. They could also scout out the stores that offered delivery to their area, since suburban stores stocked a limited range of clothing and home goods—if they stocked any at all.[64] Suburban residents browsed the city papers' entertainment ads to see if a vaudeville show or musical concert merited a weekend trip in. Some suburbs published their own papers, but their slim weekly issues could not substitute for fat metropolitan dailies. Many suburban households found city newspapers so essential to everyday life that they had two copies delivered to them every morning—one for the husband to read on the morning train, the other for the wife to read at home.[65]

To cover these new domains, Chicago publishers sent reporters along the routes that suburbanites themselves traveled. This meant that newspapers incorporated news from prosperous bedroom communities: Lake View and Evanston to the north, Grossdale and Morton Park to the west, Hyde Park to the south. Under the *Tribune*'s regular column of local news, "The City," it printed a "suburban" column, which discussed suburbs' Sunday sermons, club meetings, or new schools. The 1880s *Tribune* printed notes from the board meetings of new developments and reported on changes to suburban train service. The city's dailies covered debates over suburban annexation in detail, sometimes from the perspective of suburbanites rather than city dwellers.[66] Chicago papers integrated suburban news and announcements into their regular columns, too, mirroring the ways that urban and suburban Chicagoans themselves mixed in daily life. The residents of prosperous suburbs belonged to downtown social clubs and served on the boards of its charities, so the *Times-Herald* titled its club column "Clubs of the Town and Suburb" and listed the suburban Lake View Woman's Club alongside the urban Chicago Teacher's Club.[67] The wealthiest suburban parents debuted their daughters in downtown balls and sometimes even rented apartments downtown during the winter social season, so society columns described teas and weddings in Wilmette and Winnetka as well as in Chicago proper.[68]

Chicago suburbs depended on urban labor—and hence depended on city newspapers to connect them to labor markets. Metropolitan papers offered clearinghouses where suburban households could place ads for nannies or gardeners and where laundresses or carriage drivers could advertise both their skills and their willingness to work in the suburbs. Chicago dailies recognized that suburban readers relied on their classified listings and made efforts to hold onto that business as the metropolitan area grew. The *Tribune* opened dozens of branch offices throughout the metropolitan area; the *Daily News* enlisted hundreds of drugstore owners to take people's classified requests and phone them into the paper every day.[69] These branch arrangements kept the commerce of a huge territory flowing through city papers. Suburban residents even started to use city papers to communicate with each other. When plumbers in Evanston sought jobs nearby, when South Side dentists needed to attract local patients, or when Austin storekeepers wanted to sell their businesses, they all turned to Chicago papers' classified ads.

By the first decades of the twentieth century, Chicago's suburbs were developing somewhat more independent identities and economies. Chicago had annexed broad stretches of territory in the 1880s, but after that, the city was unable to convince many other suburbs to join. Townships—especially wealthy ones—came to value their independence and exclusivity over Chicago's city services. Suburbs established separate school systems, governments, and municipal utilities. Their economies strengthened as small stores were joined by suburban offices, banks, and branch department stores.[70] In this changed context, Chicago's newspapers had to work harder to keep themselves relevant to suburban lives.

The city's papers varied in their approaches. The *Chicago Daily News* decided to focus on urban reporting and to run advertisements aimed at an urban audience.[71] The *Chicago American* also dedicated most of its coverage to events within city limits. The *Herald*, which became the *Times-Herald*, the *Record-Herald*, and finally the *Herald and Examiner*, extended its coverage a bit wider and spoke more frequently to suburbanites' specific interests. The *Chicago Tribune* aimed to be the consummate metropolitan paper, serving urban and suburban readers alike. In 1925, the paper's suburban subscriptions totaled 104,661, about one-quarter the size of its city circulation.[72]

Newspapers actively pursued readers in distant neighborhoods and in suburbs by offering them the same prices and delivery options as city residents, meaning that Chicagoans did not have to sacrifice the quality or the speed of their news when they decided to move to the suburbs. Circulation managers enlisted horsecars, trains, trucks, and deliverymen "at an expense of several million dollars," in the case of the *Chicago Tribune*, to bring papers to suburban newsstands and doorsteps.[73] The paper paid carriers extra to deliver to far-flung subscribers, sometimes taking a steep loss on subscriptions simply to uphold the paper's reputation as a reliable news source for residents anywhere in the metropolitan area.[74] The *Daily News* concentrated its delivery routes on the city's center, but the paper employed its own suburban circulation manager, and it used four airplanes to shuttle the paper to far-off readers. It supplemented its downtown operation with plants on the West Side and the North Side, so that it could speed copies to residents in each district.[75] None of these newspapers passed on the extra transportation costs to suburban customers.

Both the *Tribune* and the *Herald and Examiner*'s politics enlisted the sympathies, and potentially the subscriptions, of Chicago's suburbanites. Each pushed an expansive and fundamentally metropolitan vision of the city. The *Tribune* printed its political platform above each day's editorials beginning around 1920:

1—Lessen the Smoke Horror.
2—Create a Modern Traction System.
3—Modernize the Water Department.
4—Build Wide Roads into the Country.
5—Develop All Railroad Terminals.
6—Push the Chicago Plan.[76]

Aside from "the smoke horror," each one of these issues dealt with connecting all the pieces and outlying areas of Chicago. (Item number six referenced Daniel Burnham and Edward H. Bennett's 1909 *Plan of Chicago*, which proposed grand public buildings, parks, and wide boulevards that would make it far easier to navigate the city by streetcar or automobile.) The *Herald and Examiner* imitated the *Tribune*'s format, and by 1929 it, too, printed an editorial platform "For Chicago, the Nation's Central Great City." It stressed many of the same issues, simply updated for 1929 technology: wide roads, fast freeways, and organized public transit.[77] Each paper's urban vision included, and even prioritized, the suburbs.

In an effective ploy to hold onto readers and advertisers all through the metropolitan area, Chicago newspapers began to act as neighborhood weeklies as well as city dailies. Beginning in 1927, the *Tribune* printed three separate editions of its Sunday metropolitan section, for Chicago's south, west, and north. Each edition covered the everyday events of its zone: charity fundraisers, high school sports matches, and Boy Scout troop meetings. The sections also sold separate advertising space.[78] In 1929, the *Herald and Examiner* created a similar service, issuing four separate editions of the daily classifieds. "The new classified shopping service," explained the paper, "is making it so convenient for readers on all four sides of the city to turn to the classified pages to find articles and services that they want and need, right in their own neighborhood, just around the corner from their homes."[79] Chicago papers established directories for local—not just downtown—services. The *Tribune* and the *Herald and Examiner* each drew up a "motion picture directory" using regional headings: Downtown, North Side, South Side, West Side, Oak Park, and Austin.[80] Because Chicago papers had secured this suburban and neighborhood audience, regional chains used them to advertise—even when most of their locations lay outside of Chicago.[81] By explicitly courting readers with neighborhood news, and by creating outlets for small and regional merchants' advertising, both the *Herald and Examiner* and the *Tribune* positioned themselves as local, neighborhood papers. This not only kept subscriptions high and kept advertising dollars flowing in to these papers, it also prevented competition from springing up in the form of neighborhood newsletters or regional newspapers.[82]

By the late 1920s, Chicago newspapers had cultivated such metropolitan—rather than strictly urban—audiences that the very feel of these papers had changed. Readers encountered stories on suburban high school sports, columns full of suburban weddings, and listings for suburban theaters. They saw images of cozy single-family homes and read about players' golf scores at suburban country clubs. Several portions of the paper no longer assumed that readers would be familiar with downtown Chicago. A 1925 Sears ad in the *Chicago Daily News* spelled out "El" and streetcar routes and driving instructions from four different directions, and department store ads mentioned their free and plentiful parking.[83] In the 1929 *Daily News*, the Pittsfield Building Shops advertised themselves to readers either unused to or exhausted by the usual hubbub of downtown shopping. "You'll be delighted with this sensation of shopping at your leisure right in the heart of the loop, yet far removed from the hurrying crowds and noise," assured the ad.[84] In their pursuit of suburban readers, editors and advertisers were incorporating suburban expectations, tastes, and values into city papers.

Yet metropolitan papers did not simply boost the profile and power of suburbs; they also kept suburbs tied to downtown. Like trains, which shuttled suburbanites downtown and back but did not carry them to the next town over, newspapers circulated information from city to suburb but not among suburbs that lay close to one another. This pattern constantly reinforced the idea that suburbs' primary relationship was with downtown Chicago—not with their neighbors. "Englewood has little in common with the Stock-Yards . . . Kenwood has little that is in common with Pullman," explained one suburban minister in a letter to the editor of the *Tribune*. "What is common to all these places? Chicago, Chicago, Chicago alone."[85] By facilitating suburbs' interactions with Chicago but not with each other, newspapers helped to create a metropolitan area utterly dependent on the city at the center, in which that city prospered from its growing suburbs.

READING SUBURBAN NEWSPAPERS

Even though several of Chicago's metropolitan dailies tried to be all things to all people, they could not provide thorough coverage of every suburb, town, and city in the metropolitan region. Other papers jumped into the news market wherever informational gaps remained. In middle- and upper-class suburbs, weeklies fostered local social and civic life and cemented the image of suburbs as enclaves of wealthy, white, nuclear families. In the largest peripheral cities, daily papers anchored small regional economies of their own, within Chicago's greater reach and influence. Each community's ratio of Chicago news to local news indicated the strength of its cultural and economic ties to the metropolis.

Commuter Suburbs

At first glance, Chicago's newspapers did not seem to leave a lot of room for competition in the suburbs. Chicago dailies saturated the prosperous communities to the north and west of the city and often staked out territory before any suburban paper had the chance to take root.[86] By the 1920s, between 70 and 90 percent of the families in these municipalities subscribed to the Sunday *Tribune* alone, not to mention the city's other Sunday and daily papers.[87] But publishers in these suburbs did spot an opportunity to gather and sell local news. They crafted weekly papers that spoke to women and mothers, older residents, and local business owners—all of whom spent their days right there in the suburbs, not in downtown Chicago. Suburban papers such as *Wilmette Life*, the *Evanston Index*, and the *Lake Shore News* provided the local and logistical information that these residents needed. At the same time, these weeklies artfully depicted the prosperous and homogenous communities that readers wanted to live in, rather than the multiracial, mixed-class suburbs that readers actually inhabited.

Suburban papers did not try to cover metropolitan papers' beats. They generally ran no international or national news, printed no business page, and covered only the most local sports. Suburban weeklies never published the fashion spreads, advice columns, feature stories, or fiction found in Chicago papers. Local editors even printed advertisements for Chicago dailies, seeing dailies as supplements rather than competitors.[88] These editors recognized that they would never develop their papers into large or highly lucrative operations. They employed just a few reporters and relied on local residents to write or phone in with their news.[89] Many suburban papers stayed afloat by operating small printing businesses on the side, using presses to run off locals' wedding invitations and birth announcements between editions of the paper.[90]

Suburban editors found their niche by focusing on local stories and local advertising but also by painting idyllic pictures of suburban life. Suburban papers played essential roles in the workings of local governments and communities. The papers covered local elections, school board motions, and club meetings, and they listed new books acquired by the library. Columns introduced readers to families moving in and alerted readers to their neighbors' illnesses or vacations. All the while, suburban editors crafted papers that reflected the communities these residents wanted to have—not necessarily the communities they did have. Suburban weeklies included almost none of the salacious or disturbing material common to metropolitan papers. Very little crime appeared in their pages, and what did appear was quite subdued, such as a 1929 *Hyde Park Herald* list of bicycle thefts and clothes stolen off of clotheslines.[91] The provocative movie ads of the metropolitan papers did not run in suburban weeklies. Instead, the Hyde Park Theater touted itself as a "house of quality" that showed only "family" films. Other ads invited readers to genteel entertainments such as teas, dinners, and dances at local clubs.[92] Suburban weeklies took pride in the wholesome content of their papers much as they took pride in the wholesome nature of their suburbs. Under its masthead, *Wilmette Life* printed the slogan: "A Clean Newspaper for a Clean Community."[93]

As publishers edited their weeklies to portray the kinds of communities they wanted their suburbs to be, they also addressed the kind of suburban audience they wanted to have. This meant that they wrote for homeowners and business owners in the fashionable parts of town. They did not write for working-class or black suburban residents, even though commuter suburbs housed gardeners, construction workers, drivers, mechanics, and live-in domestics.[94] Working-class and nonwhite suburbanites generally looked elsewhere for their news, either to Chicago dailies or to the *Chicago Defender*. The *Defender* printed an Evanston column, for example, for the African Americans who made up roughly 5 percent of that suburb's population.[95] Even the want ads in suburban weeklies barely acknowledged working-class or African American populations. Suburbanites seeking maids or gardeners placed ads in Chicago papers. Workers willing to take jobs in the suburbs posted their "situation wanted" ads there too. This arrangement made logistical sense, since domestic workers often only moved to a particular suburb once they got the job. Yet outsourcing labor markets to urban papers had the convenient effect of keeping working-class and nonwhite residents out of suburban papers' pages.

Unlike urban newspapers, which offered male- and female-oriented spaces within the larger newspaper, suburban newspapers created an overwhelmingly female space. Weeklies devoted a large proportion of their pages to schools, society, and shopping—all issues central to suburban women's lives. The 1929 *Hyde Park Herald* went so far as to report every absence at the local elementary school; *Wilmette Life* published a mini-newspaper written by the town's schoolchildren.[96] Advertisements for milliners, hair salons, and china-painting lessons targeted women readers. This news strategy made sense in an environment where more women than men spent their days. It was mostly women who supervised children's schooling, and mostly women who used suburban libraries and shopping districts. Occasionally editors revealed that they did not expect men to take as much of an interest in suburban news. "This copy of the 'home paper' on your library table identifies you and your interests in the community," stated a full-page ad in *Wilmette Life*. "Be sure that it is there every week!"[97] The ad persuaded Wilmette residents to subscribe not because they needed the information in the paper but because a subscription declared their allegiance to Wilmette.

Weeklies' advertisements assumed that their core audience did not travel downtown very often and guided suburban readers through the process in order to attract their shopping dollars. "Shoppers will find the Elevated particularly convenient," explained a 1913 ad placed by the train companies. "The Elevated will take you within a few steps of any of the large stores in the Loop district, with sheltered connections into several of them direct from station platforms."[98] The ad explained in detail which lines to take and assured suburban operagoers that there would be special late-night trains waiting to take them home from performances.[99] A 1921 ad for the Field Museum of Natural History promised "a day you will never forget!" and then walked readers through the train transfers that would take them from Wilmette to the museum entrance.[100] These ads rehearsed readers for a particularly suburban relationship to downtown, in which people took scheduled, safe, and orderly day trips for shopping and entertainment, then returned to their quieter lives by evening.

Suburban papers evolved into peculiar hybrids: one part civic institution, one part separate female sphere, and one part exclusive vision. The limited range of their articles in some ways reflected the limited range of activities that took place in commuter suburbs. But the content also rendered the kinds of lifestyles that many suburban readers wished for themselves. The articles in weeklies depicted homogenous, prosperous, domestic, wholesome places. Editors' choices of content sent messages about who and what belonged in the suburbs and shaped readers' impressions of their hometowns.

Satellite Cities

Chicago daily newspapers circulated in smaller "satellite" cities surrounding the metropolis.[101] These cities lay between thirty and fifty miles from downtown Chicago, and each grew up dependent on the larger city. Their steel plants, watch factories, and machine-building shops often imported raw materials through Chicago and then exported their finished products back through the big city. Yet cities such as Elgin, Aurora, Waukegan, Joliet, and South Chicago in Illinois, and Hammond and Gary in Indiana, functioned as urban hubs, too, with populations large enough to support real downtowns.[102] The news offerings in these satellite cities reflected, and indeed fostered, their simultaneously self-contained and dependent relationships with Chicago.

Each satellite city published one or two daily stand-alone papers, which bought national and international news from wire services, ran syndicated women's columns, covered national sports, and printed occasional feature articles. Their editorials weighed in on national politics as well as local issues. These papers also provided the logistical details necessary for daily life. The advertisements from nearby stores and firms offered a full spectrum of goods, from groceries to insurance. Chain stores did not assume that readers in Hammond or Elgin would see their ads in Chicago dailies; they placed separate ads in these newspapers.[103] Because these papers functioned as complete sources of information for local readers and served local advertisers' purposes, they usually circulated more widely in their cities than did Chicago dailies.[104]

These cities' newspapers also catered to small-town and rural people.

News articles kept readers abreast of county politics, and columns like the *Joliet Daily News*'s "From the Coal Fields and Surrounding Towns" served as central sources of information on regional social life.[105] The *Joliet Daily News* fashioned its Friday edition into a weekly, targeted at country subscribers. The paper ran its own farm column, and editors compiled an index of Joliet dairy and poultry prices for readers who sold their farm produce in town. Sunday department store ads listed the sale items for every day of the coming week, so readers could plan their shopping trips into the city.[106] The *Joliet Daily News* also offered "news bundling," a practice common in more remote areas. The paper's carriers would deliver, along with the *Daily News*, any publications that subscribers chose from a long list of options, including women's weeklies, farmers' weeklies, literary and science reviews, labor papers, and trade magazines, all with a package discount.[107]

Chicago daily newspapers never printed special columns for Elgin or Hammond the way that they did for Evanston or Hyde Park. Their society pages did not report on teas and weddings in satellite cities, and their sports pages did not say much about games there. The relatively large populations and self-contained nature of these communities discouraged Chicago editors from pushing hard for their readership, since they knew each satellite city could sustain a paper of its own. Also, if Chicago papers correlated their desired audience with people who would buy Chicago's goods, satellite city residents were not great catches. Working-class factory hands and their families tended to shop in their city's downtown, attend local theaters, and socialize in local circles. Only occasionally did they travel to Chicago, and even then, most did not spend very much money there. At first glance, it seems that residents of satellite cities would have little reason to read a Chicago newspaper.

Yet even though Chicago papers did not aggressively pursue readers in satellite cities, a majority of residents subscribed to both a local and a Chicago paper, either a daily or a Sunday edition.[108] These readers chose to learn about, and perhaps to participate in, the far-reaching economy and the sophisticated culture of the larger city. Merchants might browse Chicago stores' advertisements so that they could offer comparable products in Aurora or Waukegan. Merchants could also track Chicago prices for staple goods and plan their bulk-buying trips into the city. Satellite city residents might look to Chicago papers for style tips and world news. Many in Gary or Elgin or South Chicago thus chose to keep Chicago within their field of vision, to live within the city's cultural and economic orbit. Their Chicago newspaper subscriptions reminded them that their small-city lives unfolded on the fringes of a vast metropolis, and the papers reoriented readers' lives toward "the city" even if they spent little or no time there.

Perhaps surprisingly, small-city residents were more "metropolitan" in their news reading habits than some other residents of greater Chi-

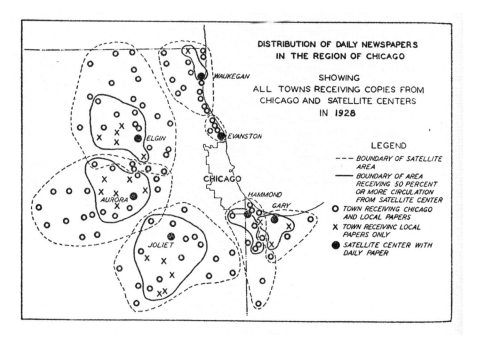

4.6 Map showing the circulations of both Chicago and satellite city newspapers in 1928. Robert E. Park, "Urbanization as Measured by Newspaper Circulation," *American Journal of Sociology* 35 (July 1929): 68.

cago. Robert Park mapped the circulations of both Chicago and satellite city newspapers in 1928 (fig. 4.6) and found spots within the region where people read only the satellite city papers. However, these spots lay not in the satellite cities themselves but beyond them. If residents of these towns wanted to travel to Chicago, they would have to go through the smaller city first. This meant that Joliet or Waukegan served as their big city, their center of gravity, the way that Chicago served as the big city for the small-city residents. "The man in the small city reads the metropolitan in preference to the local paper," Park observed. "But the farmer, it seems, still gets his news from the same market in which he buys his groceries. The more mobile city man travels farther and has a wider horizon, a different focus of attention, and, characteristically, reads a metropolitan paper."[109] Readers in satellite cities sustained their connection to Chicago, while others living nearly as close but in small villages chose not to participate in Chicago culture. So although Chicago papers dominated the information ecosystem of the metropolitan region, their reign was not uniform or complete. Residents sampled information written for a variety of audiences and on a variety of scales, and pockets of more local systems and cultures endured.

NEWSPAPERS DEFINE THE REGION

On a midwestern country road in 1907, a farmer plowing his fields struck up a conversation with a country editor passing by. They stood two hundred miles west of the Missouri River and twelve miles from a railroad as the farmer spoke: "I see by today's Kansas City papers," he began as a visitor came alongside, "that there is trouble in Russia again." "What do you know about what is in today's Kansas City papers?" "Oh, we got them from the carrier an hour ago."[110] This up-to-date farmer surprised the wandering editor because, for most of the nineteenth century, no one living in such an isolated spot could hope to read fresh news. Yet by the early twentieth century, farmers often read city papers on the same day they were printed. As these newspapers sped from Chicago into households across the Midwest, they transformed the regional economy and regional culture and cultivated a regional identity for urban and rural readers alike.

Reaching Rural Readers

People living on isolated farmsteads thirsted for news from the outside world in a way that few urban readers would understand. Women who lived far away from other wives and mothers could find companionship and advice in newspapers' women's pages. Farm children could temporarily escape from their home routines as they read the adventure stories in "junior" sections. Everyone in the family could take pleasure in the spectacle of the Sunday paper, with its color comics, photo sections, fashion spreads, and lively sports pages, all of which plunged them into a more frenetic urban world. "The newspaper was bringing me notions of the excitement and colorful variety of life in the city," explained a native of small-town Kansas, Carroll D. Clark. "I wondered how people had courage to live where bank robberies and holdups occurred almost daily and almost anything was more than likely to happen."[111] Meanwhile, city papers offered plenty of concrete, useful information for rural households. Weather maps could help farmers choose when to plant and harvest crops. Lists of prices helped them decide whether to sell their corn right away or store it for later sale, whether to send their eggs to Chicago or Indianapolis. Rail schedules told them when to arrive in town to load their produce onto freight trains.

Residents of towns and cities would seem to have fewer reasons to take big-city papers than rural readers, for their towns already printed daily papers full of local and global news. Readers in early twentieth-century Paducah, Kentucky, for example, could choose between the Paducah morning *News-Democrat* and the *Paducah Evening Sun*.[112] Yet the papers in nearby bigger cities such as Saint Louis, Nashville, Memphis, and Cincinnati offered flashier headlines, bulkier feature sections, and more current national and international news. Big-city papers especially called out to readers who found their home too provincial. With a subscription, readers could sample information from a worldlier place and declare their allegiance to a more urbane metropolis. "Paducah people want to read these metropolitan papers," noted circulation manager William Scott, "and on Sunday do read them to an amazing extent."[113]

In earlier decades, several obstacles lay between regional readers and big cities' daily papers. City dailies arrived too slowly to be very useful and cost more than most people were willing to pay. Postage added a few cents to every copy of the paper, perhaps doubling the price.[114] Papers traveled several days by train and then by horse to a town post office. There, daily issues would pile up until the subscriber—who might live several hours' journey away—made the trip to retrieve them. By the time a subscriber read news from the city, it could be weeks old. The national reporting would be stale, and the weather reports useless. If some of newspapers' appeal lay in reading information at the very same time as thousands of other people, and imagining oneself connected to that reading community, that appeal was entirely lost for small-town and rural readers. Hence in the 1870s and 1880s, recalled a former newspaper writer, "not one farmer in three hundred got a daily paper."[115]

So farm people contented themselves with other kinds of news. Most subscribed to newsweeklies, specially edited to appeal to rural people. These papers' editors assembled the highlights of the week's happenings, concentrated on state and regional politics, and paid special attention to agriculture. Editors did not bother to include anything too time sensitive, since they knew that readers might not receive their copy for days or weeks. They padded the paper with fiction and jokes that would be entertaining no matter how late the paper arrived.[116]

This scenario began to shift in the 1880s and 1890s, as newspaper publishers collaborated with post office officials to speed city dailies to faraway readers. In 1884, the post office contracted with regional railroads to run the first express mail train out of Chicago. The Chicago, Burlington and Quincy line left the city at three in the morning, loaded with mail and Chicago morning papers. Crowds greeted the train at many stations along the way and bought loads of papers. "The *Tribune* sold like hot cakes," a writer reported from Council Bluffs, Iowa, "and the supply was exhausted in ten minutes after its arrival here. Our newsdealers have quadrupled their orders for tomorrow's *Tribune*."[117] Residents in Burlington, Iowa, read Chicago papers at their breakfast tables for the first time, and those in Chariton, Iowa, rejoiced in getting "the *Tribune* for dinner every day."[118] Chicago rail lines to the east and the north of the city scrambled to set up express trains of their own, and steamboats started to speed Chicago papers up and down the Mississippi as well.[119]

Newspaper publishers wagered that if they could deliver their papers to smaller cities at the start of the working day, readers would buy copies for the still-current information inside. "When our carrier routes are established in this and other cities all readers of THE TRIBUNE within 200 miles of Chicago on either of these lines will have their papers served to them before business hours," explained the editors of the *Tribune*. "THE TRIBUNE will then be as much of a necessity to the public of Galesburg, or Burlington, or Milwaukee as to that of Chicago."[120] The strategy seemed to work even on that first day that the express trains ran, when a reporter in Creston, Iowa, declared it necessary and natural to have these Chicago papers. "The fast mail is the topic of conversation," noted the reporter, "and it seems as though something was wrong in not having it before."[121]

The post office took an active role in distributing newspapers as a part of its federal mandate to circulate information as democratically as possible. The post office's rates for newspapers had been comparatively cheap all through the nineteenth century, and in 1885, they dropped again, to one cent per pound. At this new rate, residents of Dubuque or Peoria could subscribe to Chicago papers for just slightly more than Chicago residents paid.[122] Low postal rates alone, though, could not hook rural subscribers, for they still had to retrieve all of their mail from distant post offices. Postmaster General John Wanamaker proposed Rural Free Delivery, or RFD, to change this situation. Wanamaker argued that rural people ought not to be deprived of the ideas and goods of modern life. He proposed hiring mail carriers to travel to mailboxes at rural crossroads and recommended making drastic improvements to rural roads so that mail carriers could deliver in all seasons. The idea gathered support from representatives of rural districts, from farmers' organizations such as the Grange, and from all kinds of merchants, like Wanamaker himself, who wanted to send catalogs and advertisements to potential rural customers. Congress approved the bill in 1896.

Once rural people were able to get city newspapers right at their doorstep, or in the mailbox down the road, they subscribed in droves. "The daily newspapers have never had such a boom in circulation as they have since the free rural delivery was established," commented an *Editor & Publisher* article in 1902. Many farmers, it said, subscribed to two or three dailies apiece.[123] By 1911, the post office was delivering more than one billion newspapers and magazines along rural routes each year, and periodicals outnumbered all other types of rural mail combined.[124] "Everybody can read and everybody does read," announced *Editor & Publisher*, "because periodicals are so plentiful and cheap."[125]

Even though rural people desired city newspapers, city papers did not always welcome rural subscribers. "If train schedules, distance, and other factors make it impossible for country readers to take advantage of the daily offerings of the local advertisers," explained one circulation manager, "such circulations are 90 per cent useless."[126] Instead of haphazardly sending their papers out into the countryside, circulation managers mapped out their city's "trade radius"—the area in which readers might plausibly buy advertised goods. As changes in transportation and mail delivery gradually expanded cities' reach, these managers redrew the radius. Over time, Chicago publishers managed to turn newspapers into vehicles for selling products to people living hundreds of miles away and profitably expanded into a regional market.

In the mid-nineteenth century, Chicago stores had done brisk business with shoppers from out of town, but newspapers played little part in that trade. Migrants from the east coast often outfitted themselves in Chicago before heading to their final destination, be it a homestead in eastern Iowa or a relative's house in Racine, Wisconsin.[127] Those same migrants made regular shopping trips back to the big city. Newspaper ads occasionally tried to capture these travelers' attention. "Men of the West," announced a 1901 ad in the *Chicago Daily News*. "During your visit to Chicago you are cordially invited to visit The Hub, the world's largest and best clothing house."[128] The ad appealed to country people with a picture of a ranch hand and a display of Stetson hats.

By the late nineteenth century, newspaper publishers had realized that they could advertise Chicago goods to these same shoppers before they traveled to the city. Publishers took an especially keen interest in readers living fifty miles or less from Chicago, for such people often made weekly or monthly trips in. Publishers then persuaded advertisers to take out space to speak to these potential customers.[129] Department stores hosted regular sales and advertised them ahead of time so that country readers could plan to attend.[130] Some department store ads even proposed to refund customers' railroad fares if they bought a certain amount of merchandise.[131] Advertisements aimed at country readers did not include the suggestive descriptions or stylized images that so effectively lured city residents into stores to browse. Instead, they printed realistic, detailed illustrations of their clothing and housewares (fig. 4.7). The pictures helped distant readers plan efficient shopping schedules, in which they would be sure to go home with the items they needed.

Rural Free Delivery, as it sped newspapers to country people's doorsteps, also made it far easier for those people to order Chicago goods through the mail. So Chicago retailers began to use daily and especially Sunday papers to build their mail-order business. They offered readers free catalogs and printed mail-away coupons in their ads.[132] They used guarantees to try to

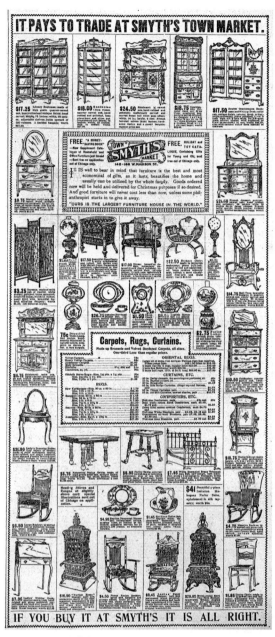

4.7 This ad for Smyth's Town Market offers free catalogs by mail but only to those who live outside of Chicago. The pictures are accompanied by detailed descriptions including the type of upholstery fabric, the variety of wood, and the color. The word "trade" rather than "shop" also seems to target country customers. *Chicago Tribune*, 21 November 1897, 31, American Newspaper Repository, Rubenstein Library, Duke University.

get readers comfortable with the idea of ordering products sight unseen. "If our goods are not as represented," stated an ad for Smyth's Town Market, "return them and get your money."[133] The passage of parcel post, in 1913, drastically lowered the shipping fees for small packages. Advertisers then began to treat newspapers as if they were themselves mail-order catalogs, printing detailed drawings of their merchandise. If a store advertised a dinner-service set, the drawings showed every single piece, down to the coffee spoons. The Sunday *Herald-Examiner* printed a special mail-order section in the 1920s, and advertisements there pictured sturdy shoes, practical housedresses, and canvas work pants intended for a rural customer base. Newspapers facilitated—and profited from—the expansion of the mail-order business, which became a staple of rural life.[134]

Cars again expanded Chicago papers' trade radius. In the 1910s and 1920s, over two million rural families bought their first cars.[135] When a 1916 federal appropriation put money toward improving rural post roads, it smoothed the drive from farms to cities, and when the 1921 Federal Highway Act invested in interstate roads, it paved clear paths from all over the Midwest to Chicago. By the mid-1920s, thanks to their automobiles, millions of residents of Illinois, Iowa, Wisconsin, Michigan, and Indiana traveled to Chicago between one and twelve times per year, and bought a huge array of products there.[136] The regional traffic through the city meant that nearly any kind of Chicago retailer could improve sales by advertising to midwestern readers.

Chicago publishers thus revamped their circulation strategies, turning their Sunday papers into substitutes for old-fashioned newsweeklies and building Sunday into more of a stand-alone edition. If editors ran serial fiction on Sunday, they printed the next installment a week later, so that Sunday subscribers could pick right up where they left off. Editors also specially timed their Sunday paper production so that they could ship editions out quickly to faraway readers. They assembled much of the Sunday material ahead of time, so on Saturday night they could wrap the front-page news sections around a stack of prepared features and ship the bundles out on the midnight train.[137] As metropolitan papers developed their Sunday editions into periodicals that combined the entertainment and the summaries of old-fashioned weeklies with the timeliness of city dailies, their Sunday circulations often swelled to more than double that of their daily editions.[138]

In Chicago, the *Tribune* and the *Herald-Examiner* both harbored grand regional ambitions. In 1925, each paper sent 25 percent of their daily sheets to country readers. On Sundays, the *Tribune* sent 39 percent of its papers into the country, and the *Herald-Examiner* sent 59 percent of its Sunday papers (over 610,000 copies) there.[139] Chicago papers even gave newspapers in other states a run for their money. The *Indianapolis News*, for example, was Indiana's biggest paper in the early twentieth century, yet it only sold about one-third more Sunday papers in its own state than did the *Chicago Tribune*.[140]

Chicago's afternoon papers, at a serious disadvantage in the country circulation game, still energetically pursued readers outside of the city. Afternoon papers printed at midday, which left them little time to stock small-town newsstands before customers walked home from work in the evening. Afternoon papers also did not publish on Sundays, the most popular day of the week among regional readers. Yet in 1925 the *Chicago American* sent 12 percent of its dailies to the country, and the *Daily News* sent 6 percent of its dailies there.[141] The *Daily News* operated delivery routes that extended not only into southern and western Illinois but also to Wisconsin, Indiana, and Michigan.[142] The paper sent salesmen to canvass towns, such as White Pigeon, Michigan, and Pine Village, Indiana, with fewer than one hundred people.[143] The paper enlisted country store owners as sales agents, paying them a 15 percent commission for any new subscribers they brought in.[144]

Because of Chicago newspapers' combined efforts to reach country people, the city's news territory expanded farther and farther outward, until it stretched hundreds of miles around the city. Robert Park made a map of all the towns taking more than half of their newspapers from Chicago in 1930. "The boundary so determined circumscribes a region with an average radius of about 200 miles," he explained.[145] Compared to the same boundary in 1920, Chicago's territory had expanded in all directions.

Becoming Regional Papers

When city newspapers pursued readers so far outside of city limits, and when regional readers started to make up significant percentages of news audiences, the papers themselves were bound to change. Because of their small proportion of country readers, the *Chicago Daily News* and the *Chicago American* did not cater much to country tastes. Their content told rural people all about the city, but told city people little about the countryside. The *Tribune* and the *Herald-Examiner*, in contrast, adjusted their content to speak to small-town and rural people. When this content mixed with all the information for city readers, it turned each paper into a truly regional medium and also encouraged a regional consciousness and identity.

Much the way that city papers had created zoned metropolitan sections and classifieds to appeal to suburban readers, papers also printed special regional editions and made tailored pitches to regional readers. In the 1920s, the *Tribune* printed a special Springfield edition, which focused on Illinois rather than Chicago politics. Printers shipped that edition off extra early so that readers in central and southern Illinois would have papers waiting on their doorsteps in the morning.[146] The *Tribune* and the *Herald-Examiner* each created and embellished features that might appeal to readers outside of the metropolitan area. They expanded their Sunday agriculture sections in the 1910s and 1920s. The *Herald-Examiner* ran a poultry page every week. The *Tribune* sold a separate *Farm and Garden* book that compiled the section's most useful tips and aired a farming broadcast on its radio station in the 1920s.[147] The *Tribune* explicitly included regional readers in the essay competitions and beauty contests it orchestrated in the 1920s by choosing regional winners for Iowa and Wisconsin as well as an overall champion.[148] Twenty departments at the *Chicago Tribune* accepted and reprinted readers' letters or questions; when midwesterners read each other's love quandaries, favorite jokes, civic opinions, and embarrassing moments, it could highlight the commonalities running through readers' lives all through the region.[149]

By gathering information from far afield and sending it right back to where it came from, Chicago newspapers kept the city at the center of the Midwest's information network, its economy, and its identity. Wisconsin people read about Wisconsin trade in a Chicago paper. Iowa farmers read about Iowa weather in a Chicago paper. At the same time, though, the inclusion of all of this regional news thrust the region into city people's consciousness. City readers now browsed, or at least flipped past, agriculture columns and mail-order ads for aprons and work boots. This material reminded readers of the others, relatively close by, who lived very different lives and whose labor provided the eggs, the wheat, and the milk they depended on. While the addition of regional news and rural advice might seem a minor accommodation to regional readers with little broader impact, it could help to cultivate a regional consciousness among all readers, every Sunday.

The *Chicago Tribune* made more overt statements, too, about regional interests. Alongside its daily political platform "For Chicago," the *Tribune* printed a platform "For the Middle West" on Sundays. Its objectives included regional highway systems, an expanded Illinois waterway, flood prevention for the Mississippi, and regional reforestation.[150] Here, the *Tribune* highlighted causes that would benefit the whole region, rather than enrich one city or state at the expense of another. The *Tribune* thus offered a sense of the Midwest as a political and economic unit, a place where all residents could get behind the same ideas. It portrayed Chicago not as the big city that drained people, attention, and resources from the rest of the region but as the true capital of the Middle West. And the paper positioned itself as the ultimate regional advocate and institution.

Newspapers strengthened regional ties as they helped—even encouraged—country people to take city jobs. Many workers and dreamers from smaller midwestern towns and rural hamlets had set out for Chicago in earlier eras, but early twentieth-century metropolitan newspapers smoothed the process. Articles about Chicago's department store girls or its factory hands gave readers a sense of how city people earned a living, and theater sections, sports news, and restaurant ads displayed the city's tempting options for evenings and weekends. Newspapers also gave country people access to city information, so that when they moved they did not have to dive entirely into the unknown. Prospective Chicagoans could reserve a room at a boarding house they spotted in the "rooms for rent" listings and scan the Chicago want ads to see what kind of positions would be open to them. The *Tribune* specifically marketed its classified columns to country parents hoping to get their children started in Chicago (fig. 4.8). As they eased the transition from country to city, newspapers likely increased the number of rural people willing to take the leap into Chicago life and, correspondingly, increased the number of families whose lives spread over the midwestern region. A 1928 *Chicago Tribune* ad spoke eloquently about the relationship that Chicago's newspapers had built with the region. The paper drew the couple into a relationship with the city (fig. 4.9), but it also cast its shadow over them. The interaction was mutually beneficial but not exactly equal.

In catering to the region around Chicago, the *Tribune* in some ways conjured it into existence—especially when it dubbed this territory "Chicagoland." Reporter James O'Donnell Bennett set out on a motoring tour of the Midwest in 1926, with this mandate from the *Tribune*:

> Travel a 200-mile radius from Chicago, north, south, east, and west, and learn that area historically, industrially, and culturally. It is Chicagoland. Make it entertaining to read about. Give the autoist some destination besides a roadhouse and some aim other than a chicken dinner.
>   . . . Get the tourists interested in *their* Mississippi valley and *their* lake coast. Make 'em sit up and look out instead of loll. Tell about interesting places and outstanding people.[151]

The term "Chicagoland," unknown before this series, appeared in every installment on Bennett's trip. The word quickly spread through the paper and entered midwesterners' vocabularies. By 1927 the *Tribune* was selling a roadmap of Chicagoland and mounted a massive Chicagoland map in its Touring Department for employees and visitors to consult as they planned out regional trips.[152] The paper narrated Chicagoland tours on its radio station, WGN. Other writers adopted the term, as when Harley Bradford Mitchell titled his 1928 book *Historical Fragments of Early Chicagoland*.[153] Though Bennett's series was mostly meant to spark Chicagoans' interest in

4.8 This ad for the *Chicago Tribune* classifieds pictures a mother in a country home and a boy in an industrial city, writing to each other. It frames the classified ads as a means to set up a son with a safe, successful Chicago life, and frames the newspaper itself as a way for families to imagine each other's lives and to stay connected. *Chicago Tribune*, 8 February 1908, 10, American Newspaper Repository, Rubenstein Library, Duke University.

4.9 The city reaches out and touches a newspaper-reading couple. The newspaper here turns the region into a network, connecting city people with those outside of it. *Chicago Tribune*, 11 November 1928, sec. 3, 8, American Newspaper Repository, Rubenstein Library, Duke University.

traveling the region (and was thus similar to many articles and maps that appeared in city newspapers' motoring sections), it also initiated a dialogue about regional identity in the places he visited. The *Peoria Transcript* received a letter from a reader who objected to Bennett's claiming the town of Nauvoo as a part of Chicagoland. The Peoria editor wrote this in reply:

> Every city and village of Illinois should be proud to be included in "Chicagoland." In addition to being the second city of the United States and the fourth city of the world, Chicago is the most democratic city in America and its great industries and enterprises enrich as well as are enriched by the small communities of Illinois.
>
> . . . Chicago, however, is now more than a city—it is a symbolism. It stands for the midwestern idea in politics, religion, education, and economics. Cook county practically dominates state politics. In many respects all Illinois is "Chicagoland," as well as many parts of Wisconsin, Iowa, Indiana, and Michigan.[154]

The editorial writer had completely adopted Chicago as his capital and had put it at the heart of his midwestern identity. Only through the regular circulation of Chicago information were people such as this Peoria editor able to feel that affinity and to proudly imagine themselves as part of Chicago's domain.

Hubs and Hinterlands

Chicago newspapers' regional ambitions continued to expand in the 1910s and 1920s with a large influx of brand advertising. Papers had carried ads for a handful of brand-name products in the nineteenth century: patent medicines, baking sodas, breakfast cocoas. But the flowering of mass-produced goods in the late nineteenth and early twentieth centuries prompted Chicago newspapers—and above all, the *Chicago Tribune*—to aggressively solicit advertisements from brand manufacturers. When newspapers carried more brand ads, they worried less about their literal "trade radius." Neither shopper nor product needed to travel through Chicago anymore; readers would likely purchase brand-name products right in their hometowns. Publishers instead started to think about targeting communities where readers would have money to buy. The seemingly small addition of brand advertisements to newspaper pages wound up reshaping newspapers' business strategies, their circulations, and eventually the whole midwestern economy.

Chicago Tribune staff studied the regional economy in an attempt to find the most prosperous, connected, and promising locations to sell the paper.

They found that regional trade was leaving small towns and concentrating in larger regional hubs. Railroads had created a new hierarchy among towns and cities. Towns with a rail depot were often instantly transformed into market centers, where farmers would travel to load their milk or grain onto freight trains and pick up the week's provisions.[155] Automobiles were also concentrating business into the region's larger towns and cities. In the 1910s and 1920s, farm families piled into their cars on Saturdays, drove to the nearest large town, and spent time and money there—buying clothes, eating ice cream, going to the movies.[156] The *Tribune* realized that with trade booming, residents of these towns had plenty to spend, both on daily paper subscriptions and on advertised goods. The paper also recognized that these towns' denser populations made for easier distribution. Sending bundles of newspapers to a few hundred towns was a far more manageable task than sending individual papers via train, mail, and carrier to thousands of different rural mailboxes across the Midwest.[157] The *Tribune* pushed hard in order to sell subscriptions in regional hubs and largely succeeded. Just under half of all the residents in these towns read the Sunday *Tribune*—impressive considering how far away many of them lay from Chicago itself.[158]

The *Chicago Tribune* taught its advertisers to think about the regional market in the same terms that the paper itself used and helped them distribute goods to high-volume markets. The *Tribune* sent its advertisers a detailed booklet titled *Book of Facts* every year from 1917 onward. As the book shared statistics about midwesterners' needs, buying habits, and incomes, it advocated a specific sales strategy. It told merchandisers to scout the region for:

(1) large bodies of people with high spending power;
(2) concentration of retailers readily accessible to salesmen and for merchandise delivery; and
(3) dominance over nearby competitive cities and towns.[159]

The *Tribune* helped merchants advertise their products and then helped persuade local stores to stock these merchants' goods. The paper sent its own salesmen to accompany advertisers' sales agents, since regional retailers would be more likely to stock a product if they knew it was being advertised in the paper.[160]

By winning over readers and retailers alike to mass-manufactured brand-name goods, the *Tribune* gradually homogenized the economies of the towns in which it circulated and built economies in which both buyer and seller—each often living hundreds of miles from Chicago—depended on Chicago information. Because they had perused newspaper advertisements, customers were more likely to arrive at their local store with opinions and preferences and were less likely to ask shopkeepers for recommendations. When the *Tribune* conducted a survey of regional retailers, many respondents said that their customers asked for products they had seen in the paper, and some customers even clipped out ads and brought them to the store. A shopkeeper in Buchanan, Michigan, reported that ads could noticeably change his customers' ways. "I have sold lots of goods by the help of *Tribune* advertising," he reported, "goods that people in my community were not in the habit of using before."[161] As a result, storekeepers, too, began to consult those ads when deciding what to stock and display. "We follow The Sunday Tribune ads," explained a merchant at E. D. Miller & Co. of Stockton, Illinois, "and on Mondays make a special display of the goods that are advertised."[162]

The *Co-Operator*, a monthly newsletter that the *Tribune* distributed to fifteen thousand retailers and merchandisers, actively pushed specific sales methods.[163] The newsletter claimed "two main objectives: one, that of helping the merchant develop better merchandising methods, and the other, that of emphasizing the wisdom and importance of handling advertised goods."[164] The newsletter profiled successful retailers and told readers how to emulate them. An article on a successful drugstore owner included photographs that showed how this owner positioned his window displays, how he arranged goods on the shelves, and how he organized the ingredients behind the soda fountain counter.[165] Due to these articles, residents of five states might each encounter identical products in identical displays on their local grocery shelves. Chicago newspapers were increasingly orchestrating the economies of small towns throughout Illinois and the Midwest.

The *Tribune* purposely ignored the Midwest's poorer and more isolated regions, and it encouraged its advertisers to do the same. The *Book of Facts* printed maps of Illinois, Indiana, Iowa, Wisconsin, and Michigan (plate 7) that ranked their counties "best," "good," "fair," and "poor," based on factors such as the number of automobiles owned by residents and their income tax returns.[166] It provided these maps to help merchants strategize about where to concentrate their own sales efforts and, also, to showcase the wealth of its subscribers. The *Tribune* boasted "mass circulation starting at the top and going down."[167] Meanwhile, the *Book of Facts* urged retailers to quit pushing their goods in struggling rural stores. "It is, at times, a tactical and costly error for a manufacturer to spend much time in intensive cultivation of the small town," it explained.[168] "Specializing on the successful dealers, the pace makers in these flourishing communities, permits discarding the old cumbersome plan of trying to sell every retailer regardless of the volume and general sales expense."[169]

The *Tribune*, and other papers, went beyond simply reinforcing existing disparities in wealth and access to information and actually reshaped the region. Through content as varied as movie reviews and Pepsodent ads, papers put a new mass culture at many readers' fingertips. But because they aggressively solicited subscriptions only in the most prosperous districts, papers also limited country people's ability to stay in touch with that culture. Papers turned certain towns into commercial centers and left other towns out of trade circuits. These strategies slowly cut out many rural readers from a growing regional economic network and carved out new hinterlands where neither urban goods nor urban information reached.

The Rural and the Regional Persist

A handful of observers began to notice, around the turn of the century, that the spread of metropolitan dailies into surrounding regions was hurting other newspapers' business. The old-time newsweeklies, written especially for country people, were fast losing their audiences.[170] Critics worried that the spread of big-city papers would kill off local dailies, too. "The proximity of large cities and fast trains is fatal to provincial dailies," declared one country editor in 1892. He saw metropolitan papers ruining the business prospects of every other daily for hundreds of miles around. For this reason, he said, "except in the case of Milwaukee, there are no really creditable dailies within two hundred miles of Chicago."[171]

Some believed that the spread of urban information might kill off distinctive local cultures entirely. In 1909 James Edward Rogers described a pattern in all towns within one hundred miles of a metropolis, in which "their inhabitants, mingling more and more with the metropolitan life, will finally become merged in the great mass."[172] The writer Sherwood Anderson depicted a world where urban information had reached into, and profoundly altered, the remotest corners of rural America:

> In our day a farmer standing by the stove in the store in his village has his mind filled to overflowing with the words of other men. The newspaper and the magazines have pumped him full. Much of the old brutal ignorance that had in it also a kind of beautiful childlike innocence is gone forever. The farmer by the stove is brother to men of the cities, and if you listen you will find him talking as glibly and as senselessly as the best city man of us all.[173]

The 1920 census, which for the first time found more Americans living inside cities than outside of them, helped to cement the public's idea that rural life and rural culture were slowly, inexorably disappearing. In 1929 Robert Park observed that, "in some parts of the country, as, for example, in New England and on the Pacific Coast, what we once called rural community and rural people has ceased to exist."[174] The city newspaper—like the mail-order catalog, like the automobile—seemed to have remade a rural republic into a nation of cities and city-centered regions.

Yet urban newspapers did not simply replace rural ways of life with urban routines. They reshaped, rather than obliterated, the local. In small cities and towns, urban newspapers dominated the morning market and covered national and international news more thoroughly than any local paper could manage. But most readers still wanted to hear something about their hometowns. So small daily papers strengthened their local news coverage and published in the afternoon, so as not to compete with metropolitan morning papers.[175] Local papers also continued to issue weeklies, often long after city papers had abandoned the practice.[176] These weeklies offered the kind of information that metropolitan papers would never print: descriptions of theatricals and revival meetings coming through town, notes of thanks from families who had received support in a time of need, and announcements of new babies born to farm families. "Although the rural carriers take each morning great packages of daily papers, brought to the village by the fast mail," explained Charles Moreau Harger, an editor from Kansas, "the people along the routes are as eager as ever for the weekly visit of the home paper."[177] These local weeklies also exerted a special nostalgic pull among people who had grown up in the region and moved away. "The city business man throws away his financial journal and his yellow 'extra,'" said Harger, "and tears open the pencil-addressed home paper that brings to him memories of new-mown hay and fallow fields and boyhood. Regardless of its style, its grammar, or its politics, it holds its reader with a grip that the city editor may well envy."[178] So as urban newspapers transformed into regional papers, they did not kill local journalism or local culture. They instead created a new division of labor, in which small papers left large-scale reporting to metropolitan newspapers and concentrated on the hometown news.

In the 1920s, city dailies' advertising departments drew up images that depicted their papers at the vital center of American metropolitan areas and broader regions (figs. 4.10 and 4.11). Newspapers' circulations appeared to ripple outward in even circles around downtown.[179] The images effectively communicated just how far city newspapers traveled and how thoroughly regional they had become. In a 1929 article, Robert Park seemed to describe this phenomenon, arguing that metropolitan newspapers' spread, alongside increasing mobility and travel, had urbanized huge swaths of the population even far outside city limits. "Urbanization may be due," he commented, "quite as much to the fact that the city is going out into the country, as to the fact that the country people are coming into the city."[180]

But metropolitan newspapers did not, in fact, urbanize their entire re-

4.10 Advertisement for the *Milwaukee Journal* in *Editor & Publisher, International Yearbook Number for 1926*, 30 January 1926, 147.

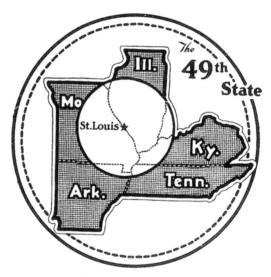

4.11 Advertisement for the *St. Louis Globe-Democrat* in *Editor & Publisher, International Yearbook Number for 1926*, 30 January 1926, 183.

gions. When newspapers crossed city limits, they did not radiate in smooth circles, nor did they pull every reader within a hundred miles into the city's economic and cultural orbit. Such images concealed the messy, uneven, and constantly shifting patterns of regional news. Within each of these circles, a combination of economics, culture, physical distance, and transportation routes determined the balance of local and regional information that residents wanted and that publishers supplied. And while city information did travel outward, smaller papers covered the events and filled the needs that metropolitan papers overlooked. The era of the entirely homogenous region, in which cities stretched on forever and everyone read the same news, never arrived.

*   *   *

Not just in Chicago but all over the nation, newspapers were the medium through which millions of Americans learned about, and were won over to, their future suburban homes. An 1899 ad for Philadelphia's Roslyn Terrace showed a cross section of the streets there, in order to fully explain all of the improvements that would make residents' lives easier—gas mains, brick gutters, macadamized streets, bright street lights.[181] Newspaper material provided rationales for suburban moves and transformed the suburban option into a common and commonsense decision for city families. "Rear your children away from the dangers of the city," suggested an ad in the 1927 *Milwaukee Journal*. "Rear them in an environment where they can develop their minds and bodies in the way in which nature intended."[182] Ads in African American papers beyond Chicago attest to the appeal of the suburban dream even among populations that many suburbs tried to exclude. A *Baltimore Afro-American* ad for Morgan Park promised an exclusive neighborhood full of illustrious neighbors: "An ideal residential community, protected by all the restrictions and with all the improvements of the best white developments."[183] With most developers uninterested in selling to African Americans, though, black suburban options remained limited. A *Pittsburgh Courier* ad touted a suburban "classy four-room bungalow": hardly the spacious retreat readers might have hoped for.[184]

The material in many cities' real estate sections kept readers focused on houses (and not apartments) with articles on gardening, decoration, construction, and renovation. "The Home Garden for Pleasure and Profit" in the *Philadelphia Public Ledger* targeted suburban gardeners; the columnist explained that he worked ten or twelve hours in the city and then came home and gardened.[185] An article in the *Baltimore Afro-American*'s home department, titled "Let Your House Show What Season It Is," taught readers that their home decor ought to change throughout the year, while newspaper ads for Hitchner wallpaper explained the art of home decor: "Wallpaper has a most important duty—to tie together the furniture, pictures and other objects in the room. Proper contrast, relation of designs and colors, size of room and lighting must all be taken into account."[186] When the *New York Sun* conducted a contest for small house plans, the headline announced that the paper "Expected to Help Solve Problem of Those Who Desire Comfortable, Artistic, Efficient Homes at Moderate Cost."[187] The *Sun*'s contest may have done that; it also handily boosted the real estate, construction, and home improvement industries.

When readers actually bought suburban homes, papers risked losing those readers' subscriptions. So metropolitan dailies tried to make themselves indispensable to suburbanites. The 1895 *Milwaukee Daily Journal*'s "news of the suburbs" section reported the visits, vacations, dinners, church services, and club meetings in prosperous communities just beyond city borders.[188] The *Philadelphia Inquirer* operated dozens of branch offices in peripheral neighborhoods such as Wissahickon, Norristown, and Riverton to keep those populations placing classified ads with them and not in neighborhood newsletters.[189] By 1927, the *New York Herald-Tribune* was printing eight pages of society news that included the boroughs, Westchester, Connecticut, and New Jersey, all to keep the city's millions of suburbanites reading.[190]

Chicago papers covered an exceptionally wide swath of territory, as the *Chicago Tribune* was keen to point out. "Chicago Rubs Elbows with No Other Metropolis!" it declared to prospective advertisers in 1927. "In every direction this titan of trade can enlarge its influence to the fullness of its destiny as master market of America."[191] Some other midwestern, southern, and western papers could market to broad hinterlands as well. The late nineteenth-century *Cincinnati Enquirer* circulated in what newspapermen called "the *Enquirer*'s Confederacy": Ohio, Indiana, Kentucky, and West Virginia.[192] The *Pittsburgh Gazette* established a newspaper train in 1885, which departed at 2:50 A.M. to deliver morning papers to Harrisburg.[193] By the 1920s, the *Des Moines Register* and *Tribune* were reprinting their front pages up to twenty times to appeal to the interests of readers in different Iowa regions.[194]

Papers along the eastern seaboard, where cities lay so close together, could not reach as far but attempted to serve as regional media nonetheless. The late nineteenth-century *Philadelphia Record* hoped to hook regional readers with an agricultural section assembled from clippings of journals like *National Farmer* and *Agricultural Review*.[195] The *New York World* offered a three-times-a-week edition specifically for New York and New Jersey rural readers in the 1890s. While posters for the daily *World* featured scandalous headlines and pictures of showgirls, posters for the country edition promised a farm department and showed a lovely girl threshing wheat.[196] In the 1920s, the *Philadelphia Public Ledger* ran pages of society notes from coal country towns like Mount Carmel, Shamokin, and Shenandoah, more than a hundred miles away.[197]

As in Chicago, city newspapers around the country only pursued regional readers when they became viable customers for advertised goods. After parcel post had created a strong incentive to reach rural readers and offer them goods by mail, a *New York World* advertisement asked: "Why Waste Money on Horses? The Do-It-All tractor will do a greater variety of work on your farm than horses because it plows, it cultivates, it hauls your loads, operates hay mowers, lawn mowers and gives you 6 H.P. for belt work."[198] The ad gave readers an address where they could write to request a catalog. When automobiles expanded papers' trade radius yet again in the 1920s, papers involved themselves even more actively in rural and regional life. The *Philadelphia Inquirer* printed lists of prizewinners at the Pennsylvania Farm Food Show, and the *Philadelphia North American* sponsored egg-laying competitions.[199] The strategies worked. "Why do I read it?" wrote a Florida farmer who subscribed to the *Jacksonville Times Union*. "Because it is the only State paper covering the whole State in its local news service. It has a fine exchange column; its farm page reports on what the Florida farmers are doing, its market reports and editorial advice to farmers interest me as a 'back-to-the-soiler.'"[200]

When trying to please their urban, suburban, and regional readers all at once, many metropolitan papers learned to highlight points of regional interest and regional pride. The *Boston Post*, which claimed the biggest Sunday circulation in New England at the turn of the century, rallied the whole region around the Harvard football team and advocated for "the advance of New England"—not just Boston—on its editorial page.[201] The *Columbia State* explored South Carolina's history in its Sunday editions. "This year it has published," explained an appreciative reader in 1911, "a secession semi-centennial number, several charming character sketches of ante-bellum life in the low country, a series of excellent articles on the birds of the State, and another series on investigations into the history of the University of South Carolina."[202] In the late 1920s, when the *Milwaukee Journal*'s rural readership was on the rise, the paper ran an exposé of companies that sold barren land to hopeful Wisconsin farmers.[203] These articles turned newspapers into guardians of regional identity and regional interests.

As city dailies spread beyond city limits, they surely had the largest impact on suburban and regional readers. Dailies drew these readers into a national system of city-centered regions, in which suburban and country people necessarily defined themselves in relation to "the city." But the expansion of metropolitan papers also influenced city readers. The addition of suburban images and viewpoints introduced many city dwellers to suburban ideals. The inclusion of rural material heightened urban readers' awareness of their farming neighbors. Metropolitan papers gave city, suburban, and country readers common vocabularies and common reading experiences. To some extent, they homogenized the different cultures present within regions such as the Midwest, the mid-Atlantic, and New England. But more than anything, these newspapers made all three types of readers aware of each other and built regional identity around the exchanges and interactions between them.

5: NATIONALIZING THE NEWS

In 1892 a New York newspaperman named John Cockerill envisioned, in *Lippincott's* magazine, "The Newspaper of the Future." News gathering had made great strides in the last few decades, he wrote, but still seemed rather inefficient. "Why should it require a stretch of the imagination," he asked, "to suppose a series of pneumatic tubes radiating from New York City to Boston, Buffalo, Rochester, Albany, Troy, Trenton, Philadelphia, Baltimore, Wilmington, and Harrisburg, by the use of which one great morning newspaper could be printed in the City of New York complete in its news and news-editorial and feature pages"?[1] Branch offices in each of these cities could then supply local news and editorials, he explained, and would send the aggregate package (through more tubes) to surrounding towns.

Cockerill's network of pneumatic tubes never came to be. But within the next few decades, news articles did in fact travel along the routes that Cockerill described. The nation's biggest newspapers—based in New York, Philadelphia, Washington, DC, Chicago, and Saint Louis—began to sell articles, full-page features, and even entire sections to papers in smaller cities. These large papers, such as the *Philadelphia Public Ledger*, the *New York Tribune*, and the *Washington Post*, formed syndicates that existed solely to redistribute articles nationwide. Newspaper chains, similarly, capitalized on economies of scale. Publishers such as William Randolph Hearst and E. W. Scripps bought up multiple papers and formed chains, which shared reports and features among themselves. As a result, the nation's news industry soon functioned much as Cockerill had forecast. Large corporations did the majority of news gathering and feature writing; local editors bought that material and merely supplemented it with local news.

Syndicates and chains did not turn early twentieth-century metropolitan newspapers into entirely generic products. Subscribers needed and expected their local newspapers to print local news, and no newspaper ever abandoned local reporting entirely. Yet editors—and their readers—found syndicated material hard to resist. Syndication offered newspapers in midsize cities such as Memphis, San Antonio, Buffalo, and Boise news they could never afford to commission themselves. On-the-ground reporting on the Russo-Japanese War, for example, or expert instruction on sprinting technique, or beauty tips from film stars—local papers could, and did, order all of these from syndicates. Meanwhile, syndication allowed the nation's biggest papers to extract another round of profits from their news material. As editors of major papers devoted increasing amounts of money, time, and staff to news they could syndicate, they undermined the local character of big-city and small-city papers alike. By the 1910s and 1920s, most of the articles that Americans read in their local papers had either been bought or sold on the national news market.

Syndicated news turned Americans into more self-consciously urbane and worldly readers. Articles that described happenings around the state, the nation, and the world gave readers the tools to envision exactly where their own cities fit in a national and global narrative. The colorful writing and detailed illustrations of cultures and events overseas fostered readers' broader curiosities. By suggesting that many other places were worth knowing about, newspapers transitioned U.S. citizens away from strict provincialism and toward more national and global concerns.

As they broadened readers' horizons, though, newspapers also homogenized Americans' vocabularies and experiences. Syndicated features created consistent news categories and stock "types" that entertained readers from coast to coast. The more often these types and categories appeared in papers, the easier it was for readers to use them as lenses to view themselves, their cities, and the world. Newspapers may have been especially effective agents in the spread of a national culture built on mass-market goods and entertainment because they gave tacit local approval to these national phenomena. When mass-produced fashion, music, and movies arrived in town, readers turned to newspapers' columnists for help interpreting and evaluating them. Standardized news necessarily diluted the local character of local newspapers, turned readers' attention away from the ethnic cultures they had grown up with, and sometimes obscured meaningful differences between regions. As they devalued the local, syndicates and chains boosted the national. Building up shared understandings among readers in disparate places, newspapers fostered a more generic but broadly intelligible national culture.

To delve into the history of news syndication, we turn to Milwaukee, Wisconsin. Milwaukee, far more than New York, Chicago, or Philadelphia, was a "typical" American city in both the size of its population and the size of its newspaper industry. Milwaukee grew from 115,587 residents in 1880 to 578,249 in 1930, climbing from the nation's nineteenth-largest city to its twelfth largest. It expanded on the strength of its iron, steel, tanning, and brewing trades. Factories lay along the Menominee and Milwaukee Rivers, and their workers—Irish, Polish, and German—lived in balloon-frame houses nearby. The houses had been built for single families but often contained three or four families between the main floors, the basement, and the attic.[2] The city's more prosperous classes lived north of downtown on Prospect Avenue's "Gold Coast" near Lake Michigan or in leafy suburbs like Brookfield and Waukesha to the west.

Milwaukee was an overwhelmingly German city in the nineteenth century. Waves of German immigrants began arriving in the 1830s, and the influx reached a peak around 1870, when one out of every three city residents had been born in Germany.[3] German engineers and architects put their stamp on the city's built landscape, as they designed stepped gables for Milwaukee mansions, put turrets on the city's hotels and theaters, and gave the 1895 city hall a tower that resembled that of the *Rathaus* in Hamburg. City social life followed German patterns as well. Many businessmen kept the rural German custom of closing up shop and going home for the main meal of the day.[4] Milwaukeeans gathered with their singing societies after work and flocked to beer gardens on weekends.[5] At parents' request, the city's public schools taught German to 93 percent of elementary school students.[6]

Milwaukee's political culture leaned noticeably to the left. Refugees from Germany's failed 1848 revolution established a radical tradition in Milwaukee, and the city's factories fostered a robust labor movement.[7] Organized workers rallied for socialist political candidates, and socialism took root more deeply in Milwaukee than in any other major American city. Two socialist mayors governed the city for a total of twenty-four years, and Milwaukee elected the United States' first socialist congressman.[8] On a less radical front, a broad swath of Milwaukee residents worked for progressive causes, from pure food to public schooling. The city touted itself as a model of good municipal government and took pride in its public health initiatives, claiming the mantle of "the healthiest city" by the 1930s.[9]

Chicago papers regarded Milwaukee as part of their trading territory, since it lay less than a hundred miles away. Indeed, the *Chicago Tribune* refused to sell its syndicated material to Milwaukee papers, since it viewed them as competitors. But because Milwaukee anchored a regional economy and because it housed a unique local culture, it formed something of an enclave of local journalism within Chicago newspapers' circulation radius. In the late nineteenth century, Milwaukee's conservative *Sentinel* and the smaller *Daily News* competed for the city's morning readers; the *Journal* and the *Evening Wisconsin* catered to the evening crowd. Four German-language dailies served the city as well, alongside a handful of weeklies written for Polish, Czech, and African American readers.[10] In the early twentieth century, the city welcomed a few start-ups: the *Free Press* began offering solid political coverage and a left-leaning editorial page in 1902, and the city's socialists founded the *Milwaukee Leader* in 1911. Milwaukee followed the national consolidating trend, though, and lost more papers than it gained. Two English-language and three German-language dailies ceased printing by 1930, and a chain took over two of the city's most established dailies. Milwaukee's population quintupled in the fifty years leading up to 1930, but its newspapers merged or bought each other out until only a few powerful dailies remained.[11]

Ads and articles in nineteenth-century Milwaukee papers—both English language and German language—reflected the markedly German, leftist character of the city. All of the city's papers reviewed German-language dramas at the Pabst Theater, ran ads for the harvest-time Jahrmarkt, and printed sports-page columns on skat, a popular German card game. Several Milwaukee newspapers printed Sunday editions long before their contemporaries in other cities, since German Catholics and Jews did not observe such strict Sunday rituals as U.S. Protestants. Papers elsewhere restricted alcohol advertisements, but Germans had brought beer drinking into the heart of Milwaukee culture and developed it into a major industry. Accordingly, Milwaukee papers freely advertised events at the Schlitz beer garden and cases of Miller High Life. Meanwhile, Milwaukee papers proudly tracked Wisconsin's contributions to a national Progressive dialogue, from Senator Bob La Follette's presidential campaign to the state university system's "Wisconsin Idea."[12]

Standardized news became viable in Milwaukee partly due to the tempering of both German and socialist influences in the early twentieth century. German immigration slowed, and World War I muted German American pride and silenced many political radicals. Yet papers did not simply mirror a Milwaukee that was losing its local culture. In running syndicated material, Milwaukee newspapers actively brought the city into line with a developing national culture. Elements of Milwaukee's politics and culture survived, of course, into the mid-twentieth century. But they did so without much support or attention from the mainstream press. As Milwaukee's idiosyncrasies made fewer appearances in the news, they risked losing their place at the center of city identity and civic pride.

FINDING MILWAUKEE'S PLACE

Starting in the 1890s, Milwaukee daily papers began circulating vivid renderings of the world that lay outside the city limits. This material ran alongside increasingly colorful, in-depth local features. The range of stories from near and far gave readers the tools to create mental maps of the world and situated Milwaukee in a network (albeit a hierarchical network) of cosmopolitan cities exchanging goods, ideas, and people.

Residents' own migrations and family histories gave them first- or second-hand knowledge of the world beyond Milwaukee. Roughly 40 percent of 1880 Milwaukee residents had been born in another country. Most of Milwaukee's turn-of-the-century black population had migrated through multiple towns and cities in the upper South and Midwest.[13] Even among native-born white families, very few had been in the city for generations; less than one-fifth of the city's 1880 residents had lived there in 1850. The city was neither a backwater nor an enclave, and newspapers were hardly Milwaukeeans' only source of place knowledge. Newspapers, however, imposed a new geography. News reports paid attention not to the places readers already knew and cared about, necessarily, but to places that editors deemed interesting and important. Papers' reporting and features scripted a "right" way to know the world and shaped how readers understood their place within that world.

Through the 1880s, Milwaukee newspapers did little to flesh out readers' impressions of places beyond Milwaukee, nor did they put Milwaukee into any clear relationship with those other places. News from the city and from elsewhere usually appeared in a jumble, with few headlines. A typical column from the front page of an 1881 paper printed side-by-side paragraphs from Platteville (Wisconsin), Saint Louis, and London.[14] Late-breaking news from multiple states and countries appeared in no particular order in telegraph columns, such as the 1889 *Evening Wisconsin*'s "Short but Newsy":

Forest fires are raging in San Mateo County, Cal.
The New York *Graphic* has suspended publication.
George Francis Train was arrested on a judgment note.
Richard Kiser, a deaf mute at Council Bluffs, was killed by the cars.
Ex-Surgeon-General Beale, of the United States navy, died at Philadelphia.
The English syndicate is negotiating for the purchase of the Eagle brewery,
    at Elgin, Ill.[15]

Newspapers' editorial pages presented similarly jumbled batches of information. Editors sifted through papers from around the country, clipped their favorite funny stories or jokes, and assembled them all on the editorial page. Readers encountered weather jokes from the *Boston Globe*, waiter jokes via the *Atlanta Constitution*, and Darwin jokes courtesy of the *Philadelphia News*.[16] The patchwork of humor may have kept readers entertained, but it did not feed their understanding of the character or qualities of other places.

By the turn of the century, newspapers began categorizing news by location, placing Milwaukee in an ordered matrix. News-gathering organizations such as the Associated Press and the United Press offered fresh, wide-ranging coverage of national events by telegraph.[17] The falling newsprint prices of the 1890s made it possible to print many more of these national and global stories, and editors began to organize them according to place. By the early twentieth century, Milwaukee editors cordoned local news into sections with titles like "Local Odds and Ends" or "The City in Brief," reserved page 2 or 3 for city and state news, and carved out a few pages of the Sunday edition for Wisconsin-specific features such as the *Journal*'s "Sunday State Page—Badger News and Features."[18] The *Journal*'s editorial-page news summary printed its stories in tiers: "Review of the Events of the Week in City, State, Nation and the World."[19] Papers' headings, subheadings, and layouts fit Milwaukee into a relationship with other places, and their ratios of local to national content spoke to the relative importance of each sphere.

Turn-of-the-century editors paid close attention to the state of Wisconsin as an important category for news, largely because state organizations began to matter more in Milwaukeeans' economic and social lives. A typical 1895 state column alerted readers to a newly incorporated company, a change in fishermen's rights, a post office recently opened in the town of Gertrude, a strike at a shoe factory, and a meeting of the dentists of southern Wisconsin.[20] This news could be put to use by readers active in broader regional sales, politics, or investing. And just as regional news in Chicago papers strengthened midwestern identity, Wisconsin news cultivated statewide identity, pride, and activism. The *Sentinel*'s front-page daily series "Mayors of Wisconsin," articles on new public libraries across the state, and notices of new municipal water works all cultivated pride in Wisconsin's progressive, active state and municipal governments.[21]

On a city rather than a state level, Milwaukee's turn-of-the-century papers moved beyond standard local news beats and printed colorful feature stories that enriched readers' sense of place. Milwaukee, though not as baffling or enormous as a city like New York, was growing beyond the immediate recognition of most readers. Between 1910 and 1920, the city annexed suburban areas and increased its square mileage by more than 50 percent.[22] New arrivals—Eastern European and Russian Jews, Greeks, and African American migrants—began moving into the Third Ward, the Sixth Ward, and Tory Hill, while the second and third generations of German, Polish, and Irish settlers moved into more prosperous peripheral neighborhoods and suburbs. Milwaukee's newspapers stepped in to explain and interpret the more sprawling, diverse, and stratified city and to define the personality of this growing place. The *Milwaukee Sentinel* sent an artist to sketch the swimmers (including the mayor) dipping into the river in the August heat of 1898 (fig. 5.1). One reporter interviewed the city's corps of messenger boys and explained their many duties.[23] The *Journal* printed a regular cartoon summary of the week's happenings and showed Milwaukeeans enduring the weather, celebrating holidays, or marching in protest.[24] These articles gave readers a working knowledge of their city and, as in New York City, formulated a coherent identity for a changing metropolis.

While editors crafted a distinct character for the city in local features, they also relegated most local news to page 3. This placement implied that Milwaukee, in the grand scheme of things, was not so important. In keeping with this message, Milwaukee newspaper coverage in many spheres paid closer attention to other cities than it did to Milwaukee itself. Milwaukee papers' business sections, for example, shifted their focus in the early twentieth century from the local market to an integrated national market centered in New York. Nineteenth-century Milwaukee editors had generally listed local stocks and agricultural prices first on their business page, followed by information from regional hubs like Chicago, Minneapolis, and Saint Louis. Charts of New York's stocks and bonds came last. This order reflected a nineteenth-century economy in which Milwaukee had received most of its goods from midwestern farmers and manufacturers and shipped those goods back out to midwestern destinations. As the nation developed more efficient freight systems and more sophisticated markets, however, the scope of Milwaukee's trade broadened. Brokers in New York City speculated on and set many of the nation's prices. Chicago's Board of Trade determined regional agricultural flows. So in the first decade of the twentieth century, each Milwaukee paper granted pride of place to Wall Street. They listed New York stocks and bonds first, Chicago prices second, and Milwaukee prices last. This simple reorganization indicated that Milwaukee business now rose and fell with the trends of Wall Street, and it depicted New York as the center of the financial universe—even for readers living hundreds of miles away in Wisconsin.

Newspapers turned Milwaukee readers' attention outward with their fashion and society features as well. Even before Milwaukee papers began printing fashion news, wealthy women there had regarded Paris and New York as fashion meccas. By importing fashion news from these places, Milwaukee newspapers catered to readers' existing preferences but also spread and reinforced the idea that Paris and New York tastes ruled the fashion world.[25] The *Milwaukee Journal* of the 1890s described the fashions seen on Paris streets.[26] The *Free Press* clipped a *New York Times* column, "In the Shops," which told readers nothing about Milwaukee shops, but instead described the styles of dishes and silverware that fashionable New Yorkers were buying.[27] Even Gimbels, a department store that had originated in Milwaukee, noted in its ads what was selling well in its New York stores.[28]

above the North avenue bridge, but it holds out its charms in vain, the space of about a block south from the bridge carrying off the honors. The swimming patronage is divided impartially between three large establishments there, just as

by having recourse to the city natatorium, but these cannot be considered as competitors of the swimming schools. A natatorium, and especially one that is enclosed, smacks too much of the bath tub to draw regular patrons away from the river. Swimming outdoors is to be pre-

up the paraphernalia. Simple as the whole affair was, it was ample for the patronage of those days, the swimmers finding it no inconvenience to walk along the clay bluff from the bridge. Eleven years ago the school was moved to its present location. A woman's department was added, and

Private Secretary Dunn Cuts no Ice—In Summer.

was the case last season, and each one appears to do a thriving business. At Rohn's, which is the pioneer establishment, a long row of new dressing rooms have had to be built to accommodate the increased business. At Whittaker's, the next in the scale of priority, there are increased facilities, while the Bechstein-Martens place, now in its second year, the original plant was so large that the season's business has been well taken care of. The weather this season has been rather cool as a rule and has had its effect on the crowds, but with warmer weather last year's record will be easily beaten. Some idea of the magnitude of the swimming activity may be had from the fact that an adding together of the largest respective Sunday records of the three establishments for last season makes a total of 2,000 persons.

The Source of Profit.

Considering these figures, it may be readily imagined that Milwaukee pays well for its proneness to swim during the summer months. A large proportion of those who go to swimming school are already able to swim, but there are many who are not yet proficient, and each season the

ferred to swimming in the house any day in the week—during the summer, months.

A Father's Reflections.

There are families in Milwaukee, especially among the German-Americans, whose members have all gone through a swimming course at one of the river schools, and a footing of the aggregate tuition fees paid would make quite a formidable figure.

"I spent thousands of dollars to have my children learn music, and hundreds of dollars, I might say, to have them learn to swim," said a well-known citizen, the other day, as he stood watching the swimmers at Whittaker's, "and now they hardly ever play and hardly ever go into the water."

Women Learn to Swim.

The number of women who learn to swim is quite large. Each one of the schools has provided a special department for them and special instructors are present during the special hours. Contrary to general opinion women are nearly as apt pupils as men. Louis Rohn says there are girls that learn quicker than some boys.

"Come over this way," he said, yesterday, pointing to the north end of his establishment, where the women do their swimming. "See that little girl out there? That girl learned to swim in three lessons,

this is taken care of by Mr. Whittaker's daughters. He has now among his patrons the sons of some of his old time customers, and he keeps just as careful watch of them as he did of their fathers.

The Mayor on the Toboggan.

There was a notable party at Whittaker's something like a week ago. It consisted of the city administration, or the component parts thereof. The mayor rode with the rest of them in an ordinary street car and his private secretary, Michael Dunn, the erstwhile iceman, held an umbrella over his head as he alighted and walked down the steps leading to the dock. The first thing the party did, when all were in bathing costumes, was to take possession of the water toboggan, an incised plane constructed of oilcloth, and then three by three they slid down into the water. For fully an hour they disported themselves, utterly oblivious to the fact that a man on the bridge was using up rolls of films in taking snap shots at them.

If you suffer from sores, boils, pimples, or if your nerves are weak and your system run down, you should take Hood's Sarsaparilla.

For new Bankruptcy law blanks address Legal Blank department, Sentinel, Milwaukee, Wis.

Department for Women at a River Swimming School.

5.1 Illustrations from "Where Milwaukeeans Swim." *Milwaukee Sentinel*, 7 August 1898, 4.

(Gimbels eventually became more famous as a New York institution than a Milwaukee one, in part through its rivalry with Macy's.) On society pages, Milwaukee papers took most of their cues from New York and Washington, with occasional updates from London. Articles such as "Olive Beauties— Famous Brunettes of New York" and "George Gould's Interesting Family" turned New York's upper echelon into national celebrities.[29] Reporters re-layed standards set in New York and Washington, from the ideal number of guests at a dinner party to the perfect country home.[30] They assumed that these standards would be inherently interesting in Milwaukee.

Special New York columns in turn-of-the-century newspapers built that city up as the national prototype for urban life. The columns, from the *Milwaukee Herold und Seebote*'s "New Yorker Zick-Zack" to the *Evening Wisconsin*'s "Seen and Heard in Gay New York," detailed that city's every-day events: real estate deals, roulette games, vaudeville shows, and street scams.[31] The columns gave the impression that nearly everything that happened in New York City was somehow notable and that this news connected Milwaukee readers to the urban cutting edge.

The detailed coverage of life in the nation's great metropolises stimulated Milwaukee's local journalism in some unexpected ways. Editors stopped assuming that Milwaukee had any intrinsic importance. Instead, they measured Milwaukee's standing by its connections to bigger, richer cities. Social columns such as "Heard in the Hotels" listed visitors to the city's elite hotels and relayed the political and business news that those travelers brought from afar.[32] In one regular *Journal* column, the author chatted with visitors, from lumbermen to prison wardens, about their areas of expertise.[33] Newspapers' theater sections turned visits from national and international stars into sources of excitement and pride. When the city hosted meetings, from the annual state teachers' convention to the meeting of German Catholic Societies, papers printed portraits of the groups' leaders and described their work in detail. These articles argued for Milwaukee's cosmopolitanism by highlighting how Milwaukee hosted, learned from, and enjoyed the very best people and ideas from elsewhere.

Milwaukee's newspapers also asserted national status by showcasing local products and people that circulated elsewhere in the wider world. This trend started in social columns, which noted families that had traveled to other cities and countries. The city's editors even scanned New York newspapers' hotel columns and reported which Milwaukeeans were staying there.[34] Eventually, articles provided in-depth profiles of residents who had earned national or international recognition, such as playwrights succeeding in New York or artists winning praise in European circles. When the 1914 *Sentinel* declared "Milwaukee Boy Best Fullback in Kansas," all of the paper's readers could delight in the native son who had made good.

5.2 The business directory for Milwaukee that ran in the *Sentinel* featured an illustration of a booming downtown. *Milwaukee Sentinel*, 27 January 1895, 13.

Major Milwaukee manufacturers, meanwhile, used newspaper advertisements to turn themselves into points of local pride. Jaeger's bread declared itself a world-class product, "Shipped from Milwaukee All over the Country. Eaten and Enjoyed Everywhere."[35] Pabst Brewing Company claimed "Our Bottled Beers Are the Standard the World over for Age, Purity and Strength, the Sales Amounting to 17,000,000 Bottles a Year."[36] Each of these ads and stories underlined the idea that national approval mattered more than local opinion.

Milwaukee's newspapers became some of the city's most avid boosters; if they could convince residents and investors of the city's promise, they stood to gain subscribers and advertisers. The *Sentinel* and the *Evening Wisconsin* published books that talked up Milwaukee as a center for business and industry.[37] The *Sentinel* printed a special industrial edition in 1906 that declared "Milwaukee Is in a Current of Progress and Prosperity—It Is a Tide That Will Flow on Triumphantly."[38] Much of this material tried to make Milwaukee seem important by ascribing to it the same qualities as bigger cities. The *Evening Wisconsin* illustrated its local news column, "About Town," with an impressive skyline—quite similar to the one heading the paper's New York column.[39] The image over the *Sentinel*'s business directory sketched a thriving, dense downtown (fig. 5.2). In a local advertising portion of the 1919 *Journal*, the paper tried to boost Milwaukee while comparing it to other places. The text simultaneously declared Milwaukee's importance and its inferiority: "Milwaukee Is the Second Largest Industrial Center in the United States. Your Every Need Can Be Supplied Right in Milwaukee."[40]

No matter how boosterish, all of this material communicated to readers that Milwaukee was not, in fact, the center of the universe. Local features did delve into the inner workings of Milwaukee, and they declared city life to be an absorbing topic in itself. But from the Paris fashion notes, Washington society columns, Wall Street stocks, and theater circuit gossip, readers would gather that other places generated more ideas, more celebrities, and more money than Milwaukee did. Even local claims to fame subtly reinforced Milwaukee's minor-city status, for they all self-consciously insisted that Milwaukee was just as good as *other* places.

As they decentered Milwaukee from readers' universes, though, newspapers offered readers wider views. In the past, only those who could afford to travel, to buy and read literature, or to subscribe to a (sometimes quite expensive) daily paper could access this kind of knowledge about the Western world's great metropolises. Turn-of-the-century newspapers suddenly allowed readers to purchase that information for only pennies a day. As one editor expressed it in 1909, "What travel and art has done for the few, the newspapers do for the many."[41] If imported newspaper material perhaps diminished Milwaukee's standing in readers' minds, it also put the city in national, even global perspective, recalibrating readers' sense of place.

SHARED AND SYNDICATED NEWS

Long before the invention of syndication, U.S. newspapers borrowed each other's material in what was called the "exchange" system. According to this system's informal ethical code, editors could borrow anything they liked so long as they also contributed original material that others might borrow in turn.[42] From the early nineteenth century onward, local editors subscribed to dozens of newspapers and magazines and reprinted the most amusing bits on their own editorial pages. Editors relied, too, on recycled pieces of classic literature.[43] A few late nineteenth-century entrepreneurs looked at the arenas where newspapers consistently borrowed material— fiction, women's columns, entertainment—and recognized that they could distribute that material quickly and efficiently. Tillotson & Son, a British syndication firm, began to sell fiction and London correspondence to U.S. newspapers in the 1870s. In 1884, S. S. McClure quit his job at *Century* magazine in order to syndicate fiction, either commissioning it or asking his wife to translate stories from French or German.[44] Irving Bacheller offered columns from New York and European correspondents, and Edward Bok distributed the New York gossip column "Bab's Babble" to an enthusiastic national audience.[45] Editors were quick to recognize the benefits of syndicate service material. "Its advantages are first, economy," noted the trade paper the *Journalist*. "The subscriber gets first class matter at from one-half to one-twentieth the price it usually pays to local writer [*sic*]. Second, it supplies better matter than what its subscribers are able to obtain."[46] Syndicates enlisted some of the world's most famous writers, such as Jack London, Ella Wheeler Wilcox, Frederick Douglass, and Rudyard Kipling. They coordinated simultaneous printings among all of their customers, allowing each subscribing paper to call the material "first-run" or "original." By the 1890s, newspapers in Milwaukee and most other U.S. cities were printing material from a host of syndicators.

Copyright laws in the late nineteenth century boosted syndicators' business because they cut down on the amount of material available for free exchange. An 1879 post office rule banned the mailing of materials that violated copyright. The editors at *Life* magazine, tired of having their copy pillaged by newspapers, used this law to file suits against newspapers.[47] The 1891 Chace Act, which allowed foreign authors to secure U.S. copyrights, ended the practice of mining British newspapers for free content.[48] Because borrowed material now carried some risk (and stigma), editors looked to source more of their articles from syndicates. If only syndicate services would sell a broader range of articles, the *Journalist* argued in 1887, "it will make the much-abused exchange editor a thing of the past and do largely away with the intellectual scissors and the encyclopedic paste-pot."[49]

Syndicates targeting nineteenth-century country newspapers often provided both text and images, but syndicates servicing the era's city papers could not illustrate their material for technical reasons. Beginning in the 1870s, a type of syndicate called newspaper unions had sold preprinted newsprint to country papers or sold heavy metal plates (called boilerplates) that country papers could use to print a page or two within their local paper.[50] Because country papers used hand-set type and flat presses, these methods saved them a good deal of labor and provided more elaborate features than they could afford to print on their own. Metropolitan editors generally did not care to run whole sheets of syndicated content, and neither half-printed newsprint nor inflexible boilerplate sheets would work in their high-volume rotary presses. Instead, city editors purchased galley proofs—unpublished paper copies of the text for sale. They would then have their own staff reset the text for printing in their high-speed presses, either by hand or, beginning in the 1880s, using a linotype machine.

The design possibilities for metropolitan syndication expanded with the invention of the stereotype plate, a thinner and more flexible printing medium. Syndicators would draw up features with elegant letters and illustrations, then cast multiple stereotype plates and send them to any subscribing newspaper. Stereotypes were easier to ship, and printers could cut them up into separate pieces, rearrange them and integrate them with local material as they saw fit. The American Press Association, a syndicate service, shipped a miter box and a saw to each newspaper office that bought its stereotype plates.[51] Over the next few years, metropolitan syndicates also began offering "mats" and "cuts," easily shipped papier-mâché castings and thin metal printing sheets that reproduced high-quality images and even photographs. These technologies turned newspapers into patchworks of syndicated and local, text and image.

As city papers began purchasing and printing reams of syndicated features, independent syndicates like Bacheller's and McClure's expanded, and the country's largest newspapers all established their own syndicate companies. Newspaper chains, too, often sold their material to any noncompetitor. Milwaukee editors could flip through the syndicates' advertisements in *Editor & Publisher* and choose from among hundreds of features on offer. Just by phoning in their order, those editors could easily create a new children's page, print an automobile column, or start a comics section from scratch. The bigger Milwaukee newspapers purchased syndicated material in part to be able to compete with what readers might find in the *Chicago Tribune* or the *Chicago Herald-Examiner*, which would gladly deliver to Milwaukee. The city's smaller papers used syndicated material to quickly catch up to their more established peers. When the *Milwaukee Free Press* launched in 1902, it did not bother trying to assemble its own women's page but, instead, purchased women's material on the news market. By 1910 it distributed a women's Sunday magazine as beautifully illustrated and as expertly written as anything its competitors offered, which it assembled entirely from syndicates.[52]

Syndicates' enticing offerings did not persuade Milwaukee editors to outsource all of their features. Instead, editors funneled their money and effort into the local stories they could not buy elsewhere. Each newspaper invested in custom-illustrated plates for column headings (such as that skyline in the *Evening Wisconsin*'s "About Town"), portraits of the politicians that dominated the headlines, and sketches of the city's new buildings or major factories. Most papers contracted with a local engraving firm to help them with this work at first; eventually they acquired the machinery and the staff to stamp out their own printing plates.[53] Between about 1895 and 1915, even though new illustration techniques raised production costs, many Milwaukee papers could craft local material that was just as compelling as their syndicated content.

At the same time, newspapers took full advantage of the specialized offerings of syndicate services. Women's pages and children's pages addressed each population's special concerns. So did columns on readers' hobbies, such as gardening, hunting, needlework, or bridge. Syndicated features spoke to housekeepers, fishermen, the lovelorn, and the unemployed. Fiction, too, began to carve out niche audiences; by the turn of the century, syndicators offered catalogs of swashbuckling adventures, murder mysteries, and domestic dramas—all aimed at different audiences within the same paper.[54] These special features, while catering to more specific audiences than ever before, remained in another sense wholly generic, for they ignored the specificities of place. Nowhere is this more obvious than in syndicated features that played on readers' common experiences of city life.

By the early twentieth century, U.S. cities shared enough basic traits that syndicates could create generic urban images that stood in for all cities. Engineers and architects took commissions in many different places, so nearly identical factories and downtown businesses sprouted up in state after state. Some builders ordered entire cast-iron buildings out of catalogs; many others hired Italian immigrants as stonemasons, so that baroque cornices and terra-cotta placards decorated buildings from Boston to New Orleans. The Olmsted firm, responsible for New York's Central Park and Prospect Park, designed thousands of parks and cemeteries over a span of more than sixty years.[55] Believers in the City Beautiful ideal constructed Greek-columned, domed public buildings set on symmetrical, Renaissance-style grounds, everywhere from Harrisburg to Denver. City planners used zoning—a tool nearly unheard of in 1900 but popular by the mid-1920s—to carry out similar agendas across the country.[56] Optimistic about the automobile's ability to disperse overcrowded neighborhoods, the planners of the 1920s built parkways—curving, landscaped freeways that enabled speedy suburban commutes.

So in spite of its peculiarities—German-inspired architecture and a long lakefront—much of Milwaukee's physical landscape would have looked familiar to urbanites across the nation. Its brewing complexes looked little different from Philadelphia's carpet mills or Pittsburgh's foundries. Its Iron Block Building on Wisconsin Avenue resembled the cast-iron buildings of New York's SoHo or Louisville's West Main district. The paths in Forest Home Cemetery meandered just like those in Brooklyn's Greenwood Cemetery and Oakland's Mountain View Cemetery. And its parkway system, designed in 1923 and approved by the city government in 1925, swirled through Milwaukee much like Eastern Parkway in the Bronx and Beach Drive in Washington, DC.

Just because urban Americans worked in similar buildings and drove on similar roads did not mean that they lived similar lives. But physical similarities between cities allowed news syndicates and national advertisers to render urban life in a way that Milwaukeeans—and Pittsburghers and Louisvillians and Washingtonians—would understand. One such generic "city life" image appeared on the back page of the 1907 *Milwaukee Journal* (fig. 5.3). The tall, narrow downtown buildings, the clock tower, and the church spire could have been spotted in Milwaukee or in nearly any other city in America.

Syndicates capitalized on cultural and ethnic commonalities in Ameri-

5.3 A syndicate probably provided this full-page image, and the *Milwaukee Journal* simply filled in the blanks with local advertisements. It shows generic urban architecture but also generic urban types: delivery boy, policeman, dapper man about town. *Milwaukee Journal*, 22 June 1907, 12.

can cities as well. Irish and German immigrants had flooded into the United States in the mid-nineteenth century, and by the early twentieth century, nearly any city dweller would have encountered these groups firsthand. (Germans and the Irish contrasted with immigrant groups such as Scandinavians, Poles, and Russian Jews, who clustered in specific regions.) This enabled William Randolph Hearst to syndicate "Mr. Dooley," a wildly popular fictional columnist who spouted commonsense wisdom in a thick Irish accent, and the *Katzenjammer Kids*, whose protagonists got into trouble every Sunday while speaking an inelegant hybrid of English and German.[57] Other syndicated features turned urban entertainments, and their audiences, into subjects readers could recognize (fig. 5.4). W. E. Hill's beautifully drawn feature *Among Us Mortals*—distributed by the *Chicago Tribune* and printed in the *Milwaukee Journal*—observed city people in broadly recognizable situations. Because the rituals of city life had developed along parallel lines in many places, readers could laugh along with the artist at the follies of the "typical" city people that appeared under headings such as "The Amateur Vaudeville," "The Apartment House," and "Modern Art."[58]

Syndicated features on country people spoofed rural ways, solidifying readers' sense of themselves as urbanites. *In Hickville* and *Punkinville Paragrafs*, both in the *Sentinel*, entertained readers with small cartoons with dialogues or sayings underneath. *Little Stories Told in Homely Rhyme* presented episodes and advice in country slang for readers who had ostensibly left such simple ways behind.[59] Even when these country folk spouted wisdom, it came out in countrified dialect: "The feller who's allus goin' around givin' free advice," explained Hickville resident Amos Crabb, "never seems to have any worth takin' which is probably why it's free."[60]

Material for city readers potentially reshaped the way readers thought about themselves. After laughing in recognition at the caricatures in features, a Milwaukee resident may have used that same visual and verbal vocabulary to understand and talk about his own urban life. After scoffing at country folks' antics, another reader might have felt more refined and more urban in comparison. Over time, these features could move newspaper readers to identify more strongly not just as Milwaukeeans or Angelenos or Atlantans but as *city* people.

NEWSPAPERS NATIONALIZE

Mass culture made syndication possible. It enabled syndicated writers to reference shared experiences—such as shopping at chain stores, watching traveling sports leagues, listening to music on records, and watching movies—and to assume that their readers' lives followed broadly simi-

5.4 A *Milwaukee Sentinel* comic strip shows theatergoers chitchatting during an intermission. Though the strip had actually been drawn up at the *New York Evening World*, the cast of types might strike any urban reader as familiar, enabling the *Sentinel* to retitle it "Somewhere in Milwaukee." *Milwaukee Sentinel*, 8 October 1918, 7.

lar patterns of work and play. The process worked both ways, though. As mass culture created audiences for syndicated features, those features supported, strengthened, and spread mass culture. Syndicated news provided the standardized diet of information that trained American audiences to buy, wear, eat, watch, and desire the same things, no matter where they lived.

Syndicates helped to turn national (rather than local) sports into a mainstay of U.S. popular culture in the twentieth century. Syndicated articles stirred up excitement about Harvard and Yale football matches even though few readers had any direct ties to those schools.[61] The same held true for national leagues. "Hundreds of thousands of newspaper readers who have never seen a major league baseball game," commented a Wisconsin journalism professor in 1916, "follow day by day the doings of the various teams and players, not merely during the playing season but throughout the greater part of the year."[62] The syndicated columns "Sportlight" by Grantland Rice and "Along the Sport Trail" by George H. Phair, together with syndicated daily sports cartoons, turned faraway athletes into household names in Milwaukee.[63] Elite sports such as golf, tennis, motorcycling, and auto racing were too expensive for most readers to try for themselves, but they could vicariously participate by reading syndicated coverage of those sports' national tournaments.[64]

In a parallel process, syndicated news acquainted Milwaukee readers with a national roster of celebrities and kept them abreast of national fads. Syndicated comics and humor columns alternately encouraged and discouraged women from cutting off their hair, publicizing the bobbed-hair trend of the 1920s. The *Milwaukee Sentinel* printed syndicated sheet music for the "Dolly Dip" so that readers could play and dance the tango right at home.[65] "Let *Wisconsin News* Teach You How to Charleston," offered the city's Hearst paper.[66] Women's sections offered interviews with theater and movie stars that discussed their personal lives and also their beauty secrets. "The Ziegfeld Follies girls are the last word in beauty and grace," said one, and then asked, "How do they do it?"[67] Syndicated how-to columns coached readers in newly popular games like basketball.[68]

While some newspaper features spread fads or boosted celebrity careers, others worked their way into the fabric of American life, becoming touchstones of popular culture themselves. Richard Outcault's comic-strip character Buster Brown endeared himself to readers all over the country and helped to sell loads of the spinoff product, Buster Brown shoes. Nell Brinkley drew beautiful wild-haired girls in features for Hearst, and soon the nation was referencing modern "Brinkley girls" and buying the Brinkley hair wavers and bob curlers that the artist endorsed.[69] The words that syndicated cartoonists invented for their characters' actions and sounds—

"plop," "grr," "kapow"—entered the American language. So did a few expressions minted by comics characters, as when Barney Google made "googly eyes" at a beautiful woman or got "the heebie-jeebies."[70] *Keeping Up with the Joneses* began as a comic strip about a family trying hard to appear as prosperous and happy as the neighbors; it struck such a chord with readers that the expression is still used today.[71] Robert LeRoy Ripley's long-lived newspaper feature "Believe it or Not" spawned a radio program and a franchise that continued through the twentieth and into the twenty-first century. Dorothy Dix's syndicated columns and advice manuals turned her into a household reference; ministers even used her words as the basis for their sermons.[72] Popular songs asked columnist Beatrice Fairfax for relationship advice; she broadcasted on the radio and her character starred in a 1916 series of silent films.[73]

A few syndicated features offered products for sale, standardizing not only readers' vocabularies and tastes but also their clothes and their houses. Every Milwaukee paper at some point offered a daily dress pattern for sale; Milwaukee women sported the same styles as home seamstresses in dozens of other cities, whether they knew it or not. Mail-order house plans, appearing in syndicated columns such as the *Evening Wisconsin*'s "Homes of Character," spread prototypical styles—bungalow, colonial, Spanish-Italian—to hundreds of urban and suburban neighborhoods.[74]

Syndicated news helped to build a more nationally uniform culture with its fads, celebrities, comics, expressions, and goods. It also offered a nationally standardized version of U.S. history. Because history features needed to market to papers in every region, they nearly always told national, not regional, tales. The *Journal* bought the comic strip *High Lights of History* from the McClure syndicate; in it, dramatic battles of the Revolution and Civil War unfolded.[75] "Today in History" singled out a nationally significant historic event for each day's editorial page, and the feature "Daily Birthday Party" celebrated the birth of some illustrious American.[76] History education in schools varied widely by region; no national curriculum existed, and some states never enforced curriculum standards.[77] Newspapers' versions of U.S. history helped to align readers' understandings of the national past.

As feature syndicates grew, they damaged local feature reporting. Milwaukee editors found it difficult to justify the expense of producing local features when they could so easily share or outsource those costs. In the 1910s and 1920s, the city's leading papers still ran special articles on Milwaukee's businesses, its politics, and its celebrations. Most kept daily or weekly local columns on issues dear to Milwaukee readers, such as bowling, skat, the outdoors, local theater, and society. Few papers launched their own regular full-page features, though, to rival those that they purchased from syndicates. The *Journal*'s "Worker's Page" was the exception that proved the rule. Immediately after the city elected a socialist roster of politicians to city office in 1910, the *Journal* designated a special editor to compile a daily feature of interest to all workers. The "Worker's Page" reported on the labor movement with articles on exploitative child labor practices in the U.S. South, the British system of old age pensions, and local department stores' salary systems. It offered detailed budgeting advice for young couples hoping to buy a home, discussed the potential profits of backyard vegetable gardens, and outlined the benefits and hazards of working for relatives. And it printed regular columns of "Workers' Tips" and "Workisms" geared to the industrial laborer:

When one roughing cut will do on lathe work, do not make two out of it.
Use shellac for the base when repainting a sign over red and the color will
    not bleed through and spoil the appearance of the job.
Never take for granted that a reamer will ream to size.[78]

A page like this required an editor to write or compile material, a staff photographer to gather images, a staff artist to design a heading and sketch some illustrations, and a printer to cast the whole thing for the press. While the *Journal* may have hoped that interest in the labor issue would increase both in Milwaukee (boosting the *Journal*'s circulation) and elsewhere (perhaps enabling it to sell material to other papers), it was not so lucky. The "Worker's Page" disappeared by 1915.[79]

Newspapers in the 1910s and 1920s worked alongside other mass media that forged a national culture and diminished American regional cultures. Radio brought broadcasts from around the country into families' living rooms, letting all listeners sing along to the same music and laugh at the same jokes. In these ways it seemed to connect and unify Americans. But radio also made listeners aware of and self-conscious about their regional accents, often for the first time. It prompted national debates over proper pronunciation, which eventually resulted in a standardized, placeless broadcast dialect.[80] The era's silent movies instantly spread national standards for beauty and fashion, sparked dance fads, and created more uniform romantic expectations.[81] After watching movies, readers may have found regional dances, clothes, and marriage traditions to be quaint or outmoded. As each of these mass media helped to build a more homogenous national culture, each also weakened the regional cultures that had developed during a less-connected age.

Despite their more specialized markets, Milwaukee's foreign-language papers were not immune to the standardizing forces of the syndicate system. Milwaukee boasted five foreign-language dailies around the turn of the century: one Polish and four German. In the 1880s, the circulations of Milwaukee's leading German-language dailies just barely trailed those of their English-language counterparts.[82] In their efforts to outshine their competitors, to provide top-notch news, and to bring in ad contracts, German-language papers in Milwaukee relied on some of the very same syndicates and agencies that English-language papers used.

German papers could subscribe to direct wire service from Germany, but many used American services. The American Press Association, primarily an English-language firm, offered a German-language syndication service.[83] The *Milwaukee Herold* contracted with the Associated Press beginning in 1875.[84] Because text could be easily translated, German-language papers syndicated fiction by writers such as Mark Twain and Bret Harte.[85] Designed features were trickier, but German-language papers still bought them. When the *Germania Abendpost* printed *Chicago Herald* cartoons, it translated the titles, but left the hand-lettered dialogue in English.[86] By the 1920s, the *Milwaukee Sonntagspost* was purchasing and translating its sports articles and its entire women's page from U.S. services.[87] German-language papers contracted with ad agencies that placed national-brand ads in local papers; Milwaukee readers browsed German-language ads for Ford automobiles, Baker's Cocoa, Stetson hats, and all of the city's department stores (fig. 5.5).[88] The *Herold und Sonntagspost* even promised to help advertisers place their products in German-owned grocery stores, so readers would easily be able to find these mass-market goods.[89]

Milwaukee's German-language papers became more "American" over time as they ran standardized material and as they imitated basic patterns in the English-language press. During the 1880s and 1890s, they adopted the narrow columns, banner headlines, and separate sports and women's sections of their English-language peers. Papers that had once championed beloved German pastimes such as orchestral music and gymnastics began covering unmistakably American entertainments such as vaudeville and baseball.[90] They eventually dropped their distinctive Fraktur script for the Roman letters that English-language papers used. Between their syndicated content, mass-market ads, and reporting that focused on the United States more than on Germany, German-language newspapers thoroughly versed their readers in U.S. culture. "It seems fairly clear that what the foreign-language press actually does, whether or not the editors desire it, is to facilitate the adjustment of the foreign born to the American environment," wrote Robert Ezra Park in 1922.[91] In this sense, Milwaukee's German-language press played a role similar to ethnic radio stations, neighborhood social clubs, and immigrant banks. Each of these institutions catered to immigrants in their native languages but ultimately assimilated immigrant communities into the U.S. mainstream.[92]

Milwaukee's German-language press survived the hostile political climate of World War I, but just barely. At first, when war broke out in Europe,

5.5 In this advertisement, some of the text remains in English, either because it includes the brand and model name or because it was technically too difficult to change (being incorporated into the border at the bottom, for example.) The smallest text is set in Fraktur type, the most common script for German-language newspapers through the 1920s. *Milwaukee Herold*, 20 January 1920, automobile section, 3.

German-language papers' circulations surged. German Americans who wanted in-depth war news (or who mistrusted the information in the English-language press) doubled the *Milwaukee Germania*'s readership during the war.[93] But German-language reporting also attracted serious suspicion. In 1917, a federal act demanded that foreign-language papers provide their local postmaster with translations, at their own expense, of all war-related articles. Wartime vigilantes took things further. Papers being shipped to subscribers disappeared off of mail cars. Cleveland Boy Scouts burned bundles of the *Wächter und Anzeiger*. Newsstands and newsboys boycotted German-language papers; so did advertisers.[94] In Milwaukee, the *Journal* began printing the *Germania*'s editorials in English, in an ongoing exposé of what they called traitorous propaganda.[95] This allowed Milwaukee, the most German city in the nation, to proclaim itself hyperpatriotic. In response, the sobered editor of the *Germania-Herold* issued a pledge of loyalty and began printing articles supplied by the Committee for Public Information, the federal propaganda service.[96] The *Germania* building, with its five copper domes in the shape of Prussian army helmets, remained standing, but the building's bronze statue, *Lady Germania*, disappeared one night in 1917 and was rumored to have been sunk to the bottom of Lake Michigan.

The consolidation of the city's German-language papers in the first decades of the twentieth century sapped Milwaukee's German communities of some of their diversity and vitality. In the 1890s, Milwaukee had offered different German-language papers for Catholics and for Lutherans, for political moderates and for radicals. By 1918, the *Seebote*, *Germania*, *Abendpost*, and *Herold* had all merged into a single paper. The circulation of the merged paper fell from 37,296 in 1918 to 27,636 in 1929.[97] Slackening demand for German-language news (due to the dwindling influx of Germans) meant that papers had to rely more heavily on English-language syndicate services; U.S.-based German-language syndicates no longer existed, and World War I had made it politically dangerous to syndicate directly from Germany. Editors had to pay staff to translate syndicated material, just at the moment that it was becoming harder to hire translators. Readers, prepared by years of American-style journalism in German, made the leap to English-language news.

It might seem that the syndication system would hurt the African American press as it did the foreign-language press, but black papers could borrow and syndicate nearly as easily as mainstream dailies. The *Wisconsin Weekly Advocate*, which served Milwaukee's small turn-of-the-century black population and African Americans throughout the state, clipped articles from dozens of other publications, from *Harper's Weekly* and *Century Magazine* to the *Cleveland Gazette* and the *Philadelphia Press*. It syndicated the gossip column "Bab's Babble" from Bok Syndicate Press and purchased feature stories such as page-long profiles of the Philippines and Puerto Rico, newly acquired U.S. colonies.[98] In the 1910s the *Chicago Defender* made a pitch for Milwaukee readers with columns titled "Along the North Shore" and "Badger State News." The *Defender*, like the *Weekly Advocate*, made use of mainstream syndicate services. It ran comic strips from the McClure syndicate and subscribed to wire services for international news. It could choose the articles that would most interest *Defender* readers and rewrite reports to reflect the paper's own politics.

While the 1924 immigration cutoff dealt a serious blow to the foreign-language press, the black press catered to an expanding, increasingly literate population. And in contrast to immigrants whose children switched over to English-language news, African American readers could remain loyal to their black weeklies for generations.[99] Recognizing an opportunity, journalists founded six news syndicates to serve black papers between 1900 and 1920. The largest of them, the Associated Negro Press, sold to over a hundred black weeklies by 1922.[100] National brands that catered to African American customers, such as Pluko hair tonic and OKeh Records, took out ad space in black weeklies across the country. Together, national-brand ads and national news services standardized the look and feel of America's black papers, though there remained a palpable difference between the papers of more militant Northern editors and those of their cautious Southern counterparts.[101]

While syndicated news and nationally distributed ads served the black press reasonably well, mass-produced illustrations did not. The *Wisconsin Weekly Advocate* purchased stock images from plate-service companies. The heading for the woman's column, then, pictured a white housewife, and the illustrations for fiction showed white protagonists. In ads for national brands, the people taking Cascarets Candy Cathartic, drinking California Fig Syrup, and eating Libby's Mince Meat were all white. The only black people who appeared in the newspaper were either the subjects of the news or the faces illustrating ads for African American brands. Almost invariably, these brands sold products to lighten skin or straighten hair—products to make black people look whiter. Syndication opened up opportunities for black journalism; the American Negro Press could thrive alongside the Associated Press. But syndicated and standardized illustrations worked against the larger messages of black papers, reminding readers (who likely needed no reminding) that mass and consumer culture held up white skin as its norm and ideal.

Syndication Americanized the news through what it destroyed as well as through what it created. By rendering local features difficult or impossible to maintain, and by contributing to the decline of the foreign-language press, it undermined local print culture. It created a cheap alternative to local, specific illustrations, which meant that minority readers rarely saw themselves depicted in features or ads. Syndicated features diverted editors' and readers' attention from regional traditions, and newspaper mergers reduced the diversity of city journalism. The features that flowered under the new syndicated system, though, forged new common vocabularies. They cultivated a stronger sense of national history and identity and spread more uniform tastes, habits, and knowledge nationwide. Newspapers—both foreign language and English language—also Americanized immigrant populations by introducing mainstream habits and goods. Journalist Will Irwin speculated that reading syndicated news "must work to unify the national psychology—to make the next generation—East, South, West, and North—think and feel alike."[102]

Thus newspapers, and their syndicated content, built a cultural foundation for much of the politics of the early twentieth century. The images, vocabularies, and values circulated in newspapers built a more solid sense of "Americanness" that allowed the nation to rally together during World War I, but that also engendered a jingoistic political climate that framed immigrants, political leftists, and pacifists as threats. It was in that climate that Congress passed the immigration restrictions of 1924—which themselves further homogenized U.S. culture by declaring any immigrants who exceeded the quotas to be illegal aliens. By the 1920s, newspaper content was helping to define an American way of life that became both a source of domestic pride and a huge export business. A 1920 newspaper ad keenly linked newspapers' process of cultural homogenization with the nation's political and global ascendance. "The place of the newspaper," it explained, was to help build "the pleasant uniformity of American life. Here, amid a multitude of opportunities, purposes and interests, obtains a striking unity of ideals, customs and thought. This is not a hundred million individuals, but a nation on the march toward its destiny."[103]

CHAINS AND BIG-BUDGET FEATURES

Newspaper chains invaded Milwaukee in 1918. William Randolph Hearst, who by that point owned newspapers in New York, Chicago, San Francisco, Atlanta, Boston, and Los Angeles, had been looking to expand his empire. He purchased Milwaukee's *Evening Wisconsin* and its *Daily News*, then merged them into the *Wisconsin News* in 1918. To improve the new paper's chances, he also bought out the *Milwaukee Free Press*—which may have been suffering for its left-leaning politics. The *Wisconsin News* began printing in Hearst's signature style, running sensational headlines in capital letters, rallying for populist causes, and privileging entertaining and sometimes

salacious material over nuanced reporting. "BURGLARS SLAY MIL-
WAUKEE GIRL—CLUBBED IN FIGHT TO SAVE JEWELS," shouted
a typical 1921 headline.[104] Hearst could not dominate the Milwaukee market with only an afternoon sheet, so in 1924 he bought the *Milwaukee Sentinel*, too.[105]

As Hearst turned the *Sentinel* and the *Wisconsin News* into colorful papers
catering to a working-class audience, he upended the standard newspaper
formula that had emerged in U.S. cities over the past three decades. Instead
of hiring a solid team of local reporters and supplementing their work with
syndicated features, he built his papers around shared material and merely
decorated them with local news. He ran the column "Today," by Arthur
Brisbane, as the front-page featured editorial of the *Sentinel*, the *Wisconsin
News*, and every other paper he owned. He wired scandalous news stories
from other papers in his chain over to Wisconsin. And his several syndicates supplied nearly all of the features for the *Sentinel* and the *Wisconsin
News*. Editors at each paper sprinkled just a few local features among the
syndicated stories such as the *Sentinel*'s "Every Day Milwaukee," which
printed a handful of city happenings each day, and the *Wisconsin News*'s
"The Inquisitive Reporter," which polled random Milwaukee citizens on
mundane questions such as "Have you found stout persons better natured
than thin ones?"[106] Hearst also tried to replace local reporting with contests and locals' contributions, which could sell copies but required little
work from reporters and editors. Milwaukee's Hearst papers offered a dollar for every printed response on topics such as "How I Earned Pin Money"
or "What are your day dreams—what is it you hope to have or be able to do
SOME day?"[107] They paid cash prizes for trivia quizzes and asked readers
to vote on the city's most popular dogs.[108]

With the transformation of the *Wisconsin News* and *Milwaukee Sentinel*, readers in Milwaukee joined those in hundreds of other U.S. cities
who got their news from chains. In 1900, the nation's ten largest chains
claimed 12–15 percent of total daily circulation. By 1923, thirty-one chains
accounted for one-third of the nation's total daily circulation, and nearly
one-half of its Sunday circulation. Ira Copley bought out the midsize cities
of California, while Gannett Newspapers seemed to control all of upstate
New York. By 1935, Hearst alone would control 11.1 percent of daily circulation in the United States.[109] Urban morning and evening papers, which had
once operated independently, often joined forces. It became increasingly
common for one owner to publish a city's morning and evening sheet; by
1930, single chains owned both morning and evening papers in Los Angeles, San Francisco, New York, Chicago, Duluth (Minnesota), and Camden
(New Jersey).[110]

The *Wisconsin News* was not the only chain operating in 1920s Milwaukee. Woolworth's had opened up on Wisconsin Avenue, just across from Gimbels, in 1912.[111] By 1924, A&P, one of the biggest grocery chains in the nation, had an outlet on Twenty-seventh and State Street.[112] Walgreens drugstores followed in 1925.[113] Universal Studios had signed the Saxe Brothers onto its theater chain by 1923; all seven of Milwaukee's Saxe-owned theaters played only Universal pictures from then on. Warner Brothers opened is first Milwaukee theater in 1931, on the site of the former Butterfly Theater, which had been locally owned and run.[114] Chain groceries and drugstores offered good selection, uniform service, and above all, low prices. Chain movie theaters offered first-run films in luxurious settings. What none of these chains (including Hearst's) offered was a product selected for or tailored to a specific Milwaukee audience.

Just as local corner stores had to rethink their business models in order to compete with the chains, Milwaukee's independent papers responded to Hearst's arrival with new strategies. In 1920 the *Journal* launched "The Green Sheet," a two-page supplement printed on green paper, nearly all of which came from syndicates, especially E. W. Scripps's Newspaper Enterprise Association. Scripps owned over twenty newspapers in midwestern and Western cities, but because he owned no Milwaukee papers, he gladly sold his features to the *Sentinel*.[115] The Green Sheet ran such sensational stories that the publishers omitted it from home deliveries, which were more likely to reach women and children.[116] By 1927 the *Journal* had toned the sheet down in order to distribute its advice columns, word puzzles, comics, serial fiction, and human-interest stories to all subscribers.

Independent papers, like chains, began to trim down their local staffs as they ran more and more syndicated material. Milwaukee papers had previously required several reporters or at least a coordinating editor for feature sections such as the children's page or the women's page. By the 1910s and 1920s, though, many papers purchased these sections wholesale or employed a single editor to merely coordinate syndicated pieces. The pre-Hearst *Sentinel* and the *Milwaukee Free Press* both bought entire Sunday magazines from the Paul Block chain.[117] The typical Sunday staff dwindled from a turn-of-the-century high of dozens to just a handful of editors in the 1920s.[118]

The mass-distribution model gave readers access to deeper expertise than strictly local papers had ever offered. Milwaukeeans read an international affairs column by Winston Churchill and an etiquette and fashion column by Queen Marie of Romania.[119] The city's 1920s sports pages offered tips from boxing champion Jack Dempsey and playing secrets from a roster of "Famous Football Stars."[120] Scientific experts explained the pressing issues of their time to the general reader. An English scientist tackled the topic of "When did the world begin and how will it end?"

in one syndicated article, while another feature explained paleontologists' process as they unearthed a trove of dinosaur bones.[121]

With the aid of syndicates, Milwaukee papers could provide readers not just print expertise but sumptuous visuals as well. The *Sentinel*'s syndicate-produced "Illustrated Sunday Magazine" stood out from the rest of the news with its higher-quality paper, stylish typeface, and elegant illustrations. Hearst's *American Weekly* (plate 8), a generic magazine included in the Sunday *Sentinel*, set the standard for visual punch. The Milwaukee papers that produced their own Sunday magazines and feature sections stocked them with full-page or two-page spreads purchased from syndicates, complete with stylized lettering, photographs, and illustrations. Before syndication, local papers found it difficult to mount full-fledged illustrated feature stories on events abroad. When the 1914 *Sentinel* printed its own article on South Asian and Middle Eastern World War I soldiers, for example, it had to cobble together a handful of outdated pictures from books.[122] The much more sophisticated illustrations and photographs in syndicated magazines and rotogravure sections turned Sunday papers into world tours.

Syndicated articles from abroad exposed Milwaukee readers to places and cultures they might never have encountered otherwise. The *Journal*'s rotogravure section ran under an image of a globe printed with the phrase "Pictorial News; World Views." As readers flipped through the section, they could visit swimmers in Australia, diplomatic meetings in China, and the landscape of the Algerian desert.[123] *Journal* readers accompanied archeologists to Egypt in the illustrated feature "Does Spell Guard Tomb of Ancients?"; they followed diamond seekers to Brazil in another: "Guianas Lure Stone Hunters."[124] Features delved into lengthy discussions of issues such as politics in the Balkans, the German education system, and Japan's role in World War I.[125] While Americans had been vicariously traveling to foreign countries for decades through slide-lantern shows, travel books, natural history museums, world's fair displays, and film shorts, only in the 1910s and 1920s were newspapers able to immerse readers in foreign ideas and far-off places.[126]

Observers hoped that syndicated articles could ignite readers' interest in foreign affairs and inspire a broader, more global consciousness. "Syndicated articles on international topics," wrote a journalism instructor in 1926, "have enlarged the mental horizons of Americans who formerly took little or no interest in politics beyond the limits of their home counties and states."[127] And even as they highlighted difference—by showing pierced Amazonian natives or coiffed Japanese geishas—feature articles often sought out the basic similarities between subjects and readers. Articles stirred sympathy for Bolivians by talking about bonds between Bolivian mothers and children or compared the task of feeding a family in West Africa to the same task in the United States. A few observers expressed hopes that this kind of reporting could render the world a more peaceful place. "In so far as the newspaper tends to focus attention daily on the doings of the whole world," noted James Edward Rogers, "it tends to do away with the prejudice and the international and internecine hatreds which are for the most part the result of ignorance and narrowness. The world is made smaller, safer, and more habitable by the press."[128]

As World War I and World War II seemed to prove, more globally aware journalism did not lead directly to a more peaceful world. But newspapers' broad scope, vivid images, and in-depth reporting did make Milwaukee a worldlier place. Syndicated news let Milwaukee readers adopt that same entitled and empowered cosmopolitanism that appeared in New York City news articles, even though Milwaukee lay a few steps more removed from international circuits of money, people, and ideas. Features commissioned and paid for by large corporations in bigger cities brought Milwaukee residents a harvest of information, impressions, and images gathered from all around the world for the purpose of American entertainment. When syndicated features piqued a reader's interest in central Asian culture, South American sports, or quantum physics, that reader's richer information diet and his heightened ambitions were both made possible by American journalism's mass market.

Turn-of-the-century syndicated features had usually identified and addressed specific audiences. Milwaukee papers continued to buy these types of features—women's material, children's pages, sports and hobby columns—through the 1920s. But they also bought a new crop of features that addressed broad, universal needs and experiences rather than particular interests. Hearst's features editor, Moses Koenigsberg, wrote that common denominators among readers should function as "a mesh for the sifting of story values—a colander through which may be strained the items of petty or local limitations, leaving only elements of universal appeal."[129] Syndicated authors earned royalties proportional to the number of papers that bought their pieces, so they worked hard to craft articles for the broadest possible audiences.[130] A 1919 writers' manual urged feature writers to stick to a few essential categories, including "(1) timely topics, (2) unique, novel, and extraordinary persons, things, and events, (3) mysteries, (4) romance, (5) adventure, (6) contests for supremacy, (7) children, (8) animals."[131]

Journalists turned these recipes into successful features and, in the process, fashioned a more placeless, generic brand of entertainment and advice. The nostalgic cartoon panels *Just Humans* by Gene Carr and *When a Feller Needs a Friend* by Clare Briggs both depicted childhood moments that most Americans would recognize, from splashing in puddles to bonding with a loyal pet terrier.[132] Vague inspirational editorials and columns called to readers' shared desires to better themselves. Hearst's *Milwaukee Sentinel* printed Dorothy Dix's homilies, Kathleen Norris's reflections on good and bad attitudes toward daily life, and an editorial-page item titled "Right Thought to Start the Day Right."[133] The *Milwaukee Journal* countered with the inspirational coaching of Elsie Robinson's "Listen, World!" and with "Sunday School, by Angelo Patri," which taught nondenominational Christian lessons.[134]

As they tried to cater to all readers at once, many syndicates' journalists stopped commenting on the urban experience: features that spoke only to big-city readers would not necessarily sell well in smaller cities, towns, or suburbs. When the city did appear in 1920s' syndicated material, journalists presented it less as a familiar context than as a fantasy setting. The lavishly illustrated series "The Adventures of Prudence Prim," running in Hearst's *American Weekly* (plate 8), chronicled the escapades of a young woman visiting New York. Rather than setting Prudence in scenarios recognizable to city readers—the office, the streetcar, the luncheonette—cartoonist Nell Brinkley sent her off to late-night cabarets and luxurious beauty parlors. In features like this, the city became a space of exotic intrigue rather than shared everyday experience.

Syndicated material that adhered to crowd-pleasing formulas could be marketed not only across the country but also across the globe. A 1926 ad insisted that Hearst's King Features "possess that universal reader-interest which attracts readers of every race and nation," and indeed, Hearst successfully sold his features in over a dozen countries.[135] Dorothy Dix, with her common-sense advice, found audiences in Canada, Latin America, the West Indies, Europe, Asia, Africa, and Australia.[136] Slapstick comic strips, such as *Mutt and Jeff* or *Felix the Cat*, tickled readers in other nations, too.[137] While writers and illustrators may have thought they were creating universal entertainment, each feature was in fact deeply rooted in U.S.—and often U.S. urban—tropes. Dorothy Dix's folksy column was meant to provide old-fashioned countryside wisdom for modern city people. *Mutt and Jeff's* humor mimicked vaudeville routines; *Felix the Cat* used minstrel shows' visual codes.[138] Syndicates, then, spread American culture through much of the newspaper-reading world.

Journalists of the era worried that syndication could undermine their own roles as local experts and sap American journalism of all local relevance. In 1925, the director of the Medill School of Journalism, Henry Franklin Harrington, warned against "excessive use of syndicate material—especially 'canned' editorials lacking pertinent application to a concrete community."[139] Will Irwin argued that syndication had made papers lazy in their pursuit of local news. "I haven't heard a managing editor boast about a beat for years," Irwin quoted a journalist friend as saying. "No, when he's talking big to me, he tells me how he got five thousand circulation away from that fellow across the street by picking 'the Gumps' instead of 'Bringing Up Father'—or vice versa."[140] Another journalist in Irwin's article compared the newspaper editor to a movie exhibitor, who did not produce or direct films but simply chose reels and ran them.[141] The local knowledge and considered opinion that had once defined good editing and reporting seemed useless in this new arrangement.

While journalists bemoaned their papers' reliance on syndicates, readers may not have even noticed that they were reading syndicated news. "Syndicates conduct their business," one 1922 manual noted, "with less noise and public attention than any other publishing concern."[142] Local readers would never encounter the same piece twice, because services were careful to sell their features to only one paper within a given city or region. "The syndicate was practically an undefinable entity to 90 percent of newspaper buyers," supposed one syndicate editor. "Not one out of ten paused to consider the difference between articles and drawings that originated with the publication's regular staff and those that were obtained from outside agencies."[143] A magazine cartoonist imagined that only by traveling would a reader ever discover that the local papers—in town after town—looked exactly the same (fig. 5.6).

Reader reaction to syndicated features and chain newspapers never boiled over into a political outcry, a rash of antitrust suits, or a flood of letters to the editor. Yet readers did seem to notice when their newspapers tilted too heavily toward generic themes and mass-produced reports. Readers may have enjoyed syndicated features and may have appreciated syndicated coverage of the wider world, but most of them still seemed to want a daily newspaper that felt firmly rooted in place.

STRIKING A BALANCE

Although William Randolph Hearst devised a highly centralized and cost-efficient system and offered an entertaining paper, his generic brand of journalism did not take over in Milwaukee. Hearst's *Wisconsin News* gained readers in its first year, but then lost over twenty thousand in circulation between 1918 and 1922. The *Sentinel* also lost over twenty thousand readers after Hearst bought it, though his Sunday editions fared better, for they outdid the independent papers in sheer spectacle.[144] Hearst's troubles stemmed from a weakness in local reporting, which his competitors quickly pointed out. An editorial in the still-independent 1922 *Milwaukee Sentinel* accused Hearst's *Wisconsin News* of coming to inaccurate conclusions on state politics, and the 1926 *Journal* poked fun at one of Hearst's token local columns in the *Wisconsin News*, "The Inquisitive Reporter," by printing a

Sad fate of cross-country traveler confronted by identical
comic strips in seven States

5.6 This cartoon, accompanying a magazine article on syndicated news, shows a traveler driven mad by the repetitive features; he speaks in crazed sentences made up of comic-strip titles. Illustration by F. G. Cooper, in Will Irwin, "Newspapers and Canned Thought," *Collier's Weekly*, 21 June 1924, 14.

spoof version with made-up responses.[145] E. W. Scripps's chain suffered from similar problems in other cities, with its papers often selling fewer copies than any of their local competitors.[146] For every four local stories that appeared in his competitors' pages, Scripps's papers ran only one. Editors at his San Francisco, Seattle, and Fresno papers all pointed out that their readers wanted more local news, which they could not supply with their meager local staffs.[147]

Hearst slowly learned that even though readers liked scandal, celebrities, and contests, they also wanted news about themselves and their neighbors. Before Hearst had bought out the *Sentinel*, that paper had solicited local news from Milwaukee readers. "Hardly a Sunday passes that there are not ten or more special matches going on in the city," announced the 1914 sports page. "Send in the scores and let the others know what you are doing."[148] Hearst eventually reintegrated local features like this. He assigned more reporters to cover basic city beats: politics, public schools, social clubs, new buildings. He fed Milwaukee residents columns on local sports victories, photo spreads of the season's brides, and regular updates from surrounding suburbs. By fleshing out the local news, Hearst grew the *Evening Wisconsin*'s circulation all through the 1920s and managed to regain the *Sentinel* readers he had lost.

John Cockerill had imagined in 1892 that an efficient national syndication system would allow local papers to supply only what they could not import from elsewhere. Indeed, a *New York World* manager claimed in 1915 that a local editor should only "garner and winnow local news where he is beyond the competition of the metropolis" and rely on syndicates for everything else.[149] But Milwaukee's successful papers did not hew to this formula. Rather, they wove local and national reporting together, so that their news more accurately mirrored the complex mix of local and national phenomena in readers' own lives.

Milwaukee editors often tailored their syndicated pieces to their readers' needs and tastes, sometimes making them appear more local than they actually were. A woman's page editor, for example, might take a syndicated food article and substitute local food prices, swap out hard-to-find ingredients, or add pictures.[150] Editors also made small print changes to help features appear homegrown at first glance. Milwaukee papers asked readers to send questions for advice columnists Dorothy Dix, William Brady (author of "Health Talks"), and Alfred P. Lane (author of "Target Tips and Hunting Helps") to the papers' own offices, as if these columnists actually worked there.[151] By disguising the fact that these authors lived elsewhere, Milwaukee papers allowed readers to think of each advice personality as a trusted friend and neighbor. Newspapers could even request that a syndicate "localize" a feature by compiling local contributions and merging them with stock content. The Cosmos Syndicate offered "a weekly page from your own young readers and a weekly prize for the best poem—and all done for you. A feature as local as your local news."[152] The weekly and monthly magazines of the 1910s and 1920s printed many of the same types of features that newspapers did: relationship advice, financial guidance, health articles, fashion spreads. So all of this tinkering added local appeal that helped to distinguish newspapers' features from magazines' offerings.

While Milwaukee residents increasingly bought products and watched movies created for a mass market, they still seemed to trust the opinion of a fellow Milwaukee resident more than an opinion from just anyone. So the spread of mass culture in the 1910s and 1920s created a surprising new niche for local columnists, who could act as interpreters and guides to the products that arrived from faraway film studios and factories. In local columns such as "On the Screen," by Nancy Lee, reviewers discussed national releases but took care to describe the particular lineup of features and shorts in Milwaukee theaters.[153] The *Journal* and the *Sentinel* kept columnists on staff to cover national sports such as football and major league baseball. These columnists became distinctive local voices whom readers trusted to give them the inside scoop from a hometown perspective.[154] "Betty Ann's" shopping service in the *Journal* featured mostly mass-produced goods, such as novel perfume bottles, but it presented them in a local way, labeling the pictures "Sketched in Milwaukee Shops Especially for The Journal."[155] A reporter who went by the name of "Brownie" at the *Milwaukee Journal* drove a different new car along the major routes and the back roads of Wisconsin every summer in the 1920s. His daily dispatches told readers the state of the local roads—muddy quagmires, new bridges, particularly scenic stretches—while also describing the performance of that make of car.[156]

Every major daily in Milwaukee, by the 1920s, offered an amalgam of syndicate and wire-service material, local reporting, and a few features that somehow spoke to local concerns. The *Milwaukee Journal*, while still following this basic formula, far outsold its competitors. The *Journal*'s intricate mix of local and nonlocal content in the 1920s shows what it took to become the paper of record in a midsize U.S. city at this time. The *Journal* also illustrates how a leading local paper could still offer a strong sense of place in an era of highly centralized and homogenized news.

In the age of wire services and feature syndicates, Milwaukee reporters did not go out and cover the globe, but they did—the *Journal* insisted—sift the news with expertise and professionalism. "Through important supplementary sources—unapproached in number or scope by those of any other newspaper for Wisconsin people—*Journal* readers benefit by enjoying special articles and news items from famous correspondents and observers in all parts of the civilized world," the paper boasted.[157] It drew its news reports from seven wire services and buttressed these with features from still more firms.[158] The *Journal* also kept multiple exchange editors in an era when most papers had eliminated that role. Equipped with blue pencils, "men and women busily sort the contemporary newspapers and magazines from all over Wisconsin, the nation and the world," explained a *Journal* brochure.[159] The paper even hired special staff to read foreign papers, so that Milwaukee readers did not have to rely on the wire services alone for their international news.[160] The paper thus cast itself as a broadly knowledgeable and discerning editor of global news, while catering to middle- and upper-class readers who prided themselves on being thoroughly informed.

The *Journal* invested in original coverage of state and national news, even though it could have bought similar news from a syndicate. The paper maintained its own bureaus in Madison, New York, and Washington, DC, and employed sports writers in cities all over the country who would report on games just for *Journal* readers.[161] It commissioned special features on national and global topics and stamped them with a logo: "The Milwaukee Journal First Run Features, First in Merit."[162] *Journal* editors wagered that these special reports would warrant the expense. The fact that the *Journal* could afford to commission reports on national and world events boosted the paper's stature in the national journalism field and among Milwaukee readers. And managing editor Martin Creager encouraged his reporters, near and far, to "write it for the man on Mitchell Street"—to always keep Milwaukee audiences in mind.[163]

The *Journal*'s editors considered a local take on the wider world enough of a marketable asset that they paid a Milwaukee native, Lindsay Hoben, to travel the globe and write about what he saw. As Hoben encountered first-hand many of the sights and situations that readers had seen in other, more anonymous news stories, his articles brought the realities of world events and world cultures a little closer to home. In daily installments called "Around the World with a *Journal* Man," Hoben described the brand-new city of Tel Aviv, the Macedonian fight for independence, Chinese torture methods, and collective farming practices in Russia.[164] On Sundays, the *Journal* fashioned Hoben's reports and photographs into full-color spreads, and encouraged readers to collect them in a specially designed travel album (fig. 5.7). The *Journal* could have turned to syndicates for more expert opinions, in-depth explanations, and striking photographs than those Hoben was able to provide on a tight budget and with limited equipment. But Hoben's status as a Milwaukee boy lent his reports a special appeal.

To secure its place as the city's leading daily, the *Journal* kept its local coverage strong. It printed poems on local characters or scenes. It employed its own illustrator to draw up front-page cartoons and sports-page sketches, and its Sunday rotogravure section included photographs of local professional dancers, neighborhood Boy Scout troops, and the city sky-line.[165] The *Journal* office issued guides to Wisconsin wildflowers, Wisconsin birds, Milwaukee history, and Wisconsin roads. Even the authors' nick-names (O. W. "Outdoors" Smith, "Wisconsin Cal") played up their local knowledge.[166] In myriad ways, from sponsoring photo contests of Wisconsin landscapes to hanging annual exhibits of Wisconsin art in its office lobby, the paper cultivated pride in all things Wisconsin.[167] So in taking the *Journal*, a reader could feel that he understood how life was lived elsewhere but that he also proudly called Milwaukee home.

No matter how rooted the *Journal* remained in Milwaukee, the constant influx of vivid, illustrated, and in-depth syndicated features changed local perceptions of place. The more that newspapers exposed readers to the world's great metropolises, the more likely readers were to measure Milwaukee against those standards. Under an image of Milwaukee on the front of the rotogravure section, a caption read: "A scene on the Milwaukee river

5.7 The first installment of the *Milwaukee Journal*'s Radio-Roto feature, "The World Voyagers Go Round the Globe," in which readers could use newspaper illustrations as accompaniments to radio broadcasts. The feature followed a Milwaukee man, Lindsay Hoben, on his travels around the world. He supplied some of the images; others came from wire services. *Milwaukee Journal*, 23 November 1930, Wisconsin Historical Society, WHS-119185.

that, on the right, suggests the picturesque buildings on the banks of the canals in Venice, and, on the left, recalls the type of architecture familiar to the waterways of Hamburg and Cologne."[168] These comparisons demonstrated the city's worldliness and perhaps helped readers to appreciate Milwaukee's beauty. But the comparison also doomed Milwaukee to provincial status, for it could never become as great a city as Venice—or London or New York—if it let those cities set the terms.

* * *

In the 1892 article in which he proposed pneumatic tubes for news, John Cockerill declared that newspapers were already sweeping away narrow-minded, provincial attitudes by expanding readers' access to all kinds of information. "There was a time when the farmer, the laboring-man, and the small shopkeeper looked to the rostrum for their annual instruction and entertainment, to the 'Village Oracle' or Oldest Inhabitant for their opinions and prophecies, and to the local politician, whom we now call a 'boss,' for their schooling in public questions. All this has to a very large extent been abolished."[169] The newspaper rendered all of these older sources of information not only uninteresting by comparison but also unimportant. "The most brilliant lecturer in the world can no longer compete with the morning newspaper. The Oldest Inhabitant finds himself ruthlessly *functus officio* by the simple process of learning from his newspaper that there are in different parts of the country ever so many Older Inhabitants.[170]

In the late nineteenth century, city newspapers began printing more and more detailed news from elsewhere, which put local people and happenings into perspective. As Cockerill saw it, that perspective could be both enlightening and deflating. The New York City and Washington, DC, columns that ran in papers around the country kept readers abreast of events in those larger and more powerful places while communicating the relative lack of importance of the local. The appearance of separate city and state sections may have done the same. The columns titled "Oregoniana" or "News of the Northwest" that replaced earlier jumbles of news from around the country and the world encouraged readers in Portland, Oregon, to follow local happenings, but the columns also classified that news as "regional" and, therefore, less important than "national" news.[171] As newspapers introduced syndicated articles, readers learned to enjoy (and came to expect) more elaborate material than local papers could produce themselves. If they did not give readers a steady diet of syndicated features, independent papers in small and midsize cities risked losing their readers to larger papers from larger cities. A reader in Grand Forks, North Dakota, found his local paper insufficiently broad. "While I like the 'Herald' for its news and its meaty editorials, and its scraps of Ole's philosophy in Norwegian dialect," he wrote, "it does not give us all the big, important news. To fill these frequent gaps we must read the Minneapolis papers, and even the Chicago 'Record-Herald.'"[172] A Pittsburgh reader insisted that none of his city's seven papers were really good enough for his cosmopolitan tastes; he felt truly at home only when reading the *New York Sun*.[173] And New Yorkers themselves hankered for a wider view than their own city could provide: "I suggest you make THE WORLD more cosmopolitan, cover a wider field," wrote an 1889 reader, illustrating the demand for what syndicates would later provide. "We are not an exclusively local people.... During the week have a letter from India or cablegrams or exciting events. Let us know what's going on in Australia."[174]

As in Milwaukee, foreign-language papers across the nation printed syndicated articles and mass-market ads—and, by extension, began to integrate American mass culture into their news. Foreign-language papers in many cities adopted the stylistic conventions of the English-language press, reviewed American films, and reported on the latest women's fashions. Hearst's German-language daily, the *New Yorker Morgen Journal*, ran translations of Hearst comic strips; by changing the characters' names, it turned them into slapstick parables of German-American assimilation.[175] Robert Ezra Park, in his 1922 study, estimated that national brands made up more than 15 percent of the advertising in large-circulation foreign-language papers such as the Italian *Il Progresso* or the Norwegian-Danish *Posten og Ved Arnen*.[176] German and Yiddish papers in major cities offered merchandising services that pushed mass-market products in simultaneous newspaper ads and ethnic grocery store displays.[177] While the circulations of foreign-language papers rose and fell with the literacy rates, the ages, and above all the sheer numbers of various immigrant groups, syndication tended to hasten papers' declines. Where struggling English-language papers could use syndicated news to attract readers, struggling foreign-language papers faced the double expense of subscribing to a syndicate and then translating its material. The most visually enticing syndicated features often proved untranslatable, since foreign-language papers could not replace the text on complex illustrated stereotype plates.

Big cities and smaller cities, as exporters and importers of syndicated news, tallied different gains and losses. Readers in exporting cities like Chicago and New York benefited when their local papers moved into the syndication business, because the papers then devoted outsize amounts of money and attention to their exportable features. The local market justified moderately expensive articles on local characters or neighborhoods; the national market paid for truly lavish news. Yet those lavish features did not tie directly to life in any one place, and big-city papers grew more generic as they geared their features toward national audiences.

Readers in smaller, importing cities received obvious benefits from the

chain and syndicate system, which provided them with more spectacular features than their local papers ever could have created on their own
and, perhaps ironically, gave them more intimate counsel than any local
writer ever had. Robert and Helen Lynd, in their study of Muncie, Indiana,
noticed how closely residents read the syndicated column by Dorothy Dix.
"Day after day two columns of syndicated advice to 'Desolate,' 'A Much-
disturbed Husband,' 'Young Wife,' etc., appear in the leading Middletown paper from this elderly lady," they wrote. "Her advice is discussed
by mothers and daughters as they sew together at Ladies' Aid meetings
and many of them say that her column is the first and sometimes the only
thing which they read every day in the paper."[178] Yet readers in small cities
also paid a higher price than their big-city counterparts. As in the cases of
Hearst and Scripps, chain papers often whittled their local coverage down
to a minimum. Small-city readers of chain papers such as the *Spokane Press*,
the *Toledo News-Bee*, or the *Muncie Star* received some of the most generic
news in the country by the 1910s and 1920s, even though their cities had
once boasted livelier local journalism.[179] With the syndicate system in
place, even independent local editors created papers with only the loosest
ties to their own cities. A reader in Albuquerque found his city's two papers
"monotonously alike."[180] The papers did not even bother to source their
syndicate material from different places, he said. "Both print practically the
same news matter, the same cuts, and sometimes even identical editorials. Like other papers of this size, they are dependent upon the great news-
gathering associations and upon the so-called plate services for much of
their material; hence their similarity to each other and to the thousand and
one other papers of the country."[181]

The material from far-off places that syndicates delivered to Americans'
doorsteps could have diminished many readers' opinions of their hometowns and other places they had known firsthand. Life at home may have
seemed a little smaller and duller after reading the news. The world beyond, though, expanded with the arrival of every Sunday paper. Colorful syndicated features could introduce readers to professional and intellectual possibilities they never would have otherwise encountered. After
reading the Sunday paper, a boy might imagine traveling to India, learning
Swahili, or becoming a deep-sea diver; a girl might decide to create an independent life for herself as a working woman, to train for a career in classical music, or to become a foreign news correspondent herself. Features
rendered the whole world as accessible and intelligible, there for Americans to understand and explore. This attitude fit neatly into the United
States' new role as a powerful actor on the world stage. Teaching readers
to take an interest in global affairs could be a first step in teaching them to
take control of those affairs.

Syndication nationalized the news. It standardized the terms in which readers thought about and understood their lives, created a sense of connection around certain common traits and passions, and highlighted affinities across ethnic and regional lines—which meant, necessarily, that it ironed over regional difference and phased out ethnic print culture. As news articles encouraged Americans to build the same houses, use the same words, and play the same games, they constructed a broadly understood American "way of life" that would become a touchstone of U.S. domestic politics and international relations through the entire twentieth century.

EPILOGUE

Decades of journalistic experiments and innovations had produced, by the 1920s, elaborate metropolitan newspapers that lay at the heart of cities' political, cultural, and economic lives. Daily papers flowed through the veins of these cities. Each day newsboys hawked papers on street corners, workers picked them up on streetcar platforms, and deliverymen deposited them on urban and suburban doorsteps. Readers then opened them up in lunchrooms, on commuter trains, at office desks or kitchen tables. Even after copies had been read once through, their information kept moving. Passengers browsed discarded papers on nearby subway seats. Neighbors discussed tragedies they had read about in the headlines. Readers tacked up newspaper pictures on their walls, cooked recipes from newspaper columns, and clipped obituaries for scrapbooks. As the information from a single issue spread through all of these channels, newspaper presses were busy churning out the next edition. The next day, the process began all over again.

Viewed through one lens, the 1920s formed metropolitan newspapers' peak decade of influence and popularity. Sociologists and scholars of that decade found that between 88 and 95 percent of all Americans regularly read newspapers, which made them the most popular reading material in the nation, more pervasive than magazines and far more common than books.[1] The news habit also reached across class and ethnicity: a 1923 Chicago study found that among its subjects, 91 percent of those with less than an eighth-grade education—and 100 percent of immigrants—were reading papers.[2] Female readership had risen steadily through the early twentieth century, until by the 1920s, roughly equal numbers of men and women read daily papers.[3] Americans' per capita newsprint consumption peaked in 1929 at sixty-two pounds.[4]

Yet the 1920s was also the decade in which newspapers settled into a comfortable pattern. Editors and journalists ceased to experiment with the energy and creativity of their predecessors. Instead they relied on a template that had emerged from the previous decades. The tumultuous changes that had begun in the late nineteenth century had produced a stable—verging on static—corporate model of the metropolitan paper.

The trend of newspaper mergers that began in eastern cities just after the turn of the century continued through the interwar decades, until it reduced a diverse field of relatively small and scrappy city papers to just a few large dailies per city. In 1914, there had been one paper for every four thousand Americans; by 1930, there was one for every nine thousand.[5] The names of cities' remaining papers showed their history of mergers: the *New Orleans Times-Picayune*, the *Buffalo Courier-Express*, the *Chicago Herald-Examiner*. Newspaper chains and partnerships further diminished the variety within American news. The *Chicago Tribune* branched into the New York market in 1919; its *New York Daily News* borrowed *Tribune* material. The *Philadelphia Public Ledger* operated under shared ownership with the *New York Evening Post*.[6] Even as newspaper readership continued to rise, Americans had far fewer papers to choose from. Between 1920 and 1953, the number of cities with more than one daily paper fell from 552 to eighty-seven.[7]

A new collection of signature newspaper buildings helped establish newspapers' roles as stable pillars of American cities. The most ambitious and experimental turn-of-the-century papers, such as the *New York World* and the *San Francisco Examiner*, built towering, gaudy, somewhat incoherent buildings. Other papers contented themselves with practical structures that blended in with the rest of downtown. Most of them clustered together in news districts, such as New York City's Park Row, San Francisco's Newspaper Corner, or Philadelphia's Chestnut Street. These districts encouraged competition, as each paper tried to post the most attention-grabbing headlines, but also allowed for exchange, since reporters generally gathered at the same clubs after work. By contrast, papers in the 1920s and 1930s often struck out for new parts of town, where their headquarters towered over all of their neighbors and became recognizable silhouettes on city skylines. The gleaming white *Philadelphia Inquirer* building, complete with clock and gold dome, stood out in the relatively low-lying district north of Vine Street. The *New York Daily News*, standing thirty-six stories tall and illuminated with eighty-four floodlights, shone in the New York City night.[8] The *Chicago Tribune*'s 1922 international competition for the design of its new headquarters ultimately produced a thirty-six-story tower topped with flying buttresses. Once construction was complete, the paper projected its daily circulation in lights up the side of the building.[9] Newspapers narrated their institutional stories in their architectural details. A frieze along the top of the *Milwaukee Journal*'s 1924 building depicted the history of communication: Egyptians writing on papyrus, Gutenberg printing out pamphlets,

6.1 *Milwaukee Daily Journal* building, 1926. To the left of the building's corner, the frieze depicts Gutenberg's press. Wisconsin Historical Society, WHS-54044.

machinists running a Hoe rotary press (fig. 6.1). The *Chicago Tribune* etched quotes on freedom of information—from Thomas Jefferson, from Milton, from the Gospels—into the stone walls of the lobby. The *Chicago Daily News* painted a mural on its lobby ceiling that showed massive machines and heroic workers carrying information to the public (fig. 6.2). Newspapers' slick, serious buildings reflected newly self-conscious and carefully managed corporate identities.

As they grew, city newspapers' internal workings began to more closely resemble those of other giant corporations. The biggest papers vertically integrated by buying up timber forests, paper factories, ink plants, photographic services, and distribution networks.[10] Newspaper publishers designed their new buildings as vertical assembly lines for news (fig. 6.3).[11] Like other large companies of the interwar years, metropolitan papers organized into business consortiums to increase their influence on politics and policy. Newspapers financed multiple lobbying groups, supported their own internal auditing bureau, and published multiple trade magazines.[12] Papers' managers worked to foster corporate cultures within their organizations. The *Chicago Tribune*, the *Chicago Daily News*, and the *New York Sun*

6.2 John Warner Norton's *Chicago Daily News* mural, circa 1929. The mural lined
the ceiling of a passageway from the *Daily News* building to the Chicago and North
Western Railway Station. It consisted of three sections: "Gathering the News,"
"Printing the News," and "Transporting the News." *Chicago Daily News* building,
Chicago, 1928–29, Holabird & Root, Architects, Historic Architecture and Landscape Image Collection, Ryerson and Burnham Archives, Art Institute of Chicago,
digital file #31005.

THIS "phantom" view, with various floors of Tribune Tower laid open to permit viewing the activities inside, shows how thoroughly The Tribune is organized to serve its three-quarters of a million customers daily, and nearly a million and a quarter buyers every Sunday. The entire lower portion—down from the third floor above the boulevard, is devoted to manufacturing activities. Note how news comes in on the fourth floor, and flows downward through the composing room to the presses. Paper comes up from storage to meet the news at the presses, rises to the mailing room, and thence goes on its way to Tribune readers. These arrangements give maximum efficiency and speed in producing Tribunes.

Above the editorial floor are business, feature, and executive offices—with some well-known Tribunites even perched high above the city in the very tip of the tower! This arrangement permits concentration of all manufacturing activities on the lower stories, and at the same time removes the business and executive departments from the rush and distraction inevitable in the business of turning out a paper like The Tribune. The resulting economies in time, effort, and money all help The Tribune maintain its position as foremost among the world's great newspapers.

Tribune Tower, Chicago

6.3 Cross section of the *Chicago Tribune* tower. Editors sat at the top of the skyscraper, dictating ideas to the reporters below, who in turn sent their copy to proofreaders and typesetters on lower floors. Meanwhile, workers in the basement unloaded newsprint from railroad cars or river barges. Chicago Tribune, *Book of Facts, 1927: Data on Markets, Merchandising, Advertising, with Special Reference to the Chicago Territory and Chicago Newspaper Advertising* (Chicago: Chicago Tribune, 1927), 4.

each produced internal newsletters that kept these papers' staffs of thousands up-to-date on company doings.[13] The clatter and chaos of turn-of-the-century newsrooms and pressrooms gave way to far larger, more coordinated, and increasingly corporate operations.

Accordingly, newspapers of the interwar decades ceased to nurture novel modes of urban behavior; newspaper jobs instead came to resemble other corporate jobs. Editors more carefully divided newsroom labor, leaving reporters less freedom to follow their own hunches. While turn-of-the-century newswomen pushed the boundaries of acceptable public behavior and assumed new professional duties, women's work at newspapers of the 1920s, 1930s, and 1940s mostly mirrored women's roles at other corporate workplaces. A few women took on skilled professional and public positions, but many more performed clerical roles. At the *Chicago Tribune*, for example, just over a dozen women wrote for news departments, while hundreds of women employees handled billing inquiries, operated switchboards, and served as secretaries for male executives.[14] Newsboys still worked on street corners in the 1930s and 1940s, but in many cities they no longer seemed the quintessential urban hustlers. Many states passed child labor laws that forced papers to rely on adult vendors and newsstand operators rather than newsboys. When newspapers did hire children or teenagers, it was to deliver papers in neighborhoods rather than to sell copies downtown. By the 1950s, the paperboy on his bicycle had become a symbol not of determined urban survival but of wholesome suburban life.[15]

Portrayals of news reporters in film, comic books, and fiction retained some of the glamour of newspapers' most innovative decades, but they could also reflect the more humdrum nature of reporting in an era of large corporate papers. After the transition to "talkies," many former reporters wrote movie screenplays; Hollywood produced hundreds of films set in newsrooms in the 1930s, 1940s, and 1950s.[16] Some movies' versions of newsrooms seemed to offer their characters fame, glory, and upward mobility. On screen, working-class reporters often rubbed shoulders with the powerful, wooed wealthy women, and heroically revealed the truth to the public.[17] The 1930s' and 1940s' comic book characters Superman, the Crimson Avenger, Captain Zero, the Ray, Bob Phantom, the Destroyer, Patriot, and the Fox worked as reporters in their daytime lives and enjoyed modest successes in their corporate newsrooms. Yet each of these characters escaped the workaday world of editors and copywriting and truly came into their own only through their superhuman alter egos.[18]

Newspapers had always been private businesses that played essential public roles. But in the interwar period, newspapers created public spaces that fully fused the pursuit of profit with civic responsibility. Wide plazas and revolving doors welcomed visitors to the newspaper buildings of the

6.4 Entrance and public plaza of the 1929 *Chicago Daily News* building at 400 West Madison Street, MMS Field Enterprises, Newberry Library, Chicago.

1920s and 1930s (figs. 6.4 and 6.5). Once inside, visitors could send packages, place calls on public telephones, apply for fishing or driving licenses, visit notaries, or get help with income taxes. They could look up information in the offices' files of past articles, or even borrow reference books from the papers' libraries.[19] Just as publishers created women's sections to get ads in front of female readers, they also outfitted lobbies to be comfortable places for women to spend time and money. Papers imitated department stores by building public lounges—secluded, female-friendly environments in the midst of busy downtowns. The *Chicago Tribune* even partitioned off a women's section in their "want ad store," so that women placing ads felt comfortable and safe.[20] Motor and travel bureaus in newspapers' lobbies distributed advertisers' brochures. Papers put on fashion shows, home-decorating workshops, cooking schools, and electrification demonstrations that featured advertisers' products.[21] Like newspapers themselves, newspaper buildings continuously blurred the line between public life and private commerce.

In the interwar years, advertising so suffused newspapers' operations that publishers and readers alike may not have been able to imagine city news untouched by ads or uninfluenced by manufacturers' selling goals. In 1930, about 480 dailies offered merchandising services, which enlisted stores to stock, display, and push the products advertised in the newspaper.[22] One of these dailies, the *Detroit News*, placed full-color panels of newspaper ads in store windows, with a slogan above reading: "Here are the goods! Advertised in The Detroit News."[23] Like the *Chicago Tribune*, several other newspapers so fully embraced their roles as vehicles for advertising that they carried out extensive consumer research and distributed it to advertisers.[24] Journalists such as Genevieve Jackson Boughner argued that advertisements and shopping-service columns (which incorporated paid mentions of goods) were just as valuable as more neutral news. "This department is a distinct service to the reader," she said, "who thus learns of merchandise that might not otherwise be brought to her attention."[25] As in previous decades, many readers continued to rely on newspapers for commercial information as much as for news. When New York City newspaper carriers went on strike in 1945, some readers said it was the absence of stock listings, movie schedules, and department store ads that most pained them.[26]

6.5 Lobby of the *Chicago Tribune* Public Service Office at Dearborn and Madison. The services shown include out-of-town directories, back-issue sales, a resort and travel bureau, a large state map, public phones, and *Tribune*-published booklets at the back counter. From 1930 brochure *Ask Us Another!* in Public Service Pamphlets, Tribune Company Archives, Col. McCormick Research Center.

6.6 In the *New York Daily News* building lobby, the marble floor displays longitudes of major cities; the clocks on the wall display time zones around the world. Author's own photograph.

In an expansion, rather than a continuation, of their turn-of-the-century roles, metropolitan papers of the 1920s, 1930s, and 1940s cultivated images of expertise and power consonant with the United States' rising place in the world. Newspapers' headquarters demonstrated their global prowess. The clocks in the *New York Daily News* lobby displayed the times in major cities around the world (fig. 6.6), and visitors could marvel at a twelve-foot diameter rotating globe sunk into the floor, which workers kept up-to-date by repainting national borders and city names as they changed.[27] The *Chicago Tribune* collected pieces of world monuments such as the Parthenon, the Taj Mahal, and the Great Wall of China, and embedded them in the exterior of its 1925 building so that visitors could see and touch them all. The *Chicago Daily News*, on its public tour, made sure to point out that the paper kept foreign correspondents stationed in twenty-seven different countries.[28] Many newspapers highlighted their global presence and expertise by listing the addresses of their bureaus in Rome, Shanghai, and Mexico City on their mastheads.[29] Several papers invited readers to treat their foreign bureaus as a "home away from home" while traveling; the bureaus offered comfortable reading rooms stocked with American newspapers and provided free travel planning and advice.[30] As papers drew attention to the global nature of their work, they invited readers to enjoy and participate in the United States' global reach and power.

Only one new competitor—radio—threatened to dislodge newspapers from their seat as the most popular and influential media of the interwar years. Radio had fascinated tinkerers and hobbyists in the late 1910s and early 1920s but became a mainstream medium in the late 1920s. A poll taken in 1930 found about twelve million receiving sets in the United States, enough for nearly half of the nation's families.[31] Radio stations were able to broadcast breaking news more quickly than newspapers could print and distribute it, so newspaper publishers worried that radio would steal away their audiences, and then their advertisers. And indeed, in the 1930s, advertisers spent proportionally less money on newspaper space. Papers received 54 percent of all U.S. advertising expenditures in 1929, 50 percent in 1935, and 38 percent by 1939. In the meantime, radio's share steadily increased.[32] Newspapers responded to the threat not by launching counteroffensives but by swiftly establishing their own radio stations. Papers' extensive news-gathering networks gave them a head start in the broadcasting business, and they saw radio news as a logical extension of the authority and expertise they had developed.[33] Papers even had some of the necessary infrastructure in place, for they had constructed radio receiving stations to collect news dispatches that they then turned into print.[34] In 1930, newspapers owned just 5.9 percent of radio stations, but these were some of the most respected newspapers and powerful stations on the air. By 1942, newspapers owned 36 percent of all stations.[35]

Successful newspaper publishers had bought out and merged with their competitors for decades. As they applied similar strategies of ownership and consolidation to radio and television, publishers created the nation's first multimedia empires. Papers moved into the FM radio station market in the 1940s and 1950s; they held between 20 and 38 percent of stations in those decades. Publishers moved quickly into the new medium of television as well. The *Detroit News*, the *St. Louis Post-Dispatch*, and the *Fort Worth Star-Telegram* all bought television stations in 1946, and by 1953 newspapers owned more than half of all stations.[36] When newspapers branched out, they spread reporting and administrative expenses across media outlets, streamlining their costs while broadening their revenue base. This multiplatform business model kept newspaper companies powerful and profitable through midcentury.

Yet even as new varieties of media blossomed in the interwar decades, Americans continued to treat newspapers as their primary and most trustworthy sources of news. For most Americans living in the 1930s and 1940s, radio served as a complement to newspapers rather than as a substitute. Many people listened to the radio in the presence of others, gathered around the sole set in the house. Listeners had little control over what kind of news they heard and when they heard it; they had to live by broadcasters' schedules.[37] When Americans wanted a moment to themselves, and when they wanted to dive into the news that interested them most, they still turned to their newspapers.[38] The daily newspaper ritual also remained the foundation of many people's everyday interactions. "You have to read in order to keep up a conversation with other people," said one respondent to a 1945 survey. "It is embarrassing not to know if you are in company who discuss the news."[39] For these reasons, dailies' circulations continued to outpace population growth between 1920 and 1955. In 1920, the nation printed one copy of a daily paper for every four people; by 1955, the ratio was one to three.[40]

At midcentury, generations of readers still thought of their papers as friends, advisers, entertainers, critics, and conduits to the wider world. Readers surveyed during New York City's 1945 news carriers' strike expressed many of the same feelings about their newspapers as did the readers who wrote into the *Collier's Weekly* contest in 1911. "You get used to certain people; they become part of your family, like Dorothy Kilgallen," said one fan of the *New York Daily News* columnist.[41] Another reader explained that the paper connected him to both his neighbors and the world. "I like the feeling of being in touch with the world at large. If I don't know what's going on next door, it hurts me."[42] Readers felt passionately attached to their papers, even in a media landscape that had expanded to include newsreels, glossy mass-audience magazines, and radio broadcasts. "Life is more monotonous without the paper. I didn't know what to do with myself," said one person surveyed during the strike. "I am suffering! Seriously!" said another. "I could not sleep, I missed it so."[43]

* * *

Six decades later, the era of the newsprint metropolis feels far away. Some papers disappeared in the 1960s, 1970s, and 1980s as their deindustrializing cities, such as Detroit and Cleveland, lost residents. But even where urban populations have stabilized or boomed, the number of metropolitan papers continues its steep drop. Most major American cities now publish only one daily paper, if that. Papers in some of the nation's largest and most culturally rich cities, such as Chicago, Philadelphia, and San Francisco, have declared bankruptcy or come close to extinction.

Shorn of the revenue they collected from advertising and classified listings, newspapers search for a new business model that incorporates an Internet presence but still provides income. The National Public Radio show "On the Media" discusses possible models for monetizing the newspaper industry so often that they have given the topic its own theme tune. A few national papers such as the *New York Times* and the *Wall Street Journal* seem to be successfully managing the transition, but the option of creating powerful newspaper-controlled Internet sites akin to what newspapers did with radio stations does not appear likely in a medium already dominated by search-engine companies.[44]

Many of newspapers' former functions have been segmented and picked up by the Internet and other non-news outlets. What was once called the classified section now exists entirely online, in clearinghouse sites such as craigslist.org and in specialized job, real estate, and dating websites. The categories in these clearinghouse sites have flowered more creatively than those in print classified sections, giving rise to urban barter economies, markets for short-term sublets, personal ads for evangelical Christians, and poetic laments over missed connections. Magazines now compile more thorough entertainment listings than newspapers do, and Internet sites such as Yelp and TripAdvisor provide customer reviews of far more goods and services than could be covered in print. Sites and apps tailored to specific demographics offer guides to urban eating, shopping, and nightlife. The niche audiences first shaped by newspaper sections such as the sports pages, women's pages, and home decor sections now fuel the business of hundreds of television stations, magazines, and blogs.

The daily-life advice that newspapers once provided survives in several different spheres today, though we now mostly take our advice from national celebrities rather than local guides. Syndicated advice columns on relationships, manners, and home life continue to run in newspapers. Papers still dispense fashion, health, and beauty advice as well, but magazines and websites have attracted most of the advertising money in those spheres. Television personalities, rather than newspaper columnists, tell Americans how to relate to their families and how to conduct their finances. Churches have also taken on more everyday advising of the kind newspapers used to provide, with many offering marriage counseling and financial planning. When newspapers first brought private life out into a public medium, they allowed readers to compare their lives to the examples in newspaper pages. Such windows into Americans' private lives have become far more common—even inescapable—today. Reality television shows, celebrity gossip magazines, and social media feeds have all created a level of intimacy with strangers not considered polite or possible in the 1910s. Yet we use these views of others' lives in much the same way that newspaper readers of the early twentieth century did. They become the material with which we piece together definitions of modern manhood, womanhood, manners, sophistication, and success.

Nonprofit news sources such as ProPublica and the *Texas Tribune* have picked up the reins on investigative reporting, and their dedication to serious journalism stands as an online counterpoint to sites that pander with clickbait. When they share their findings with other news sources, they ensure that their work reaches a wide audience but also strengthen the expectation that all news is now free. A handful of nonprofit print and online news agencies, however, cannot fully cover all of the beats and bureaus that metropolitan newspapers once did. The decisions of many state legislatures, for example, go unreported now that newspapers in state capitals have laid off reporters or closed down entirely. So far, online media have failed to cover local issues and provide the shared base of knowledge that binds city dwellers together with a sense of community and civic identity. Currently, blogs and online news media most often gather readers who live far apart from one another but who share interests and political views. It is much less often that they draw together readers who live in a single neighborhood or city but who hold widely differing interests and opinions.

The Internet has unquestionably opened up the news landscape, making room for a huge diversity of voices that was never possible when a few major papers dominated the dialogue within each city. Proponents of "crowdsourced" news and "citizen media" argue that private citizens can collectively assemble information that is comprehensive and keyed to populations' real curiosities and needs. Certainly, citizen videos of police violence have demonstrated the power of social media to report events that newspapers often fail (and have been failing for decades) to adequately cover. At the same time, blogs and Twitter feeds will never replace the investigations and syntheses that mainstream media, such as newspapers, are able to commission. Many have pointed out that search engines and social media sites censor, filter, and hide information as often as any newspaper, while masquerading as entirely open and free platforms.[45]

As a variety of new media have taken over newspapers' past functions, the media-consuming public has lost common ground. The layout of newspapers encouraged broad curiosity. Entertainment articles ran on pages that faced political articles, so that subscribers who read one kind of article would always see the other. Newspapers sat around on peoples' kitchen counters or coffee tables, and readers would often pick them up in whatever idle time they found during the day to read the sections they had missed in the morning. Readers who took no special interest in the war in Korea or the crisis in the public schools still occasionally (and often accidentally) learned about these topics. By contrast, today's Internet news makes it exceedingly easy to read only the stories we already know we are interested in and to ignore stories we would rather not know about. Search engines, able to gauge our interests, point us toward topics and products related to what we already read and already buy.[46]

We must be careful not to idealize metropolitan newspapers' contents. Their editors' power to decide what their millions of readers should know carried both benefits and dangers. Out of ignorance or by strategy, editors omitted important stories and played down others. Their decisions to devote so much space to commerce-friendly or gender-stereotyped topics had decidedly mixed consequences for American culture and the economy. Still, when editors placed local, national, and international stories in their papers, they forced those stories into readers' consciousness and created a baseline level of public knowledge. The shared vocabulary created by syndicated news in the 1910s and 1920s, and the shared understanding of American actions abroad created by midcentury mass media coverage, is conspicuously missing today.

In the past, newspapers weathered dramatic changes in the media landscape and in their readers' preferences and often responded with creative and unexpected solutions. Instead of ceding their audiences to magazines, newspapers began publishing magazines of their own. When they feared losing readers who moved to suburbs, they started reporting on those suburbs and became metropolitan rather than strictly urban media. City newspapers identified markets in small-town and rural America and managed to sell subscriptions far outside of city limits. And when readers began to expect the kind of international coverage and entertaining features that big-city papers offered, small-city papers bought that material from syndicates and managed to hold onto their readers.

We do not know yet whether metropolitan newspapers will become stable and profitable digital businesses and whether those businesses will be recognizable as newspapers. But even as their heyday recedes, newspapers continue to influence expectations of news media. Americans assume that their media will speak to them as consumers and as citizens, will blend entertainment and information, and will offer material with which to patch together individual identities and form community allegiances. We owe all of these expectations—and much, much more—to turn-of-the-century newspapers.

ACKNOWLEDGMENTS

A wide circle of people have, over the life of this project and even longer, nurtured my love of the past and pushed me to think harder about what that past meant. It is a pleasure to thank them here.

My parents, day by day, ushered this project into existence; this book is for them. My mother, Valerie Weller, has been an endlessly patient and discerning reader. Her support and her pride in my work have made every achievement sweeter and more meaningful. My father, Carl Guarneri, has puzzled through hundreds upon hundreds of historical questions with me. Quietly intelligent, giving, and compassionate, he has provided me the best possible model of what it means to be a historian.

At Cornell University, Barry Maxwell paid real attention to my writing in my first college semester, demonstrating that within a large research university there was a personal, challenging, and electric undergraduate education waiting for me. I am still, happily, answering questions that I learned to ask in Anette Schwarz's wonderful class on the idea of the metropolis. And I count myself extraordinarily lucky to have written an undergraduate honors thesis under Michael Kammen's meticulous guidance and to have been mentored by him until the end of his life. His omnivorous and playful approach to history will inspire me always.

Glenda Gilmore insisted on the soundness and importance of this project from the beginning of my time as a doctoral student at Yale University. She pushed me to ask big questions and to work on a large scale; at the same time, her careful attention to each draft always brought me closer to the truth of my sources. Seth Fein set uncommonly high expectations for this project, and then expressed the utmost confidence that I would meet them. His wholehearted involvement and palpable excitement about his students' work is a true gift. Matthew Jacobson's spirit of collaboration, his creativity, and his infectious enthusiasm inspired me throughout my time in graduate school. He spotted and cultivated the project's strengths at moments when I could not tell strengths from weaknesses. I cannot imagine what this project would look like without Mary Lui's generosity and her expertise; to her I owe crucial suggestions for how to embed this story more deeply in cities' populations and physical landscapes. I am grateful for the tireless advocacy and levelheaded professional advice I received from all four of these mentors.

For their valued feedback and excellent company I thank my friends and fellow graduate students Helen Curry, Kathryn Gin, Taylor Spence, Robin Morris, Catherine McNeur, Sara Hudson, and Francesca Ammon. Others who began their PhDs a year or two ahead of me have graciously answered what now adds up to a decade's worth of questions about this profession; thanks to Rebecca McKenna, Helen Veit, Sam Schaffer, Julia Irwin, Steve Prince, Alison Greene, and Jason Ward.

Conferences, research trips, and workshops have brought me into conversation with excellent scholars of media and of cities, including David Paul Nord, David Henkin, Christine Pawley, James Danky, and Jim Grossman. Each has been generous with time and advice. Jay Gitlin pointed me toward Milwaukee and reminded me that academic writing could still convey how much *fun* newspapers are.

I am grateful for support from an Andrew W. Mellon Fellowship in Humanistic Studies, from Yale University, from the American Council of Learned Societies for a New Faculty Fellowship at the University of Pittsburgh, and from the University of Cambridge. Additionally, the Yale Club of Philadelphia, the Newberry Library, the James P. Danky fellowship at the Wisconsin Historical Society, and a Gilder-Lehrman research fellowship all enabled research travel. A program of the J. M. Kaplan Fund, titled Furthermore, and the Neil Harris Endowment Fund at the University of Chicago Press subsidized the cost of illustrations.

I have never met Nicholson Baker, but I need to thank him; it is only because he rescued an astounding archive from the British Library that I know what the earliest color newspaper sections looked like. I owe the discovery of several of the images in this book, and many of the articles, to his collection of reprints, *The World on Sunday*. Those newspapers now sit in the American Newspaper Repository at Duke University, and Elizabeth Dunn made gathering images from that archive a breeze. Thanks also to the Interlibrary Loan staff at Yale University and the University of Pittsburgh, especially Benjamin Rubin at Pittsburgh, who accommodated my many requests with care and speed.

I revised this manuscript while working at four different institutions; each helped the project along in a different way. My students at City College—ambitious, contentious, and utterly competent—reminded me how much there is to love about New York City and New Yorkers. Colgate University provided immersive teaching experience, a tight-knit community, and a gorgeous landscape in which to write and think. At the University of Pittsburgh, Lara Putnam and Laura Gotkowitz offered up exciting ideas and questions about the meanings of newspapers. At the University of Cambridge, the American History subject group and the fellows and staff at Fitzwilliam College have extended a warm welcome and have provided much-appreciated guidance through an unfamiliar academic system. I made the final revisions to this book in the Olisa Library and in the dining room of the Emma Darwin house. I am grateful to Fitzwilliam College for the use of those quiet and beautiful spaces.

At the University of Chicago Press, Timothy Mennel has been a responsive and committed editor; I thank both him and Timothy Gilfoyle for carefully reading and energetically advocating for this book. Feedback from two anonymous reviewers provided an excellent roadmap for revisions. Rachel Kelly's editorial assistance and Yvonne Zipter's copyediting sped the book to a finish and improved it along the way.

On research trips, I was kindly hosted by Melanie Macbride, Paul and Joann Guarneri, Theresa and Joe Gould, and Kathy Peiss and Peter Agree. Andrew Rotter and Padma Kaimal, Carol Kammen, Christopher and the late Jane Breiseth, my father-in-law Timothy Connor, and my late grandparents, Alice and George Weller, all fortified me with their interest and faith in this project. Walks and talks with my friends Melina Shannon-DiPietro, Corinne Benedek, and Lydia Breiseth have brought me both comfort and joy. My sister, Anna Guarneri, has supported me with many Philadelphia visits, countless conversations, and true sympathy for my love of old things.

Finally, I want to acknowledge my husband John Theodore Connor, whose deep knowledge, curiosity, and commitments I admire and adore, and who brings theoretical sophistication and a sense of justice to our conversations about history. My friend, my love, my camerado—thank you.

APPENDIX

ARCHIVES

Col. McCormick Research Center
  Chicago Tribune Departmental Papers
  Tribune Company Archives
      Everett McClane Collection
      Frances Peck Grover (Mae Tinee) Papers
Columbia University Rare Books and Manuscripts
  Joseph Pulitzer Papers
  New York World Papers
Fresh Air Fund Headquarters Office, New York City
  Fresh Air Fund Papers
Milwaukee Historical Society
  Evening Wisconsin Company File
  Milwaukee Journal File
  Wisconsin Printing Company File
Newberry Library
  MMS Field Enterprises Collection
      Chicago Daily News Collection
  Ring Lardner Papers
  Victor Freemont Lawson Papers
New-York Historical Society
  Art Posters Collection
  William Thompson Dewart Collection of Frank A. Munsey and *New York Sun*
      Papers
New York Public Library
  Art and Architecture Collection
      Newspaper Posters
  Schomberg Center
      T. Thomas Fortune Scrapbooks
Philadelphia Free Library
  Print and Picture Collection
  Notes and References Relating to the History of Philadelphia Newspapers
University of Chicago Special Collections
  Robert Ezra Park Papers
Wisconsin Historical Society
  August C. Backus Papers

Lindsay Hoben Papers
John Goadby Gregory Papers
Newscarriers' Addresses
"Newspapers" File
W. J. Anderson Papers

PERIODICALS

Editor & Publisher
American Newspaper Directory (New York: George P. Rowell & Co)
The Journalist
N. W. Ayer & Son's American Newspaper Annual (Philadelphia: N. W. Ayer & Son)
The Newspaper Maker
Pettingill & Company's Newspaper Directory
Printer's Ink
The Trib

NEWSPAPERS

For each of the four case-study cities, I read a sampling of the most popular mainstream daily newspapers. For each of the papers below, I researched the entire span from 1880 to 1930, or I researched the shorter span of years within that timeframe that the newspaper remained in business and widely read. I read a minimum of one week of issues, including the Sunday paper if it existed, at intervals of at most every four years.

Philadelphia Daily News, 1925–30
Philadelphia Evening Bulletin, 1895–1930
Philadelphia Evening Item, 1898–1906
Philadelphia Evening Public Ledger, 1914–30
Philadelphia Inquirer, 1877–1930
Philadelphia North American, 1899–1925
Philadelphia Public Ledger, 1880–1930
Philadelphia Record, 1880–1930
New York Daily News, 1919–30
New York Herald-Tribune, 1926–30
New York Journal (including the Sunday *American*), 1896–1930
New York Sun, 1880–1930
New York Times, 1895–1930
New York Tribune, 1880–1926
New York World, 1883–1930
Brooklyn Eagle, 1892–1930
Chicago American (including the Sunday *Journal and American*), 1900–1930
Chicago Daily News, 1880–1930
Chicago Herald-Examiner, 1918–30
Chicago Record-Herald, 1902–14
Chicago Times-Herald, 1895–1901
Chicago Tribune, 1880–1930
Milwaukee Journal, 1882–1930

Milwaukee Sentinel, 1880-1930
Evening Wisconsin, 1880-1917
Wisconsin News, 1918-30

I did additional research in the following newspapers:

Baltimore Afro American   *Milwaukee Herold*
Chicago Defender   *Milwaukee Herold und Seebote*
Chicagoer Freie Presse   *Milwaukee Sonntagspost*
Evanston Index   *New York Amsterdam News*
Hyde Park Herald   *Philadelphia Tribune*
Illinois Staats-Zeitung   *Pittsburgh Courier*
Joliet Daily News   *South Chicago Daily Calumet*
Joliet Evening Herald News   *Wilmette Life*
Lake Shore News   *Wisconsin Weekly Advocate*
Milwaukee Germania

NOTES

INTRODUCTION

1. *Collier's Weekly*, 18 February 1911, 7.

2. Letter from Egmont H. Arens in *Collier's Weekly*, 30 September 1911, 34. Arens's essay, along with many others, appeared in a series of *Collier's* columns titled "The American Newspaper" that ran through the summer and fall of 1911. The magazine commissioned articles by journalists for the series, too, some of which also appeared under the title "The American Newspaper."

3. Letter from Curtis C. Brown in *Collier's Weekly*, 2 September 1911, 23.

4. Letter from O. H. Chamberlain in *Collier's Weekly*, 19 August 1911, 18.

5. Ibid.

6. Letter from Edward Broderick in *Collier's Weekly*, 18 November 1911, 6.

7. Letter from May V. Godfrey in *Collier's Weekly*, 2 September 1911, 22.

8. Ibid.

9. Letter from Curtis C. Brown in *Collier's Weekly*, 2 September 1911, 23.

10. Letter from O. H. Chamberlain in *Collier's Weekly*, 19 August 1911, 18.

11. Letter from Marjorie Van Horn in *Collier's Weekly*, 2 September 1911, 22. When I have quoted Marjorie Van Horn's essay here and elsewhere, I have kept the original spelling and syntax.

12. Ibid.

13. Will Irwin, "The American Newspaper: A Study of Journalism and Its Relation to the Public," pt. 5, "What Is News?" *Collier's Weekly*, 18 March 1911, 16. Irwin started as a feature writer at the *New York Sun* and during the 1920s wrote syndicated pieces for Metropolitan Features.

14. *Collier's Weekly*, 8 April 1911, 9, and *Collier's Weekly*, 18 February 1911, 7.

15. Thomas C. Leonard, *News for All: America's Coming-of-Age with the Press* (New York: Oxford University Press, 1995), 178, drawn from U.S. Census reports and *Editor & Publisher*.

16. Carl F. Kaestle, Helen Damon-Moore, Lawrence C. Stedman, and Katherine Tinsley, *Literacy in the United States: Readers and Reading since 1880* (New Haven, CT: Yale University Press, 1991), 164. The census indicates high literacy rates among most U.S. populations by the late nineteenth century. In 1880, 9 percent of native-born whites over the age of ten reported that they could not write. Among foreign-born whites, the number was 12 percent. An astonishing 70 percent of black respondents reported that they could not write, but that percentage declined rapidly over the next few decades. Carl F. Kaestle, "Seeing the Sites: Readers, Publishers, and Local Print Cultures in

1880," in *A History of the Book in America*, vol. 4, *Print in Motion: The Expansion of Publishing and Reading in the United States, 1880–1940*, ed. Carl F. Kaestle and Janice A. Radway (Chapel Hill: University of North Carolina Press, 2009), 28–29.

17. William R. Merriman, director, prepared under the supervision of S. N. D. North, *Twelfth Census of the United States, Taken in the Year 1900*, vol. 9, *Manufactures*, pt. 3: *Special Reports on Selected Industries* (Washington, DC: U.S. Census Office, 1902), 1051.

18. John L. Given, *Making a Newspaper* (New York: Henry Holt, 1907), 1–2.

19. The role that newspapers played in creating nations was famously outlined by Benedict Anderson in *Imagined Communities: Reflections on the Origin and Spread of Nationalism* (New York: Verso, 1991) and has been debated ever since. For discussions of newspapers' roles (nation-building and otherwise) in the early national United States, see David Paul Nord, "Newspapers and American Nationhood, 1776–1826," in *Communities of Journalism: A History of American Newspapers and Their Readers* (Urbana: University of Illinois Press, 2006); Paul Starr, *The Creation of the Media: Political Origins of Modern Communications* (New York: Basic Books, 2004), pt. 1; Jeffrey L. Pasley, *"The Tyranny of Printers": Newspaper Politics in the Early American Republic* (Charlottesville: University Press of Virginia, 2001); and Carol Sue Humphrey, *The Press of the Young Republic, 1783–1833* (Westport, CT: Greenwood Press, 1996). In speaking about the public sphere, I am joining the many media historians who have adopted and worked with Jurgen Habermas's term. Habermas, *The Structural Transformation of the Public Sphere: An Inquiry into a Category of Bourgeois Society* (Cambridge, MA: MIT Press, 1989). For an incisive discussion of how the idea of a public sphere relates to media and journalism history, see Michael Schudson, "News, Public, Nation," *American Historical Review* 107, no. 102 (April 2002): 481–95. Richard Butsch analyzes media audiences as "publics" in *The Citizen Audience: Crowds, Publics, and Individuals* (New York: Routledge, 2007).

20. On 1830s and 1840s penny papers and their local urban reporting, see James L. Crouthamel, *Bennett's "New York Herald" and the Rise of the Popular Press* (Syracuse, NY: Syracuse University Press, 1989); Michael Schudson, *Discovering the News: A Social History of American Newspapers* (New York: Basic Books, 1978), chap. 1; John D. Stevens, *Sensationalism and the New York Press* (New York: Columbia University Press, 1991), 1–53; and Andie Tucher, *Froth and Scum: Truth, Beauty, Goodness, and the Ax Murder in America's First Mass Medium* (Chapel Hill: University of North Carolina Press, 1994).

21. On the diversifying readership of turn-of-the-century newspapers, see Leonard, *News for All*; Gerald J. Baldasty, *The Commercialization of News in the Nineteenth Century* (Madison: University of Wisconsin Press, 1992); and David Paul Nord, "Working-Class Readers: Family, Community, and Reading in Late Nineteenth-Century America," in *Communities of Journalism*. On women's increasing presence on newspaper staffs, see Alice Fahs, *Out on Assignment: Newspaper Women and the Making of Modern Public Space* (Chapel Hill: University of North Carolina Press, 2011); and Jan Whitt, *Women in American Journalism: A New History* (Urbana: University of Illinois Press, 2008). There has been little written on immigrant journalists as a group, but their ranks include Joseph Pulitzer, editor of the *New York World*; S. S. McClure, founder of the McClure syndicate; Prosper Fiorini (pen name: Maurice Ketten) and Valerian Gribayedoff, *New York World* cartoonists; and Rudolph Dirks, creator of the *Katzenjammer Kids* comic strip.

22. The most concrete evidence of this special influence comes from a sociologist's survey performed after the scope of this study, in 1945. New Yorkers described what they missed about their daily newspapers during a seventeen-day news carriers'

strike; many of them spoke most passionately about features, columnists, and listings rather than specific current events. Bernard Berelson, "What 'Missing the Newspaper' Means," in *Communications Research, 1948–1949*, ed. Paul Felix Lazarsfeld and Frank Stanton (New York: Harper & Brothers, 1949), 111–29. Most journalism histories mention the birth of features such as the women's page and the comic strips, but few delve into the actual content of those features. Among the journalism histories that incorporate discussions of feature news are Gerald J. Baldasty, *E. W. Scripps and the Business of Newspapers* (Urbana: University of Illinois Press, 1999); George Juergens, *Joseph Pulitzer and the New York World* (Princeton, NJ: Princeton University Press, 1966); and Peter Conolly-Smith, *Translating America: An Immigrant Press Visualizes American Popular Culture, 1890–1918* (Washington, DC: Smithsonian Books, 2004). Gunther Barth, though he writes in general ways about newspapers, does claim that features were some of the most important innovations in late nineteenth- and early twentieth-century news. See Barth, *City People: The Rise of Modern City Culture in Nineteenth-Century America* (New York: Oxford University Press, 1980), 58–109.

CHAPTER ONE

1. William T. Stead, *The Americanization of the World* (New York: Horace Markley, 1901), 290.

2. Ibid., 292.

3. Whitelaw Reid, *Some Newspaper Tendencies: An Address Delivered Before the Editorial Associations of New-York and Ohio* (New York: Henry Holt, 1879), 5.

4. On nineteenth-century Americans' distrust of advertising, see Neil Harris, *Humbug: The Art of P. T. Barnum* (Chicago: University of Chicago Press, 1981); Steven Fox, *The Mirror Makers: A History of American Advertising and Its Creators* (New York: Morrow, 1984), 15–19; and Frank Presbrey, *The History and Development of Advertising* (Garden City, NY: Doubleday, Doran & Co., 1929), 211–26, 289–301.

5. Daniel J. Boorstin, *The Americans: The Democratic Experience* (New York: Vintage, 1974), 138.

6. On nineteenth-century reading habits, see Ronald J. Zboray and Mary Saracino Zboray, *Everyday Ideas: Socioliterary Experience among Antebellum New Englanders* (Knoxville: University of Tennessee Press, 2006); William J. Gilmore-Lehne, *Reading Becomes a Necessity of Life: Material and Cultural Life in Rural New England, 1780–1835* (Knoxville: University of Tennessee Press, 1989); David M. Henkin, *City Reading: Written Words and Public Spaces in Antebellum New York* (New York: Columbia University Press, 1999); Thomas C. Leonard, *News for All: America's Coming-of-Age with the Press* (New York: Oxford University Press, 1995), 13, 20–21; and Ellen Gruber Garvey, "The Power of Recirculation: Scrapbooks and the Reception of the Nineteenth-Century Press," in *New Directions in American Reception Study*, ed. Philip Goldstein and James L. Machor (New York: Oxford University Press, 2008), 211–31.

7. Glenn S. Williamson, "The Mechanical Department," in *Journalism: Its Relation to and Influence upon the Political, Social, Professional, Financial, and Commercial Life of the United States of America*, ed. New York Press Club (New York: New York Press Club, 1905), 48. On nineteenth-century methods of newsprint processing, see Joel Munsell, *Chronology of the Origin and Progress of Paper and Paper Making* (Albany, NY: J. Munsell, 1876; reprint, New York: Garland, 1980); and David C. Smith, "Wood Pulp and Newspapers, 1867–1900," *Business History Review* 38 (1964): 328–45.

8. Alfred McClung Lee, *The Daily Newspaper in America: The Evolution of a Social Instrument* (New York: Macmillan, 1937), 323.

9. Williamson, "The Mechanical Department," 47–49. The *New York Tribune* operated the first commercial linotype in 1886, and the machines became commonplace in metropolitan newspapers over the next decade.

10. Ibid., 47.

11. Thorin Tritter, "Paper Profits in Public Service: Money Making in the New York Newspaper Industry, 1830–1930" (PhD diss., Columbia University, 2000), 191.

12. M. A. Steigers to Joseph Pulitzer, 19 July 1902, Pulitzer Papers, Columbia University Rare Books and Manuscripts.

13. Will C. Conrad, Kathleen F. Wilson, and Dale Wilson, *The Milwaukee Journal: The First Eighty Years* (Madison: University of Wisconsin Press, 1964), 45.

14. William Leach, *Land of Desire: Merchants, Power, and the Rise of a New American Culture* (New York: Pantheon, 1993), 42. This ratio of advertising to national income would stay the same for the next sixty years.

15. Among the most useful studies on the growth of the advertising industry in the late nineteenth and early twentieth centuries are Leach, *Land of Desire*; Roland Marchand, *Advertising the American Dream: Making Way for Modernity, 1920–1940* (Berkeley: University of California Press, 1985); Pamela Laird, *Advertising Progress: American Business and the Rise of Consumer Marketing* (Baltimore: Johns Hopkins University Press, 1998); and Presbrey, *History and Development of Advertising*. On advertising agencies in particular, see Daniel Pope, *The Making of Modern Advertising* (New York: Basic Books, 1983), 112–82; Fox, *The Mirror Makers*; and Lee, *The Daily Newspaper in America*, 338–53.

16. M. M. Gilliam, "The Wanamaker Advertising Idea," *Printers' Ink: A Journal for Advertisers* 6, no. 1 (January 6, 1892): 4–7.

17. On experiments within newspapers' advertising rules, see Presbrey, *History and Development of Advertising*, 227–52; and Boorstin, *The Americans: The Democratic Experience*, 137–48.

18. Richard Ohmann, *Selling Culture: Magazines, Markets, and the Class at the Turn of the Century* (London: Verso, 1996), 29. Also on the magazines of this era, see Jennifer Scanlon, *Inarticulate Longings: The Ladies' Home Journal, Gender, and the Promise of Consumer Culture* (New York: Routledge, 1995); Helen Damon-Moore, *Magazines for the Millions: Gender and Commerce in the Ladies' Home Journal and the Saturday Evening Post, 1880–1910* (Albany: State University of New York Press, 1994); and Mark J. Noonan, *Reading the Century Illustrated Monthly Magazine: American Literature and Culture, 1870–1893* (Kent, OH: Kent State University Press, 2010).

19. Presbrey, *History and Development of Advertising*, 473–74, and Upton Sinclair, *The Brass Check: A Study of American Journalism* (Pasadena, CA: published by the author, 1919), 295–96.

20. Willard Holcomb, *The Merry-Go-Round: A Volume of Verse Suitable for the Silly Season*, vol. 2, no. 6 of *Bauble* (July 1896): 83, as quoted in Frank Luther Mott, *A History of American Magazines*, vol. 4, *1885–1905* (Cambridge, MA: Harvard University Press, 1938), 150. On readers clipping advertisements, see Ellen Gruber Garvey, *The Adman in the Parlor: Magazines and the Gendering of Consumer Culture, 1880s to 1910s* (New York: Oxford University Press, 1996), 16–50.

21. William R. Scott, *Scientific Circulation Management for Newspapers* (New York: Ronald Press, 1915), 36.

22. Richard L. Kaplan, "From Partisanship to Professionalism: The Transformation

of the Daily Press," in *A History of the Book in America*, vol. 4, *Print in Motion: The Expansion of Publishing and Reading in the United States, 1880-1940*, ed. Carl F. Kaestle and Janice A. Radway (Chapel Hill: University of North Carolina Press, 2009), 125.

23. Tritter, "Paper Profits in Public Service," 167.

24. A few slogans predated this era; since 1833, *New York Sun* readers had seen in the nameplate, "It Shines for All." Some newspaper nameplates had included small illustrations since the eighteenth century, but pictures became more common and typefaces became more distinctive over the course of the nineteenth century.

25. Scott, *Scientific Circulation Management*, 17-23.

26. Lee, *The Daily Newspaper in America*, 283.

27. Presbrey, *History and Development of Advertising*, 507.

28. This practice started in the 1830s but only became common by the turn of the century. Lee, *The Daily Newspaper in America*, 282. Examples include *New York Herald* ad in the *New York Sun*, 20 August 1893, 8; *Philadelphia Inquirer* ad in the *Philadelphia Evening Bulletin*, 21 March 1916, 12; and ad for the *Philadelphia Evening Bulletin* in the *Philadelphia Public Ledger*, 26 March 1916, 12.

29. These posters survive in "Circulation Department General" series, Chicago Tribune Departmental Papers, Col. McCormick Research Center, Wheaton, IL.

30. The onlooker was describing the electric sign over the *New York Times* building entrance, erected in 1895. Unattributed quote taken from *Printer's Ink*, in Presbrey, *History and Development of Advertising*, 507.

31. For a study of the chaotic visual and textual world of American cities in the antebellum era, see Henkin, *City Reading* (n. 6 above, this chap.).

32. Lee, *The Daily Newspaper in America*, 283. Twelve cents was the *Philadelphia Public Ledger*'s rate from 1880 through the early 1900s.

33. Scott reprints an example of this kind of list in *Scientific Circulation Management for Newspapers*, 104-5.

34. *New Orleans States-Item*, 8 November 1885, quoted in John Wilds, *Afternoon Story: A Century of the New Orleans States-Item* (Baton Rouge: Louisiana State University Press, 1976). Newsboys' shouting grew so loud and alarming during World War I that some publishers and city governments put bans on the practice. Leonard, *News for All*, 155.

35. Don C. Seitz, *Training for the Newspaper Trade* (Philadelphia: J. B. Lippincott, 1916), 139.

36. Tritter, "Paper Profits in Public Service," 146, 160; John L. Given, *Making a Newspaper* (New York: Henry Holt, 1907), 9.

37. Given, *Making a Newspaper*, 59, 61, 62.

38. Will Irwin, "The American Newspaper: A Study of Journalism and Its Relation to the Public," pt. 7, "The Reporter and the News," *Collier's Weekly*, 22 April 1911, 21. The only time editors had commissioned such thorough reporting during the mid-nineteenth century was during the Civil War. By the 1890s and 1900s, however, the crush of newspaper competition within big cities inspired editors to devote as much time and money to urban events as they had to war zones.

39. Dana calculated these numbers in 1882. Frank M. O'Brien, *The Story of the Sun, New York, 1833-1918* (New York: George H. Doran, 1918), 180. On the importance of scoops, see Lincoln Steffens, "The Business of a Newspaper," *Scribner's Magazine*, October 1897, 461-62; "Morning and Evening Newspapers," in *Journalism*, ed. New York Press Club, 173.

40. Tritter, "Paper Profits in Public Service," 146, 160.

41. Given, *Making a Newspaper*, 64–65.

42. Ibid., 302–3.

43. "Morning and Evening Newspapers," 173. Given mentions the same process in *Making a Newspaper*, 303.

44. Harold A. Williams, *The Baltimore Sun, 1837–1987* (Baltimore: Johns Hopkins University Press, 1987), 227, and the *Philadelphia Evening Item*, 20 June 1902, 4.

45. Charles D. Platt, "The Circulation Department," in *Journalism*, ed. New York Press Club, 173. Posters publicizing upcoming Sunday editions often advertised these special inserts; see newspaper posters in the Art and Architecture Collection, New York Public Library, and in the Art Posters Collection, New-York Historical Society.

46. This reporter was Elizabeth Cochrane, writing as "Nellie Bly." She traveled around the world in seventy-three days in 1889 and 1890.

47. Letter from Marjorie Van Horn in *Collier's Weekly*, 2 September 1911, 2.

48. See John Henry Hepp, *The Middle-Class City: Transforming Space and Time in Philadelphia, 1876–1926* (Philadelphia: University of Pennsylvania Press, 2003), 140; Charles Johanningsmeier, *Fiction and the American Literary Marketplace: The Role of Newspaper Syndicates, 1860–1900* (New York: Cambridge University Press, 1997), 187–92; and Zboray and Zboray, *Everyday Ideas*.

49. William Dean Howells, "What Should Girls Read?" *Harper's Bazaar* 36, no. 11 (November 1902): 960.

50. Nathaniel Fowler, "Reaching the Men through the Women," *Printer's Ink*, 22 July 1892, quoted in Presbrey, *History and Development of Advertising*, 317.

51. *New York World*, 27 October 1889, 21. This suggestion was one of many submitted (and then printed) during a contest in which the *World* asked readers how it could improve itself and gave cash prizes for the best ideas.

52. Presbrey, *History and Development of Advertising*, 480–81.

53. Platt, "The Circulation Department," 171–72.

54. *Evening Wisconsin*, 22 March 1893, front page. For an older overview of the birth of women's pages in U.S. daily newspapers, see George Juergens, *Joseph Pulitzer and the New York World* (Princeton, NJ: Princeton University Press, 1966), xi, 132–72; for a new one, see Julie Golia, "Courting Women, Courting Advertisers: The Woman's Page and the Transformation of the American Newspaper, 1895–1935," *Journal of American History* 103, no. 3 (December 2016), 606–28.

55. On the working-class readership of these penny papers, see Alexander Saxton, "Problems of Class and Race in the Origins of the Mass Circulation Press," *American Quarterly* 36, no. 2 (Summer 1984): 211–34.

56. Kaplan, "From Partisanship to Professionalism," 121. Kaplan also notes that afternoon papers accounted for 74 percent of dailies in 1910. This figure can be a bit misleading, since morning newspapers' circulations were often larger. The morning field, by 1910, was dominated by a few mass-readership papers; the afternoon offered smaller and more locally based papers. For more on the differences in audience and content between morning and afternoon papers, see Steffens, "The Business of a Newspaper," 449–50, and "Morning and Afternoon Newspapers," in *Journalism*, ed. New York Press Club, 30–32.

57. Ross Gregory, ed., *Almanacs of American Life: Victorian America, 1876–1913* (New York: Facts on File, 1996), 80.

58. Mark S. Littman, *A Statistical Portrait of the United States: Social Conditions and Trends* (Lanham, MD: Bernan Press, 1998), 15.

59. The illiteracy rate among foreign-born Americans ranged between 12 and 13.1 percent from 1880 to 1920. The illiteracy rate among native-born whites dropped from 8.7 to 2 percent over this span. Don Dodd, *Historical Statistics of the United States, 1790–1970* (Tuscaloosa: University of Alabama Press, 1973), 1:382. Literacy and newspaper habits also varied widely from one ethnic group to another. Germans were some of the most avid newspaper readers, while Italians often picked up the habit years or even generations after emigrating.

60. Quote is from Gerald J. Baldasty, *E. W. Scripps and the Business of Newspapers* (Urbana: University of Illinois Press, 1999), 124.

61. I draw my description of Pulitzer's newspapers from my own research and from Juergens, *Joseph Pulitzer and the New York World*, 30, 94–115.

62. For a sampling of the *New York World*'s spectacular color Sunday sections, see Nicholson Baker and Margaret Brentano, eds., *The World on Sunday: Graphic Art in Joseph Pulitzer's Newspaper (1898-1911)* (New York: Bulfinch Press, 2005).

63. Baldasty, *E. W. Scripps and the Business of Newspapers*, 133, 158.

64. Juergens, *Joseph Pulitzer and the New York World*, 96, 115–17. On the history of the newspaper comic strip, see Judith O'Sullivan, *The Great American Comic Strip: One Hundred Years of Cartoon Art* (Boston: Little, Brown, 1990); Jerry Robinson, *The Comics: An Illustrated History of Comic Strip Art* (Milwaukie, OR: Dark Horse, 2011); Bill Blackbeard and Martin Williams, eds., *Smithsonian Collection of Newspaper Comics* (1977; repr., Washington, DC: Smithsonian Institution Press, 1984); and Brian Walker, *The Comics: The Complete Collection* (New York: Abrams ComicArts, 2011).

65. Edwin Emery and Michael Emery, *The Press and America: An Interpretive History of the Mass Media*, 4th ed. (Englewood Cliffs, NJ: Prentice-Hall, Inc., 1978), 247.

66. Seitz, *Training for the Newspaper Trade*, 89–90.

67. Ralph Berengren, "The Humor of the Colored Supplement," *Atlantic*, August 1906, reprinted in Willard Grosvenor Bleyer, ed., *The Profession of Journalism: A Collection of Articles on Newspaper Editing and Publishing, Taken from the Atlantic Monthly* (Boston: Atlantic Monthly Press, 1918), 238, 242.

68. Platt, "The Circulation Department," 172.

69. On the strike, see Lee, *The Daily Newspaper in America*, 402. On other criticisms, see James Edward Rogers, *The American Newspaper* (Chicago: University of Chicago Press, 1909), 157–58.

70. *Philadelphia Public Ledger*, 26 March 1916, 5.

71. On these tactics, see Given, *Making a Newspaper*, 3–4, and Jason Rogers, *Newspaper Building: Application of Efficiency to Editing, to Mechanical Production, to Circulation and Advertising* (New York: Harper & Brothers, 1918), 143. For examples of color-printed cut-out games, dioramas, and activities in the turn-of-the-century *New York World*, see Baker and Brentano, eds., *The World on Sunday*, 28, 42, 51, 53, 54, 90, 92, 94, 100.

72. Leonard, *News for All*, 163.

73. Ibid., 165.

74. Given, *Making a Newspaper*, 308.

75. *Philadelphia North American*, 20 June 1909, news section, page 5.

76. As quoted in Kaplan, "From Partisanship to Professionalism," 128.

77. An exchange in the files of the *St. Louis Post-Dispatch* makes this logic clear; the managing editor mentions that the paper's new music column will not run if the paper cannot enlist enough advertisers to support it. Don C. Seitz, memorandum on Post-Dispatch Music, 13 September 1899, Pulitzer Papers, September 1899, Columbia University Rare Books and Manuscripts.

78. Scott, *Scientific Circulation Management for Newspapers*, 206.

79. *Advertising World* (Columbus, Ohio), 14 June 1897, 1. I owe this reference to Gerald J. Baldasty and Jeffrey Rutenbeck, "Money, Politics, and Newspapers: The Business Environment of Press Partisanship in the Late Nineteenth Century," *Journalism History* 15 (1988): 66.

80. "Morning and Afternoon Newspapers," 29-30.

81. Hepp, *The Middle-Class City*, 101. On changing leisure habits in the late nineteenth century, see John F. Kasson, *Amusing the Million: Coney Island at the Turn of the Century* (New York: Hill and Wang, 1978); David Nasaw, *Going Out: The Rise and Fall of Public Amusements* (Cambridge, MA: Harvard University Press, 1999); and Roy Rosenzweig, *Eight Hours for What We Will: Workers and Leisure in an Industrial City, 1870-1920* (New York: Cambridge University Press, 1983).

82. Lee, *The Daily Newspaper in America*, 396.

83. Scott, *Scientific Circulation Management for Newspapers*, 199. Lincoln Steffens says the same in "The Business of a Newspaper," 464. On the rise of the Sunday newspaper, see Arthur Benington, "The Sunday Newspaper," in *Journalism*, ed. New York Press Club; Emery and Emery, *The Press and America*, 246; Robert Ezra Park, "The Natural History of the Newspaper," in *The City*, ed. Robert Ezra Park, Ernest Watson Burgess, Roderick Duncan McKenzie, and Louis Wirth (Chicago: University of Chicago Press, 1923), 96; Gunther Barth, *City People: The Rise of Modern City Culture in Nineteenth-Century America* (New York: Oxford University Press, 1980), 79; Gerald J. Baldasty, *The Commercialization of News in the Nineteenth Century* (Madison: University of Wisconsin Press, 1992), 122; and Lee, *The Daily Newspaper in America*, 380-404.

84. *New York World*, 27 October 1889, 13.

85. As indicated by masthead circulation statistics pre-1914 and by Audit Bureau of Circulations numbers post-1914.

86. Lloyd Wendt, *Chicago Tribune: The Rise of a Great American Newspaper* (Chicago: Rand McNally & Co., 1979), 456.

87. Given, *Making a Newspaper*, 313.

88. *Philadelphia Record*, 4 November 1907, 8. For other ads that illustrated why and how to use classifieds, see the *New York World*, 16 March 1885, cartoons at the top of the front page; *Philadelphia Public Ledger*, 6 May 1908, 14; and the *Evening Wisconsin*, 28 June 1913, 5.

89. Quote from *New York World*, 13 August 1905, Manhattan section, page 1. Two cents was the rate that the *Philadelphia Public Ledger* offered in 1908.

90. W. Ward Damon, "Advertising," in *Journalism*, ed. New York Press Club; and Wendt, *Chicago Tribune*, 454.

91. Nathaniel Fowler, *How to Sell, Being a Series of True-to-Life Dialogues between Salesmen and Customers, Covering Many Classes of Wholesale and Retail Selling and Buying in the Store, the Office, and on the Road* (Chicago: A. C. McClurg & Co., 1915), 201-7. Other books that advised these space salesmen include Marco Morrow, *Things to Tell*

the Merchant (Lawrence: University of Kansas, Department of Journalism Press, 1914); and Joseph E. Chasnoff, *Selling Newspaper Space* (New York: The Ronald Press, 1913).

92. Fowler, *How to Sell*, 194.

93. *Chicago Defender*, 5 April 1913, 2.

94. *Philadelphia North American*, 26 October 1913, third news section, 15.

95. Lee, *The Daily Newspaper in America*, 235, 355.

96. These were all ideas suggested by Truman DeWeese in *Keeping a Dollar at Work: Fifty "Talks" on Newspaper Advertising Written for the N.Y. Evening Post* (New York: New York Evening Post, 1915).

97. R. Roy Shuman, "Filling the 'Ad' Columns," in *Practical Journalism: A Complete Manual of the Best Newspaper Methods*, ed. Edwin L. Shuman (New York: D. Appleton and Company, 1903), 192. For another source on the roles newspapers played in advertising in the first decades of the twentieth century, see Nathaniel Fowler, *How to Sell*, chap. 22.

98. Address of Frank Munsey before the Sphinx Club at the Waldorf-Astoria, New York, 12 October 1898, 16, William Thompson Dewart Collection of Frank A. Munsey and *New York Sun* Papers, New-York Historical Society.

99. Edward C. Drew, "The Merchants and the Press," *Journalism*, ed. New York Press Club, 138.

100. *Collier's Weekly*, 2 September 1911, 22.

101. That year, the Scripps-McRae chain refused $500,000 worth of ad copy. Lee, *The Daily Newspaper in America*, 328. Also on ad censorship, see Presbrey, *History and Development of Advertising*, 474, 481, 531; Scott, *Scientific Circulation Management for Newspapers*, 33; and Shuman, "Filling the 'Ad' Columns," 198–99.

102. Letter from Curtis C. Brown in *Collier's Weekly*, 2 September 1911, 23.

103. Magazines set the standard here, too. Warren wrote in his letter to Lawson: "That is one reason the L. H. Journal can get their price for advertising—they have a clean publication which everybody loves to look over." Victor Freemont Lawson Papers, Newberry Library.

104. Rogers, *Newspaper Building*, 243. Lincoln Steffens claimed that the most profitable papers were those who were strictest with their advertisers; Steffens, "The Business of a Newspaper," 465.

105. Stead, *The Americanization of the World*, 290.

106. Ibid., 290.

107. Both the *New York World* building, completed in 1890, and the *San Francisco Call* building, completed in 1898, had baroque domes; the *Milwaukee Germania* building, completed in 1896, sported turrets; both the *San Francisco Chronicle* building, completed in 1889, and the *New York Herald* building, completed in 1893, had signature clocks. Many of these structures were much larger than they needed to be to house a newspaper; they rented the extra space to other firms.

108. On the *Tribune*'s marble top, see Mona Domosh, "A Method for Interpreting Landscape: A Case Study of the New York World Building," *Area* 21, no. 4 (1989): 328–29; on the *World*'s view and brochure, see Angela M. Blake, *How New York Became American, 1890–1924* (Baltimore: Johns Hopkins University Press, 2009), 49, 53–55; and for the *Evening Wisconsin* print, see "Newspapers" file, Milwaukee Historical Society. For more on newspaper buildings, see Mona Domosh, "The Symbolism of the Skyscraper: Case Studies of New York's First Tall Buildings," *Journal of Urban History* 14, no. 3 (May

1988): 321–45; and Aurora Wallace, *Media Capital: Architecture and Communications in New York City* (Urbana: University of Illinois Press, 2012).

109. Chauncey Depew, quoted in the *New York World*, 11 October, 1889. I owe this reference to Mona Domosh's article "A Method for Interpreting Landscape," 348.

110. Photos of this practice include an image of the *Milwaukee Journal* office, by J. Robert Taylor, Classified File "Newspapers," 876 A, Wisconsin Historical Society, and one of the *New York Journal* building, in Bill Blackbeard, ed., *R. F. Outcault's The Yellow Kid: A Centennial Celebration of the Kid Who Started the Comics* (Northampton, MA: Kitchen Sink Press, 1995), 62. Mary Antin mentions the crowd studying the bulletin board outside the *Boston Herald* in her memoir *The Promised Land* (1912; repr., Princeton, NJ: Princeton University Press, 1969), 236.

111. Hy B. Turner, *When Giants Ruled: The Story of Park Row, New York's Great Newspaper Street* (New York: Fordham University Press, 1999), 127. The *Herald* would do something similar for baseball games between 1911 and 1913, setting up a diamond and moving the ball according to reports. Wallace, *Media Capital*, 77.

112. The estimate of freelancers comes from Steffens, "The Business of a Newspaper," 447. On the numbers and types of newspaper employees, see Tritter, "Paper Profits in Public Service," 136, 164; Directory of Public Ledger Employees, 1902, in *Notes and References Relating to the History of Philadelphia Newspapers, 1937*, 6:823, Philadelphia Public Library; and *Chicago Daily News* Staff List, 1895, folder 60, "Administrative and Operations," Chicago Daily News Collection, MMS Field Enterprises, Newberry Library.

113. "Art in Printers' Ink," *Milwaukee Sentinel*, 22 May 1892, 10.

114. Steffens, "The Business of a Newspaper," 463.

115. For a sampling of these behind-the-scenes articles, see Harold King, "Four and Twenty Hours in a Newspaper Office," *Once a Week Magazine*, 26 September 1863; "The Metropolitan Newspaper," *Harper's Monthly* 56 (December 1877): 43–59; and Elizabeth G. Jordan, "The Newspaper Woman's Story," *Lippincott's Monthly Magazine*, March 1893, 340–47.

116. Newsboy training became common in the 1880s; Scott, *Scientific Circulation Management for Newspapers*, 289.

117. Tritter, "Paper Profits in Public Service," 200.

118. Scott, *Scientific Circulation Management for Newspapers*, 100.

119. These tactics are suggested in James Philip MacCarthy, *The Newspaper Worker: A Manual for All Who Write* (New York: The Press Guild, 1906; repr., New York: Frank-Maurice, Inc., 1925), 10.

120. Kaplan, "From Partisanship to Professionalism," 137; and Given, *Making a Newspaper*, 272–73.

121. Shuman, ed., *Practical Journalism*, 28.

122. Given, *Making a Newspaper*, 272–73. Manuals and articles consistently discouraged young hopefuls from even trying to write for newspapers; see Given, *Making a Newspaper*; Shuman, ed., *Practical Journalism*; Edwin L. Shuman, *Steps into Journalism: Helps and Hints for Young Writers* (Evanston, IL: Evanston Press, 1894); Jordan, "The Newspaper Woman's Story"; and Flora McDonald, "The Newspaper Woman: One Side of the Question," *Journalist*, 26 January 1889, 13.

123. I take this John Reed quote from Richard O'Connor, *Heywood Broun: A Biography* (New York: Putnam, 1975), 22, and I owe the reference to Kaplan, "From Partisanship to Professionalism," 137.

124. Theodore Dreiser, "Out of My Newspaper Days," pt. 5, "I Quit the Game," *Bookman* 54, no. 8 (April 1922): 118, 124.

125. Will Irwin, "The American Newspaper: A Study of Journalism and Its Relation to the Public," pt. 6, "The Editor and the News," *Collier's Weekly*, 1 April 1911, 29.

126. These writers began working for newspapers in the 1840s through the 1860s. Croly mostly wrote domestic reflections and advice; Greenwood often worked as a correspondent; and Fern wrote about women's lives, sometimes with a feminist bent. For a survey of women journalists of the 1870s and 1880s, see the "Women's Issue" of the trade magazine the *Journalist*, 26 January 1889.

127. Shuman, ed., *Practical Journalism*, 148.

128. In 1880, 288 out of 12,308 journalists in the United States were women, and in 1900, 2,193 out of a total of 30,098 were women. By 1920 the numbers had risen, with women making up 16.8 percent of the nation's reporters and editors. U.S. census data, cited in Deborah Chambers, Linda Steiner, and Carole Fleming, *Women and Journalism* (London: Routledge, 2004), 15.

129. For histories of women journalists in this era, see Alice Fahs, *Out on Assignment: Newspaper Women and the Making of Modern Public Space* (Chapel Hill: University of North Carolina Press, 2011); Agnes Hooper Gottlieb, "Grit Your Teeth, Then Learn to Swear: Women in Journalistic Careers, 1850–1926," *American Journalism* 18, no. 1 (2001): 53–72; Jean Marie Lutes, *Front Page Girls: Women Journalists in American Culture and Fiction, 1880–1930* (Ithaca, NY: Cornell University Press, 2007); Jan Whitt, *Women in American Journalism: A New History* (Urbana: University of Illinois Press, 2008); and Barbara Belford, *Brilliant Bylines: A Biographical Anthology of Notable Newspaperwomen in America* (New York: Columbia University Press, 1986).

130. A *New York Sun* code of conduct from 1894 needed to explicitly state that spitting on the floor, using obscene language, and arriving at work intoxicated were all prohibited. "Some Rules of Style for the Guidance of Compositors and Proof Readers Employed on The Sun," Broadside, New-York Historical Society.

131. Flora McDonald, "The Newspaper Woman: One Side of the Question," 13.

132. Jordan, "The Newspaper Woman's Story," 342.

133. Isabel Worrell Ball as quoted in Ida Husted Harper, "The Training of Women Journalists," in *The International Congress of Women of 1899*, vol. 4, *Women in the Professions* (London: T. Fisher Unwin, 1900), 54.

134. *Journalist*, 26 January 1889; quote taken from Gottlieb, "Grit Your Teeth, Then Learn to Swear," 53.

135. James H. Collins, "The American Grub Street," *Atlantic*, November 1906. On the rise of freelance writing, also see Lee, *The Daily Newspaper in America*, 404, 588.

136. On some women's preference for freelance writing, see Collins, "The American Grub Street," 261–62.

137. Lewis V. Bogy, *How to Be a Newspaper Correspondent and Feature Story Writer* (Washington, DC: Press Correspondence Bureau, 1910).

138. Fred L. Wenner, of Guthrie, Oklahoma, in the *Journalist*, 2 April 1892, 15.

139. See *New York Herald* ad in *New York Sun*, 20 August 1893, 8.

140. On newspaper workers' hours, see Louis M. Lyons, *Newspaper Story: One Hundred Years of the Boston Globe* (Cambridge, MA: Belknap Press, 1971), 214–15; Tritter, "Paper Profits in Public Service," 125, 127, 215; and Shuman, ed., *Practical Journalism*, 18.

141. On the practice of issuing many daily editions, see Given, *Making a Newspaper*, 19; and Lee, *The Daily Newspaper in America*, 276–81. In my research I encountered

morning editions, "Home" editions, five o'clock editions, "Night Special" editions, "Final Night Extras," and "Tenth Extra Racing" editions.

142. *Collier's Weekly*, 2 September 1911, 22. On the increasing amount of work done during the night in this time, see Peter C. Baldwin, *In the Watches of the Night: Life in the Nocturnal City, 1820–1930* (Chicago: University of Chicago Press, 2012).

143. For an overview of how the partisan-paper model worked, see David M. Ryfe, "News, Culture, and Public Life: A Study of Nineteenth-Century American Journalism," *Journalism Studies* 7, no. 1 (2006): 60–77.

144. On newspapers' evolution toward the joint-stock corporation model, see Tritter, "Paper Profits in Public Service," 101–16, 143–61. On newspapers' expenses outpacing the ability of political parties to cover them, see Baldasty and Rutenbeck, "Money, Politics, and Newspapers," 65.

145. Shuman, ed., *Practical Journalism*, 16–17.

146. Tritter, "Paper Profits in Public Service," 143.

147. Steffens, "The Business of a Newspaper," 458–59.

148. MacCarthy, *The Newspaper Worker*, 16.

149. Nelson Antrim Crawford, *The Ethics of Journalism* (New York: Alfred A. Knopf, 1924). The pamphlet was issued in several earlier editions as well. On reporters who refused to register with a party, see Michael Schudson, "Persistence of Vision: Partisan Journalism in the Mainstream Press," in *A History of the Book in America*, ed. Kaestle and Radway, 4:140–50. On the rise of a new standard of objectivity, see Richard L. Kaplan, *Politics and the American Press: The Rise of Objectivity, 1865–1920* (New York: Cambridge University Press, 2002); Michael Schudson, *Discovering the News: A Social History of American Newspapers* (New York: Basic Books, 1978); Ted Curtis Smythe, *The Gilded Age Press, 1865–1900* (Westport, CT: Praeger, 2003); Emery and Emery, *The Press and America*, 219–36; and Hazel Dicken Garcia, *Journalistic Standards in Nineteenth-Century America* (Madison: University of Wisconsin Press, 1989).

150. Melville E. Stone, *Fifty Years a Journalist* (Garden City, NY: Doubleday, Page, 1921), 53.

151. Will Irwin, "The American Newspaper: A Study of Journalism and Its Relation to the Public," pt. 12, "The Foe from Within," *Collier's Weekly*, 1 July 1911, 17.

152. For example, railroad magnate Jay Gould bought stock in the *New York Tribune* in the 1870s, and John D. Rockefeller, owner of Standard Oil, invested $10,000 in the *Cleveland Herald* in 1879. Linda Lawson, *Truth in Publishing: Federal Regulation of the Press's Business Practices 1880–1920* (Carbondale: Southern Illinois University Press, 1993), 15–16.

153. Sinclair, *The Brass Check*, 236.

154. Lee, *The Daily Newspaper in America*, 667–68; Editorial, *Journalist*, 18 August 1888, 8.

155. John A. Cockerill credited press clubs with boosting professional morale and standards in "The Newspaper of the Future" (Journalist Series), *Lippincott's Monthly Magazine*, August 1892. On press clubs, see William H. Freeman, *The Press Club of Chicago: A History* (Chicago: Press Club of Chicago, 1894); *Journalist*, 29 March 1884, 3; and *Journalist*, 4 December 1897. For a reminiscence about the socializing among reporters at such a press club, see Charles H. Dennis, "Whitechapel Nights," *Chicago Daily News*, 29 July 1936.

156. On press clubs, see Hamilton Holt, *Commercialism and Journalism* (Boston:

Houghton Mifflin, 1909), 77 78; and Bessie Louise Pierce, *A History of Chicago*, vol. 3, *The Rise of a Modern City, 1871–1893* (New York: Alfred A. Knopf, 1957), 410.

157. Invitation from Milwaukee Press Club to John Goadby Gregory, 11 July 1906, "Correspondence," John Goadby Gregory Papers, Wisconsin Historical Society.

158. For these and similar examples of careers that spanned news and business, see the personal notes in issues of the trade journal the *Journalist* in the 1890s, as well as Ethel M. Colson Brazelton, *Writing and Editing for Women: A Bird's-Eye View of the Widening Opportunities for Women in Newspaper, Magazine and Other Writing Work* (New York: Funk & Wagnalls Company, 1927), 85; Lee, *The Daily Newspaper in America*, 460; Lyons, *Newspaper Story*, 83; and Fanny Butcher, *Many Lives—One Love* (New York: Harper & Row, 1972), 112.

159. Lee, *The Daily Newspaper in America*, 443.

160. Collins, "The American Grub Street," 252; Will Irwin, "The American Newspaper: A Study of Journalism and Its Relation to the Public," pt. 10, "The Unhealthy Alliance," *Collier's Weekly*, 3 June 1911, 17–19, 28–29, 31, 34; and Genevieve Jackson Boughner, *Women in Journalism: A Guide to the Opportunities and a Manual of the Technique of Women's Work for Newspapers and Magazines* (New York: D. Appleton, 1926), 165.

161. Collins, "The American Grub Street," 263.

162. For a list of journalism schools and their founding dates as well as program offerings, see *Editor & Publisher, International Yearbook Number for 1926*, 30 January 1926, 218–20.

163. How-to books that covered both journalism and copywriting include Arnold Bennett, *Journalism for Women: A Practical Guide* (New York: J. Lane, 1898); Shuman, ed., *Practical Journalism*; Boughner, *Women in Journalism*; and Robert Cortes Holliday and Alexander Van Rensselaer, *The Business of Writing: A Practical Guide for Writers* (New York: George H. Duran, 1922).

164. Anonymous, "Confessions of a Managing Editor," *Collier's Weekly*, 28 October 1911, 19.

165. Will Irwin, "The American Newspaper: A Study of Journalism and Its Relation to the Public," pt. 9, "The Advertising Influence," *Collier's Weekly*, 20 May 1911, 16, 23–24; Holt, *Commercialism and Journalism*, 76, and Anonymous, "Confessions of a Managing Editor," 19, 20, 24, 26.

166. Sinclair, *The Brass Check*, 213.

167. The *Day Book* ran from 1911 to 1917. Duane C. S. Stoltzfus, *Freedom from Advertising: E. W. Scripps's Chicago Experiment* (Urbana: University of Illinois Press, 2007).

168. F. D. Corley to Victor Lawson, 7 December 1918. Victor Freemont Lawson Papers, Newberry Library. For a list of sums that companies spent on newspaper advertising, see Holt, *Commercialism and Journalism*, 13.

169. Lee, *The Daily Newspaper in America*, 438.

170. Joseph Pulitzer's files contain multiple railroad passes; Joseph Pulitzer Papers, Columbia University Rare Books and Manuscripts. Also see Lee, *The Daily Newspaper in America*, 434 and 459. For journalists' stories about pushy press agents, see T. Campbell-Copeland, *The Ladder of Journalism: How to Climb It* (New York: Allan Forman, 1893), 31–33; and Stone, *Fifty Years a Journalist*, 55.

171. Sinclair, *The Brass Check*, 285.

172. Given, *Making a Newspaper*, 309–10. See also Will Irwin, "The American Newspaper: A Study of Journalism and Its Relation to the Public," pt. 11, "Our Kind of

People," *Collier's Weekly*, 17 June 1911, 17–18; Anonymous, "Confessions of a Managing Editor," 20, 24; and Lee, *The Daily Newspaper in America*, 463.

173. Jason Rogers, editorial, *Editor & Publisher* 6:46, 4 May 1907, 4. Other sources on the press agent include Anonymous, "Confessions of a Managing Editor," 18; Baldasty, *The Commercialization of News*, 70–71; Given, *Making a Newspaper*, 309–10; Irwin, "The American Newspaper," pt. 10, "The Unhealthy Alliance," 13; and Sinclair, *The Brass Check*, 282–85.

174. "What Milwaukee Merchants Are Offering," *Milwaukee Sentinel*, 29 January 1903, front page.

175. Sinclair, *The Brass Check*, 213.

176. Gilliam, "The Wanamaker Advertising Idea," 4–7.

177. On Wanamaker's newsy strategy, see Joseph Appel, *Growing Up with Advertising* (New York: Business Bourse, 1940), 25, 43, 92, 97. Appel served as an advertising manager with Wanamaker.

178. Wanamaker's ad, *Philadelphia Record*, 19 April 1887, 3.

179. Shuman, ed., *Practical Journalism*, 186.

180. This talk was given at the University of California and reprinted in Holt, *Commercialism and Journalism*.

181. Anonymous, "Confessions of a Managing Editor," 20, 24, 26.

182. Lee, *The Daily Newspaper in America*, 436, 444.

183. Ibid., 445–46.

184. Lawson, "When Publishers Invited Federal Regulation to Curb Circulation Abuses," *Journalism Quarterly* 71 (1994): 114. Also on the Newspaper Publicity Act see Lawson, *Truth in Publishing*; and Timothy E. Cook, *Governing with the News: The News Media as a Political Institution* (Chicago: University of Chicago Press, 1998), 43–44.

185. *Philadelphia North American*, 20 March 1909, as quoted in Holt, *Commercialism and Journalism*, 92.

186. Scott, *Scientific Circulation Management for Newspapers*, 34.

187. Unnamed correspondent, *Collier's Weekly*, 19 August 1911, 18.

188. Baldasty, *E. W. Scripps and the Business of Newspapers*, 133, 147–48.

189. Hearst's papers held larger circulations than Scripps's papers in San Francisco, Chicago, and Los Angeles. Baldasty, *E. W. Scripps and the Business of Newspapers*, 152.

190. The *New York World* claimed the biggest circulation in the country in this era; it reached 1,500,000 readers every day by 1898. Juergens, *Joseph Pulitzer and the New York World*, vii.

CHAPTER TWO

1. Ad for the *Inquirer Almanac*, *Philadelphia Inquirer*, 24 February 1899, 13.

2. I draw this background on advice literature from Arthur M. Schlesinger, *Learning How to Behave: A Historical Study of American Etiquette Books* (New York: MacMillan, 1946), and Judy Hilkey, *Character Is Capital: Success Manuals and Manhood in Gilded Age America* (Chapel Hill: University of North Carolina Press, 1997).

3. Clara S. J. Moore, *Sensible Etiquette of the Best Society*, 10th rev. ed. (Philadelphia: Porter & Coates, 1878).

4. Schlesinger, *Learning How to Behave*, 34.

5. *Good Manners: A Manual of Etiquette in Good Society* (Philadelphia: Porter & Coates, 1870), iii. I owe this quote to Arthur M. Schlesinger, *Learning How to Behave*, 34.

6. Among the scholars who have considered newspapers as assimilators are Gunther Barth, *City People: The Rise of Modern City Culture in Nineteenth-Century America* (New York: Oxford University Press, 1980), 59–61; and Robert Ezra Park, "The Natural History of the Newspaper," in *The City*, ed. Robert Ezra Park, Ernest Watson Burgess, Roderick Duncan McKenzie, and Louis Wirth (Chicago: University of Chicago Press, 1923). For an overview of the foreign-language press in America, see Robert Ezra Park, *The Immigrant Press and Its Control* (New York: Harper & Brothers, 1922); Peter Conolly-Smith, *Translating America: An Immigrant Press Visualizes American Popular Culture, 1890–1918* (Washington, DC: Smithsonian Books, 2004); and Janet E. Steele, *The Sun Shines for All: Journalism and Ideology in the Life of Charles A. Dana* (Syracuse University Press, 1993), 119–20.

7. Barbara Mary Klaczynska, "Working Women in Philadelphia, 1900–1930" (PhD diss., Temple University, 1975).

8. The port reached its peak in the early twentieth century, between trade and new demands for ships for the post–Spanish American War navy; it was fading by the 1920s. Domenic Vitiello, *Engineering Philadelphia: The Sellers Family and the Industrial Metropolis* (Ithaca, NY: Cornell University Press, 2013), 154, 208.

9. Lincoln Steffens, "Philadelphia: Corrupt and Contented," *McClure's Magazine*, July 1903, 249–63.

10. Caroline Golab, "The Immigrant and the City: Poles, Italians, and Jews in Philadelphia, 1870–1920," in *The Peoples of Philadelphia: A History of Ethnic Groups and Lower-Class Life, 1790–1940*, ed. Allen F. Davis and Mark H. Haller (Philadelphia: Temple University Press, 1973), 203; and Nathaniel Burt and Wallace E. Davies, "The Iron Age, 1876–1905," in *Philadelphia: A 300 Year History*, ed. Nicholas B. Wainwright and Edwin Wolf (New York: W. W. Norton, 1982), 488.

11. Background on Philadelphia populations comes from Burt and Davies, "The Iron Age, 1876–1905"; Davis and Haller, eds., *The Peoples of Philadelphia*; and Fredric M. Miller, Morris J. Vogel, and Allen F. Davis, *Still Philadelphia: A Photographic History, 1890–1940* (Philadelphia: Temple University Press, 1983).

12. Vitiello, *Engineering Philadelphia*, 144; and Miller, Vogel, and Davis, *Still Philadelphia*, 66.

13. Klaczynska, "Working Women in Philadelphia," 5.

14. Ibid., 74–76; Miller, Vogel, and Davis, *Still Philadelphia*, 97.

15. Ray H. Abrams, "Residential Propinquity as a Factor in Marriage Selection," *American Sociological Review* 8 (June 1943): 292.

16. *Rowell's & Ayer's American Newspaper Directory* (New York: Geo. P. Rowell, 1891).

17. John F. Sutherland, "Housing the Poor in the City of Homes: Philadelphia at the Turn of the Century," in *The Peoples of Philadelphia*, ed. Davis and Haller, 182; and Miller, Vogel, and Davis, *Still Philadelphia*, 223.

18. Fourteen of those papers were in English, five in German. Newspaper numbers come from *Geo. P. Rowell & Co.'s American Newspaper Directory* (New York: George P. Rowell, 1880. This chapter does not study the advice material in the foreign-language press. The role of that press in immigrant assimilation deserves separate studies. Existing scholarship includes Conolly-Smith, *Translating America*; and Park, *The Immigrant Press and Its Control*. See also Isaac Metzker, ed., *A Bintel Brief: Sixty Years of Letters from the Lower East Side to the "Jewish Daily Forward"* (Garden City, NY: Doubleday & Company, 1971), for translations of advice columns that appeared in New York City's largest Yiddish-language newspaper.

19. "The Fashions," *Philadelphia Record*, December 9, 1882, 2. This article was reprinted from a women's magazine, *The Delineator*.

20. As recounted by Childs in a later anniversary edition of the paper, *Philadelphia Public Ledger*, 24 April 1893, 15. The *Ledger*'s claim to have run the first women's column is reinforced by various journalism histories, but newsweeklies and magazines were working along similar lines. One year before the *Ledger* began its "Women's Interests" column, Cyrus Curtis assembled clippings for a four-page magazine published out of Philadelphia, the *Tribune and Farmer*. The column "Woman and the Home" was the magazine's most popular feature and inspired him to found the *Ladies' Home Journal* in 1883. This column of clippings likely inspired the *Ledger*'s own.

21. *Philadelphia Public Ledger*, 30 November 1889, 5.

22. Within Philadelphia, the *North American* syndicated the advice column "Marion Harland Advises on Matters of Etiquette" in 1901 and ran a regular column "Advice on Social Customs" in 1909. A column titled "Social Problems" appeared in the *Philadelphia Evening Bulletin* by 1902, and a more specific "Points in Etiquette" column ran there by 1916. The *Public Ledger* printed the column "Good Form" by 1916.

23. "Dear Household," *Philadelphia Public Ledger*, 3 November 1902, 7.

24. On the mapping (and policing) of respectable urban space for women, see Karen Halttunen, *Confidence Men and Painted Women: A Study of Middle-Class Culture in America, 1830–1870* (New Haven, CT: Yale University Press, 1982); Mary Ting Yi Lui, *The Chinatown Trunk Mystery: Murder, Miscegenation, and Other Dangerous Encounters in Turn-of-the-Century New York City* (Princeton, NJ: Princeton University Press, 2005); and Mona Domosh, "Those 'Gorgeous Incongruities': Polite Politics and Public Space on the Streets of Nineteenth-Century New York City," *Annals of the Association of American Geographers* 88, no. 2 (1998): 209–26. John Hepp writes about public transit creating middle-class female space in Philadelphia: *The Middle-Class City: Transforming Space and Time in Philadelphia, 1876–1926* (Philadelphia: University of Pennsylvania Press, 2003), 25–47.

25. For a study of single women's city lives in this era, see Joanne Meyerowitz, *Women Adrift: Independent Wage Earners in Chicago, 1880–1930* (Chicago: University of Chicago Press, 1988). Women also had to leave the house more often for errands because fewer vendors traveled from door to door in turn-of-the-century urban neighborhoods. Ruth Schwartz Cowan, *More Work for Mother: The Ironies of Household Technology from the Open Hearth to the Microwave* (New York: Basic Books, 1985).

26. "Luncheon and Soups," *Philadelphia Public Ledger*, 7 February 1880, 2.

27. The face-washing routine is described in the *Philadelphia Public Ledger*, 2 November 1902, 10.

28. "In the Household," *Philadelphia Public Ledger*, 28 February 1880, supplement section, 1.

29. "Always Wear, for Beauty," *Philadelphia Public Ledger*, 24 April 1893, 15.

30. "The Fashionable Figure," *Philadelphia Public Ledger*, 1 March 1900, 7.

31. "Women's Interests," *Philadelphia Public Ledger*, 22 December 1892, 6. The column gathered this information from sources like the *London Daily News* and women's periodicals, such as the *Woman's Journal* and the *Woman's Tribune*.

32. On settlement houses in Philadelphia, see John F. Sutherland, "Origins of Philadelphia's Octavia Hill Association: Social Reform in the 'Contented City,'" *Pennsylvania Magazine of History and Biography* 99, no. 1 (January 1975): 20–44; and Rosina McAvoy Ryan, "Settlement Houses," Encyclopedia of Greater Philadelphia, http://philadelphia

encyclopedia.org/archive/settlement-houses/, accessed 27 May 2014. On the Civic Club, see Cary Hutto, "Civic Club," *Question of the Week* (blog), Historical Society of Pennsylvania website, September 12, 2011, https://hsp.org/blogs/question-of-the -week/organized-in-1894-by-prominent-philadelphia-women-what-club-sought-to -promote-%E2%80%9Cby-education-and-acti.

33. "Women's Interests," *Philadelphia Public Ledger*, 22 December 1892, 6.

34. "The Interesting Sex" was running by 1895.

35. The *Philadelphia Call*, another working-class paper, shut down in 1895. The *Item* closed in 1912; the *Record* published through 1947.

36. Miller, Vogel, and Davis, *Still Philadelphia*, 77; and Philip Scranton and Walter Licht, *Work Sights: Industrial Philadelphia, 1890–1950* (Philadelphia: Temple University Press, 1986), 133–35.

37. Classified ad, *Philadelphia Record*, 25 September 1895, 3.

38. "In the Swim," *Philadelphia Evening Item*, 3 April 1898, 5.

39. Ibid.; and *Philadelphia Record*, 20 April 1887, 2.

40. *Philadelphia Evening Item*, 20 June 1902, 6.

41. *Philadelphia Evening Item*, 20 June 1902, front page.

42. Circulation records do not exist to document any specific audience for turn-of-the-century Philadelphia papers. Classified ads, though, help piece together readership. In classified columns in all of the major Philadelphia dailies, employers posted ads for "colored" workers, and workers seeking positions identified themselves as colored.

43. The *Philadelphia Tribune* did not write for an audience far beyond the city itself and did not discuss behavior very openly. African American papers that circulated from northern cities through southern communities—especially the *Chicago Defender*— spoke more explicitly about urban life and gave more guidance on how to adjust. On this process, see James Grossman, "Blowing the Trumpet: The *Chicago Defender* and Black Migration during WWI," *Illinois Historical Journal* 78 (1985): 84.

44. Society column, *Philadelphia Record*, April 23, 1887, 7.

45. Ad for picture series "The Paris Salon," *Philadelphia Inquirer*, 18 May 1895, 3. On self-cultivation in middle-class culture, see Joseph F. Kett, *The Pursuit of Knowledge under Difficulties: From Self-Improvement to Adult Education in America, 1750–1990* (Stanford, CA: Stanford University Press, 1994); Andrew C. Rieser, *The Chautauqua Moment: Protestants, Progressives, and the Culture of Modern Liberalism* (New York: Columbia University Press, 2003); and Cindy S. Aron, *Working at Play: A History of Vacations in the United States* (New York: Oxford University Press, 1999), 101–26.

46. List of subjects is from the *Philadelphia Inquirer*, 23 February 1899, 9. The *Inquirer* bought the "Home Study Circle" from the *Chicago Record*, which syndicated the series for over a dozen newspapers. The *Chicago Record* reported forty thousand attendees at a series of seventy-five lectures that it hosted in connection with the series. Donald I. Abramoski, "The Chicago Daily News: A Business History, 1875–1901" (PhD diss., University of Chicago, 1963), 181–85.

47. Examples of classified ads come from the *Philadelphia Evening Bulletin*, 25 and 30 September 1895, and the *Philadelphia Inquirer*, 2 October 1907, 14.

48. For one example, see the ad for "The Record" School Information Bureau, *Philadelphia Record*, 12 May 1915, 12.

49. "The Well-Bred Girl," *Philadelphia Inquirer*, 20 September 1892, 7.

50. The *Philadelphia Inquirer* was more demure, refraining from printing letters it

deemed "purely personal" and sending individual responses to those questions. This was the policy both for "Everybody's Column" and for "Womanly Answers to Womanly Questions," found in the early 1900s' *Inquirer*.

51. Letter from John W. F. W., *Philadelphia Evening Bulletin*, 10 October 1906, 8.

52. Letter from Edna Holloway, *Philadelphia Evening Bulletin*, 1 July 1902, 10, and letter to "Everybody's Column," *Philadelphia Inquirer*, 7 July 1903, 8.

53. *Philadelphia Inquirer*, 15 May 1895, 3.

54. *Philadelphia Inquirer*, 26 March 1911, sec. 3, 7.

55. James J. Flink, in *America Adopts the Automobile, 1895–1910* (Cambridge, MA: MIT Press, 1970), reports that the *Inquirer* and the *North American* were the first newspapers to use automobiles for delivery, when they took newspapers to the Jersey shore in 1901. For department store delivery, see Strawbridge & Clothier advertisement in the *Philadelphia Evening Bulletin*, 12 July 1910, 5.

56. "Don'ts for Travellers," *Philadelphia Evening Bulletin*, 12 July 1910, 7.

57. Ibid.

58. For an example of a feature that showcased summer adventures, see "Leaves from the Diary of a Summer Girl," *Philadelphia Evening Bulletin*, 12 July 1910, 7. For an example of illustrations modeling vacation behavior, see the *Philadelphia Inquirer*, 19 May 1895, 14.

59. On the rise of this aspirational, visually alluring consumer culture in turn-of-the-century cities, see William Leach, *Land of Desire: Merchants, Power, and the Rise of a New American Culture* (New York: Pantheon, 1993); T. J. Jackson Lears, *Fables of Abundance: A Cultural History of Advertising in America* (New York: Basic Books, 1994); Pamela Laird, *Advertising Progress: American Business and the Rise of Consumer Marketing* (Baltimore: Johns Hopkins University Press, 1998); and Roland Marchand, *Advertising the American Dream: Making Way for Modernity, 1920–1940* (Berkeley: University of California Press, 1985).

60. "Right and Wrong Way of Watering Plants," *Philadelphia Inquirer*, 6 October 1907, 2, women's magazine; and "Do You Know How to Sweep?" *Philadelphia Inquirer*, 15 May 1895. The rise of home economics and domestic science partly account for the new precision expected in homemaking; see Janice Williams Rutherford, *Selling Mrs. Consumer: Christine Frederick and the Rise of Household Efficiency* (Athens: University of Georgia Press, 2003); Megan Elias, *Stir It Up: Home Economics in American Culture* (Philadelphia: University of Pennsylvania Press, 2010); Helen Zoe Veit, *Modern Food, Moral Food: Self-Control, Science, and the Rise of Modern American Eating in the Early Twentieth Century* (Chapel Hill: University of North Carolina Press, 2013); and Laura Shapiro, *Perfection Salad: Women and Cooking at the Turn of the Century* (New York: Farrar, Straus, and Giroux, 1986).

61. Quoted in Marian Martineau, "How to Have Lily White Hands in Spite of a Hot July Sun," *Philadelphia Evening Bulletin*, 5 July 1902, 3.

62. Women's magazine, *Philadelphia Inquirer*, 26 March 1911, 3.

63. "Harmony in Homecraft," *Philadelphia Record*, 16 May 1915, sec. 4, 3.

64. For fashion show, see Leach, *Land of Desire*, plate 13; on cooking classes, see *Philadelphia Public Ledger*, 7 November 1920, women's section, 2. Few papers kept records on the number of letters they received on questions of beauty, but a few 1920s sources indicate high numbers. For example, the *Chicago Tribune*, which kept tallies for the year 1926, received the most letters (24,047) asking for health advice; beauty was the second-largest category, with 14,570 letters. Chicago Tribune, *Book of Facts, 1927:*

Data on Markets, Merchandising, Advertising, with Special Reference to the Chicago Territory and Chicago Newspaper Advertising (Chicago: Chicago Tribune, 1927), 170.

65. For example, see *Philadelphia Record*, 26 March 1911, magazine section, 10.

66. *Philadelphia Evening Bulletin*, 10 October 1906, 16. The title "Nicckel-out Magazine" suggests that the *Bulletin* borrowed this joke from a foreign newspaper. Newspaper humor sections—both print and illustrated—often borrowed from other publications, both American and foreign.

67. "Dorothy Dix: Reminds Us That with Success There Is a Price," *Philadelphia Evening Bulletin*, 25 March 1916, 7.

68. The decline in the *Ledger*'s share of the market is evident in statistics from *George P. Rowell's Newspaper Directory*, years 1880–1901, and *Pettingill & Company's Newspaper Directory*, 4th ed. (Boston: Pettingill & Co., 1896), 280. A reporter in *Printer's Ink* told potential advertisers that "the *Public Ledger* holds a small conservative clientele among the business and moneyed classes, making it an excellent medium for financial and high grade real estate advertising." *Printer's Ink* 48, no. 1 (July 6, 1904): 2–3.

69. Information about the *North American* under Thomas Wanamaker comes from Harry B. Whitcraft, "Fifty Years of Journalism in Philadelphia," pt. 3, "The *North American* under the Ownership and Management of Thomas B. Wanamaker and Edward A. Van Valkenburg," *Beehive: A Monthly Magazine of Germantown, Philadelphia's Richest Suburb* 25, no. 3 (July 1934): 3–7, 20–21. The *Philadelphia Press* was considered a newspaper for "the classes" as well. I concentrated on the *Ledger* and the *North American* because the *Press* did not last quite as long as they did (the *Ledger* bought it in 1920) and because the *Press*'s circulation dwindled between 1900 and 1920.

70. "Peggy Shippen's Letter," *Philadelphia Public Ledger*, 26 March 1916, 6: "These Americans are marvelous." The real Peggy Shippen was a prominent Philadelphian in the time of the Revolutionary War who had married Benedict Arnold.

71. "University Activities. News Notes of Campus and Classroom and Philadelphia's Big Educational Center," *Philadelphia North American*, 26 October 1913, 7.

72. The "College Notes" column appeared in 1896. It chronicled new courses, college budgets, and professors' research trips at top-tier colleges across the nation. For an example, see *Philadelphia Public Ledger*, 10 November 1896, 16.

73. Scranton and Licht, *Work Sights*, 133–35.

74. "Guide for Americans Abroad," *Philadelphia Public Ledger*, 6 May 1908, 7. The *North American* ran a bureau with resort information; see *Philadelphia North American*, 18 June 1909, 9.

75. For examples, see advertisements for J. E. Caldwell, the Chestnut Street jewelers, in every day's *Philadelphia Public Ledger* during the 1910s.

76. The *Philadelphia Public Ledger* occasionally used the heading "Women's Interests" after 1900 but no longer ran notes about women's professional and political achievements under that heading.

77. On the history of such columns, see Julie Golia, "Advising America: Advice Columns and the Modern American Newspaper, 1895–1955" (PhD diss., Columbia University, 2011); David Gudelunas, *Confidential to America: Newspaper Advice Columns and Sexual Education* (New Brunswick, NJ: Transaction Publishers, 2008); Harnett T. Kane, with Ella Bentley Arthur, *Dear Dorothy Dix: The Story of a Compassionate Woman* (Garden City, NY: Doubleday & Company, 1952); Laura Claridge, *Emily Post: Daughter of the Gilded Age, Mistress of American Manners* (New York: Random House, 2009); and Schlesinger, *Learning How to Behave*.

78. One Chicago reader occasionally bought working-class papers "to gratify a low taste for Mutt, Jeff, the Katzenjammer Kids, and the others. I class my reading the Hearst papers with my occasional eating of pig's feet." Letter from O. H. Chamberlain Jr., *Collier's Weekly*, 19 August 1911, 18.

79. In 1880, one Philadelphia newspaper copy circulated for every four city residents. By 1900, there were five dailies issued for every six Philadelphians. Hepp, *The Middle-Class City*, 99. Because not all Philadelphians read a newspaper (due to poverty, illiteracy, youth, or lack of interest), these statistics indicate that those city residents who did read sometimes took multiple papers.

80. Truman DeWeese, *Keeping a Dollar at Work: Fifty "Talks" on Newspaper Advertising Written for the N.Y. Evening Post* (New York: New York Evening Post, 1915), 49, 29-30.

81. On these changes in food supply, see Harvey A. Levenstein, *Revolution at the Table: The Transformation of the American Diet* (New York: Oxford University Press, 1988), chap. 3. On the nineteenth-century meatpacking industry, see William Cronon, *Nature's Metropolis: Chicago and the Great West* (New York: W. W. Norton, 1991), 207-59.

82. "Hot-Weather Soup," *Philadelphia Evening Bulletin*, 7 July 1902, 7.

83. Horn & Hardart Baking Company ad, *Philadelphia Daily News*, 8 September 1925, 14.

84. Baker's Sugar Corn ad, *Philadelphia Evening Bulletin*, 3 July 1902, 7.

85. Heckers' Old Homestead Pancake Flour ad, *Philadelphia Inquirer*, 8 November 1915, 4.

86. General Electric refrigerator ad, *Philadelphia Evening Public Ledger*, 8 March 1928, 8. On the new household technologies of the era and their impact on women's lives, see Cowan, *More Work for Mother*; and Susan Strasser, *Never Done: A History of American Housework* (New York: Pantheon Books, 1982).

87. "Mrs. Scott's Food Talks," *Philadelphia North American*, 12 May 1925, 8.

88. Oysterettes ad, *Philadelphia Inquirer*, 2 October 1907, 9. For more on the changing food rituals in the Progressive era, see Shapiro, *Perfection Salad*.

89. United Gas Improvement Company ad, *Philadelphia Tribune*, 10 January 1920, 6.

90. Philadelphia Gas Works Company ad, *Philadelphia Daily News*, 24 April 1929, 18.

91. Miller, Vogel, and Davis, *Still Philadelphia*, 173.

92. See the *Philadelphia Inquirer*, 26 March 1911, sec. 2, 10, and the *Philadelphia Public Ledger*, 7 November 1920, sec. 1, 16.

93. For example, see "Laws and Facts for Motorists," *Philadelphia Inquirer*, 26 March 1911, sec. 2, 10. On early regulation of automobiles, see Flink, *America Adopts the Automobile*, chap. 6. On the history of the automobile in early twentieth-century America, see Clay McShane, *Down the Asphalt Path: The Automobile and the American City* (New York: Columbia University Press, 1994); Cotton Seiler, *Republic of Drivers: A Cultural History of Automobility in America* (Chicago: University of Chicago Press, 2008); and Flink, *The Automobile Age* (Cambridge, MA: MIT Press, 1988).

94. On the Bush Hill auto district, see Vitiello, *Engineering Philadelphia*, 199-215. On the construction of the parkway, see Miller, Vogel, and Davis, *Still Philadelphia*, 201.

95. The first three examples come from the 1923 *Philadelphia Inquirer*, the last from the 1925 *Philadelphia North American*.

96. "Answers to Radio Questions," *Philadelphia Evening Bulletin*, 18 October 1922, 31.

97. "The Home-Maker's Page," ed. Gertrude M. O'Reilly, *Philadelphia Public Ledger*, 21 March 1916, 10.

98. Wanamaker's ad, *Philadelphia Record*, 17 February 1899, 10.

99. While few scholars have investigated the ways that advertisements schooled readers on how to shop, a number have looked at the ways that stores' environments guided shoppers' behavior. See Leach, *Land of Desire*, 72–75; Alan Trachtenberg, *The Incorporation of America: Culture and Society in the Gilded Age* (New York: Hill and Wang, 1982), 130–35; Jan Whitaker, *Service and Style: How the American Department Store Fashioned the Middle Class* (New York: Macmillan, 2006); and Susan Porter-Benson, *Counter Cultures: Saleswomen, Managers, and Customers in American Departments Stores, 1890–1940* (Urbana: University of Illinois Press, 1987), chaps. 2 and 3.

100. The Lit Brothers' department store, for example, printed a directory of its fifty-seven departments in its full-page ad; *Philadelphia Evening Item*, 20 June 1902, 3.

101. Lit Brothers department store ad, *Philadelphia Daily News*, 7 September 1925, 5.

102. Hepp, *The Middle-Class City*, 133.

103. On Philadelphia's early trend toward deindustrialization and service jobs, see Domenic Vitiello, "Machine Building and City Building: Urban Planning and Industrial Restructuring in Philadelphia, 1894–1928," *Journal of Urban History* 34, no. 3 (March 2008): 399–434; Miller, Vogel, and Davis, *Still Philadelphia*; and Scranton and Licht, *Work Sights*.

104. Richard L. Kaplan, "From Partisanship to Professionalism: The Transformation of the Daily Press," in *A History of the Book in America*, vol. 4, *Print in Motion: The Expansion of Publishing and Reading in the United States, 1880–1940*, ed. Carl F. Kaestle and Janice A. Radway (Chapel Hill: University of North Carolina Press, 2009), 127. For specific operations and startup costs, see Given, *Making a Newspaper*, 306–7. On the broader trend of mergers and acquisitions in the late nineteenth and early twentieth centuries, see Naomi Lamoreaux, *The Great Merger Movement in American Business, 1895–1904* (New York: Cambridge University Press, 1985); and Alfred Chandler, *The Visible Hand: The Managerial Revolution in American Business* (Cambridge, MA: Belknap Press, 1977).

105. For a chronicle of these mergers, see Hepp, *The Middle-Class City*, 129–38.

106. Cyrus Curtis started another tabloid in Philadelphia, the *Illustrated Sun*, but it lasted only from 1925 to 1928.

107. Hepp, *The Middle-Class City*, 127.

108. "Mrs. Scott's Food Talks," *Philadelphia Inquirer*, 17 August 1927, 10.

109. The best evidence that Philadelphians read the *Pittsburgh Courier* is the space the paper devoted to Philadelphia news. Patrick Washburn also reports that the *Courier*'s national edition rose in popularity in the 1920s, as the *Chicago Defender* declined. Patrick S. Washburn, *The African American Newspaper: Voice of Freedom* (Evanston, IL: Northwestern University Press, 2006), 126. The *Baltimore Afro American* also pitched itself as a national weekly and would seem like a logical (nearby) choice for Philadelphians, but that paper devoted little if any space to Philadelphia news.

110. Statistics on chains come from Miller, Vogel, and Davis, *Still Philadelphia*, 228; and Stephen Nepa, "Automats," Encyclopedia of Greater Philadelphia, http://philadelphiaencyclopedia.org/archive/automats-2/, accessed 2 June 2014.

111. Fruit-Nut cereal ad, *Philadelphia Evening Bulletin*, 14 October 1922, 9.

112. "Phila. Society Women to Restrict Meals," *Philadelphia North American*, 17 April 1917, 3.

113. Ross Gregory, ed., *Almanacs of American Life: Modern America, 1914–1945* (New York: Facts on File, 1995), 113, 117, 122. Farm incomes rose in this era, too, but did not keep pace with growth in other sectors.

114. Klaczynska, "Working Women in Philadelphia," 41, 88.

115. Gimbels ad, *Philadelphia Inquirer*, 7 January 1923, sec. 2, 14.

116. Integrity Trust Company ad, *Philadelphia Evening Bulletin*, 21 January 1930, 30. On the spread and democratization of investing in the early twentieth century, see Julia C. Ott, *When Wall Street Met Main Street: The Quest for an Investors' Democracy* (Cambridge, MA: Harvard University Press, 2011); and Steve Fraser, *Every Man a Speculator: A History of Wall Street in American Life* (New York: Harper Perennial, 2006).

117. These questions are from "Money Problems of Women," *Philadelphia Record*, 10 August 1927, 7, and 12 August 1927, 7.

118. "M'Liss Explains Mysteries of Society's Inner Circle," *Philadelphia Evening Public Ledger*, 23 March 1916, 6.

119. Deborah Rush, "Good Form," *Philadelphia Evening Public Ledger*, 21 March 1916, 8.

120. "How's Your Grammar?" *Philadelphia Evening Bulletin*, 27 December 1926, 15.

121. Deborah Rush, "Good Form," *Philadelphia Evening Public Ledger*, 21 March 1916, 8. Letter-writing templates had appeared in early nineteenth-century American manuals; see *The Fashionable Letter Writer; or, Art of Polite Correspondence with Forms of Complementary Cards and a New and Easy English Grammar* (New York: George Long, No. 71, Pearl-Street, 1818).

122. See Manheim Rising Academy ad, *Philadelphia North American*, 9 October 1921, sports section, 3, and "Revue des Deux Mondes" ad, *Philadelphia Public Ledger*, 21 September 1924, literary review section, 11.

123. Rolls-Royce ad, *Philadelphia Public Ledger*, 21 September 1924, sec. 4, 16.

124. See Gimbels ad, *Evening Ledger*, 6 April 1928, 10.

125. Bourjois cosmetics ad, *Philadelphia Inquirer*, 21 August 1927, 3.

126. "Adventures with a Purse," *Philadelphia Evening Ledger*, 16 September 1924, 12.

127. The feature was called "Modish Mitzi"; for an example, see *Philadelphia North American*, 2 May 1925, 21.

128. Eleanor Gilbert, "The Business Girl," *Philadelphia Public Ledger*, 15 July 1917, 10.

129. Philadelphia School of Filing ad, *Philadelphia Evening Bulletin*, 18 October 1922, 26.

130. These columns ran in 1905. The *Philadelphia North American* consistently offered advice for working women earlier than Philadelphia's other newspapers; this is partly because it drew a larger percentage of female readers. On the *North American*'s audience, see *Printer's Ink* 48, no. 1, 6 July 1904.

131. "Vivian Shirley," *Philadelphia Evening Ledger*, 5 April, 1928, 4, and 6 April, 1928, 4.

132. For an in-depth analysis of another of these strips, *Winnie Winkle, the Breadwinner*, see Ian Gordon, *Comic Strips and Consumer Culture, 1890–1945* (Washington, DC: Smithsonian Institution Press, 1998), 118–27. On women's entrance into office work, see Margery W. Davies, *Woman's Place Is at the Typewriter: Office Work and Office Workers, 1870–1930* (Philadelphia: Temple University Press, 1982); Sharon H. Strom, *Beyond the Typewriter: Gender, Class, and the Origins of American Office Work, 1900–1930* (Urbana: University of Illinois Press, 1992); and Jerome P. Bjelopera, *City of Clerks: Office and Sales Workers in Philadelphia, 1870–1920* (Urbana: University of Illinois Press, 2005).

133. "The Modern Well-Dressed Woman of Business," *Philadelphia Inquirer*, 7 January 1923, 5.

134. For example, see "Getting On at the Office," *Philadelphia Evening Bulletin*, 19 October 1922, 7.

135. *Philadelphia Inquirer*, 5 January 1923, 20.

136. For "The Woman Citizen," see the *Public Ledger*, 6 April 1928, 20; for "Money Problems," see the *Philadelphia Record*, 11 August 1927, 7.

137. For example, see the "Women of Mark" column, *Philadelphia North American*, 26 October 1913, magazine, 7.

138. For examples, see "The Story of My First Job," *Philadelphia Record*, 8, 9, 10, 11 August 1927, all on page 8.

139. *Philadelphia Public Ledger*, 16 September 1924, 4.

140. Egalitarian rhetoric in political news articles could also obscure class differences among male readers. See Alexander Saxton, "Problems of Class and Race in the Origins of the Mass Circulation Press," *American Quarterly* 36, no. 2 (Summer 1984): 211–34.

141. "You and Your Habits Are Masters of Your Fate," *Philadelphia Evening Ledger*, 23 March 1916, 13. This was a syndicated feature. On models of American male success in this era, see Hilkey, *Character Is Capital* (n. 2 above, this chap.); Brian Luskey, *On the Make: Clerks and Quest for Capital in Nineteenth-Century America* (New York: New York University Press, 2010); and Richard Weiss, *The American Myth of Success: From Horatio Alger to Norman Vincent Peale* (Urbana: University of Illinois Press, 1998).

142. "You and Your Habits are Masters of Your Fate," *Philadelphia Evening Ledger*, 23 March 1916, 13.

143. Ovaltine ad, *Philadelphia Evening Ledger*, 6 April 1928, 15.

144. Louis Mark Shoes ad, *Philadelphia Public Ledger*, 5 November 1920, 16.

145. On men's relationship to consumer culture in this era, see Tom Pendergast, *Creating the Modern Man: American Magazines and Consumer Culture, 1900–1950* (Columbia: University of Missouri Press, 2000). Lisa Jacobson argues that advertisements constructed the ideal boy consumer as rational and economical as compared with fanciful and fickle girls; see Lisa Jacobson, *Raising Consumers: Children and the American Mass Market in the Early Twentieth Century* (New York: Columbia University Press, 2005), chap. 3.

146. On working-class culture and political radicalism in the same era, see Roy Rosenzweig, *Eight Hours for What We Will: Workers and Leisure in an Industrial City, 1870–1920* (New York: Cambridge University Press, 1983); and Francis Couvares, *The Remaking of Pittsburgh: Class and Culture in an Industrializing City, 1877–1919* (Albany: State University of New York Press, 1984). On male culture more broadly in this era, see Howard P. Chudacoff, *The Age of the Bachelor: Creating an American Subculture* (Princeton, NJ: Princeton University Press, 1999); and E. Anthony Rotundo, *American Manhood: Transformations in Masculinity From the Revolution to the Modern Era* (New York: Basic Books, 1994). On corporate efforts to shape male leisure time, see Lizabeth Cohen, *Making a New Deal: Industrial Workers in Chicago, 1919–1939* (New York: Cambridge University Press, 1990), chap. 4; and Cindy S. Aron, *Working at Play: A History of Vacations in the United States* (New York: Oxford University Press, 1999), 194–205.

147. "Tremendous Stamina Alone Saved Tilden," *Philadelphia Daily News*, 11 September 1925, 22.

148. For examples, see: George H. Brooke, "How to Play Football," *Philadelphia Inquirer*, 6 October 1907, 12; series of articles by John F. Moakley, Cornell track coach, in the *Philadelphia Public Ledger*, 26 March 1916, sports magazine, 2; series on swimming strokes in the *Philadelphia Evening Bulletin*, 9 July 1910, 15; Chic Evans, "Golf Simplified," *Philadelphia Daily News*, 8 September 1925, 19; Press Publishing Co., "Expert Tells How to Play Basketball," *Philadelphia Inquirer*, 7 January 1923, 19.

149. Young women in the comic strips did not get the same treatment; they were usually drawn similarly to women in fashion illustrations or advertisements, perhaps appearing even more beautiful or buxom. Only henpecking housewives were drawn in caricature.

150. The critique leveled in comic strips perhaps most resembled the one that surfaced in the male counterculture investigated by Todd DePastino in *Citizen Hobo: How a Century of Homelessness Shaped America* (Chicago: University of Chicago Press, 2003), chaps. 3-5.

151. These two examples are from "What Does Your Husband Do?" and "What Does Your Wife Do?" *Philadelphia Record*, 26 January 1923, 6, and 25 January 1923, 7, respectively.

152. "The Marriage Game," *Philadelphia Daily News*, 8 September 1925, 8, and "The Marriage Game," *Philadelphia Public Ledger*, 6 April 1928, 21. Other strains in 1920s' culture, from Freudian analysis to *True Story* magazine, also encouraged the airing of personal details.

153. *Philadelphia Evening Ledger*, 23 March 1916, 15.

154. *Philadelphia Tribune*, 17 January 1920, 6.

155. Bill Blackbeard and Martin Williams, eds., *The Smithsonian Collection of Newspaper Comics* (1977; repr., Washington, DC: Smithsonian Institution Press, 1984), 52.

156. "The Padded Cell," *Philadelphia Evening Ledger*, 23 March 1916, 15.

157. Marriage age statistic from Gregory, ed., *Almanacs of American Life: Modern America, 1914-1945*, 68. The "raised expectations" argument about marriage in the 1920s and its relationship to popular culture was first made by Elaine Tyler May in *Great Expectations: Marriage and Divorce in Post-Victorian America* (Chicago: University of Chicago Press, 1980).

158. Cobbett S. Steinberg, *Film Facts* (New York: Facts on File, 1980), 40-41. On the cultural impact of movies in the 1910s and 1920s, see Robert Sklar, *Movie-Made America: A Cultural History of American Movies* (New York: Vintage Books, 1975), pts. 1 and 2; and David Nasaw, *Going Out: The Rise and Fall of Public Amusements* (Cambridge, MA: Harvard University Press, 1999), chaps. 12-16.

159. Herbert Blumer, *Movies and Conduct* (New York: Macmillan Company, 1933), 149.

160. Beatrice Fairfax, "Marriage Vacations," *Philadelphia Evening Bulletin*, 27 December 1926, 10.

161. From column "Listen World," by Elsie Robinson, *Philadelphia Daily News*, 7 September 1925, 10.

162. "The Psychometer" in the *Philadelphia Record*, 14 January 1923, magazine section, 4. Also see questions printed in "Legal Queries" in the *Philadelphia Evening Bulletin*, 25 March 1916, 11, and 14 October 1922, 22. On divorce in the early twentieth century, see May, *Great Expectations*, and J. Herbie Difonzo, *Beneath the Fault Line: The Popular and Legal Culture of Divorce in Twentieth-Century America* (Charlottesville: University of Virginia Press, 1997).

NOTES TO PAGES 96-98   281

163. "Dorothy Dix Thinks the One-Man Woman and the One-Woman Man are Extremely Rare Specimens," *Philadelphia Evening Bulletin*, 20 October 1922, 7.

164. World Wide News Service, "The 'Next Best' Husband," *Philadelphia Record*, 21 January 1923, magazine section, 5.

165. The column was written by Edna Ewing; these topics appeared on the women's page in August 1927.

166. These topics appeared in the syndicated feature "Our Children," by Angelo Patri, in the *Philadelphia Evening Bulletin*, 27 December 1926, 9, and 29 December 1926, 9.

167. Letter from "Anna" to Deborah Rush, "Good Form," *Philadelphia Evening Ledger*, 23 March 1916, 6. Edward Bok, working in both newspapers and magazines in the late nineteenth century, picked up on the demand for such articles early on. According to his autobiography, he "divined the fact that in thousands of cases the American mother was not the confidante of her daughter, and reasoned if an inviting human personality could be created on the printed page that would supply this lamentable lack of American family life, girls would flock to such a figure. But all depended on the confidence which the written word could inspire." Bok, *The Americanization of Edward Bok*, 169.

168. Jay V. Jay, "Modish Mitzi," *Philadelphia North American*, 12 May 1925, 14.

169. Letter from "Twenty-Six" to "Please Tell Me What to Do, by Cynthia," *Philadelphia Evening Ledger*, 16 September 1924, 12. On changing dating practices in the 1920s, see Paula Fass, *The Damned and the Beautiful: American Youth in the 1920s* (New York: Oxford University Press, 1977); and Beth Bailey, *From Front Porch to Back Seat: Courtship in Twentieth-Century America* (Baltimore: Johns Hopkins University Press, 1989).

170. Ad for *Book of Good Manners*, *Pittsburgh Courier*, national ed., 18 October 1924, 10.

171. Letter from "Fiance" to Mary Strong, "Friendly Advice to Girls," *Pittsburgh Courier*, national ed., Saturday 22 September 1928, sec. 1, 6.

172. Letter to by Mary Strong, "Friendly Advice to Girls," *Pittsburgh Courier*, national ed., Saturday 22 September 1928, sec. 1, 6.

173. Letter from "Brokenhearted, G. B." to Mary Strong, "Friendly Advice to Girls," *Pittsburgh Courier*, national ed., Saturday 11 August 1928, sec. 1, 6.

174. Letter to Mary Strong, "Friendly Advice to Girls," *Pittsburgh Courier*, national ed., Saturday 11 August 1928, sec. 1, 6.

175. Unprinted letters to advice columns also show what was excluded, but very few of those letters survive. Julie Golia has mined the collection of letters—some printed in the newspaper, some not—sent to Beatrice Fairfax, "Advice to the Lovelorn," in the 1930s. Golia, "Advising America," chap. 2.

176. James Edward Rogers, *The American Newspaper* (Chicago: University of Chicago Press, 1909), 145. Rogers also worked as a leader in the movement for playgrounds and supervised recreation, one of Progressives' main avenues of reform.

177. Ibid., 151. Several turn-of-the-century editors also spoke about their newspapers as vehicles for education and uplift. See Alexander K. McClure, former editor of the *Philadelphia Public Ledger*, "Foreword" in *Journalism: Its Relation to and Influence upon the Political, Social, Professional, Financial, and Commercial Life of the United States of America*, ed. New York Press Club (New York: New York Press Club, 1905), iii–v; editorial, *New York Sun*, 18 August 1893, 4; and Will Irwin, "The American Newspaper:

A Study of Journalism and Its Relation to the Public," pt. 5, "What Is News?" *Collier's Weekly*, 18 March 1911, 16.

178. "The Woman's Hour" began in 1881; women's material later ran under the headings "Housekeeper's Column" and later, in the 1920s, "Confidential Chat." Louis M. Lyons, *Newspaper Story: One Hundred Years of the Boston Globe* (Cambridge, MA: Belknap Press, 1971), 40, 115.

179. George Juergens, *Joseph Pulitzer and the New York World* (Princeton, NJ: Princeton University Press, 1966), 148. The series began in November 1883.

180. An announcement for this series of articles ran in the *Atlanta Constitution*, 12 April 1903, 42.

181. Summer School at Home ad, *Rocky Mountain News*, 9 May 1897, 20.

182. "A Five O'clock Tea in Town," *New York Sun*, 6 January 1889, 9.

183. Letter from Frederick Thomas Bowers in *Collier's Weekly*, 2 September 1911, 22.

184. Letter from Edward Broderick in *Collier's Weekly*, 18 November 1911, 6.

185. *Advertiser's Handy Guide 1896* (New York: Lyman D. Morse Advertising Agency, 1896), 669.

186. Lee, *The Daily Newspaper in America*, 272-73.

187. Kaplan, "From Partisanship to Professionalism," 127. Other articles cite slight variations on this number and date; see Moses Koenigsberg, *King News: An Autobiography* (Philadelphia: F. A. Stokes Company, 1941), 365; and Edwin Emery and Michael Emery, *The Press and America: An Interpretive History of the Mass Media*, 4th ed (Englewood Cliffs, NJ: Prentice-Hall, Inc., 1978), 430.

188. "Evening Journal Investors' Service," *New York Journal*, 15 May 1930, 36.

189. Peggy Hoyt Hats ad, *New York Times*, 28 March 1920, 10.

190. "Husbands under Scrutiny," *Chicago Tribune*, 4 November 1928, pt. 6, 12.

191. Golia, "Advising America," 127, 128, 140.

192. Harold A. Williams, *The Baltimore Sun, 1837-1987* (Baltimore: Johns Hopkins University Press, 1987), 140.

193. Chicago Tribune, *Book of Facts, 1927*, 170.

CHAPTER THREE

1. Charles H. Cooley, *Social Organization: A Study of the Larger Mind* (New York: Charles Scribner's Sons, 1909), 83-84.

2. Ibid., 192. A handful of other observers noticed newspapers updating what they portrayed as old-fashioned, small-town community in the early decades of the twentieth century. Frank L. Blanchard wrote in 1905 that the newspaper had replaced the church as the central source of local gossip. Blanchard, "Pulpit and Press," in *Journalism: Its Relation to and Influence upon the Political, Social, Professional, Financial, and Commercial Life of the United States of America*, ed. New York Press Club (New York: New York Press Club, 1905), 177. Sociologist Robert Park noted in 1925 that newspapers allowed readers to get to know their cities the way that people once knew their villages. Robert Ezra Park, "The Natural History of the Newspaper," in *The City*, ed. Robert Ezra Park, Ernest Watson Burgess, Roderick Duncan McKenzie, and Louis Wirth (Chicago: University of Chicago Press, 1923), 84-85.

3. There is a varied literature on the idea of print community, with the scale of that community ranging from global diasporas to small groups devoted to a hobby or a cause. Only a few scholars have looked at print community in the United States on a

city-wide level. These include David Paul Nord, "The Public Community: The Urbanization of Journalism in Chicago" and "Readership as Citizenship in Late Eighteenth-Century Philadelphia," in *Communities of Journalism: A History of American Newspapers and Their Readers* (Urbana: University of Illinois Press, 2006); Gunther Barth, "Metropolitan Press," in *City People: The Rise of Modern City Culture in Nineteenth-Century America* (New York: Oxford University Press, 1980); and Park, "The Natural History of the Newspaper."

4. Scholars who have examined the link between American journalism and civic identity include Neil Harris, "Covering New York: Journalism and Civic Identity in the Twentieth Century," in *Budapest and New York: Studies in Metropolitan Transformation, 1870-1930*, ed. Thomas Bender and Carl Schorske (New York: Russell Sage Foundation, 1994); Neil Harris, "Introduction," in *The Chicagoan: A Lost Magazine of the Jazz Age*, ed. Neil Harris (Chicago: University of Chicago Press, 2008); and Richard Junger, *Becoming the Second City: Chicago's Mass News Media, 1833-1898* (Urbana: University of Illinois Press, 2010).

5. Population statistics drawn from 1890 and 1900 census numbers.

6. Charles Lockwood, *Manhattan Moves Uptown: An Illustrated History* (New York: Barnes and Noble Books, 1995); and Sven Beckert, *The Monied Metropolis: New York City and the Consolidation of the American Bourgeoisie, 1850-1896* (New York: Cambridge University Press, 2001), 56–57, 294.

7. Jacob A. Riis, *How the Other Half Lives* (New York: C. Scribner's Sons, 1890; repr., New York: Dover, 1971).

8. Contours of Harlem taken from 1920, 1925, and 1930 boundaries mapped at the website Digital Harlem: Everyday Life 1915-1930, http://heuristscholar.org/digital _harlem/.

9. See Clifton Hood, *722 Miles: The Building of the Subways and How They Transformed New York* (Baltimore: Johns Hopkins University Press, 2004).

10. Information about New York's neighborhoods comes from Deborah Dash Moore, "Class and Ethnicity in the Creation of New York City Neighborhoods: 1900–1930," in *Budapest and New York*, ed. Bender and Schorske, 139–60.

11. Between 1880 and 1900, New York City printed more than one daily newspaper for every two residents. New York shared this level of newspaper saturation with four other cities in 1880 and with twelve others in 1900. William S. Rossiter, *Printing and Publishing, Twelfth Census of the United States, 1900*, vol. 9, *Manufactures*, pt. 3, *Special Reports on Selected Industries*, ser. no. 79 (Washington: U.S. Census Office, 1902), 1053.

12. Hy B. Turner, *When Giants Ruled: The Story of Park Row, New York's Great Newspaper Street* (New York: Fordham University Press, 1999), 119.

13. On the distinctive readerships of this era, see ibid.; Phyllis Kluger and Richard Kluger, *The Paper: The Life and Death of the New York Herald Tribune* (New York: Knopf, 1986); George Juergens, *Joseph Pulitzer and the New York World* (Princeton, NJ: Princeton University Press, 1966); Janet E. Steele, *The Sun Shines for All: Journalism and Ideology in the Life of Charles A. Dana* (Syracuse University Press, 1993); Frank Michael O'Brien, *The Story of the Sun, New York, 1833-1918* (New York: George H. Doran, 1918); Elmer Holmes Davis, *The History of the New York Times, 1851-1921* (New York: New York Times, 1921); William R. Scott, *Scientific Circulation Management for Newspapers* (New York: Ronald Press, 1915), 163–69; and Jason Rogers, *Newspaper Building: Application of Efficiency to Edition, to Mechanical Production, to Circulation and Advertising* (New York: Harper & Brothers, 1918), 242–45.

14. This description comes from listings in *N. W. Ayer & Son's American Newspaper Annual* (Philadelphia, various years.) The foreign language count comes from 1882; the number of foreign-language dailies increased through the 1910s.

15. Andie Tucher, *Froth and Scum: Truth, Beauty, Goodness, and the Ax Murder in America's First Mass Medium* (Chapel Hill: University of North Carolina Press, 1994); and Patricia Cline Cohen, *The Murder of Helen Jewett: The Life and Death of a Prostitute in Nineteenth-Century New York* (New York: Vintage, 1998). On the penny papers that were the first to break from the partisan mold, see O'Brien, *The Story of the Sun*; Steele, *The Sun Shines for All*; and James J. Crouthamel, *Bennett's "New York Herald" and the Rise of the Popular Press* (Syracuse, NY: Syracuse University Press, 1989).

16. Lincoln Steffens, "The Business of a Newspaper," *Scribner's Magazine*, October 1897, 461.

17. See *New York Evening Journal*, "Night Special" edition, 3 August 1898, front page; the *New York World*, 27 October 1901, front page; and photographs of the *Journal* building in Bill Blackbeard, ed., *R. F. Outcault's The Yellow Kid: A Centennial Celebration of the Kid Who Started the Comics* (Northampton, MA: Kitchen Sink Press, 1995), 62.

18. This quote first appeared in the *New York World* on 10 May 1883. The *World* printed it at the top of its editorial page every day during the 1910s and 1920s.

19. The *New York Herald* adopted a populist, independent political stance even before the *World* and the *Journal*, but it was the latter two papers that turned this stance mainstream in New York. See Crouthamel, *Bennett's "New York Herald."* Midwestern newspapers were also writing in a more populist, politically independent mode during the late nineteenth century; see David Paul Nord, *Newspapers and New Politics: Midwestern Municipal Reform, 1890–1900* (Ann Arbor: UMI Research Press, 1979).

20. Note soliciting letters for a future column called "The Grumbler," *New York World*, 16 October 1889, 5.

21. Examples come from *New York World*, 20 October 1889, 13, and 27 October 1889, 21.

22. Partisan papers did occasionally expose problems within the opposing party, as when the Republican *New York Times* and *Harper's Weekly* took on the Democratic political machine, Tammany Hall, in the 1870s. Thomas C. Leonard, *The Power of the Press: The Birth of American Political Reporting* (New York: Oxford University Press, 1986), 97–131.

23. On muckraking campaigns, see Juergens, *Joseph Pulitzer and the New York World*, chaps. 8 and 9; Harris, "Covering New York"; Leonard, *The Power of the Press*, chaps. 3 and 4; and John M. Harrison and Harry H. Stein, eds., *Muckraking: Past, Present, and Future* (University Park: Pennsylvania State University Press, 1973).

24. Loren Ghiglione, *The American Journalist: The Paradox of the Press* (Washington, DC: Library of Congress, 1990), 49.

25. On Jacob Riis's reporting, his photographs, and his influence on the Progressive movement more broadly, see Bonnie Yochelson and Daniel Czitrom, *Rediscovering Jacob Riis: The Reformer, His Journalism, and His Photographs* (New York: New Press, 2008); and Peter B. Hales, *Silver Cities: The Photography of American Urbanization, 1839–1915* (Philadelphia: Temple University Press, 1984), chap. 4.

26. "Drag Up the Slums," *New York World*, 6 June 1897, main news section, 6.

27. On the trend of viewing cities as interconnected organisms, see Keith D. Revell, *Building Gotham: Civic Culture and Public Policy in New York City, 1898–1938* (Baltimore:

Johns Hopkins University Press, 2003); Paul S. Boyer, *Urban Masses and Moral Order in America, 1820–1920* (Cambridge, MA.: Harvard University Press, 1978); Robert Hamlett Bremner, *From the Depths: The Discovery of Poverty in the United States* (New York: New York University Press, 1956); and Maureen A. Flanagan, *America Reformed: Progressives and Progressivisms* (New York: Oxford University Press, 2007), 24–27. For discussions of new models of engagement and citizenship encouraged by newspapers' muckraking journalism, see Michael Schudson, *The Good Citizen: A History of American Civic Life* (New York: Free Press, 1998), chap. 4; Nord, *Newspapers and New Politics*; and Leonard, *The Power of the Press*.

28. See Leonard, *The Power of the Press*, chaps. 3 and 4, and Harrison and Stein, eds., *Muckraking*.

29. Crandall A. Shifflett, *Almanacs of American Life: Victorian America, 1876 to 1913* (New York: Facts on File, 1996), 78.

30. The Fresh Air Fund first campaigned in the *Brooklyn Daily Union*, in 1877, and moved to the *Tribune* in 1882. See Julia A. Guarneri, "Changing Strategies for Child Welfare, Enduring Beliefs about Childhood: The Fresh Air Fund, 1877–1926," *Journal of the Gilded Age and Progressive Era* 11, no. 1 (January 2012): 27–70.

31. Clipped articles from 1 July 1900, Fresh Air Fund scrapbook, Fresh Air Fund Papers, Fresh Air Fund headquarters office, New York City.

32. The *New York Times*'s Neediest Cases campaign started in 1912; the *Brooklyn Eagle*'s campaign was in operation by the 1920s. Other drives focusing on New York's needy included the *New York Evening Mail*'s Save-a-Home Fund; the *New York Post*'s Old Folks Christmas Fund; the *New York Journal*'s Christmas baskets campaign, and the *New York American*'s Playgrounds Fund. See also Charles O. Burgess, "The Newspaper as Charity Worker: Poor Relief in New York City, 1893–1894," *New York History* 43, no. 3 (July 1962): 249–68; and John W. Perry, "Newspaper Funds Alleviate Suffering," *Editor & Publisher*, 21 December 1929, 9, 10, 48, 50.

33. For an example of a newspaper collection fund for an officer's widow and children, see the "Guarnieri Hero Fund" in the *New York American*, 26 April 1914, L-11.

34. "New York's 100 Neediest Cases," *New York Times*, 15 December 1918, 75. The nose description could well have been meant to communicate that Jimmy Sharp was white.

35. *New York Tribune*, 11 August 1890, 6.

36. *New York Tribune*, 17 July 1890, 7.

37. *New York Times*, 14 December 1924, sec. 8, front page.

38. "100 Neediest Cases after 3 Months' Aid," *New York Times*, 21 April 1918, 25.

39. Editorial, *New York Tribune*, 27 May 1890, 6.

40. I owe this image reference to Joseph W. Campbell, *Yellow Journalism: Puncturing the Myths, Defining the Legacies* (Westport, CT: Praeger, 2001).

41. On Brace and the operations of his Newsboys' Lodging House, see Charles Loring Brace, *The Dangerous Classes of New York and Twenty Years' Work among Them* (New York: Wynkoop & Hallenbeck, 1872), 101–13. On Horatio Alger, see Edwin P. Hoyt, *Horatio's Boys: The Life and Works of Horatio Alger, Jr.* (Radnor, PA: Chilton Book Co., 1974), 80–89.

42. Mrs. Louisa Baker to Joseph Pulitzer, 7 February 1886, Pulitzer Papers, Columbia University Rare Books and Manuscripts. "Begging letters" from the poor to the rich were in fact fairly common in late nineteenth- and early twentieth-century New York;

see David Huyssen, *Progressive Inequality: Rich and Poor in New York 1890–1920* (Cambridge, MA: Harvard University Press, 2014), chap. 6. The requests sent to Pulitzer, however, more often asked for publicity than for money.

43. Irving Dillard, "Foreword," in *Muckraking*, ed. Harrison and Stein, 4.

44. Neil Harris, "Covering New York," 250–51.

45. Tribune Fresh Air Fund annual reports, New York Public Library.

46. *New York Herald*, 11 May 1835, as quoted in Helen MacGill Hughes, "Human Interest Stories and Democracy," *Public Opinion Quarterly* 1 (1937): 73–83.

47. The *New York Sun* ran a version of this column from roughly 1874 to 1889. The *Sun*'s reporters relied so often on an interview-based method of reporting that some called it the "Sun style." O'Brien, *The Story of the Sun*, chap. 15.

48. "What Is Going on To-Day," *New York Tribune*, 19 April 1887, 8. Benedict Anderson was the first to claim that simultaneity bound the events in a newspaper's pages together and could ultimately bind readers together, too, though Anderson was discussing national ties, not civic ones. Anderson, *Imagined Communities: Reflections on the Origin and Spread of Nationalism* (New York: Verso, 1991), 33, 63.

49. "Fun in the Holland Society," *New York Sun*, 7 April 1897, 3.

50. "The Life-Savers at Work," *New York World*, 27 October 1889, 15.

51. "Baldness in New York," *New York Tribune*, 8 July 1883, 4.

52. "The Life-Savers at Work," *New York World*, 27 October 1889, 15.

53. "Stage News of the Week," *New York American and Journal*, 14 January 1906, 38.

54. The *New York American* started this practice in its Sunday paper around 1910 and continued it through the 1920s. In 1910 the paper also ran a column titled "Best Jokes at New York's Theaters" and attributed each joke to the show it was taken from. *New York American*, 2 October 1910, 5M.

55. Letter from May V. Godfrey, printed in "The American Newspaper," *Collier's Weekly*, 2 September 1911, 22.

56. Titles taken from the *New York Times*, 3 September 1896, 8, and the *New York American*, 2 October 1910, 8CE.

57. "Selecting Figurantes," *New York Sun*, evening edition, 2 January 1889, 5; "How Tully Marshall Starts Hysterics in the Second Act of 'The City,'" *New York World*, 19 December 1909, metropolitan section, 2; "The Gentle Art of Faking," *New York Times*, 21 January 1912, Part 7, 7.

58. "Opera Season Will Have a Brilliant Opening," *New York Times*, 20 November 1904, magazine section, 3.

59. "New York's Real First-Nighters," *New York World*, 30 March 1913, magazine section, 10.

60. A few publications printed colorful, in-depth sports news in the mid-nineteenth century. For discussions of this sports journalism, see Patricia Cline Cohen, Timothy J. Gilfoyle, and Helen Lefkowitz Horowitz, *The Flash Press: Sporting Male Weeklies in 1840s New York* (Chicago: University of Chicago Press, 2008); Gene and Jane Barry Smith, eds., *The National Police Gazette* (New York: Simon and Schuster, 1972); and John A. Dinan, *Sports in the Pulp Magazines* (Jefferson, NC: McFarland & Company, 1998). The reporting in these weeklies likely inspired mainstream daily newspapers to expand and alter their coverage.

61. "Courtney Breaks Down, and Is Therefore Compelled to Forfeit the Handball Match," *New York Sun*, evening edition, 2 January 1889, 6.

62. Ibid., 6.

63. For example see "New York's Joy, Brooklyn's Sorrow," *New York World*, 19 October 1889, 1–2, and "Story of Fight Told by Rounds," *New York Evening Journal*, tenth extra racing ed., 20 January 1906, 7.

64. George B. Underwood, "St. Nicks Triumph in Extra Period," *New York Sun*, 22 February 1917, 10.

65. "Giants Earn Victory in Tenth Inning Rally," *New York Times*, 14 June 1908, sec. 4, front page.

66. For individual statistics and photographs, see "Yankees? Giants? Take your Pick," *New York American*, 9 October 1910, sec. L II, 5. For portrait illustrations of the Yankees, see the *New York World*, 23 April 1893, 32. "How the Stars of the Brooklyn Superbas, National League Winners, Handle Ball and Bat," *New York Daily News*, 28 September 1920, 9.

67. These nicknames (for Dodgers coach Wilbert Robinson and for Babe Ruth) appeared in the "Giants Get Even Break; Brooklyn Clinches Pennant," *New York Daily News*, 28 September 1920, 14.

68. "A Tale of Sister Cities!" *New York World*, 19 October 1889, 1.

69. "What Brokers Think of the Market Outlook," *New York American and Journal*, 14 January 1906, 73.

70. "Topics of the Day in Wall Street," *New York Times*, 3 June 1930, 42. The "Chat from Wall Street" column ran in the *New York World* in 1885, and changed into "Business and Financial Matters Talked about on Wall Street," which ran at least until 1901. "Gossip from Wall Street" ran in the *New York Sun* from roughly 1909 to 1917.

71. "New York Photographed by Steeple Jacks from the Spires of St. Patrick's Cathedral," *New York World*, 11 May 1902, magazine section, 12, as reprinted in Nicholson Baker and Margaret Brentano, eds., *The World on Sunday: Graphic Art in Joseph Pulitzer's Newspaper (1898–1911)* (New York: Bulfinch Press, 2005); 52; "Times Square and the Theatrical District as Seen from the Air, Looking Northward," *New York Times*, 28 March 1920, picture section, 2; "Unfamiliar New York from the Air, No. 3," *New York Herald Tribune*, 23 August 1927, rotogravure section, 10.

72. "Unfamiliar New York from the Air, No. 3," *New York Herald Tribune*, 23 August 1927, rotogravure section, 10. On the history of urban views in the United States, see John W. Reps, *Bird's Eye Views: Historic Lithographs of North American Cities* (New York: Princeton Architectural Press, 1998); and Hales, *Silver Cities*, chaps. 2 and 3.

73. I draw some of these concepts and this vocabulary from Kevin Lynch's *The Image of the City* (Cambridge, MA: MIT Press, 1960), 1–10. Though Lynch intended his book for city planners and mostly discusses the visual experience and design of cities, newspapers feed his idea that people integrate new information into their preexisting "image" of the city.

74. "Adventures in Sewers," *New York Sun*, 31 March 1901, sec. 4, page 8; "Under the Hudson River," *New York Tribune*, 8 July 1883, 10; "New River Bed under City Is a Marvel of Boring," *New York World*, 30 March 1913, second news section, 2.

75. Special subway supplement, *New York World*, 2 October 1904. John Kasson and others have written about recurring "mole's eye" and "bird's eye" depictions of city life. Kasson, *Rudeness and Civility: Manners in Nineteenth-Century Urban America* (New York: Hill & Wang, 1990), 72–80.

76. Hype Igo, "New Madison Square Garden Is Greatest of All Arenas," *New York World*, 22 November 1925, second news section, 21.

77. Dreiser, "Out of My Newspaper Days," pt. 5, "I Quit the Game," *Bookman* 54, no. 8 (April 1922): 118.

78. John L. Given, *Making a Newspaper* (New York: Henry Holt, 1907), 160.

79. Dreiser, "Out of My Newspaper Days."

80. George P. Rowell & Co., *Centennial Newspaper Exhibition, 1876* (New York: George P. Rowell & Co., 1876), 199.

81. Given, *Making a Newspaper*, 169.

82. Letterbook, The World Papers, Columbia University Rare Books and Manuscripts.

83. "One Minute, Please!" ran regularly in the *New York Tribune* from February 1915 to April 1916.

84. Julia McNair Wright, *Practical Life; or, Ways and Means for Developing Character and Resources* (Philadelphia: Bradley, Garretson, 1882), 214–19, 218–19. As quoted in Thomas C. Leonard, *News for All: America's Coming-of-Age with the Press* (New York: Oxford University Press, 1995), 92.

85. "Home News," *New York Tribune*, 8 July 1883, 12. Castle Garden was New York's immigration center before Ellis Island.

86. "One Year's 'Eats' of New York Dwellers," *New York World*, 30 March 1913, sec. 2, 2, and "763,574,085 on 'L' and 'Sub' in a Year," *New York World*, 3 September 1917, 7.

87. *New York World*, 7 June 1897, 3.

88. "Open a Boulevard over Jamaica Bay; City Officials Take Part in Exercises at New $5,000,000 Causeway," *New York Times*, 12 October 1924, 25.

89. On the proliferation of printed words in the urban streetscape in the antebellum era, see David M. Henkin, *City Reading: Written Words and Public Spaces in Antebellum New York* (New York: Columbia University Press, 1999). This sensory overload was one of the main subjects of several neo-Romantic and Weimar German writers; for a start, see Walter Benjamin, "On Some Motifs in Baudelaire" (1939), in *Illuminations* (New York: Harcourt Brace, 1968), 155–20; and Georg Simmel's "The Metropolis and Mental Life" (1902), in *Simmel on Culture*, ed. David Frisby and Mike Featherstone (London: Sage Publications, 1997), 174–86.

90. John Dos Passos, *Manhattan Transfer* (1925; repr., New York: Penguin, 1986), 334.

91. "Murder in New York 15 Minutes After 1889 Began," *New York Sun*, 2 January 1889, front page.

92. "Starved for Family," *New York Tribune*, 7 June 1903, front page.

93. "The American Sky-Scraper Is a Modern Tower of Babel" (cartoon), *New York World*, 20 February 1898, front page of comic weekly.

94. First printed in the *New York World*, 7 July 1895, and reprinted in Blackbeard, ed., *R. F. Outcault's The Yellow Kid*, Plate 4.

95. On the movement toward more "scientific" reform in the late nineteenth and early twentieth centuries, including the birth of social sciences that used surveying techniques to define and assess urban problems, see Thomas Haskell, *The Emergence of Professional Social Science: The American Social Science Association and the Nineteenth-Century Crisis of Authority* (Urbana: University of Illinois, 1977); Thomas Bender, *Intellect and Public Life: Essays on the Social History of Academic Intellectuals in the United States* (Baltimore: Johns Hopkins University Press, 1997), chaps. 3 and 4; and Daniel Rodgers, *Atlantic Crossings: Social Politics in a Progressive Age* (Cambridge, MA: Harvard University Press, 1998), chaps. 4–6.

96. "Cupid's Work with an Egg," *New York Sun*, 18 July 1881, front page.

97. Grant Milnor Hyde, *Newspaper Reporting and Correspondence: A Manual for Reporters, Correspondents, and Students of Newspaper Writing* (New York: D. Appleton and Company, 1924), 236. On the history of the human interest genre, see Frank Luther Mott, *The News in America* (Cambridge, MA: Harvard University Press, 1952), chap. 7; Hughes, "Human Interest Stories and Democracy"; and Helen MacGill Hughes, *News and the Human Interest Story* (1940; repr., New Brunswick, NJ: Transaction Press, 1980).

98. "Pussy Obstructs the Streets," *New York Sun*, 17 November 1885, 4.

99. *New York World*, 18 October 1901, 9.

100. "Hetta Holst Has a Good Time," *New York Sun*, 8 April 1897, 4.

101. This series is discussed and quoted in H. F. Harrington, *Chats on Feature Writing, by Members of the Blue Pencil Club of Professional Writers* (New York: Harper and Brothers, 1925), 310–13.

102. "Interesting Gossip of the Day," *New York Sun*, 2 January 1889, 4; "She Left $5,000 in Her Satchel on 'L' Train," *New York World*, 14 December 1909, front page; and "Mrs. Gray Gets Back her $5,000 Pearl," *New York Sun*, 17 November 1913, 3.

103. "The Hofstatters, 'Coffee and Sandwich Angels' of New York Firemen," *New York World*, 31 January 1904, magazine section, 3. On a selfless rescue worker, see "Life-Saving Chaplain Is a Modest Hero," *New York World*, 27 October 1901, 27, and on a socialite who became a nurse, see "From the Gayeties of Fifth Avenue . . . to the Slums of Water Street," *New York World*, 13 June 1897, 34.

104. "This Shows New York Is Not So Black as Its Painted," *New York Times*, 14 June 1908, magazine section, 11.

105. Hyde, *Newspaper Reporting and Correspondence*, 235.

106. I draw my basic definition of cosmopolitanism from much more detailed definitions that appear in Walter Mignolo, "The Many Faces of Cosmo-polis: Border Thinking and Critical Cosmopolitanism," *Public Culture* 12, no. 3 (2001): 721; and Bruce Robbins, "Introduction, Part I: Actually Existing Cosmopolitanism," in *Cosmopolitics: Thinking and Feeling beyond the Nation*, ed. Pheng Cheah and Bruce Robbins (Minneapolis: University of Minnesota Press, 1998), 3.

107. "Little Paris in Gotham," *New York Sun*, 27 August 1893, pt. 2, 6.

108. Jane Dixon, "New York Night's Entertainments Off Beaten Track," *New York Sun*, 4 March 1917, sec. 5, 11.

109. "New 'Bohemia' Discovered on East Side," *New York Times*, 13 November 1904, magazine section, 3.

110. "Three Year Old Boy Gone; Search for Him in Vain," *New York Times*, 8 June 1908, 5.

111. "Sealed Grocer in His Own Barrel," *New York World*, 2 August 1905, 8.

112. "New 'Bohemia' Discovered on East Side," *New York Times*, 13 November 1904, magazine section, 3.

113. "New York Night's Entertainments off Beaten Track," *New York Sun*, 4 March 1917, sec. 5, 11.

114. On the "travelogue" style and exoticism, see Sabine Haenni, *The Immigrant Scene: Ethnic Amusements in New York, 1880–1920* (Minneapolis: University of Minnesota Press, 2008), chaps. 1, 4, and 5; and Esther Romeyn, *Street Scenes: Staging the Self in Immigrant New York, 1880–1924* (Minneapolis: University of Minnesota Press, 2008), chap. 1.

115. T. Thomas Fortune Scrapbooks, Manuscripts and Archives, The Schomberg

Center, New York Public Library. Fortune wrote for the *Sun*, with varying frequency, from 1884 through 1900. Emma Lou Thornbrough, *T. Thomas Fortune: Militant Journalist* (Chicago: University of Chicago Press, 1974); and Shawn Leigh Alexander, ed., *T. Thomas Fortune, the Afro-American Agitator: A Collection of Writings, 1880–1928* (Gainesville: University Press of Florida, 2008).

116. Patrick S. Washburn, *The African American Newspaper: Voice of Freedom* (Evanston, IL: Northwestern University Press, 2006), 126; and Ellen Gruber Garvey, *Writing with Scissors: American Scrapbooks from the Civil War to the Harlem Renaissance* (Oxford: Oxford University Press, 2013), 134.

117. See Horace Kallen, "Democracy versus the Melting-Pot: A Study of American Nationality," pts. 1 and 2, *Nation* (February 18, 1915), 190–94, and (February 25, 1915), 217–20, respectively; and Randolph Bourne, "Trans-National America," *Atlantic Monthly* 118 (July 1916): 86–97. On debates over citizenship and diversity in the early twentieth-century United States, see Matthew Frye Jacobson, *Barbarian Virtues: The United States Encounters Foreign Peoples at Home and Abroad, 1876–1917* (New York: Hill and Wang, 2000), chap. 5; and Jonathan M. Hansen, *The Lost Promise of Patriotism: Debating American Identity, 1890–1920* (Chicago: University of Chicago Press, 2003), chap. 4.

118. *New York Daily News*, 28 September 1920, 20.

119. For examples, see the church news page, *New York World*, 28 January 1929, 4; and "Topics of the Preachers in the Pulpits of the City and Suburbs Yesterday," *New York Times*, Brooklyn/Queens edition, 9 June 1930, 24.

120. "Chinatown's Last Pigtail," *New York Times*, 28 March 1920, sec. 7, 9.

121. Jean Piper, "30,000 Boro Lithuanians Toy with Their Beads and Long for Trees of Homeland," *Brooklyn Daily Eagle*, 22 February 1925, A9.

122. New York City, unlike most other U.S. cities, had its own weekly society newspaper, *Town Talk*. Daily papers certainly catered to elite readers, but their society pages drew a high proportion of curious middle-class and working-class readers as well.

123. The "Chat from Wall Street" column gave similar profiles of a handful of powerful businessmen. *New York World*, 22 March 1885, 18. For a history of the field of celebrity journalism, see Charles L. Ponce de Leon, *Self-Exposure: Human-Interest Journalism and the Emergence of Celebrity in America, 1890–1940* (Chapel Hill: University of North Carolina Press, 2002).

124. For example, see photographs in "Mrs. Whitelaw Reid a Distinguished Hostess," *New York Times*, 21 January 1912, pt. 7, 1.

125. See the article on Broadway "Progressive supper," *New York World*, 19 December 1909, metropolitan section, 2; "Bankers of Manhattan at the Banquet Table," the *New York Times*, 7 February 1900, front page; and "Cholly Knickerbocker," *New York American*, 2 October 1910, 12L.

126. Dos Passos, *Manhattan Transfer*, 226.

127. "The Bridal Romance of the Largest Private House in New York," *New York World*, 6 June 1897, metropolitan section.

128. "Every House and Every Foot of the Astor Real Estate on Manhattan Island," *New York World*, 27 March 1898, magazine section, pages 34–35, as reprinted in Baker and Brentano, eds., *The World on Sunday*, 20–21.

129. "Reconciliation between Mrs. Roche and Her Father a Tacit Admission That a '400' Leader Must Spend $375 A DAY," *New York American and Journal*, 14 January 1906, 54.

130. Stephen Crane is one of the most famous of these writers; he covered the Tenderloin for the *New York Journal*. On the genre of the urban travelogue that delved into poor neighborhoods, see Stuart Blumin's introduction to George Foster, *New York by Gas-Light and Other Urban Sketches* (Berkeley: University of California Press, 1990); Jacobson, *Barbarian Virtues*, 121–27; and Keith Gandal, *The Virtues of the Vicious: Jacob Riis, Stephen Crane, and the Spectacle of the Slum* (New York: Oxford University Press, 1997).

131. "Murderers' Alley to Go," *New York World*, 6 June 1897, main news section, 8. This article pictured people and buildings around the alley. A second article on the same subject, "Murderers' Alley to Be Wiped Out," *New York World*, 13 June 1897, 38, included a map.

132. For mafia article, see "Red-Handed Mafia Lurks in New York," *New York World*, 20 March 1898, magazine section, 2, as reprinted in Baker and Brentano, eds., *The World on Sunday*, 6. For gambling terminology, see the *New York Evening Journal*, "Night Special" ed., 3 August 1898, 3. For the "Moll" article, see John T. Quimby, "The Moll and the Mob," *New York World*, 3 April 1921, magazine section, 4–5.

133. "Red-Handed Mafia Lurks in New York," *New York World*, 20 March 1898, magazine section, 2, as reprinted in Baker and Brentano, eds., *The World on Sunday*, 6; "The Ordeal of New York's 'Black Path,'" *New York World*, 11 October 1908, front page of magazine section; "Inmates of Blackwell's Island Penitentiary Play Ball at the Celebration of the First Anniversary of John J. Murtha as Warden," *New York Times*, 6 August 1916, picture section, 7.

134. For example, see "Doctor Lowered by Rope into Shaft to Save Woman Who Fled from Husband," *New York Evening Journal*, tenth extra racing ed., 18 January 1906, 2.

135. "Gangsters Buy Death in Pills 'Good as Coke,'" *New York Tribune*, 14 April 1915, front page. For an earlier example, see *New York Evening Journal*, "Night Special" ed., 3 August 1898, 3. These articles built on a long tradition of using printed dialect, meant to signal region, class, ethnicity, or race, as entertainment. On the use of dialect in American literature at this time, see Gavin Jones, *Strange Talk: The Politics of Dialect Literature in Gilded Age America* (Berkeley: University of California Press, 1999); and Michael North, *Dialect of Modernism: Race, Language, and Twentieth-Century Literature* (New York: Oxford University Press, 1998). Similar dialect-based passages appeared in a few other metropolitan newspaper features, such as Peter Finley Dunne's Irish "Mr. Dooley," and Dorothy Dix's African American "Mirandy."

136. Examples come from "Catching the Criminals of the Railroads," *New York Times*, 14 June 1908, magazine section, 9, and "How the 'House Men' Guard the Hotels," *New York Times*, 21 January 1912, pt. 7, 14.

137. *New York American and Journal*, 14 January 1906, 75.

138. M. B. Levick, "Our Town and Its Folk," *New York Times*, 12 October 1924, sec. 9, 2.

139. "Mickey at a Recital," *New York World*, 14 April 1895, as reprinted in Blackbeard, ed., *R. F. Outcault's The Yellow Kid*, 138.

140. "Chinamen at the Natural History Museum," *New York World*, 7 June 1897, 3.

141. For an example of such a scandal in turn-of-the-century New York, see Mary Ting Yi Lui, *The Chinatown Trunk Mystery: Murder, Miscegenation, and Other Dangerous Encounters in Turn-of-the-Century New York City* (Princeton, NJ: Princeton University Press, 2005). Until recently, scholars defined cosmopolitanism as a trait only possible through choice—and hence as a quality often limited to elite groups. More recently,

scholars have shifted the definition, claiming that poor and working-class people, immigrants, and refugees can be just as fluent in different cultures as any prosperous world travelers or scholars. Sheldon Pollock, Homi K. Bhabha, Carol A. Breckenridge, and Dipesh Chakrabarty, "Cosmopolitanisms," *Public Culture* 12, no. 3 (2000): 582; and Robbins, "Introduction, Part I: Actually Existing Cosmopolitanism," 2-3.

142. For an array of comics that, similarly, lampooned society with glee, see Peter Maresca, ed., *Society Is Nix: Gleeful Anarchy at the Dawn of the American Comic Strip, 1895-1915* (Palo Alto, CA: Sunday Press, 2013).

143. The first titled "metropolitan" section of the *New York World* that I have seen ran in 1905. Smaller, earlier columns set a precedent: the *World* ran a column called "The Metropolis Day by Day" in the 1890s, and the *Sun* printed a column of local news called "Life in the Metropolis" in the 1880s.

144. The Sunday editor for the *New York World*, Herbert Bayard Swope, was at the center of one such urban circle, and he employed friends to write feature material for the *World*. Harris, "Covering New York," 258-59.

145. For chronicles of New York's more flamboyant, less political culture in the 1920s, see Ann Douglass, *Terrible Honesty: Mongrel Manhattan in the 1920s* (New York: Farrar, Straus and Giroux, 1995); and Chad Heap, *Slumming: Sexual and Racial Encounters in American Nightlife, 1885-1940* (Chicago: University of Chicago Press, 2010).

146. The city's largest paper in the 1920s, the *New York Daily News*, did less of this kind of urban branding. It tended to involve readers by printing personal stories, covering neighborhood news, and inviting reader participation rather than by offering a burnished image of the city that readers belonged to. Even so, common themes emerged in the *Daily News* and the rest of the city's dailies. Neil Harris also discusses these qualities in "Covering New York," 261-65.

147. On this process, see Angela M. Blake, *How New York Became American, 1890-1924* (Baltimore: Johns Hopkins University Press, 2006).

148. See Wanda Corn, "The Artist's New York, 1900-1930," in *Budapest and New York*, ed. Bender and Schorske, 275-303; and Thomas Bender, "Modernist Aesthetics and Urban Politics," in *The Unfinished City: New York and the Metropolitan Idea* (New York: New Press, 2002).

149. Ad for Sunday edition, *New York American*, 18 May 1930, 14-M.

150. The *Tribune* section appeared beginning in 1919. M. B. Levick wrote "Our Town and Its Folk," which started around 1924, and "Listen, Folks Listen" appeared under the name Jim Hayseed, starting in 1928.

151. From the regular column by Leo T. Heatley, "Wit and Without," *New York Journal*, 15 May 1930, 7.

152. Jean B. Quant weaves this theme through *From the Small Town to the Great Community: The Social Thought of Progressive Intellectuals* (New Brunswick, NJ: Rutgers University Press, 1970). It appears in a handful of other autobiographies and biographies of these reformers as well.

153. Examples from "One Year's 'Eats' of New York Dwellers," *New York World*, 30 March 1913, second news section, 3, and "Auto Drivers Increased 110,000 Here in Year," *New York Times*, 3 June 1930, front page. Newspapers' habit of reporting these aggregate statistics became common enough that the 1920 *World* parodied it; a cartoon showed the city's total raisin consumption and the city's collective wad of gum. *New York World*, 9 May 1920, metropolitan section, front page.

154. *Facts about New York, with a Complete Index*, 6th ed. (New York: The Sun, 1928).

155. Igo, "New Madison Square Garden Is Greatest of All Arenas," 21.

156. "Mirror of City Life" and "Bits of Life in the Metropolis" both appeared in the metropolitan section in the 1920s *New York World* and the feature "Our Town and Its Folk" in the 1920s' *New York Times*.

157. Eva Weinstein's letter to the editor appearing in the *New York Tribune*, 13 October 1919, 8; and Charles Romm's letter to the editor appearing in the *New York Tribune*, 11 October 1919, 10.

158. Many historians have investigated the reality and the cultural trope of the threatening nineteenth-century city. See Cohen, *The Murder of Helen Jewett*; Timothy Gilfoyle, *City of Eros: New York City, Prostitution, and the Commercialization of Sex, 1790–1920* (New York: W. W. Norton, 1994), and *A Pickpocket's Tale: The Underworld of Nineteenth-Century New York* (New York: W. W. Norton, 2007); Kasson, *Rudeness and Civility*; Karen Halttunen, *Confidence Men and Painted Women: A Study of Middle-Class Culture in America, 1830–1870* (New Haven, CT: Yale University Press, 1982); William Cronon, *Nature's Metropolis: Chicago and the Great West* (New York: W. W. Norton, 1991), chap. 8; and Alan Trachtenberg, *The Incorporation of America: Culture and Society in the Gilded Age* (New York: Hill and Wang, 1982), chap. 4.

159. *New York Times*, 17 November 1904, 7; *New York World*, 20 March 1898, 2, as reprinted in Baker and Brentano, eds., *The World on Sunday*; *New York American*, 26 April 1914, 4CE.

160. *New York American and Journal*, 14 January 1906, 70.

161. "Once a Waiter, Now to Be an Operatic Star," *New York World*, 13 June 1897, 38; *New York World*, 20 October 1901, magazine section, 5.

162. *New York World*, 2 August 1905, 8; and "Every House and Every Foot of the Astor Real Estate on Manhattan Island," *New York World*, 27 March 1898, magazine section, 34–35, as reprinted in Baker and Brentano, eds., *The World on Sunday*, 20–21.

163. "The White Collar Squad," *New York Times*, 19 October 1919, magazine section, 8.

164. Karl K. Kitchen, "Protesting against New York's New Neighborly Spirit That Co-Operative Apartments Are Bringing About," *New York World*, 27 March 1921, metropolitan section, front page.

165. Ad for Weber and Heilbroner, *New York World*, 27 March 1913, 5.

166. Ad for *New York American*, *New York American*, 18 May 1930, 14M. For a sampling of scholarship treating New York's identity as capital of the modern world in the early twentieth century, see Corn, "The Artist's New York, 1900–1930," 275–303; Douglass, *Terrible Honesty*; and Christine Stansell, *American Moderns: Bohemian New York and the Creation of a New Century* (New York: Metropolitan Books/Henry Holt and Co., 2000).

167. *New York Tribune*, 4 September 1899, 7. In a similar vein, Angela Blake found that New York's 1923 "Silver Jubilee," organized by a business bureau, had trouble mustering local enthusiasm or support, because New Yorkers felt that such self-celebration was unnecessary. Blake, *How New York Became American*, chap. 5.

168. *The Journalist*, 26 January 1889, 2.

169. Letter from Curtis C. Brown in *Collier's Weekly*, 2 September 1911, 23.

170. Letter from E. S. Hull in *Collier's Weekly*, 14 October 1911, 35.

171. "North American Porch Parties for Crippled Children," *Philadelphia North American*, 9 October 1921, 4.

172. John W. Perry, "Newspaper Funds Alleviate Suffering," *Editor & Publisher*, 21 December 1929, 9–10.

173. Roy D. Pinkerton letter to *Collier's Weekly*, 30 September 1911, 34.

174. One of the more extreme and famous cases of demonizing is the way that California newspapers depicted Chinese immigrants. Yet the depictions of the "yellow peril" often coexisted with articles that treated Chinese Californians as colorful additions to the social landscape. See Jules Becker, *The Course of Exclusion, 1882-1924: San Francisco Newspaper Coverage of the Chinese and Japanese in the United States* (San Francisco: Mellen Research University Press, 1991).

175. Theodore Dreiser, "Out of My Newspaper Days," pt. 2, "St. Louis," *Bookman* 54, no. 5 (January 1922): 431.

176. Society column, *Milwaukee Journal*, 23 December 1919, 8.

177. Letter from R. F. Walker in *Collier's Weekly*, 30 September 1911, 33.

178. "Found $1,000 Pin. Liveryman Picked up Piece of Jewelry Where He Lost It," *Philadelphia Evening Bulletin*, 9 July 1910, 9.

179. Letter from "Opinion" to *Collier's Weekly*, 16 Sept 1911, 30.

180. "Girard's Topics of the Town," "Peggy Shippen's Diary," and "Anne Rittenhouse" all appeared in the *Philadelphia Public Ledger* in the 1910s and 1920s.

181. Harold A. Williams, *The Baltimore Sun, 1837-1987* (Baltimore: Johns Hopkins University Press, 1987), 140.

182. Ibid., 227.

CHAPTER FOUR

1. James Edward Rogers, *The American Newspaper* (Chicago: University of Chicago Press, 1909), 37.

2. As shown in circulation statistics for major city dailies in *Editor & Publisher* in the 1920s, when the trade journal first broke circulations down into "city," "suburban," and "country" categories.

3. I draw this background largely from William Cronon, *Nature's Metropolis: Chicago and the Great West* (New York: W. W. Norton, 1991); Bessie Louise Pierce, *A History of Chicago*, vol. 3, *The Rise of a Modern City, 1871-1893* (New York: Alfred A. Knopf, 1957); Donald L. Miller, *City of the Century: The Epic of Chicago and the Making of America* (New York: Simon & Schuster, 1997); and Jon Teaford, *Cities of the Heartland: The Rise and Fall of the Industrial Midwest* (Bloomington: Indiana University Press, 1993).

4. Chicago played a leading role in realist urban novels such as Theodore Dreiser's *Sister Carrie* (1900), Upton Sinclair's *The Jungle* (1906), and Frank Norris's *The Pit: A Story of Chicago* (1902). Chicago journalists specializing in human interest reporting included George Ade, Ben Hecht, Henry Justin Smith, and Robert Casey.

5. For example, see an 1884 *Chicago Tribune* column by "Urban" that complained about the practice of tying up horses in the city streets. *Chicago Tribune*, 12 October 1884, 23.

6. From census figures, as cited in Neil Harris, ed., *The Chicagoan: A Lost Magazine of the Jazz Age* (Chicago: University of Chicago Press, 2008), 2.

7. Because of its unparalleled expansion around the turn of the century, Chicago has generated a rich body of scholarship on urban development and suburban growth. Among these works are Cronon, *Nature's Metropolis*; Ann Durkin Keating, *Building Chicago: Suburban Developers and the Creation of a Divided Metropolis* (Columbus: Ohio State University Press, 1988), and *Chicagoland: City and Suburbs in the Railroad Age* (Chicago: University of Chicago Press, 2005); Michael Ebner, *Creating Chicago's North*

Shore: A Suburban History (Chicago: University of Chicago Press, 1988); and Harold M. Mayer and Richard C. Wade, *Chicago: Growth of a Metropolis* (Chicago: Chicago University Press, 1969).

8. Examples include *Chicago Tribune* editor Robert McCormick, who lived at his Wheaton estate, Cantigny, for most of his publishing career; *Washington Post* owner John R. McLean, who owned a seventy-five-acre estate called Friendship outside of Washington DC; Frank Munsey, owner of the *New York Sun* and of a Long Island estate; and *St. Louis Post-Dispatch* publisher Joseph Pulitzer II, who spent his time on a hundred-acre estate called Lone Tree Farm.

9. Chicago's largest annexation, in 1889, added 125 square miles and 225,000 people, but the city annexed smaller pieces of land both before and after. Louis P. Cain, "Annexation," in the Encyclopedia of Chicago, http://www.encyclopedia.chicagohistory .org/pages/53.html, accessed 3 December 2010.

10. For detailed descriptions of suburban neighborhoods' landscapes, see Keating, *Chicagoland*; and Dominic Pacyga and Ellen Skerrett, *Chicago, City of Neighborhoods: Histories and Tours* (Chicago: Loyola University Press, 1986). In this chapter I define "suburb" as a densely populated area adjacent to a large city, taking my cue from 1910 and 1920 census definitions of metropolitan districts.

11. This argument about the suburban dream, and my description of working-class suburbs more generally, is drawn from Richard Harris, "Chicago's Other Suburbs," *Geographical Review* 84, no. 4 (October 1994): 394–410.

12. Samuel E. Gross ad, *Chicago Daily News*, 26 October 1889, supplement section, 8.

13. Realtor ad, *Sunday Record-Herald*, 4 May 1913, 5.

14. "Some of the Many Phases of the Annual Mayday Hegira," *Chicago Tribune*, 25 April 1897, 37. I owe this reference to Perry Duis, who uses it in *Challenging Chicago: Coping with Everyday Life, 1837–1920* (Urbana: University of Illinois Press, 1998), 79.

15. Ad for real estate classifieds, *Sunday Record-Herald*, 4 May, 1913, sec. 2, 8. On the gradual spread of the norm of homeownership in Chicago, see Margaret Garb, *City of American Dreams: A History of Home Ownership and Housing Reform in Chicago, 1871–1919* (Chicago: University of Chicago Press, 2005); Elaine Lewinnek, *The Working Man's Reward: Chicago's Early Suburbs and the Roots of American Sprawl* (New York: Oxford University Press, 2014); and Joseph C. Bigott, *From Cottage to Bungalow: Houses and the Working Class in Metropolitan Chicago* (Chicago: University of Chicago Press, 2001).

16. For examples, see ads in *Chicago Herald*, 27 April 1889, 10, and *Chicago Tribune*, 10 October 1884, 7.

17. Ad for Edgewater development, *Chicago Tribune*, 15 April 1888, 29.

18. Ad for real estate classifieds, *Sunday Record-Herald*, 4 May, 1913, sec. 2, 8.

19. Ad for Auburn Park, *Chicago Tribune*, 15 April 1888, 31.

20. Samuel E. Gross ad, *Chicago Daily News*, 26 October 1889, supplement section, 8.

21. Ad for West Side properties, *Chicago Herald*, 28 April 1889, 23.

22. Ad for Auburn Park, *Chicago Herald*, 28 April 1889, 13; ad for Home Addition, *Chicago Tribune*, 27 June 1920, pt. 1, 10.

23. *Chicago Record*, September 18, 1890. I owe this source to Duis, *Challenging Chicago*, 32.

24. Ad for Washington Boulevard lots, *Chicago Herald*, 27 April 1889, 10. This idea became more entrenched in later decades and was formalized in the property codes of the Home Owners' Loan Corporation.

25. For example, see ad for Samuel Gross's Avondale subdivision on the front page

of the *Illinois Staats-Zeitung*, 7 July 1891, and for the Lucy M. Green Addition in the *Illinois Staats-Zietung*, 8 July 1891, 8.

26. These groups would get their suburban chance only later, during the boom in construction after World War II.

27. For an advertisement for a subdivision full of such standard-issue homes, see ad for Portage Park in the *Chicago Daily News*, 5 September 1925, 14. On developers' processes in the region in this era, see Keating, *Building Chicago*, chaps. 3 and 4.

28. Andrew Wiese, *Places of Their Own: African American Suburbanization in the Twentieth Century* (Chicago: University of Chicago Press, 2002), 41–42, 64. In its news columns, the *Chicago Defender* occasionally waged battles against discrimination in housing and real estate. For examples, see *Chicago Defender*, 21 April 1917, 1, and "South Shorers in Move to Bar 'Undesirables;' Seek Signers for Old Illegal Pact," *Chicago Defender*, 6 April 1929, pt. 1, 6. For an article on this issue in a suburban paper, see "Negroes Unable to Secure Homes Here," *Evanston Index*, 2 January 1918, front page.

29. "Lilydale 'The Beautiful,'" *Chicago Defender*, 5 April 1913, 3.

30. W. M. Farrow, "Art and the Home," *Chicago Defender*, 19 September, 1925, pt. 2, 4.

31. Ibid., 4.

32. In Chicago's dailies, properties for sale equaled or outnumbered rentals, from the 1890s onward. In the *Defender*, rental listings far outnumbered for-purchase listings in the same period. Black homeownership rates were much lower than white rates in Chicago in this era; see Garb, *City of American Dreams*, chap. 7; and Lewinnek, *The Working Man's Reward*, chap. 6.

33. For ads for African American developments, see *Chicago Defender*, 5 February 1921, 6 (Gary, Indiana), and *Chicago Defender*, 18 May 1929, pt. 1, 3 (the far South Side). For a broader history of African Americans and suburbanization, see Wiese, *Places of Their Own*.

34. Ad for South Side real estate, *Chicago Defender*, 5 April 1913, 6.

35. Classified ad for South Side real estate, *Chicago Daily News*, 20 June 1921, 29. I.C.R.R. stands for Illinois Central Railroad.

36. The *Chicago Tribune* printed regular real estate news starting in the 1880s; the *Herald* in the 1890s; and the *Daily News* in the 1920s.

37. Ad for Englefield, *Chicago Tribune*, 17 September 1916, Sec. I, 11.

38. "Chicago Building Pace Called Dizzy," *Chicago Daily News*, 5 September 1925, 15.

39. Ad for Frederick H. Bartlett Realty Company, *Chicago Herald*, 29 April 1917, 8.

40. For more on the history of consumer credit—for both homes and household purchases—see Lendol Caldor, *Financing the American Dream: A Cultural History of Consumer Credit* (Princeton, NJ: Princeton University Press, 2001).

41. Advertisement for Frederick H. Bartlett Realty Company, *Chicago Herald and Examiner*, 5 May 1929, pt. 1, 4.

42. Chicago Tribune, *Chicago Tribune Book of Homes: Containing Nineteen Prize Winning Plans and Eighty Other Plans Submitted in the $7,500 Competition*, conducted by the Home Builders' Department of the Chicago Tribune (Chicago: Chicago Tribune, 1927), 6.

43. Louise Bargelt, "Home Building and Remodeling," *Chicago Tribune*, 11 November 1928, sec. 3, 3.

44. Chicago Tribune, *Book of Facts, 1927: Data on Markets, Merchandising, Advertising, with Special Reference to the Chicago Territory and Chicago Newspaper Advertising*

(Chicago: Chicago Tribune, 1927), 17, 103. On the birth and expansion of the home-improvement industry, see Richard Harris, *Building a Market: The Rise of the Home Improvement Industry, 1914–1960* (Chicago: University of Chicago Press, 2012); and Carolyn M. Goldstein, *Do It Yourself: Home Improvement in 20th-Century America* (New York: Princeton Architectural Press, 1998).

45. In the *Chicago Tribune*, 20 April 1924, pt. 7, 4, a question-and-answer column titled "The Home Harmonious" advised readers on coordinating living room upholstery and choosing colors for a bedroom. Roland Marchand discusses the "ensemble" as a 1920s sales technique in *Advertising the American Dream: Making Way for Modernity, 1920–1940* (Berkeley: University of California Press, 1985).

46. "Novel Hints for Furnishing Homes," *Chicago Times-Herald*, 7 November 1897, 47.

47. Pirie Scott & Company ad, *Chicago Daily News*, 5 September 1925, 15.

48. The *Chicago Daily News*'s home decor column received about a dozen letters per week. Letter from Margaret H. Mann, *Chicago Daily News*, in response to a syndicate circular, no date, estimated between 1917 and 1924, Victor Freemont Lawson Papers, Newberry Library, Chicago.

49. Dorothy Ethel Walsh, "Getting the House Ready for Warm Weather," *Chicago Daily News*, 24 February 1917, 8.

50. *Suburban Gardening* by Frank Ridgway is advertised in Chicago Tribune, *Book of Facts, 1927*.

51. The *Chicago Herald*, for example, began printing regular gardening columns during the war.

52. Carson Pirie Scott & Company ad, *Chicago Herald*, 24 April 1917, 3, and *Chicago Daily News*, 18 April 1929, 11.

53. Wittbold Gardeners ad, Sunday *Record-Herald*, 4 May, 1913, 3.

54. For an example, see ad for the "Jeffery Four" in the *Chicago Tribune*, 17 September 1916, pt. 1, 7.

55. "Help for the Man Who Wants to Build" was a syndicated feature, written by the Architects' Small House Service Bureau and run in the *Chicago Daily News* in the 1920s.

56. These questions appeared in the column "What You May Want to Know about Building," *Chicago Daily News*, 5 September 1925, 15.

57. The 1920s *Herald and Examiner* offered a free booklet on the fine points of home construction, and Sears, Roebuck, & Company advertised its mail-order homes in Chicago newspapers as well. For both see *Chicago Herald and Examiner*, 5 May 1929, real estate and business section, 1.

58. Chicago Tribune, *Book of Facts, 1927*, 41.

59. Chicago Tribune, *Chicago Tribune Book of Homes*, 7.

60. "Events of a City Day," *Chicago Tribune*, 8 August 1896, 5; and "What Some of the Chicago Preachers Said," *Chicago Tribune*, and 3 August 1896, 12.

61. These stories were later collected in a book: Franklin J. Meine, ed. *Chicago Stories, by George Ade, Illustrated by John T. McCutcheon and Others* (Chicago: Henry Regnery Company, 1963). The same feature ran in the *Chicago Record-Herald* for several years in the 1900s.

62. "Tales They Tell in the Loop" and "Our Neighbors across the Way," *Chicago Herald*, 29 April 1917, humor and city life section.

63. For example, see "The Restless Age," *Chicago Tribune*, 21 June 1920, front page.

64. For an ad that offered suburban delivery, see *Chicago Daily News*, 5 January

1905, 16. For a map showing how Chicago department stores calibrated their delivery routes to the incomes and neighborhoods of their desired customers, see Lewis Copeland, "The Limits and Characteristics of Metropolitan Chicago" (PhD diss., University of Chicago, 1937), 67, 70. Regena Marie Beckmire also discusses suburban delivery in "The Study of Highland Park as a Residential Suburb" (MA thesis, University of Chicago, 1932), 113.

65. Beckmire, "The Study of Highland Park as a Residential Suburb," 111.

66. The *Herald* subtitled one 1889 article on annexation "Valuable Hints for Suburbanites" and walked readers through the complicated new laws surrounding the process. "To Get Into Chicago; the New Plan for Annexation," *Chicago Herald*, 28 April 1889, 10.

67. The example of club lists comes from the *Chicago Times-Herald*, 3 November 1897, 9. There are fewer records of suburban social mixing in the late nineteenth century than there are for the early twentieth century. Lewis Copeland tracked membership in social clubs in "The Limits and Characteristics of Metropolitan Chicago," 211, 213. He found that the Union League was 57 percent suburban in 1935, the University Club was about 50 percent suburban in 1926, and the City Club was 27.5 percent suburban in 1935. The Chicago names appearing in the 1926 *Social Register* were 35.9 percent suburban.

68. Beckmire, "The Study of Highland Park as a Residential Suburb," 110-11. Other examples of mixed urban and suburban news include the *Tribune*'s weekly listings of religious services, and many papers' columns on amateur leagues, which reported on teams such as the Lake Views, the Garden Cities, and the Evanston Boys, who regularly played urban teams. *Chicago Herald*, 17 July 1893, 7.

69. An 1888 *Tribune* listed dozens of branch offices, with seven in suburbs. List of branch offices, *Chicago Tribune*, 10 April 1888, 10. In 1890, two hundred druggists worked for the *Daily News*; by 1905, the number had risen to six hundred. Charles H. Dennis, *Victor Lawson: His Time and His Work* (Chicago: University of Chicago Press, 1935), 35, 136. Around the turn of the century, most Chicagoans did not own telephones, but many druggists kept a phone in their stores—hence the need for this arrangement.

70. On the decentralization of work and retail in the Chicago area and beyond, see Robert Bruegmann, "Schaumburg, Oak Brook, Rosemont, and the Recentering of the Chicago Metropolitan Area," in *Chicago Architecture and Design, 1923-1993*, ed. John Zukowsky (Munich: Prestel-Verlag; Chicago: Art Institute of Chicago, 1993), 161; Neil Harris, "The City That Shops: Chicago's Retailing Landscape," in *Chicago Architecture and Design*, ed. Zukowsky, 179-80; and Richard Harris and Robert Lewis, "The Geography of North American Cities and Suburbs, 1900-1950: A New Synthesis," *Journal of Urban History* 27, no. 3 (March 2001): 262-92.

71. The *Daily News* articulated its urban focus in an editorial on 30 October 1876, quoted in Dennis, *Victor Lawson*, 33, and later also in its Employee's Manual, 1928, 26, MMS Field Enterprises Collection, Newberry Library, Chicago.

72. For comparison: in the 1920s, the *American*, the *Herald and Examiner*, and the *Daily News* all sold between twenty-eight and thirty-eight thousand papers to the suburbs every day. Circulation statistics are for 1925 and come from *Editor & Publisher, International Yearbook Number for 1926*, 30 January 1926, 35.

73. Chicago Tribune, *Pictured Encyclopedia of the World's Greatest Newspaper* (Chicago: Tribune Company, 1928), 122-23.

74. The *Tribune* said that it paid a carrier, for example, $3.50 per week to deliver a newspaper that cost the subscriber sixty cents per week. Chicago Tribune, *Pictured Encyclopedia*, 124.

75. The suburban circulation manager is listed in the employee manual, 1928, 12, MMS Field Enterprises Collection, Newberry Library, Chicago. The airplanes and branch plans are mentioned in "'Story of a Newspaper'—a Conducted Tour through the Chicago Daily News Plant," script, no date—likely 1929, 8, Victor Freemont Lawson Papers, Newberry Library, Chicago. Several New York City papers, including the *Sun*, *Telegram*, *Journal*, and *Daily News*, set up branch plants in the 1920s and 1930s as well. These plants became especially necessary as automobile traffic clogged city streets, and trucks could not deliver papers to suburbs on time. Alfred McClung Lee, *The Daily Newspaper in America: The Evolution of a Social Instrument* (New York: Macmillan, 1937), 281.

76. "The *Tribune*'s Platform for Chicago," *Chicago Tribune*, 21 June 1920, 8.

77. "For Chicago, the Nation's Central Great City." *Chicago Herald and Examiner*, 3 May 1929, 10.

78. For the first year and a half of its existence, the metropolitan section printed different advertisements for the three zones, but the same articles. In 1928 it started running separate news content as well. *The Trib* (internal newsletter for *Chicago Tribune* employees), October 1928, 6–7. Regional advertising rates are explained in Chicago Tribune, *Pictured Encyclopedia*, 108.

79. Advertisement for zoned classified ads in the *Chicago Herald and Examiner*, 5 May 1929, Part 4, 8.

80. These regional headings appeared in the *Chicago Tribune*, 18 September 1916, 13. The *Tribune* explained its directory's purpose and advertising success in 1927: "When it first appeared, thirteen years ago, skeptics were positive that it could not possibly succeed because of the 'waste circulation.' No movie theatre outside the loop has in its immediate neighborhood more than 25,000 *Tribune* subscribers out of a total of more than 1,000,000. Yet, the movie theatres outside the loop find it profitable to use *Chicago Tribune* space 365 days in the year. In fact, their advertising totals far more than that of all legitimate loop theatres which are, of course, in a position to draw upon the entire city." Chicago Tribune, *Book of Facts, 1927*, 162. The *Chicago Herald and Examiner* printed a regionally organized listing page by 1929.

81. The Harris Brothers' home improvement chain, for example, operated more stores in Chicago's periphery than in Chicago proper, but it still placed two-page ads in the Sunday *Herald and Examiner*. *Chicago Herald and Examiner*, 5 May 1929, pt. 1, 24. For other examples of chains advertising all of their branches in Chicago dailies, see the ad for Harman's in the *Chicago Tribune*, 4 November 1928, pt. 1, 14–15, and ads for Spiegel's department stores in both the *Chicago Tribune*, 20 April 1924, 6–7, and the *Chicago Defender*, 13 April 1929, pt. 1, 5.

82. Lee, *The Daily Newspaper in America*, 281.

83. For "El" instructions and parking publicity, see the Sears ad in the *Chicago Daily News*, 4 September 1925, 22, as well as multiple full-page advertisements in the *Chicago Herald and Examiner*, 5 May 1929.

84. Pittsfield Building Shops ad, *Chicago Daily News*, 17 April 1929, midweek features section, 2.

85. Rev. Henry C. Kinney, "The Towns All Need Chicago," *Chicago Tribune*, 23 June 1889, 5. I owe this reference to Michael P. McCarthy, "The New Metropolis: Chicago,

the Annexation Movement and Progressive Reform," in *The Age of Urban Reform: New Perspectives on the Progressive Era*, ed. Michael H. Ebner and Eugene M. Tobin (Port Washington, NY: Kennikat Press, 1977), 45.

86. A few suburbs boasted newspapers almost from the date of their founding, but these were booster papers, created to attract buyers rather than to communicate news. For example, see the *Riverside Gazette* (1871) and the *Evanston Real Estate News* (1871–73).

87. Chicago Tribune, *Book of Facts, 1927*, 49.

88. University Bookstore advertised Chicago dailies in the *Evanston Index*, 1 May, 1880, front page. Full-page ads for the *Herald and Examiner* appeared in the *Evanston Index*, 18 July 1925, 3, and the *Hyde Park Herald*, 22 May 1925, 8.

89. For an invitation to phone in news, see the masthead of the *Evanston Index*, 20 July 1925, front page.

90. Newspapers advertised their printing services in their own pages: see the *Hyde Park Herald*, 2 February 1884, 10, and the *Lake Shore News*, 10 June 1921, 8.

91. Police news, *Hyde Park Herald*, 14 June 1929, 10.

92. Hyde Park Theater ad, *Hyde Park Herald*, 6 September 1918, 2.

93. For an example of its slogan, "A Clean Newspaper for a Clean Community," see, e.g., *Wilmette Life*, 4 January 1924.

94. During the Great Migration, one in six African Americans moving to the urban north moved to a suburb. Wiese, *Places of Their Own*, 5. This population included people who settled in working-class suburbs near industrial jobs as well as those who lived and worked in prosperous, predominantly white suburbs.

95. One thousand one hundred African Americans lived in Evanston in 1910, when the total population was twenty-five thousand. The number climbed steeply in the next three decades. Wiese, *Places of Their Own*, 21, 61.

96. Junior section, *Hyde Park Herald*, 14 June 1929, 17; "Junior Life," in *Wilmette Life*, 14 June 1929, 5.

97. Ad for *Wilmette Life*, *Winnetka Talk*, and *Glencoe News* in *Wilmette Life*, 14 June 1929, 49.

98. Ad for Northwestern Elevated trains, *Lake Shore News*, 18 December 1913, 8.

99. Regena Beckmire also documented this "opera train," which ran at 11 P.M. to take suburban operagoers home. Beckmire, "The Study of Highland Park as a Residential Suburb," 106.

100. Field Museum of Natural History ad, *Lake Shore News*, 10 June 1921, 12.

101. The phrase "satellite city" was first coined by Graham Romeyn Taylor, *Satellite Cities: A Study of Industrial Suburbs* (New York: D. Appleton, 1915), then picked up by N. Carpenter in *The Sociology of City Life* (New York: Longmans, Green & Company, 1931), and by many Chicago School sociologists, including Robert Ezra Park, Charles Newcomb, and Roderick McKenzie. See *The City*, ed. Robert Ezra Park, Ernest Watson Burgess, Roderick Duncan McKenzie, and Louis Wirth (Chicago: University of Chicago Press, 1923); Park and Newcomb, "Newspaper Circulation and Metropolitan Regions," in *The Metropolitan Community*, ed. Roderick D. McKenzie (New York: McGraw-Hill Book Company, Inc., 1933); and Park, "Urbanization as Measured by Newspaper Circulation," *American Journal of Sociology* 35 (July 1929): 60–79.

102. South Chicago, though annexed to Chicago in 1889, functioned as a satellite city through the turn of the century; it had its own downtown district, industrial employers, and self-contained social life.

103. For example, an ad for the South Chicago branch of the Bee Hive in the *South Chicago Daily Calumet* (15 July 1892, 2) told readers that in the branch they would find German, Swedish, and Polish clerks.

104. In 1892, the *Joliet Daily News* claimed "a larger home circulation, and consequently a greater home popularity than any other daily paper" (14 January 1892, 2). In 1892, the *Daily Calumet* declared on its front page, "The Calumet has a larger circulation in the 33d ward than all the other Chicago papers combined" (15 July 1892, front page). No official circulation statistics exist for the 1880s through the 1910s, but by 1928, nearly all of the satellite cities took more local than Chicago papers. Park and Newcomb, "Newspaper Circulation and Metropolitan Regions," 103.

105. "From the Coal Fields and Surrounding Towns," *Joliet Daily News*, 20 May 1910, 2. The *South Chicago Daily Calumet* reported on Indiana social life since it lay so close to the border; it called the column "Across the River." *South Chicago Daily Calumet*, 11 July 1887, 4.

106. For agricultural material, see F. C. Grannis, "Weekly Farm Letter" and "Joliet Local Mart Reports," *Joliet Evening Herald News*, 2 March 1916, 13; for Friday advertisements including weekend or next-week prices, see ad for L. F. Beach & Company, *Joliet Daily News*, 15 January 1892, 3, and ads for the Spot Cash and the Boston Store, *Joliet Daily News*, 20 May 1910, 1, 8.

107. *Joliet Daily News*, 14 January 1892, 6.

108. Robert Park and Charles Newcomb found that, in 1928, Gary received 50.1 percent of its newspapers from Chicago, Elgin 46 percent, Joliet 45 percent, Hammond 42 percent, and Aurora 40 percent. Park and Newcomb, "Newspaper Circulation and Metropolitan Regions," 103. The *Chicago Tribune* alone reported subscription rates of 54–70 percent in these cities in 1924—though some of the subscriptions were just for Sunday. Chicago Tribune, *Book of Facts, 1927*, 77.

109. Park, "Urbanization as Measured by Newspaper Circulation," 75.

110. Charles Moreau Harger, "The Country Editor Today," *Atlantic Monthly* 99 (January 1907): 93. I owe this reference to Wayne Fuller, *RFD: The Changing Face of Rural America* (Bloomington: Indiana University Press, 1964), 293–94.

111. Carroll D. Clark, "My 'Newspaper Life History,'" 13, Robert Ezra Park Papers, University of Chicago Special Collections.

112. *N. W. Ayer & Son's American Newspaper Annual and Directory, 1916* (Philadelphia: N. W. Ayer & Son, 1916), 359.

113. William R. Scott, *Scientific Circulation Management for Newspapers* (New York: Ronald Press, 1915), 123.

114. Until 1885, newspapers cost two cents per pound to send through the mail.

115. John M. Stahl, *Growing with the West: The Story of a Busy, Quiet Life* (London: Longmans, Green, and Co., 1930), 101, as quoted in Charles Johanningsmeier, *Fiction and the American Literary Marketplace: The Role of Newspaper Syndicates, 1860–1900* (New York: Cambridge University Press, 1997), 189.

116. Daily papers sometimes published separate weeklies for rural readers. Other weeklies were independent publications. Chicago dailies that published a weekly edition in 1880 include the *Chicagoer Neue Freie Presse*, the *Chicago Evening Journal*, the *Illinois Staats-Zeitung*, the *Chicago Inter-Ocean*, the *Chicago Daily News*, the *Chicago Skandinaven*, the *Chicago Svornost* (called the *Amerikan* in its weekly version), the *Chicago Telegraph*, the *Chicago Times*, and the *Chicago Tribune*. *American Newspaper Directory, 1880* (New York: George P. Rowell & Co., 1880), 62–63.

117. *Chicago Tribune*, 12 March 1884, 2. The story of this first express train appears in Cronon, *Nature's Metropolis*, 333.

118. "The Fast Mail: The Run from Chicago to Burlington Accomplished in Less Than Five Hours," *Chicago Tribune*, 12 March 1884, 2.

119. On the additional rail lines, see "Fast Mails," *Chicago Tribune*, 13 March 1884, 7. Special newspaper trains still ran in the 1930s; see the Chicago Tribune, *Pictured Encyclopedia*, 119. On steamboats for Chicago newspapers, see E. W. Howe, "Country Newspapers," *Century Magazine* 42, no. 5 (September 1891): 782.

120. "Editorial : The *Tribune*'s 'Boom,'" *Chicago Tribune*, 13 March 1884, 6.

121. "The Fast Mail: The Run from Chicago to Burlington Accomplished in Less Than Five Hours," *Chicago Tribune*, 12 March 1884, 2.

122. A yearly subscription to the *Chicago Tribune* in 1896, for example, cost country readers $6.00 per year, only twenty-eight cents more than in the city. On the history of the post office and its distribution of news, see Richard R. John, *Spreading the News: The American Postal System from Franklin to Morse* (Cambridge, MA: Harvard University Press, 1995); Richard B. Kielbowicz, *News in the Mail: The Press, the Post Office, and Public Information, 1700s–1860s* (Santa Barbara, CA: Greenwood Press, 1989); and David Henkin, *The Postal Age: The Emergence of Modern Communications in Nineteenth-Century America* (Chicago: University of Chicago Press, 2006), chap. 2.

123. Fuller, *RFD*, 294–95.

124. *Postmaster General's Report*, 1911, 613, as cited in Fuller, *RFD*, 294–95.

125. *Editor & Publisher*, 23 November 1901, as quoted in Lee, *The Daily Newspaper in America*, 387.

126. Scott, *Scientific Circulation Management for Newspapers*, 122.

127. For Chicago's history as a crossroads for travelers and homesteaders, see Cronon, *Nature's Metropolis*, prologue through chap. 2.

128. Ad for the Hub, *Chicago Daily News*, 29 November 1901, 14.

129. Scott, *Scientific Circulation Management for Newspapers*, 122.

130. For examples, see ad for Rothschild's semiannual sale in the *Chicagoer Freie Presse*, 7 August 1898, 8, and Mandel Brothers ad in the Sunday *Chicago Tribune*, 15 April 1888, 2. William Scott talks about these practices in *Scientific Circulation Management for Newspapers*, 122.

131. Though I have not seen this technique in Chicago newspaper ads, it did appear in an ad for Frank A. Lappen & Co. in the *Milwaukee Daily Journal*. "We Pay Railroad Fare from any place in the state within 150 miles of Milwaukee for any customer whose purchase amounts to $100.00," it said. "Should amount purchased be $200 or over, we pay railroad fare both ways." *Milwaukee Daily Journal*, 6 April 1891, 8. William Scott describes this as common practice in Indianapolis in *Scientific Circulation Management for Newspapers*, 122.

132. For examples of ads offering catalogs, see Speigel & Co. Furniture ad, *Chicago Herald*, 28 April 1889, 14; several ads in the *Chicago Tribune*, 15 April 1888, 3, 4, 12; and Siegel and Cooper ad, *Chicago Times-Herald*, 7 November 1897, 37.

133. Smyth's Town Market ad, *Chicago Times-Herald*, 7 November 1897, 37.

134. By 1920, families living on rural delivery routes were receiving an average of seventeen packages per year. Fuller, *RFD*, 252. Rural Free Delivery did not deliver packages for free, but it smoothed the mail-order process. Companies such as Sears, Roebuck & Co. and Montgomery Ward had pioneered the mail-order business in the

mid-nineteenth century, concentrating strictly on the rural market by advertising in religious weeklies and in publications such as *Comfort* and *Home Monthly* that circulated almost entirely in rural households. Boris Emmet and John E. Jeuck, *Catalogues and Counters: A History of Sears, Roebuck and Company* (Chicago: University of Chicago Press, 1950).

135. U.S. farmers owned eighty-five thousand cars total in 1911; by 1920 they owned 2,146,512. By 1930 about half of all the registered automobiles in the United States were in rural areas; over half of farms had at least one car. Hal S. Barron, *Mixed Harvest: The Second Great Transformation in the Rural North, 1870–1930* (Chapel Hill: University of North Carolina Press, 1997), 195. The Midwest had a higher rate of automobile ownership than most U.S. regions. In 1926 Illinois, Iowa, Wisconsin, Michigan, and Indiana held 17.1 percent of the nation's population and 21.1 percent of the nation's cars. Chicago Tribune, *Book of Facts, 1927*, 17.

136. Lloyd Wendt, *Chicago Tribune: The Rise of a Great American Newspaper* (Chicago: Rand McNally & Co., 1979), 458. Wendt's information comes from the Chicago Tribune's *Book of Facts*; he gives no year.

137. On the assembly of the Sunday paper, see Lee, *The Daily Newspaper in America*, 397.

138. This is based on my survey of circulation statistics in 1920s editions of *Editor & Publisher*.

139. Circulation numbers come from *Editor & Publisher, International Yearbook Number for 1926*, 30 January 1926, 35.

140. In 1925 the *Indianapolis News* held a Sunday circulation of 125,827, while the *Chicago Tribune*'s Sunday circulation in Indiana was 89,761. Indiana statistics from *Editor & Publisher, International Yearbook Number for 1926*, 30 January 1926, 42. *Tribune* circulation numbers from *Book of Facts, 1927*, 73.

141. Circulation numbers come from *Editor & Publisher, International Yearbook Number for 1926*, 30 January 1926, 35.

142. Circulation manager position listed in the Employee Manual, 1928, 12, Chicago Daily News–Administration and Operations, MMS Field Enterprises, Newberry Library. Delivery routes shown in Copeland, "The Limits and Characteristics of Metropolitan Chicago," 42. These were the delivery routes on or before 1937. There are no data on the routes before that year.

143. From a chart documenting a circulation drive, dated 17 November 1914, Reports and Documents, Circulation—1905, 1921, Victor Freemont Lawson Papers, Newberry Library.

144. Form letter dated 11 March 1921, Reports and Documents, Circulation—1905, 1921, Victor Freemont Lawson Papers, Newberry Library.

145. Robert Ezra Park, "Newspaper Circulation in the Chicago Region and Its Relation to the Organization of the Regional Community Pattern," unpublished typescript, Robert Ezra Park Papers, University of Chicago Special Collections. Park incorporated some of this information into maps that appeared in Park and Newcomb, "Newspaper Circulation and Metropolitan Regions," 102.

146. Chicago Tribune, *Pictured Encyclopedia*, 195–97.

147. Radio broadcast referenced in "Farm and Garden," *Chicago Tribune*, 20 April 1924, pt. 2, 14.

148. The *Tribune*'s essay contest was for schoolchildren and ran in 1923; its beauty

contest, for fifty midwestern "peaches," ran in 1927. Descriptions of contests come from letters and articles in Series XI-125, Circulation Department General, 1921–1939, Chicago Tribune Departmental Papers, Col. McCormick Research Center, Wheaton, IL.

149. Departments as listed in the Chicago Tribune, *Book of Facts, 1927,* 41.

150. The objectives changed slightly over the course of the decade. These are drawn from Sunday papers in 1924; from the platforms reprinted in the Chicago Tribune's *Pictured Encyclopedia,* 204; and from the Chicago Tribune's *The WGN: A Handbook of Newspaper Administration* (Chicago: Chicago Tribune, 1922), 170.

151. James O'Donnell Bennett, "Chicagoland's Shrines: A Tour of Discoveries; Our Own Historic Midwest Revealed," *Chicago Tribune,* 27 July 1926, front page.

152. *The Trib* (internal newsletter for *Chicago Tribune* employees), April 1929, 2.

153. As referenced by Keating in *Chicagoland,* 19. The book collected Bradford's newspaper columns on regional history; none of these earlier columns had used the phrase.

154. Reprinted in *Chicago Tribune,* 2 September 1926, 8.

155. Ann Durkin Keating discusses rural market centers relatively close to Chicago in *Chicagoland,* chap. 3. For an overview of the transformation that trains wrought on the human landscape, see John R. Stilgoe, *Metropolitan Corridor: Railroads and the American Scene* (New Haven, CT: Yale University Press, 1983).

156. Hal Barron describes the impact of automobiles on early twentieth-century rural culture in *Mixed Harvest,* chap. 6, and the ritual of Saturday "farmers' nights" in regional towns on pages 204–5. The *Tribune* described the trend of farm families making shopping trips to larger "trading centers" in its *Book of Facts, 1927,* 71, and supported it with reports from the U.S. Department of Commerce.

157. The *Tribune* explained that 204 towns housed 53.4 percent of the region's families, and that these towns provided 75.1 percent of the region's tax returns. Chicago Tribune, *Book of Facts, 1927,* 73.

158. Ibid.

159. Ibid., 69.

160. Ibid., 479.

161. The 1922 *Tribune* survey asked shopkeepers "Do you believe advertising in the *Tribune* helps the sale of advertised brands in your community?" Their responses appear in the Chicago Tribune, *Book of Facts, 1927,* 60.

162. Chicago Tribune, *Book of Facts, 1927,* 60. The 1922 *Tribune* survey found that 65 percent of retailers in Illinois, Indiana, Iowa, Michigan, and Wisconsin read the *Tribune,* and 72 percent felt the effect of *Tribune* ads on their sales. Chicago Tribune, *The WGN,* 201.

163. Chicago Tribune, *Pictured Encyclopedia,* 62.

164. Ibid., 170.

165. Ibid.

166. These maps came from Crowell Publishing Company. Chicago Tribune, *Book of Facts, 1927,* 95.

167. Ibid.

168. Ibid., 70.

169. Ibid., 72.

170. Weeklies still made up 70 percent of all publications in 1900, according to the U.S. Census, but their numbers had been shrinking since 1880. William S. Rossiter, *Printing and Publishing, Twelfth Census of the United States, 1900,* vol. 9, *Manufactures,*

pt. 3, *Special Reports on Selected Industries*, ser. no. 79 (Washington: U.S. Census Office, 1902), 1037–1119. One analysis found that weeklies' circulation stagnated from 1902 to 1916 and then declined. Lee, *The Daily Newspaper in America*, 208.

171. Howe, "Country Newspapers," 782.

172. James Edward Rogers, *The American Newspaper*, 39–40.

173. Sherwood Anderson, "Godliness," in *Winesburg, Ohio* (1919; repr., New York: Random House, 1950), 43.

174. Park, "Urbanization as Measured by Newspaper Circulation," 64.

175. Howe, "Country Newspapers," 782; Lee, *The Daily Newspaper in America*, 281, 387; and Harger, "The Country Editor Today," 93.

176. About a thousand of the nation's 2,580 dailies still published a weekly edition in 1914. Lee, *The Daily Newspaper in America*, 387. On the persistence of local weeklies, see Harger, "The Country Editor Today," 93–94; and Fuller, *RFD*, 296–300.

177. Harger, "The Country Editor Today," 93. Also on rural readers of local weeklies, see Fuller, *RFD*, 296–97.

178. Harger, "The Country Editor Today," 94. Sally Foreman Griffith found that the *Emporia Gazette*, in Kansas, held subscribers of this type, too. Griffith, *Home Town News: William Allen White and the Emporia Gazette* (New York: Oxford University Press, 1989), 233. On the nineteenth-century practice of sending hometown newspapers to loved ones, see Henkin, *The Postal Age*, chap. 2.

179. These radial images echo urban and suburban maps from previous eras. Ann Durkin Keating examines Chicago maps from 1874 and 1909 that depict this radial pattern in *Chicagoland*, 15–18. Urban sociologists Ernest Burgess and Robert Park used such images to explain and predict urban growth in Park et al., *The City*. For a discussion of the evolution and accuracy of this kind of mapping, see Elaine Lewinnek, "Mapping Chicago, Imagining Metropolises: Reconsidering the Zonal Model of Urban Growth," *Journal of Urban History* 36 (March 2010): 197–225.

180. Park, "Urbanization as Measured by Newspaper Circulation," 65.

181. Roslyn Terrace ad, *Philadelphia Inquirer*, 21 May 1899, sec. 1, 4.

182. Suburban Homes Realty Co. ad for Fern Heights, *Milwaukee Journal*, 22 May 1927, real estate section, 10.

183. Ad for Morgan Park, *Baltimore Afro-American*, 20 September 1918, 8.

184. Ad for Crestas development, *Pittsburgh Courier*, National Edition, Saturday 15 September 1928, sec. 1, 12.

185. "The Home Garden for Pleasure and Profit," *Philadelphia Evening Public Ledger*, March 21, 1916, 9.

186. Hitchner Wallpaper ad, *Baltimore Afro-American*, 17 November 1928, and *Philadelphia Evening Bulletin*, 14 October 1922, 10.

187. "Third Competition Problem Calls for Perspective, Plans and Plot Plan for Dwelling That Can Be Erected for $6,000," *New York Sun*, 25 February 1917, 14.

188. "News of the Suburbs," *Milwaukee Daily Journal*, 5 October 1895, 8.

189. *Philadelphia Inquirer*, 15 May 1895, 8.

190. Society pages, *New York Herald Tribune*, 23 August 1927, late city edition, sec. 5, 2–7.

191. Chicago Tribune, *Book of Facts, 1927*, 14.

192. Chalmers M. Roberts, *The Washington Post: The First 100 Years* (Boston: Houghton Mifflin Company, 1977), 77.

193. J. Cutler Andrews, *Pittsburgh's Post-Gazette: "The First Newspaper West of the Alleghenies"* (Boston: Chapman & Grimes, 1936), 196.

194. Lee, *The Daily Newspaper in America*, 281.

195. Examples come from *Philadelphia Record*, 9 December 1882, 7.

196. Poster for "New York World Thrice-a-Week Edition," 1895, Art and Architecture Collection, New York Public Library.

197. Society notes, *Philadelphia Public Ledger*, 7 November 1920, 3, 4, 5.

198. Tractor advertisement, *New York World*, 27 March 1921, second news section, 3.

199. "Farm Food Show Has Many Winners," *Philadelphia Inquirer*, 7 January 1923, 5; poultry section, *Philadelphia North American*, 17 May 1925, second news section, 5.

200. Letter from "a Florida farmer" in *Collier's Weekly*, 30 September 1911, 34.

201. Louis M. Lyons, *Newspaper Story: One Hundred Years of the Boston Globe* (Cambridge, MA: Belknap Press, 1971), 154.

202. Letter from Louis Parke Chamberlayne in *Collier's Weekly*, 19 August 1911, 18.

203. Will C. Conrad, Kathleen F. Wilson, and Dale Wilson, *The Milwaukee Journal: The First Eighty Years* (Madison: University of Wisconsin Press, 1964), 119.

CHAPTER FIVE

1. John A. Cockerill, "The Newspaper of the Future" (Journalist Series), *Lippincott's Monthly Magazine*, August 1892, 226. Cockerill worked as managing editor of the *St. Louis Post-Dispatch* beginning in 1879, became Sunday editor of the *New York World* in the 1880s, and then held a position at the *New York Advertiser*.

2. John McCarthy, "The Reluctant City: Milwaukee's Fragmented Metropolis, 1920–1960" (PhD diss., Marquette University, 2005), 25, 31–32.

3. On the communities and culture that German immigrants established in Milwaukee, see Kathleen Conzen, *Immigrant Milwaukee, 1836–1860: Accommodation and Community in a Frontier City* (Cambridge, MA: Harvard University Press, 1976); and Anke Ortlepp, "*Deutsch-Athen* Revisited: Writing the History of Germans in Milwaukee," in *Perspectives on Milwaukee's Past*, ed. Margo Anderson and Victor Greene (Urbana: University of Illinois Press, 2009), 109–30.

4. Robert C. Nesbit, *The History of Wisconsin*, vol. 2, *Urbanization and Industrialization, 1873–1893* (Madison: State Historical Society of Wisconsin, 1985), 541–42n118.

5. Bayrd Still, *Milwaukee: the History of a City* (Madison: The State Historical Society of Wisconsin, 1948), 259. On Milwaukee's beer gardens and other German features, see Megan E. Daniels, *Milwaukee's Early Architecture* (Mount Pleasant, SC: Arcadia Publishing, 2010); and Larry Widen, *Entertainment in Early Milwaukee* (Mount Pleasant, SC: Arcadia Publishing, 2007).

6. Louis J. Swichkow and Lloyd P. Gartner, *The History of the Jews of Milwaukee* (Philadelphia: Jewish Publication Society of America, 1963), 258.

7. German immigration information comes from Still, *Milwaukee: The History of a City*, 112–13. On Milwaukee's laborers and labor politics, see Eric Fure-Slocum, "Milwaukee Labor and Urban Democracy," in *Perspectives on Milwaukee's Past*, ed. Anderson and Greene, 48–78.

8. These were Mayor Emil Seidel, Mayor Daniel Hoan, and Congressman Victor Bergen. For an overview of the history and historiography of Milwaukee socialism, see Aims McGuinness, "The Revolution Begins Here: Milwaukee and the History of Socialism," in *Perspectives on Milwaukee's Past*, ed. Anderson and Greene, 79–106.

9. Judith W. Leavitt, *The Healthiest City: Milwaukee and the Politics of Health Reform* (Madison: University of Wisconsin Press, 1996).

10. These were the *Germania* (which began as a semiweekly but became a daily in 1897), the *Seebote*, the *Herold*, and the *Abendpost*. Information about the city's German-language press comes from Carl Heinz Knoche, "The German Immigrant Press in Milwaukee" (PhD diss., Ohio State University, 1969), 123–48; and from Charles Austin Bates, ed., *American Journalism from the Practical Side: What Leading Newspaper Publishers Say Concerning the Relations of Advertisers and Publishers and about the Way a Great Paper Should be Made* (New York: Holmes Publishing Company, 1897), 185–96.

11. Milwaukee in 1905 had eight daily newspapers with circulations between 10,000 and 40,000. By 1929 the readers were less equally distributed among fewer daily newspapers. The *Journal* dominated the city with around 170,000 daily readers; the *Wisconsin News* had just over 100,000. The *Sentinel* held around 75,000, and the *Leader*, the *Herold*, and the *Kuryer Polski* each held under 50,000. Newspaper numbers come from *N.W. Ayer & Son's American Newspaper Annual* and from *Editor & Publisher*. Population statistics come from the U.S. Census.

12. The "Wisconsin Idea" maintained that the state university system should benefit the state's population as broadly as possible, often through the sharing of academic expertise with state legislators.

13. Joe William Trotter Jr., *Black Milwaukee: The Making of an Industrial Proletariat, 1915–1945* (Urbana: University of Illinois Press, 1985), 8.

14. *Evening Wisconsin*, 17 June 1881.

15. "Short But Newsy," *Evening Wisconsin*, 25 September 1889, 4. In the 1880s, the *Evening Wisconsin* also ran a column titled "Miscellaneous Telegrams," the *Milwaukee Journal* ran a front-page column called "Telegraphic Sparks," and the *Milwaukee Germania* had a telegraph column drawing news from all over the world.

16. All are from the column "A Little Nonsense" in the *Milwaukee Daily Sentinel*, 25 July 1881, 4.

17. On the history of the Associated Press and the United Press, see Victor Rosewater, *History of Coöperative News-Gathering in the United States* (New York: D. Appleton and Company, 1930).

18. "Local Odds and Ends" and "The City in Brief" were the titles of daily columns in the *Milwaukee Free Press* in 1902. "Sunday State Page—Badger News and Features," *Milwaukee Daily Journal*, 3 October 1895, pt. 4, 1.

19. "Review of the Events of the Week in City, State, Nation and the World," *Milwaukee Journal*, 28 December 1919, pt. 4, 8.

20. "State News in Brief," *Milwaukee Daily Journal*, 2 October 1895, 7.

21. See "Mayors of Wisconsin" on the front page of the *Milwaukee Sentinel*, week of 16 May 1892; "State News in Brief," *Milwaukee Daily Journal*, 21 November 1899, 2; and "Gossip of the State," *Milwaukee Daily Journal*, 3 October 1895, 10.

22. Trotter, *Black Milwaukee*, 40.

23. "The Messenger Boy 'Who in His Time Plays Many Parts' Caring for Babies, Acting as Escort, Washing Dishes and Playing Detective," *Milwaukee Free Press*, 25 September 1906, Sunday magazine section, 1.

24. "As Cartoonist Bernau Saw Happenings of the Week," *Milwaukee Journal*, 4 February 1911, 1.

25. For a deeper investigation into this phenomenon of U.S. women following European fashions, see Kristin L. Hoganson, *Consumers' Imperium: The Global Production*

of American Domesticity, 1865–1920 (Chapel Hill: University of North Carolina Press, 2007), chap. 2.

26. "The Fashions of Paris," *Milwaukee Daily Journal*, 6 April 1891, 2; and "Parisian Fashions for the Hair as Described by a Recent Observer," *Milwaukee Journal*, 25 November 1899, 8.

27. "In the Shops," *Milwaukee Free Press*, 5 August 1902, 6.

28. Gimbels ad, *Milwaukee Daily Journal*, 21 November 1899, 5. Adam Gimbel opened the very first Gimbels as an Indiana dry goods shop, but his son Jacob Gimbel opened the first Gimbels department store in Milwaukee in 1887. Other Gimbel brothers opened stores in Philadelphia in 1894, New York in 1910, and several other cities. Paul Geenen, *Schuster's and Gimbels: Milwaukee's Beloved Department Stores* (Charleston, SC: History Press, 2012).

29. "Olive Beauties" appeared in the illustrated Sunday magazine of the *Milwaukee Sentinel*, 30 December 1906, 15; "George Gould" ran on the same day in the "Special Features," sec. 4, 4.

30. Examples taken from "What Society Talks Of," *Milwaukee Daily Journal*, 3 October 1895, 9. Both were paraphrased from other papers—the *Washington Evening Star* and the *New York Journal*.

31. For these columns, see *Evening Wisconsin*, 23 April 1901, 4, and 19 January 1906, 6; and *Milwaukee Herold und Seebote*, 27 August 1899, 9, and 13 November 1904, sec. 2, front page. For other New York columns in Milwaukee see "New Yorker Plauderei" ("New York Chat") in the *Milwaukee Sonntagspost*, 6 October 1912, 3; and "New York Every Day" in the *Wisconsin Weekly Advocate*, 28 February 1907, 4. These New York columns were written exclusively for Milwaukee papers, but other New York columns came from syndicate services. Some of the first such columns were offered by the American Printers' Warehouse in 1875 and by Irving Bacheller's New York Press Syndicate in 1884. Lee, *The Daily Newspaper in America*, 582; and Elmo Scott Watson, *A History of Newspaper Syndicates* (Chicago: printed by author, 1936), 42.

32. "Heard in the Hotels" ran in the *Milwaukee Sentinel*, 27 December 1906; the *Journal* also had a hotel column.

33. For the two given examples, see the "The Man with the Hoe," *Milwaukee Journal*, 21 November 1899, 4, and 22 November 1899, 6.

34. *Milwaukee Sentinel*, 27 January 1895, 6.

35. Ad for Oswald Jaeger Baking Co., *Milwaukee Journal*, 15 April 1923, rotogravure section, 8.

36. Ad for Pabst Brewing Co., *Milwaukee Daily Journal*, 6 April 1891, 8.

37. See *An Illustrated Description of Milwaukee: Its Homes, Social Conditions, Public Institutions, Manufactures, Commerce, Improvements, and Its Unparalleled Growth* (Milwaukee: Milwaukee Sentinel, 1890); *Milwaukee, Wisconsin, the Cream City: Its Unexampled Growth and Brilliant Prospects; A Glance at Its History, a Review of Its Commerce and a Description of Some of Its Business Enterprise* (Milwaukee: Evening Wisconsin, 1891); and *The Book of Milwaukee: Development, Resources, Enterprise and Beauty of the Peerless Cream City* (Milwaukee: Evening Wisconsin, 1901).

38. Ad for upcoming industrial issue in the *Milwaukee Sentinel*, 28 December 1906, 11.

39. "About Town," *Evening Wisconsin*, 19 January 1906, 12.

40. "The Milwaukee Market," *Milwaukee Journal*, 28 December 1919, part three, 7.

41. Rogers, *The American Newspaper*, 162.

42. Laura J. Murray, "Exchange Practices among Nineteenth-Century US Newspaper Editors: Cooperation in Competition," in *Governing Knowledge Commons*, ed. Brett M. Frischmann, Michael J. Madison, and Katherine J. Strandburg (New York: Oxford University Press, 2014).

43. For an example of recycling, see the Charles Dickens story in the *Milwaukee Free Press*, 13 December 1908, Sunday magazine, 5.

44. Watson, *A History of Newspaper Syndicates*, 44. U.S. copyright did not extend to foreign authors, so these stories were free for the taking.

45. On the early history of news syndicates for city papers, see ibid., 42–46; Lee, *The Daily Newspaper in America*, 580–86; and Charles Johanningsmeier, *Fiction and the American Literary Marketplace: The Role of Newspaper Syndicates, 1860–1900* (New York: Cambridge University Press, 1997), 32–35, 48–81. Bok and McClure both talk about their time in the syndication business in autobiographies; see Edward Bok, *The Americanization of Edward Bok: The Autobiography of a Dutch Boy Fifty Years After* (New York: Charles Scribner's Sons, 1921), 111–14, and S. S. McClure, *My Autobiography* (New York: Frederick A. Stokes Company, 1914).

46. "The Extension of Syndicate Work," *Journalist*, 9 July 1887, 8.

47. Lee, *The Daily Newspaper in America*, 583.

48. On copyright laws and suits, see Johanningsmeier, *Fiction and the American Literary Marketplace*, 39; Lee, *The Daily Newspaper in America*, 578, 583; and "Does Stealing Pay?" *Journalist*, 18 August 1888, 8.

49. "The Extension of Syndicate Work," *Journalist*, 9 July 1887, 8.

50. On the birth of the term "boilerplate," see Eugene C. Harter and Dorothy Harter, *Boilerplating America: The Hidden Newspaper* (Lanham, MD: University Press of America, 1991), 33. One of the first newspaper unions operated out of Milwaukee and sold to country papers throughout the region. By the 1870s it had moved to Chicago and become the Chicago Newspaper Union; it ultimately became a branch of the American Newspaper Union. On newspaper unions and their origins, see Watson, *A History of Newspaper Syndicates*, 26–30; and Johanningsmeier, *Fiction and the American Literary Marketplace*, 37–38.

51. American Press Association, *Hand-book Containing Description of Service, List of Features, with a Variety of . . . Suggestions about Plates* (New York: American Press Association, 1890). On the evolution of syndication technology, see Watson, *A History of Newspaper Syndicates*, 33–35; Lee, *The Daily Newspaper in America*, 581; and Johanningsmeier, *Fiction and the American Literary Marketplace*, 42–44, 48, 159–60.

52. For another example, all of the women's material in the Sunday magazine of the *Milwaukee Sentinel*, 20 December 1914, came from syndicates. A similar catching-up process occurred at the *Herold*. It added a sports page quite late; when it did, it bought (and translated) nearly the whole thing from syndicates. See the *Milwaukee Herold*, 23 November 1929, 8.

53. The *Sentinel* took readers on an illustrated tour of its engravers' offices on Sunday, 22 May 1892, 10. By 1925, the *Milwaukee Journal*, the *Wisconsin News*, and the *Milwaukee Leader* all owned their own engraving plants. See *Editor & Publisher, International Yearbook Number for 1926*, 30 January 1926, 102.

54. Charles Johanningsmeier documents newspaper editors requesting a variety of fiction genres in *Fiction and the American Literary Marketplace*, 167–69.

55. Matthew Klingle, *Emerald City: An Environmental History of Seattle* (New Haven, CT: Yale University Press, 2007), 122, 151.

56. On Progressive-era city planning and planners, see Alison Isenberg, *Downtown America: A History of the Place and the People Who Made It* (Chicago: University of Chicago Press, 2004).

57. The *Milwaukee Journal* printed syndicated "Mr. Dooley" columns, by Finley Peter Dunne, sporadically between 1894 and 1899, before they fell under Hearst's control. *The Katzenjammer Kids*, also syndicated by Hearst, ran in the 1918 *Free Press* and in the *Milwaukee Sentinel* after 1924. Scripps papers had their own German comic characters, Osgar and Adolf, in the strip *A Bit of Vaudeville*.

58. These titles come from an anthology of this feature: William Ely Hill and Franklin Pierce Adams, eds., *Among Us Mortals; Pictures and Legends by W. E. Hill* (Boston: Houghton Mifflin Company, 1917). The *Chicago Tribune* and the *New York Tribune* each distributed this feature at various points during the 1910s and 1920s.

59. *Little Stories Told in Homely Rhyme* appeared in the *Philadelphia Public Ledger*, 21 March 1916, 10.

60. "In Hickville," *Milwaukee Sentinel*, 15 December 1914, 6.

61. See Michael Oriard, *Reading Football: How the Popular Press Created an American Spectacle* (Chapel Hill: University of North Carolina Press, 1993).

62. Willard Grosvenor Bleyer, *Types of News Writing* (Boston: Houghton Mifflin Co., 1916), 200.

63. "Sportlight" appeared in the *Milwaukee Journal* from at least 1919 through the 1920s; it was distributed by the *New York Tribune*. "Along the Sport Trail" appeared in the *Wisconsin News* in 1921; it appears syndicated but was not attributed. For syndicated sports cartoons, see the *Sunday Sentinel*'s "Big Peach" (its sports section printed on peach-colored paper), 1922, and the *Evening Sentinel*, 15 December 1914, 11.

64. For syndicated golf column, see Grantland Rice, "Tales of a Wayside Tee," *Milwaukee Journal*, 28 December 1919, pt. 3, 4. King Features and Ledger Feature Syndicate offered tennis columns; see Moses Koenigsberg, *King News: An Autobiography* (Philadelphia: F. A. Stokes Company, 1941), 447; and *Editor & Publisher, International Yearbook Number for 1926*, 30 January 1926, 176. For a national motorcycle column, see "Motorcycle Notes," *Milwaukee Sentinel*, 20 December 1914, 3.

65. "A Touch of Tango Makes the Whole World Spin," from the *New York Herald* Syndicate, *Milwaukee Sentinel*, 20 December 1914, magazine, 10.

66. "Let *Wisconsin News* Teach You How to Charleston," *Wisconsin News*, 6 October 1925, 13. The *News* published photographs of Milwaukee dancer Lester Mayhew Jr. in this series on the Charleston and then aired his instructions in nightly radio broadcasts.

67. As cited in Genevieve Jackson Boughner, *Women in Journalism: A Guide to the Opportunities and a Manual of the Technique of Women's Work for Newspapers and Magazines* (New York: D. Appleton, 1926), 167.

68. For basketball example, see *Milwaukee Sentinel*, 20 December 1914, pt. 3, 2.

69. Trina Robbins, *Nell Brinkley and the New Woman in the Early 20th Century* (Jefferson, NC: McFarland & Company, 2001), 39–41, 51.

70. On words that originated in comic strips, see H. L. Mencken, *The American Language: An Inquiry into the Development of English in the United States*, supp. 1 (New York: Knopf, 1945), 333.

71. The *New York World* syndicated this strip. For its appearance in Milwaukee, see the *Milwaukee Journal*, 3 September 1915, 7.

72. Harnett T. Kane, with Ella Bentley Arthur, *Dear Dorothy Dix: The Story of a Com-*

passionate Woman (Garden City, NY: Doubleday & Company, 1952), 11–12, 264. On sermons, see Robert S. Lynd and Helen Merrell Lynd, *Middletown: A Study in Contemporary American Culture* (New York: Harcourt, Brace and Co., 1929), 116, and Kane, *Dear Dorothy Dix*, 11.

73. Fairfax gets questioned in George Gershwin's 1930 song "But Not for Me," and Bert Kalmar, Edgar Leslie, and Pete Wendling's 1919 song "Take Your Girlie to the Movies." Fairfax's radio show ran in the 1930s, and she became the basis of a series of comic books in the 1950s as well. Fairfax was distributed through the Hearst syndicate.

74. For "Homes of Character" by John Henry Newson, see the *Evening Wisconsin*, 28 June 1913, 6. Another mail-order column, "Help for the Man Who Wants to Build," appeared in the *Milwaukee Journal* (and in many other papers, including, as appeared in chap. 3, the *Chicago Daily News*.) The style examples come from booklets offered by the Architects' Small House Service Bureau through the *Milwaukee Journal*, 22 May 1927, real estate section, 37. Americans built houses from ready-made patterns that they got through a variety of other sources, too; see Daniel D. Reiff, *Houses from Books: Treatises, Pattern Books, and Catalogs in American Architecture, 1738–1950: A History and Guide* (University Park: Pennsylvania State University Press, 2000).

75. See, for *High Lights of History*, the *Milwaukee Journal*, 24 May 1927, 28. I have also seen this feature in the *Philadelphia North American* in 1925 and the *Philadelphia Daily News* in 1929.

76. "Today in History" and "Daily Birthday Party," *Milwaukee Journal*, 31 January 1911, 8. The *Journal* was not the only Milwaukee paper running historical features; Hearst's *Sentinel* ran a weeklong contest in 1926 that asked readers to piece together the faces of famous U.S. historical figures, from John C. Calhoun to Horace Greeley. *Milwaukee Sentinel*, 14 February 1926, sec. 4, 4–5.

77. The National Education Association committees merely made recommendations all through this era. See Edward A. Krug, *The Shaping of the American High School* (New York: Harper & Row, 1964), 54, 353–58. The U.S. South seems like it would be least receptive to these standardized versions of U.S. history. While I have not looked in every Southern paper, my searches of digitized archives of Charlotte and New Orleans papers turned up no trace of these syndicated features.

78. "Workisms," *Milwaukee Journal*, 4 February 1911, 6.

79. Truly dedicated members of Milwaukee's labor movement could turn instead to the *Milwaukee Leader*, the socialist daily newspaper. Other much shorter labor columns appeared in the city's mainstream papers at various times; see "In the Labor World," *Evening Wisconsin*, 12 June 1909, 7; and "Labor News," *Wisconsin News*, 2 February 1921. Mainstream daily papers in other cities devoted similarly sporadic attention to workers' interests. The *New York World* published a column called "Here and There in the Labor World" in 1885 and reprinted clippings from other publications in 1925 columns called "Voice of Union Labor and the Radical Press." In 1905, the *Chicago Tribune* briefly published a "Worker's Magazine" on Sundays, but it was geared more to success in the workplace than to labor activism. The only syndicated material for workers appeared earlier, during the heyday of the Populist movement. The American Press Association offered a syndicated biweekly column titled "The Farmer's Movement" as well as a biweekly "Labor Page." American Press Association, *Hand-book*.

80. Susan J. Douglas, *Listening In: Radio and the American Imagination* (New York: Times Books, 1999), 102–3.

81. Robert Sklar, *Movie-Made America: A Cultural History of American Movies* (New York: Vintage Books, 1975), chaps. 6 and 8, and Herbert Blumer, *Movies and Conduct* (New York: Macmillan Company, 1933).

82. Circulation statistics from *N. W. Ayer & Son's American Newspaper Annual*.

83. American Press Association, *Hand-book*.

84. Knoche, "The German Immigrant Press in Milwaukee." Many German-language papers subscribed to the New York Associated Press; Carl Wittke, *The German-Language Press in America* (Knoxville: University of Kentucky Press, 1957), 212.

85. Peter C. Merrill, *German-American Urban Culture: Writers and Theaters in Early Milwaukee*, Studies of the Max Kade Institute for German-American Studies (Madison: University of Wisconsin, 2000), 73.

86. See cartoon titled "Wurst wider Wurst," *Milwaukee Germania Abendpost*, 3 October 1912, 6.

87. On nineteenth-century translated fiction, see Merrill, *German-American Urban Culture*, 73.

88. These agencies could be either those that also served the English-language press or the American Association of Foreign-Language Presses, an agency that contracted with seven hundred papers nationwide in twenty-nine languages. Wittke, *The German-Language Press in America*, 227; and Robert Ezra Park, *The Immigrant Press and Its Control* (New York: Harper & Brothers, 1922), 376-77. Ford ad, *Milwaukee Herold*, 15 January 1922, 12; Baker's ad in *Milwaukee Germania*, 1 September 1891, 7; Stetson hat ad, *Milwaukee Herold* 20 January 1922, 9. Department store ads were ubiquitous; good examples are in *Milwaukee Germania und Sonntags-Post*, 5 October 1901.

89. *Editor & Publisher, International Yearbook Number for 1930*, 25 January 1930, 218.

90. Wittke, *The German-Language Press in America*, 197, 201, 213; Peter Conolly-Smith, *Translating America: An Immigrant Press Visualizes American Popular Culture, 1890-1918* (Washington, DC: Smithsonian Books, 2004), 61-62.

91. Park, *The Immigrant Press and Its Control*, 87.

92. For a study of such immigrant institutions, see Lizabeth Cohen, *Making a New Deal: Industrial Workers in Chicago, 1919-1939* (New York: Cambridge University Press, 1990), chap. 3.

93. Wittke, *The German-Language Press in America*, 244.

94. Ibid., 271.

95. The *Journal* won a Pulitzer Prize for this reporting in 1919. On this episode between the *Journal* and the *Germania-Herold*, see Will C. Conrad, Kathleen F. Wilson, and Dale Wilson, *The Milwaukee Journal: The First Eighty Years* (Madison: University of Wisconsin Press, 1964), 87-90; and Robert W. Wells, *The Milwaukee Journal: An Informal Chronicle of Its First Hundred Years* (Milwaukee: Milwaukee Journal, 1981), 102.

96. Wittke, *The German-Language Press in America*, 265-66.

97. The statistics for 1918 are from *N. W. Ayer & Son's American Newspaper Annual* and from *Editor & Publisher*; 1930 statistics are from *Editor & Publisher, International Yearbook Number for 1930*, 25 January 1930. The mergers themselves did not hurt German-language circulation in the city; in the 1920s, the *Herold* carried roughly the same collective circulation as the separate papers had in the 1910s.

98. For "Bab's Babble," see *Wisconsin Weekly Advocate*, 21 May 1898, 7; for stories on the Philippines and Puerto Rico, see "Rich Island Group: The Oriental Colony Which Is Lost to Spain," 14 May 1898, 8; and "Porto Rico, Our Future Possession," 28 May 1898, 8, respectively.

99. For statistics on the growth of the black press in this period, see Melissa Mae Elliott, "News in the Negro Press" (MA thesis, University of Chicago, 1931), 32–33.

100. George W. Gore Jr., *Negro Journalism: An Essay on the History and Present Conditions of the Negro Press* (Greencastle, IN: Journalism Press, 1922), 15.

101. Ibid., 18.

102. Will Irwin, "Newspapers and Canned Thought," *Collier's Weekly*, 21 June 1924, 14.

103. Ad for the *Minneapolis Journal* in *Editor & Publisher*, 15 January 1920, sec. 2, xxiv.

104. "BURGLARS SLAY MILWAUKEE GIRL—CLUBBED IN FIGHT TO SAVE JEWELS," *Wisconsin News*, 2 February 1921, 1.

105. To disguise his involvement, Hearst enlisted a local judge to front the purchase. See article in *Chicago Daily Tribune*, 5 June 1924, and letter from 5 June 1924 in August C. Backus papers, Wisconsin Historical Society. Hearst used this tactic in many cities; see Koenigsberg, *King News*, 349–50, who says the strategy was useful in retaining advertisers who did not want to buy space twice a day from the same publisher.

106. For "Every Day in Milwaukee," see *Milwaukee Sentinel*, 11 February 1926; for "The Inquisitive Reporter," see the *Wisconsin News*, 2 February 1921, 2, and 5 February 1921, 2.

107. "How I Earned Pin Money," *Wisconsin News*, 2 February 1921, 12; and "What Are Your Day Dreams," *Wisconsin News*, 5 February 1921, 11.

108. "How Much Do You Know?" *Wisconsin News*, 2 February 1921, 14; and "Popular Dog Contest," *Milwaukee Sentinel*, 11 February 1926, 2.

109. Lee, *The Daily Newspaper in America*, 215, 217.

110. According to Will Irwin, these singly owned morning and evening papers accounted for 15 percent of national circulation. Irwin, "Newspapers and Canned Thought," 14. Information on 1930 chains comes from *Editor & Publisher, International Yearbook Number for 1930*, 25 January 1930, 138–39.

111. F. W. Woolworth Company Building 3rd and Wisconsin Avenue, Milwaukee Historic Photos, Milwaukee Public Library, http://content.mpl.org/cdm/singleitem /collection/HstoricPho/id/3625/rec/1, accessed 5 June 2014.

112. Interior view of two men behind counter of A&P grocery, Milwaukee Historic Photos, Milwaukee Public Library, http://content.mpl.org/cdm/singleitem/collection /HstoricPho/id/4344/rec/3, accessed 5 June 2014.

113. Miranda H. Ferrara and Jay Pederson, eds., *International Directory of Company Histories*, vol. 65 (Detroit: St. James Press, 2005).

114. Larry Widen, *Milwaukee Movie Theaters* (Mount Pleasant, SC: Arcadia Publishing, 2010), 26, 46, and *Entertainment in Early Milwaukee*, 98.

115. E. W. Scripps ran his chain of newspapers on a similar economic model to that of Hearst. Hearst tended to dominate in bigger U.S. cities, while Scripps targeted midsize cities in the West and Midwest. See Gerald J. Baldasty, *E. W. Scripps and the Business of News* (Urbana: University of Illinois Press, 1999); and Edward E. Adams and Gerald J. Baldasty, "Syndicated Service Dependence and a Lack of Commitment to Localism: Scripps Newspapers and Market Subordination," *Journalism and Mass Communications Quarterly* 78, no. 3 (Autumn 2001): 519–32.

116. Conrad, Wilson, and Wilson, *The Milwaukee Journal: The First Eighty Years*, 116.

117. This was only one of several such magazines available for purchase in this era. Other magazines available included the *Associated Sunday Magazine* and Hearst's

American Weekly. William R. Scott, *Scientific Circulation Management* (New York: Ronald Press, 1915), 209. Paul Block Inc.'s *Illustrated Sunday Magazine* claimed more than five million readers and 1,300,000 in circulation in 1914; it had offices in New York, Chicago, Boston, and Detroit. See advertisement in *Milwaukee Sentinel*, 20 December 1914, magazine, 13.

118. Staff information is hard to come by, but one account told of the *Philadelphia Inquirer*'s Sunday staff, which shrank from forty to sixty in the early 1900s to only a handful by 1934. Lee, *The Daily Newspaper in America*, 404, 599.

119. See Churchill in the *Wisconsin News*, 2 February 1921, 13, and "Queen's Counsel" in the *Milwaukee Sentinel*, 11 February 1926, 5.

120. See Jack Dempsey's article in *Milwaukee Sentinel*, 14 February 1926, sec. 3, 4; and Ed Thorpe, "Famous Football Stars' Playing Secrets," *Wisconsin News*, 6 October 1925, 16.

121. Sir Oliver Lodge, "When Did the World Begin and How Will it End?" *Milwaukee Sentinel*, 14 February 1926, sec. 4, 2, and *Milwaukee Sentinel*, 5 April 1930, features section, 1.

122. *Milwaukee Sentinel*, 20 December 1914, magazine, 5.

123. *Milwaukee Journal*, 15 April 1923, "roto-art" section.

124. "Does Spell Guard Tomb of Ancients?" and George T. Bye, "Guianas Lure Stone Hunters," *Milwaukee Journal*, 15 April 1923, pt. 5, 6 and 7.

125. See *Milwaukee Journal*, 22 May 1927, sec. 8; "Germany's Intellectual Leaders on Way to the Poorhouse," *Milwaukee Journal*, 15 April 1923, pt. 6, 2; and "Wilson Discussed Chance of War with Japan," *Milwaukee Sentinel*, 14 February 1926, sec. 4, 1.

126. On these other kinds of exposure to foreign lands and peoples, see Hoganson, *Consumers' Imperium*, chap. 4; Alison Griffiths, *Wondrous Difference: Cinema, Anthropology, and Turn-of-the-Century Visual Culture* (New York: Columbia University Press, 2001); and Catharine A. Lutz and Jane L. Collins, *Reading National Geographic* (Chicago: University of Chicago Press, 1993).

127. Boughner, *Women in Journalism*, 312–13.

128. Rogers, *The American Newspaper*, 162–63.

129. Koenigsberg, *King News*, 394.

130. Ethel M. Colson Brazelton, *Writing and Editing for Women*, 176.

131. Bleyer, *How to Write Special Feature Articles: A Bird's-Eye View of the Widening Opportunities for Women in Newspaper, Magazine and Other Writing Work* (New York: Funk & Wagnalls Company, 1927), 39.

132. *Just Humans* was distributed by the McClure syndicate; *When a Feller Needs a Friend* was distributed by the *New York Tribune*. Briggs also drew up typical daily joys and sorrows in his regular cartoons *Someone's Always Taking the Joy Out of Life* and *Ain't It a Grand and Glorious Feeling?*

133. For a Dorothy Dix column, see *Milwaukee Sentinel*, 2 April 1930, 11; for Kathleen Norris, see *Milwaukee Sentinel*, 5 April 1930, 4D; for "A Right Thought to Start the Day Right," see *Milwaukee Sentinel*, 11 February 1926, 7. Hearst's competitor, E. W. Scripps, distributed similar editorials such as "Don't Apologize for Yourself," or "Laugh and the World Laughs with You" through his Newspaper Enterprise Association syndicate. Baldasty, *E. W. Scripps and the Business of Newspapers*, 140.

134. Angelo Patri's feature included no copyright but was syndicated; it also appeared in the *Milwaukee Sentinel* in 1930 and the *Philadelphia Evening Bulletin* in the 1920s.

135. *Editor & Publisher, International Yearbook Number for 1926*, 30 January 1926, 188–89.

136. *Editor & Publisher, International Yearbook Number for 1930*, 25 January 1930, 14–15; and Kane, *Dear Dorothy Dix*, 11. A few features found an audience abroad as early as the turn of the century; W. T. Stead reported that "Mr. Dooley" and the humorist Sam Slick were being printed in British newspapers by 1900. William T. Stead, *The Americanization of the World*, (New York: Horace Markley, 1901), 286.

137. Information about exported and international comics comes from Maurice Horn, ed., *World Encyclopedia of Comics* (New York: Chelsea House Publishers, 1976), 15–20.

138. On the minstrelsy roots of comic-strip and animated characters, see Nicholas Sammond, *Birth of an Industry: Blackface Minstrelsy and the Rise of American Animation* (Chapel Hill, NC: Duke University Press, 2015).

139. H. F. Harrington, *Chats on Feature Writing, by Members of the Blue Pencil Club of Professional Writers* (New York: Harper and Brothers, 1925), 560.

140. Irwin, "Newspapers and Canned Thought," 14.

141. Ibid.

142. Robert Cortes Holliday and Alexander Van Rensselaer, *The Business of Writing: A Practical Guide for Writers* (New York: George H. Duran, 1922), 246.

143. Koenigsberg, *King News*, 365.

144. Circulation statistics come from *N.W. Ayer & Son's Newspaper Annual and Directory* (New York: 1918, 1919, 1920, 1922), and from *Editor & Publisher, International Yearbook Number for 1926*, 30 January 1926, 152, and *International Yearbook Number for 1930*, 25 January 1930, 114.

145. Editorial, *Milwaukee Sentinel*, 16 August 1922, 6; and "Our Nosy Reporter," *Milwaukee Journal*, 15 April 1923, pt. 2, 6.

146. Adams and Baldasty, "Syndicated Service Dependence and a Lack of Commitment to Localism," 519.

147. Ibid., 522.

148. J. J. Delany, "On the Bowling Firing Line," *Milwaukee Sentinel*, 20 December 1914, pt. 3, 4.

149. Don C. Seitz, *Training for the Newspaper Trade* (Philadelphia: J. B. Lippincott, 1916), 160.

150. Boughner, *Women in Journalism*, 82–83.

151. These columnists (and instructions on how to write to them) appear in the *Milwaukee Sentinel*, 2 April 1930, 11; *Evening Wisconsin*, 25 October 1917, 9; and the *Milwaukee Journal*, 5 September 1915, Peach Sunday Sheet, 2.

152. *Editor & Publisher, International Yearbook Number for 1926*, 30 January 1926, 164–65. The *Milwaukee Free Press* ran such a semilocal children's page, where children were invited to write a story about an image published each week. *Milwaukee Free Press*, 28 March 1915, women's section.

153. For Nancy Lee, see "On the Screen," *Milwaukee Journal*, 22 May 1927, sec. 7, 4.

154. For examples of these sports columns: "From Tee to Green, with Billy Sixty," *Milwaukee Journal*, 24 May 1927, 24; "Following through with Downer," *Milwaukee Journal*, 28 December 1919, 2, and *Milwaukee Sentinel*, 11 February 1926, 9; Chet Slam-Em [pseud.], "Biffs and Bangs," *Milwaukee Sentinel* (evening edition), 15 December 1914, 11.

155. For Betty Ann's column, see *Milwaukee Journal*, 11 April 1923, 12, and 15 April 1923, 8.

156. For examples of Brownie's motor columns, see *Milwaukee Journal*, 5 September 1915, Peach Sunday Sheet, 3; 22 May 1927, sec. 4, 1; and 24 May 1927, 21.

157. 1924 *Milwaukee Journal* brochure, 3, Milwaukee Historical Society.

158. The *Sentinel* and the *Wisconsin News*, by comparison, subscribed to three wire services each in the 1920s. *Editor & Publisher, International Yearbook Number for 1930*, 25 January 1930, 114.

159. 1924 *Milwaukee Journal* brochure, 32, Milwaukee Historical Society.

160. The *Journal* claimed to be the only U.S. paper with an international exchange staff (ibid.).

161. 1924 *Milwaukee Journal* brochure, 3, 29, Milwaukee Historical Society.

162. For special coverage of national and global topics, see *Milwaukee Journal*, 9 January 1927, feature section.

163. The *Journal* recruited Creager from another locally oriented paper, the *Kansas City Star*, and hoped that his local emphasis would win readers away from the more generic Hearst papers. Wells, *The Milwaukee Journal: An Informal Chronicle*, 153.

164. Information on Hoben taken from scrapbooks in the Lindsay Hoben papers, Wisconsin Historical Society. A few similar local takes on international events had run in earlier decades; in these cases, Milwaukee papers turned to recently returned residents as easy sources for international events. See "Wisconsin Man Likes Porto Rico," *Milwaukee Daily Journal*, 21 November 1899, 1, and "Wisconsin Man Writes of a Day at Lourdes," *Milwaukee Sentinel*, 30 December 1906, special features section, 1.

165. Rotogravure section *Milwaukee Journal*, 15 April 1923. Though the heyday of Milwaukee illustrators was actually the 1910s, local cartoons still appeared sporadically in the 1920s.

166. A list of the *Journal*'s special booklets appears on the inside of the back cover of James W. Barton, *That Body of Yours* (Milwaukee: Milwaukee Journal, 1930), Milwaukee Historical Society. Author names appear in Matt Clohisy, *Wisconsin Wild Flowers*, 2nd ed. (Milwaukee: Milwaukee Journal, 1927).

167. For photo contest, see *Milwaukee Journal*, 15 April 1923, rotogravure section, 3. On Wisconsin art exhibits, see 1928 brochure, *The Milwaukee Journal's Gallery of Wisconsin Art: Twentieth Exhibit, October 15, 1928 to January 10, 1929*, Milwaukee Historical Society.

168. *Milwaukee Journal*, 15 April 1923, Roto-Art section, page 1.

169. Cockerill, "The Newspaper of the Future," 221.

170. Ibid., 221.

171. Both columns appeared in the *Portland Oregonian* in the 1880s; I thank Harry H. Stein for these references.

172. Letter from James E. Doyle in *Collier's Weekly*, 18 November 1911, 6.

173. Letter from Edward Broderick in *Collier's Weekly*, 18 November 1911, 6.

174. Letter from E. A. Treadwell in the *New York World*, 27 October 1889, 21.

175. Conolly-Smith, *Translating America*, 84.

176. Park, *The Immigrant Press and Its Control*, 375.

177. *Editor & Publisher, International Yearbook Number for 1930*, 25 January 1930, 218.

178. Lynd and Lynd, *Middletown*, 116n10.

179. The *Press* and the *News-Bee* were Scripps papers; the *Star* was part of the Shaffer Group. Baldasty, *E. W. Scripps and the Business of Newspapers*, and *Editor & Publisher, International Yearbook Number for 1930*, 25 January 1930, 138–39.

180. Letter from Egmont H. Arens in *Collier's Weekly*, 30 September 1911, 34.

181. Ibid., 34.

EPILOGUE

1. William S. Gray and Ruth Monroe, *The Reading Interests and Habits of Adults: A Preliminary Report* (New York: Macmillan, 1929), 262, as cited in Carl F. Kaestle and Helen Damon-Moore, *Literacy in the United States: Readers and Reading since 1880* (New Haven, CT: Yale University Press, 1991), 181. Gray and Monroe cite statistics from the 1920s putting newspaper readership at 95 percent, magazine readership at 75 percent, and book readership at 50 percent. Alfred Lee put the percentage of families buying Sunday papers in 1930 at 88 percent. Alfred McClung Lee, *The Daily Newspaper in America: The Evolution of a Social Instrument* (New York: Macmillan, 1937), 368. The 1927 *Chicago Tribune* cited statistics from the U.S. Chamber of Commerce, which stated that 95.7 percent of U.S. families bought newspapers, 46 percent bought magazines, and 15.4 percent bought books. Chicago Tribune, *Book of Facts, 1927: Data on Markets, Merchandising, Advertising, with Special Reference to the Chicago Territory and Chicago Newspaper Advertising* (Chicago: Chicago Tribune, 1927), 36–38.

2. Rhey Boyd Parsons, "A Study of Adult Reading" (PhD diss., University of Chicago, 1923), 45, 65, 74, as cited in Kaestle and Damon-Moore, *Literacy in the United States*, 188, 193.

3. Parsons found that 98 percent of Chicago men and 93 percent of Chicago women read newspapers (ibid., 195).

4. Lee, *The Daily Newspaper in America*, 323.

5. Robert Ezra Park, "Newspaper Circulation in the Chicago Region and Its Relation to the Organization of the Regional Community Pattern," unpublished typescript, Robert Ezra Park Papers, University of Chicago Special Collections. These numbers are based on census figures. This article also includes a map of the falling numbers of newspapers.

6. I draw information about chain newspapers in 1930 from *Editor & Publisher, International Yearbook Number for 1930*, 25 January 1930, 138–39.

7. Michael Stamm, *Sound Business: Newspapers, Radio, and the Politics of New Media* (Philadelphia: University of Pennsylvania Press, 2011), 193.

8. Thorin Tritter, "Paper Profits in Public Service: Money Making in the New York Newspaper Industry, 1830–1930" (PhD diss., Columbia University, 2000), 270.

9. A picture of the Tribune tower with the circulation in lights appeared in *The Trib* (internal newsletter for *Chicago Tribune* employees), November 1928, 4.

10. The *Chicago Tribune* was the most enthusiastic vertical integrator in the 1920s newspaper scene; on its many components, see Lloyd Wendt, *Chicago Tribune: The Rise of a Great American Newspaper* (Chicago: Rand McNally & Co., 1979), 471, and Chicago Tribune, *Pictured Encyclopedia of the World's Greatest Newspaper* (Chicago: Tribune Company, 1928).

11. See Tritter, "Paper Profits in Public Service," 264–66.

12. The American Newspaper Publishers' Association and the American Society of Newspaper Editors each lobbied for newspapers' interests, alongside dozens of state and regional press associations. The Audit Bureau of Circulations, financed by papers themselves, tracked circulation statistics. Trade magazines in operation in 1930 in-

cluded *Editor & Publisher, Printers' Ink*, the *Author & Journalist, National Printer Journalist*, and several journals issued by journalism schools, such as the *Columbia Journalist* and the *Iowa Journalist*.

13. The *Chicago Tribune*'s newsletter, *The Trib*, began publishing in 1919; the *Chicago Daily News*'s letter, *The C.D.N. Circle*, started up in 1927; and the *Sun*'s newsletter, *The Sun Rays*, began in 1926.

14. For a detailed description of the kinds of jobs held by women at newspapers in the 1920s, see Chicago Tribune, *Women of the World's Greatest Newspaper* (Chicago: Public Service Office of the Chicago Tribune, 1927), Frances Peck Grover (Mae Tinee) Papers, 1895–1940, Col. McCormick Research Center, Wheaton, IL.

15. This transition is already noticeable in a 1918 newsboys' newsletter put out by the *Milwaukee Journal*. The letter addressed newsboys' parents, as well as the boys themselves, and offered prizes such as baseball bats for good sales records. Milwaukee Journal, *Newsy News for Journal Newsies*, vol. 3, no. 4 (April 1918), Milwaukee Historical Society.

16. For a detailed account of movies from the 1920s through the 1970s that feature journalist characters, see Alex Barris, *Stop the Presses! The Newspaperman in American Film* (South Brunswick, NJ: A. S. Barnes and Company, 1976). For a broader survey of journalist characters in popular culture, see Matthew C. Erlich and Joe Saltzman, *Heroes and Scoundrels: The Image of the Journalist in Popular Culture* (Urbana: University of Illinois Press, 2015).

17. On the plotlines and common themes in movies about newspaper reporters, see Barris, *Stop the Presses!*; Thomas C. Leonard, *News for All: America's Coming-of-Age with the Press* (New York: Oxford University Press, 1995), 210–16, and Loren Ghiglione, *The American Journalist: The Paradox of the Press* (Washington, DC: Library of Congress, 1990), pt. 2.

18. Jeff Rovin, *The Encyclopedia of Superheroes* (New York: Facts on File, 1985).

19. I draw this list of services from Chicago Tribune, *Book of Facts, 1927*, 41; Chicago Tribune, *Pictured Encyclopedia*, 610–11; Robert W. Wells, *The Milwaukee Journal: An Informal Chronicle of Its First Hundred Years* (Milwaukee: Milwaukee Journal, 1981), 165; "Automotive Topics," *Milwaukee Journal*, 28 December 1919, pt. 4, 3; and "'Story of a Newspaper'—a Conducted Tour through the Chicago Daily News Plant," undated script, Victor Freemont Lawson Papers, Newberry Library, Chicago.

20. Chicago Tribune, *Pictured Encyclopedia*, 783.

21. Lee, *The Daily Newspaper in America*, 357. For a listing of cooking schools willing to collaborate with newspapers see *Editor & Publisher, International Yearbook Number for 1930*, 25 January 1930, 252.

22. *Editor & Publisher, International Yearbook Number for 1930*, 25 January 1930, 218.

23. *Editor & Publisher*, 30 January 1926, v. Also on merchandising services, see Truman DeWeese, *Keeping a Dollar at Work: Fifty "Talks" on Newspaper Advertising Written for the N.Y. Evening Post* (New York: New York Evening Post, 1915), 215; and Jason Rogers, *Newspaper Building: Application of Efficiency to Editing, to Mechanical Production, to Circulation and Advertising* (New York: Harper & Brothers, 1918), 238–39.

24. The *Milwaukee Journal*, for example, gave away grocery bags worth $3 to women who answered a merchandising survey. *Editor & Publisher*, 6 February 1926, 45. Many newspapers used consumer research statistics to market their audiences to advertisers; see, for instance, the *Philadelphia Record* advertisement in *Editor & Publisher, International Yearbook Number for 1926*, January 30, 1926, 85.

25. Genevieve Jackson Boughner, *Women in Journalism: A Guide to the Opportunities and a Manual of the Technique of Women's Work for Newspapers and Magazines* (New York: D. Appleton, 1926), 233.

26. Bernard Berelson, "What 'Missing the Newspaper' Means," in *Communications Research, 1948-1949*, ed. Paul Felix Lazarsfeld and Frank Stanton (New York: Harper & Brothers, 1949), 118.

27. Tritter, "Paper Profits in Public Service," 270; and Hy B. Turner, *When Giants Ruled: The Story of Park Row, New York's Great Newspaper Street* (New York: Fordham University Press, 1999), 208.

28. "'Story of a Newspaper'—a Conducted Tour," 3.

29. For example, see the *New York World*, 22 March 1921, 11, and the *Chicago Tribune*, 18 April 1924, 8.

30. See postcards from the *Chicago Daily News*'s foreign offices in Berlin and London, MMS Field Enterprises, Newberry Library, Chicago; "The World's Aid to Tourists," *New York World*, 22 March 1921, 11; and images in Chicago Tribune, *Pictured Encyclopedia*, 263-67.

31. Lee, *The Daily Newspaper in America*, 368.

32. Edwin Emery and Michael Emery, *The Press and America: An Interpretive History of the Mass Media*, 4th ed. (Englewood Cliffs, NJ: Prentice-Hall, Inc., 1978), 399.

33. Stamm, *Sound Business*, 10.

34. Wendt, *Chicago Tribune*, 472. Among the first newspaper companies to enter the radio business were the *Chicago Tribune*, the Hearst chain, and the Scripps-Howard chain. On the history of newspaper-owned radio stations, see Stamm, *Sound Business*.

35. Stamm, *Sound Business*, 195.

36. Ibid., 186, 195. On early competition between newspapers and television, see James L. Baughman, "Wounded but Not Slain: The Orderly Retreat of the American Newspaper," in *A History of the Book in America*, vol. 5, *The Enduring Book: Print Culture in Postwar America*, ed. David Paul Nord, Joan Shelley Rubin, and Michael Schudson (Chapel Hill: University of North Carolina Press, 2009), 122, 127.

37. On Americans' radio habits, see Susan J. Douglas, *Listening In: Radio and the American Imagination* (New York: Times Books, 1999).

38. One sociologist found in the 1930s and 1940s that many people who first heard news on the radio had the desire to then read about that topic. Stamm, *Sound Business*, 4.

39. Berelson, "What 'Missing the Newspaper' Means," 120. For more on the endurance of the newspaper through the radio era, see Baughman, "Wounded but Not Slain," 119.

40. Stamm, *Sound Business*, 4. This ratio began to fall in the 1960s and 1970s; see Emery and Emery, *The Press and America*, 436.

41. Berelson, "What 'Missing the Newspaper' Means," 121.

42. Ibid., 125.

43. Ibid., 122, 125.

44. Columbia University's School of Journalism has issued reports on the state of journalism that include suggestions for how news platforms can stay financially afloat. See Chris Anderson, Emily Bell, and Clay Shirky, "Post Industrial Journalism: Adapting to the Present," 3 December 2014, http://towcenter.org/research/post-industrial -journalism-adapting-to-the-present-2/; and Bill Grueskin, Ava Seave, and Lucas Graves, "The Story So Far: What We Know about the Business of Digital Journalism,"

3 December 2014, http://towcenter.org/research/the-story-so-far-what-we-know
-about-the-business-of-digital-journalism/.

45. Prominent "Internet utopians" include Jim VandeHei, editor of Politico; Michael Wolff, founder of news aggregator newser.com; Biz Stone, cofounder of Twitter; Jay Rosen, editor of *Pressthink* blog; and Dan Gillmor, founder of Center for Citizen Media. For a book that waxes optimistic about Internet information, see Clay Shirky, *Here Comes Everybody: The Power of Organizing without Organizations* (New York: Penguin, 2009). Books by "Internet dystopians" include Evgeny Morozov, *The Net Delusion: The Dark Side of Internet Freedom* (New York: PublicAffairs, 2011); and Eli Pariser, *The Filter Bubble: What the Internet Is Hiding from You* (New York: Penguin, 2011). For a structured debate between these two viewpoints, see Intelligence Squared, "Good Riddance to Mainstream Media" Tuesday, 27 October 2009, http://www.intelligencesquaredus.org/debates/good-riddance-mainstream-media.

46. On the Internet's ability to tailor news and information to users' habits and interests, see Pariser, *The Filter Bubble*; and Clive Thompson, "If You Liked This, You're Sure to Like That," *New York Times Magazine*, 23 November 2008.

INDEX

The letter *f* following a page number denotes a figure.

editors (*continued*)
roles within corporate newspapers, 45–46; syndication and, 220, 224, 225. *See also names of individual editors*
Evanston Index, 169
evening editions, 44, 81
Evening Wisconsin, 26, 196, 198, 202, 203, 212, 218
exchange system, 204

Fairfax, Beatrice, 2–3, 95, 212, 311n73
fashion news: advice, 58, 90, 96; in foreign language press, 231; illustrations, 84, 89; nineteenth-century, 58, 200; patterns, 212; in shopping columns, 84, 89, 200; in society news, 133, 145; syndicated, 212, 220
feature news: birth of, 30–31; commercial nature of, 7, 11, 14, 30–31, 34, 52, 101; growth of, 1–2, 6–7, 31–32, 82, 206–7; importance of, 4, 6–7; legacy of, 245–47; local, 113–22, 197–204, 213, 225–30; reader experience of, 6–7, 52–53, 101, 163; syndicated, 81, 194–95, 205–12, 214, 216–24, 230–33. *See also* advice columns; business news; cartoons; children's sections; comic strips; fashion news; fiction; home décor sections; human interest; metropolitan sections; real estate news; rotogravure; society news; sports pages; Sunday papers; theater news; travel news; women's pages
Felix the Cat, 223
Fern, Fannie, 41, 267n126
fiction: in African American press, 157, 217; in foreign language press, 214; in magazines, 19; reporters in, 239; serial, 31, 95, 157, 179, 220; Sunday, 31, 52; syndicated, 204, 206–7, 214; in weeklies, 175; on women's page, 90
financial news. *See* business news
foreign-language press: advertising in, 156, 214, 215f, 231; assimilation and, 26–27, 214, 216, 231, 271n18; in Chicago, 156, 301n116; circulation of, 10; German-language, 105, 156, 197, 202, 213–16; in Milwaukee, 197, 202, 213–16;

in New York City, 105; syndication and, 214, 216, 231
Fortune, Timothy Thomas, "The Afro American," 131
Fort Worth Star-Telegram, 243
Fresh Air Fund, 109–11, 113

Gannett Newspapers, 219
gardening sections, 160–61, 191, 206
Germania Abendpost, 214, 216
German-language press. *See under* foreign-language press
Gimbels, 85, 200, 202, 308n28
Given, John, 4, 24, 30, 48, 122, 123
Green Sheet, *Milwaukee Journal*, 220
Greenwood, Grace, 41, 267n126
Gumps, The, 224

Harper's Weekly, 19, 216, 284n22
Hearst, William Randolph: *New York Journal* and, 21, 28, 106, 136; as sole proprietor of his newspapers, 45
Hearst media: *American Weekly*, 221, 223, plate 8; King Features (Hearst media's syndicate), 209, 223; *Milwaukee Sentinel*, 218–19, 221, 224, plate 8; national chain, 194, 211, 221, 223–24, 231, 313n115, 319n34; *Wisconsin News*, 211, 218–19, 224
Hecht, Ben, 294n4
Hill, W. E., *Among Us Mortals*, 209
Hoben, Lindsay, 228, 229f
Hogan's Alley, 28, 125, 134, 136–37, plate 6
Holt, Hamilton, 51
home décor sections, 159–60, 191, 245
human interest, 126–29, 145–46, 150
Hyde Park Herald, 169, 170

Illinois Staats-Zeitung, 156, 301n116
illustrations in newspapers: innovations, 27, 115; syndicated, 217–18, 221, 228, 229, 231, 261n24; technology, 16, 205–6, 231, 309n53. *See also* cartoons; comic strips; printing; rotogravure
immigrant characters, 28, 29, 209
immigrant journalists, 27, 258n21
immigrant newspapers. *See* foreign-language press

Munsey's, 19
Mutt and Jeff, 95, 223, 225f, 276n78

"Neediest Cases," 109–11
Nelson, Nell, 144
Newcomb, Charles, 147, 148f
New Orleans Times-Picayune, 235
newsboys: during World War I, 216,
    261n24; evolution into paper boys, 239;
    as urban types, 23, 139f; working con-
    ditions of, 37–38, 111
newspaper buildings: growth of, 81, 82f,
    83f, 235–43; as self-promotion, 106,
    235–36, 236f, 237f, 242–43, 242f; as
    urban hubs, 36f, 35–37, 237f, 239–41,
    240f, 241f, 265n107; as visitor attrac-
    tions, 18, 240–43; as visually distinc-
    tive, 35, 235, 238f
newspaper charities, 109–13, 144
newspaper corner (San Francisco), 235
newspaper delivery: by mail, 37, 175–76;
    by newsboys and paper boys, 38, 239;
    regional, 147–48, 172, 192, 206; to re-
    sort towns, 69; rural, 174–76, 180, 192;
    suburban, 164, 166, 299n75; Sunday,
    148
Newspaper Enterprise Association, 220,
    319n34
Newspaper Publicity Act of 1912, 52
newspapers: as advisors, 54–101, 150–
    63; civic role of, 59, 102–46, 199–200,
    239–40, 246–47; class and, 55–56, 62–
    75, 84–88, 98–100, 103, 129–37, 150–51,
    168–71; commercial nature of, 5–7, 19–
    22, 29–35, 45–53, 69–75, 151–63, 185–88,
    239–40; corporate model of, 45–47,
    234–44; decline of, 244–45; growth of,
    3–4, 13–14, 16–35, 234, 244; homogeni-
    zation of, 9, 80–82, 194–233; intended
    audience of, 9–10, 103, 129–37, 150–
    51, 164–93; mass culture and, 75–88,
    209–33; partisan model of, 5, 15, 45, 54,
    106–7; regional spread of, 8–9, 147–93.
    See also names of individual newspapers
newspaper unions, 205, 309n50
newsprint, 14–17, 38f, 199, 205, 233, 236,
    238f
New York Age, 131

New York American: advertising for, 138,
    143; charity, 110; features, 115, 118f,
    119, 120f, 139f
New York American and Journal, 115, 116f,
    136
New York City: built environment, 104–
    6, 119–22, 207; as business and finan-
    cial center, 52, 149, 200, 204; chain
    newspapers and, 218, 219; as generator
    of national news, 26, 194, 200, 202,
    204, 227, 230; immigration to, 57, 104–
    5, 130–32; innovations in journalism,
    5, 21, 106–13; newscarrier strike, 241,
    244, 258–59n22; as newspaper industry
    center, 2, 4, 36, 42, 147, 194; rendered
    in its newspapers, 104–43. *See also
    names of New York City newspapers*
New York Commercial Advertiser, 25
New York Daily News (1855–1906), 27
New York Daily News (1919–): building,
    242, 242f; delivery, 299n75; features,
    117, 132, 135; ownership of, 235; reader-
    ship, 105, 244, 292n146
New Yorker, 137
New Yorker Morgen Journal, 231
New York Evening Globe, 105
New York Evening Mail, 285n32
New York Evening Post, 2, 99, 105, 235
New York Herald, 17f, 44, 106, 109, 113–
    14, 265n107, 266n111
New York Herald Tribune, 119, 128, 192
New York Independent, 51
New York Journal: charity, 109–10, 112f,
    285n32; comics, 28, 136–37; features,
    43f, 100, 135, 138; populist politics,
    106–7; readership, 2, 29, 105–7; self-
    promotion, 21, 22f; sensationalism,
    24, 135
New York Morning Journal, 47, 105
New York Sun: advertising in, 20f; "The
    Afro American," 131; city news, 108,
    114, 125, 140; delivery, 299n75; edi-
    tors, 123, 295n8; employees, 123, 236,
    239; features, 99, 117, 130, 131, 191;
    human interest reporting, 126, 128;
    populist politics, 106, 107; readership,
    105, 231; reporters, 23, 24, 41, 131; self-
    promotion, 261n24